Multicultural
Education

Multicultural Education

Raising Consciousness

Gloria Boutte, Ph.D.
University of South Carolina

Wadsworth Publishing Company

I(T)P®*An International Thomson Publishing Company*

Belmont, CA • Albany, NY • Boston • Cincinnati • Johannesburg
London • Madrid • Melbourne • Mexico City • New York
Pacific Grove, CA • Scottsdale, AZ • Singapore • Tokyo • Toronto

NOTICE TO THE READER

Cover Design: Courtesy of Timothy J. Conners

Delmar Staff:
Publisher: Bill Brottmiller
Acquisitions Editor: Jay Whitney
Associate Editor: Erin J. O'Connor Traylor
Marketing Manager: Denise Davis
Editorial Assistant: Mara Berman
Production Coordinator: Barbara A. Bullock
Art and Design Coordinator: Timothy J. Conners

COPYRIGHT © 1999
By Wadsworth Publishing Company
an International Thomson Publishing Company

The ITP logo is a trademark under license.

Printed in the United States of America

For more information, contact:

Wadsworth Publishing Company
10 Davis Drive
Belmont CA, 94002
http://www.wadsworth.com

International Thomson Editores
Campos Eliseos 385, Piso 7
Col Polonco
11560 Mexico D F Mexico

International Thomson Publishing Europe
Berkshire House
168-173 High Holborn
London, WC1V 7AA
England

International Thomson Publishing South Africa
Building 18, Constantia Square
138 Sixteenth Road, P.O. Box 2459
Halfway House, 1685 South Africa

Thomas Nelson Australia
102 Dodds Street
South Melbourne 3205
Victoria, Australia

International Thomson Publishing Asia
60 Albert Street
#15-01 Albert Complex
Singapore 189969

Nelson Canada
1120 Birchmount Road
Scarborough, Ontario
Canada, M1K 5G4

International Thomson Publishing Japan
Kyowa Building, 3F
2-2-1 Hirakawa-cho
Chiyoda-ku, Tokyo 102
Japan

6 7 8 9 10 XXX 05
ISBN 0-8273-8159-X

Library of Congress Cataloging-in-Publication Data

Boutte, Gloria.
     Multicultural education: raising consciousness / Gloria Boutte.
        p. cm.
     Includes bibliographical references and index.
     ISBN 0-8273-8159-X
     1. Multicultural education—United States. I. Title.
  LC1099.3.B68   1998
  370.117'0973—DC21

                                                  97–36020
                                                CIP

Contents

Preface

ONCE...
    . . . in the seemingly distant past, lords in Europe controlled and resided in huge manors; peasants provided the physical labor and lived in huts. Peasants were considered to be part of the lords' property.
    . . . indentured servants were common in Europe and the United States. As slavery increased, this practice subsided.
    . . . millions of Native Americans were stripped of their tribal homes, land, and ways of life. Europeans tried to force Native Americans to adopt European ways. Native Americans were prohibited from practicing their religions. European "civilization" resulted in the genocide of millions of Native Americans.
    . . . Africans were unwillingly and forcefully brought to America in unprecedented numbers, enslaved, and treated inhumanely. Many died en route to America. Slave women were routinely raped. Physical abuse of slaves was rampant. These atrocities lasted almost three hundred years.
    . . . hundreds of thousands of Chinese were brought to America to mine gold and build railroads. They were subjected to pervasive legal anti-Asian discrimination and often lived in virtual slavery.
    . . . approximately 110,000 Japanese were unconstitutionally confined to detention camps.
    . . . approximately six million European Jews were murdered; millions of Jews were forced to leave their homes and were imprisoned in concentration camps.
    . . . schools existed primarily for white males from upper-income families.
    . . . women and African Americans were not allowed to vote.
    . . . disabled students were not allowed to attend public schools.
    . . . interracial marriages were illegal in the United States of America.
    . . . in India, people were divided by castes. Caste system prejudice is still present today.
    Although the examples presented here are by no means comprehensive, they demonstrate that virtually no culture, ethnicity, class, religion, gender, or exceptional group has escaped the effects of injustices. Regardless of whether the individuals

involved were the perpetrators or recipients of injustices, the effects of racism, classism, sexism, and other "isms" had a powerful impact. During all of the aforementioned times, many people undoubtedly thought that the future looked dismal. However, many held on to the hope that times would change. Indeed, history has taught us that change is inevitable (Banks and Banks, 1993).

We look back in horror at many historical events and it is likely that future generations will look back with disdain at many of our current trends. Our ancestors surely could not envision our lives today. Likewise, our predictions for the future probably do not come close to changes that will occur in the next century. But we can be certain that times will change. Knowledge is increasing exponentially and North American culture is continuously being redefined. The world is changing. The United States is changing. Schools are changing. Ensuring success for the diverse populations that schools serve calls for continual reexamination of traditional assumptions, expectations, and biases (Guild, 1994). Systemic reform, which is required, should be viewed as an evolutionary process with each change necessitating other changes (Kahle, 1994). Therefore, the goal of ultimate multiculturalism is an infinite one.

We would be deluding ourselves if we did not acknowledge that the oppression and victimization of various groups of people still exists. The rise of hate groups and hate crimes is evidence of this. However, racism, sexism, and other "isms" often manifest themselves in different forms than they did in the past. As we will illustrate in this book, institutional "isms" (e.g., racism, classism, sexism) are thriving. Ironically, it seems that the more things change, the more they remain the same. On the other hand, we realize that each generation poses new problems in human relations that must be addressed differently than they were in the past. If we as humans are to continue to coexist on this planet, we must learn to be tolerant of differences. We must also reckon with the fact that change is an inevitable part of life. Although we are not responsible for the crimes of the past, we bear an obligation to change those things that we have the power to change. Hopefully, we can learn from our history instead of repeating the same mistakes.

Multiculturalism is only one tiny aspect in the evolutionary equation, but based on historical events, it has proven to be an important one, since people have and will continue to demand their human rights. Given the rapidly changing demographics in the United States, tolerance toward other lifestyles and cultures seems inevitable. This book discusses some of the multicultural implications that change has on schools and society.

Teachers, parents, students, administrators, employers, employees, and society at large encounter multicultural issues on a daily basis. Since these issues may sometimes be controversial and cause some level of discomfort, they are typically addressed on a superficial level. Many of the topics in this book have been previously discussed; however, the etiologies of the issues are seldom addressed. This book examines underlying issues and makes recommendations for moving beyond discussion. A developmental approach is used because each stage of the life span affects or is affected by previous or subsequent stages of human development. As Jonathan Kozol (1991) poignantly illustrates, whether children succeed or fail usually does not happen by chance. Schools and other institutions are powerful contributors to success or failure later in life. Therefore, readers need to read the entire book, including chapters about grade levels or environments that they are not directly involved with. It is important to see the connections between the various grade levels and institutions (e.g., schools, families, workplaces, testing) in order to truly understand children and what happens prior to and after particular stages of development. Without a full understanding of the interdependence of various life stages, educators may have little long term-effect on the students they teach, or may fail to recognize the significance of their teaching and interactions with children. In order to ward off failure and to encourage success, it is crucial for educators to have an awareness of development and possible trajectories prior to and after each stage of development.

The importance of diversity issues in today's society is evidenced by the emphasis placed on it in restructuring movements and in accreditation standards across the nation. Indeed, change is imminent—albeit slow. A major assumption of this book is that there are no simple solutions or recipes. This book will address highly sensitive issues such as racism, classism, and sexism (both institutional and personal) because multiculturalism cannot be discussed in a meaningful way without discussing these integral issues. Equity issues will be addressed from five different perspectives outlined by Kahle (1994).

- *Equity in access*—who studies what—e.g., high-or low-level science courses

- *Equity in education*—who has the curriculum, materials, and instruction for optimal education

- *Equity in outcomes*—who achieves to his or her fullest potential

- *Equity in resources*—who has optimal and equal facilities and other types of support
- *Equity in leadership*—who has access to and success in a myriad of leadership roles

Throughout the book, it will be important for readers to personally reflect on issues and to view the role that they play in multicultural education. While this book focuses on the role of individuals in multicultural education, it also focuses on institutional racism and other forms of discrimination in the larger society and in schools. The implication is schools do not exist in a vacuum; therefore, simply addressing issues at the school level is insufficient. However, individuals can collectively change the complex systems that prohibit progress toward becoming a society where diversity is respected and appreciated.

This book can be used in survey multicultural or diversity courses for both undergraduate and graduate education students. Because of the developmental nature of the book, it can be used with students from a variety of education majors (e.g., early childhood education, elementary, secondary, administration, counseling). Both present and future educators will benefit from the numerous recommended activities presented at the end of each chapter.

❖ Acknowledgements

I extend my sincere gratitude to the contributing authors who helped make this book a reality. I dedicate this book to my legacies, Stephanie and Jonathan, who continuously inspire me to continue my work on diversity in the hopes of making schools and society agreeable and fair places for them and for all children.

❖ REFERENCES

Banks, J. A., and C. A. M. Banks. 1993. *Multicultural education: Issues and perspectives* 2nd ed. Boston: Allyn and Bacon.

Guild, P. 1994. The culture/learning style connection. *Educational Leadership* 51(8): 16–21.

Kahle, J. B. 1994. Ohio's statewide systemic initiative: Lessons from the trenches. Building the System: Making Science Education Work, National Science Foundation National Invitational Conference, Washington, D. C.

Kozol, J. 1991. *Savage inequalities: Children in America's schools.* New York: Harper.

❖ List of Reviewers

J. Perry Carter, Richland College, Dallas, TX

Maureen Gillette, Ph. D., College of St. Rose, Albany, NY

Mary Hughes, Ed.D., Iona College, New Rochelle, NY

Jan Hintz, Ph.D., St. Cloud State University, St. Cloud, MN

Jann James, Ed.D., Troy State University, Goshen, AL

Joseph Pizzillo, Ph.D., Rowan College, Glassboro, NJ

Delia Richards, Ed.D., Prince George Community College, Largo, MD

❖ List of Contributors to Boutte/Multicultural Education

Chapter   Name/Affiliation

1,2	Gloria S. Boutte, Ph.D., University of South Carolina, Columbia, SC
3	Desiree DeFlorimonte, Ph.D., Morgan State University, Baltimore, MD
	Sally Lapoint, Ed.D., University of South Carolina–Beaufort, Beaufort, SC
	Gloria S. Boutte
4	Carolyn Whetstone, Richland Northeast High School, Columbia, SC
	Gloria S. Boutte
5	Barbara D. Davis, The University of Memphis, Memphis, TN
6	Janice Belton-Owens, Ph.D., South Carolina State University, Orangeburg, SC
7	Michael L. Clemons, Ph.D., Old Dominion University, Norfolk, VA
	Michael Boatwright, Ph.D., American College Testing, Iowa City, IA
	Gloria S. Boutte
8	James T. McLawhorn, President, CEO, Columbia Urban League, Columbia, SC
	Gloria S. Boutte
9	Gloria S. Boutte

Introduction and Overview

Appreciation of both similarities and differences must be stressed in multicultural classrooms.

"An individual has not started living until he can rise above the narrow confines of his individualistic concerns to the broader concerns of all humanity."

—Martin Luther King, Jr.

INTRODUCTION

It is futile to discuss any level of schooling without discussing how it fits in the total scheme of life. Development cannot be isolated from prior and subsequent stages, or from the many dynamics that affect individuals at any given point and time. This point cannot be overemphasized. Attempts to explain one level of schooling in isolation will result in oversimplification of the issues involved. Throughout this book, we will emphasize the complexities surrounding the role of education in a multicultural society. In order to do so, we will examine prior and subsequent levels of student development, societal influences, families, communities, the workplace, and a host of other factors. Additionally, the complex interplay between all factors will be recognized and acknowledged.

The genius of the United States lies in the ability of its citizens to embrace basic, common values while accepting diversity (Schlesinger, 1994). The appreciation of similarities and differences will be emphasized throughout the book.

❖ OVERVIEW OF BOOK

This book contains nine chapters which cover development from infancy through adulthood. The role of multiculturalism throughout the life span is examined. The intent of this book is to facilitate the implementation of the multicultural process and to deepen understanding of related issues. Emphasis is placed on the complex interplay between each level of development and social, cognitive, intellectual, economic, and emotional factors. Each chapter begins with a real scenario and concludes with recommended activities. Readers should keep a reflective journal. Guidance for journal entries is provided in each chapter as the first activity; **however, students are encouraged to write about ANY insights gleaned or reactions that they have to the chapter.** These activities emphasize reflecting on the role that educators play in children's long term development and helping educators view the issues beyond the walls of their classrooms and/or offices.

Chapter One—Overview And Introduction

This chapter provides an overview of major concepts, conceptual frameworks, and a discussion of the role of power. Chapter One emphasizes that at some point we must realize that as humans our destinies are inevitably linked. What happens to one of us affects all of us in the long run. Therefore, the ultimate goal of multiculturalism is to seek global unity. We have a long way to go toward meeting this goal, and there are no simple solutions. This chapter stresses addressing institutionalized "isms" and current power structures in this country and the world.

When thinking about diversity in classrooms, families, and workplaces, several dimensions should be considered: gender, ethnicity, religion, socioeconomic status, exceptionality, age, language, and others. The interactions between these factors must always be considered.

This chapter emphasizes that the first step in becoming a multicultural educator is to closely examine one's own culture and beliefs. Then other cultures and diverse perspectives can be explored and appreciated. This chapter points out that, contrary to popular belief, multicultural education is beneficial to all children—including white children from mainstream environments.

Chapters Two Through Five—Schools

Chapters Two through Five discuss multicultural issues developmentally from the early years to adulthood. The emphasis is on making schools, colleges, and universities more inclusive for all ethnic groups, socioeconomic statuses, genders, religions, and ability groups. Authentic (as opposed to superficial) multicultural approaches, parents' and teachers' awareness of subtle and covert issues, and anti-bias methods are discussed. All four of these chapters examine issues globally within the context of the general society, as well as within specific settings. Although the chapters are presented separately, they are not mutually exclusive.

Schools are primary gatekeepers in the allocation of social resources (Sleeter, 1993). Along with families, they often have the power to relegate children to higher or lower status positions later in life. These chapters demonstrate that schools do not operate as isolated entities, as many would have us believe. What happens in schools is influenced by families, communities, government, the media, and society at large.

The powerful impact of tracking in schools (e.g., placing students in compensatory education classes for the duration of their school career) will be discussed throughout this book, with a special emphasis in these four chapters. Tracking is a mechanism which perpetuates systematic discrimination in our society. It is undemocratic because it unjustly precludes segments of the population from achieving their fullest potential. However, tracking is so deeply entrenched in school systems that many schools cannot even begin to conceive of strategies for eliminating it even though an abundance of literature opposes it (Oakes and Lipton, 1990).

These chapters highlight changing demographics which indicate that educators must be prepared to teach a more diverse student population. Many children in the United States currently do not receive the level of education that they deserve.

Chapter Three emphasizes that multicultural education is synonymous with effective teaching. Educators cannot be effective without considering both individual and cultural influences on children's development and learning.

Chapter Two—The Early Childhood Years. This chapter examines multicultural issues during the early childhood years (birth to eight years). Family, school, and societal factors are addressed. Teacher expectations and curricular issues are also discussed.

The early childhood years are among the most impressionable times in an individual's life. The messages and values conveyed during this period can potentially last a lifetime. As soon as a child is born, he or she begins to be indoctrinated into a society filled with systematic "isms." How families, schools, and society handle these "isms" will affect the child's future in unforeseen ways.

Chapter Two, "The Early Childhood Years," examines systematic ways that educators contribute (sometimes unwittingly) to the child's future successes or failures. Institutional discrimination is examined in the discussion of covert and overt school issues. The grouping patterns that begin during the early childhood years could well determine the child's trajectory throughout school. Educators must continuously reflect on their practices and attitudes to ensure that they are not contributing to systematic discrimination.

Although components of authentic multicultural classrooms are discussed in the chapter on early childhood, they are important for all levels of schooling. Five components of multicultural classrooms (Modeling by Teachers, Curriculum Inclusion of Multicultural Heritage, Multicultural Literature, Multilinguistic Experiences, and Resource Persons from Different Cultures) are revisited in other chapters as well. Strategies for making classrooms multicultural are presented in this chapter; however, it is emphasized that multiculturalism is an attitude rather than a collection of activities. No classroom can be multicultural unless the teacher truly believes in basic tenets of fairness, equity, and appreciation of cultures. Both similarities and differences among individuals must be considered.

Chapter Three—The Elementary Years. Multicultural issues encountered during the elementary years (fourth through eighth grades) are discussed. As with the early childhood years, children in elementary school are still very impressionable. Although the peer group becomes more important during this period, parents and educators have a tremendous amount of influence on elementary school children. The elementary school years are a period where children must develop a sense of competence and accomplishment (Tribe, 1982). This sense of competence can be developed in the home, school, or community. It is especially important during the elementary years for parents and teachers to work together to help elementary school children feel successful. If children receive the message that they cannot achieve in school, they are likely to feel inferior in this domain and seek satisfaction elsewhere (Hale-Benson, 1986).

For many groups of children, the longer they stay in school, the farther they fall behind. The message that many children receive is that they do not belong in school. For example, after fourth grade, many children of color begin to fall behind their white counterparts (Kunjufu, 1990). Additionally, females and males begin to take decidedly different trajectories. Factors contributing to performance differences among children include the failure of educators to teach relevant information and to teach according to children's learning styles. Instead of teaching primarily from a linguistic and logical-mathematical orientation, schools must also focus on other intelligences as well.

By junior high school (middle school), teachers have developed sex-stereotyped attitudes about characteristics of "good" male and female students (Berk, 1994). "Good" male students are described as active, assertive, curious, energetic, enterprising, independent, and inventive. "Good" female students are conscientious, appreciative, considerate, cooperative, mannerly, sensitive, dependable, poised, obliging, efficient, and thorough. Unfortunately, teachers are often unaware of how their expectations contribute to sex-role stereotypes and the development of different academic abilities and behaviors in students (Berns, 1994). As in the early childhood years, the "hidden curriculum" of elementary school often teaches children what their place is in school and society.

Chapter Four—The High School Years. By high school, the cumulative effect of schooling is apparent. Low, average, and above-average groups have solidified. High school students are typically placed in either vocational or college preparatory tracks.

Nationally, school restructuring endeavors include recommendations for diversifying the curriculum in schools. However, suggestions for pluralizing the curriculum have come under attack by critics like E. D. Hirsch. Hirsch and other conservatives call for a return to "universal" works of Western civilization and a move away from a curriculum that reflects multiple voices (Hillis, 1996). Asa Hilliard (1992), a renowned expert in the area of African American studies and multicultural education, agrees with Hirsch's assertions that the development and presentation of certain common content for all children is desirable. However, Hilliard objects to the approach Hirsch used to arrive at a common core. Unlike Hirsch, who recommends focusing on "the classics," Hilliard asserts that the canon must be decided upon jointly by all stake holders. Hilliard further points out that this nation was founded by individuals who fled the cultural totalitarianism of Europe to seek religious and political freedom. Hilliard poses the question, "Do the critics of pluralistic curriculums wish to require 'universalism' in religion and politics?" (p. 13) Obviously, such actions would be undemocratic.

In high schools that appreciate diversity, math, science, and other content areas undergo scrutiny to ensure that diverse perspectives are included. Additionally, schools must find strategies which help children from all ethnic, socioeconomic status, gender, and ability groups succeed in school.

The high school years are typically reputed to be a turbulent period. Problems such as teenage pregnancy, premature sexual activity, drugs, gang membership, and violence are likely to arise during these years. Educators must seek to understand the root of these problems and seek strategies for preventing them before they interfere with learning and with students' futures.

Chapter Five—Higher Education. Diversity issues as they relate to college students, professors, and administrators are presented in this chapter. Issues such as tenure and promotion of faculty members are addressed, as well as recruitment and retention of students, faculty, and staff.

Many students never make it to college. Cutbacks on federal grants make it difficult for many students from low income homes to attend college. Additionally, low SAT and ACT scores prevent many African Americans and Latino/a Americans from being eligible for scholarships. Historically Black Colleges and Universities (HBCUs) traditionally have done an outstanding job educating and graduating students who may have had difficulty getting admitted to a predominantly white college. However, this does not imply that the quality of education at HBCUs is lower. Often, HBCUs are simply more committed to working with students who may encounter difficulties in college. Yet white university officials continue to rate HBCUs as substandard—even the more prestigious colleges that are highly regarded in African American communities (e.g., Spellman, Morehouse, and Howard).

Like other levels of schooling, the curriculum of higher education is dominated by European perspectives. There have been many attempts in recent years to make programs more multicultural in nature. Graff (1992) notes that universities intend to welcome diversity and innovation, but they neutralize the conflicts which result from them. Instead of ignoring and avoiding conflicts, Graff suggests that conflicts be used as central points for discussion.

Universities are deeply contradictory places (Graff, 1992). On one hand, the university is expected to preserve, transmit, and honor traditions. Yet, at the same time it is supposed to produce new knowledge, which means questioning ideas and revising traditional ways of thinking. Academic disputes over Western and non-Western culture reflect serious and broader social conflicts over race, ethnicity, and privilege (Graff, 1992). Opposing viewpoints are rarely debated and on the rare occasions when debate occurs, it is usually filled with hostility and confusion. There is a lack of respectful disagreement in higher education. Paradoxically, such disagreement is supposed to be the strength of democracies and educational institutions. Students need to see connections between different interpretations, ideas, and values in curriculum if they are to enter actively into academic discussions (Graff, 1992). Likewise, faculty need to be able to respectfully argue issues. Hillis (1996) agrees with Graff's notion that engaging in intellectual debate is crucial if students are to learn to examine their assumptions and biases.

The number of faculty members from diverse cultures and/or ethnicities is low nationwide. While many universities have attempted to address this shortage through Affirmative Action, other universities are eliminating the practice (e.g., public universities in California). Without some mechanism for ensuring equity in hiring practices, it is unlikely that people of color will be better represented than they currently are at university levels. In fact, because racial and other types of discrimination are prevalent in our society, it is likely that people of color will be less represented.

Chapter Six—Parents And Families

This chapter presents information on multicultural issues confronted by parents and families. Emphasis is placed on valuing diversity among families.

It is almost a cliché to say that families and schools must work together in order to have effective schools, yet it is true. Both institutions must work together for the mutual benefit of the child. Families from all walks of life must be respected and valued by schools. Educators need to examine assumptions that most of the students they teach will come from heterosexual two-parent homes. Because of changing demographics, families are just as likely to be comprised of single parents, divorced parents, foster parents, legal guardians, teenage parents, grandparents, homosexual parents, or interracial parents. Instead of viewing these "non-traditional" families from a deficit and pathological perspective, educators must focus on the strengths that each family brings to school.

Chapter Seven—Testing

This chapter is included because testing is a significant factor that is intricately related to multicultural issues at all developmental levels. Testing in schools, colleges, and the workplace is examined. Implications for each level are discussed.

A testing craze pervades our society. From the moment of birth when we receive our first test (APGAR) until we enter the workplace, we are tested. Some view IQ tests as one of psychology's greatest achievements (Scarr, 1981). Others view the tests as one of its most shameful achievements. Opponents of testing argue that the outcomes of testing should not result in disproportionate numbers of minority group members who fail. Proponents counter that fairness means giving everyone a chance to compete (albeit that many are unprepared).

Since the early 1960s, researchers have reported that children from typically economically depressed ethnic groups (such as African, Latino/a, and Native Americans) tend to score lower than their white counterparts on various measures of cognitive ability and academic success. Poor children and children of color often receive less educationally, but are judged by the same tests (Kozol, 1991). The literature on these findings is extensive and reveal that these children are disproportionately placed in special classes for the mentally retarded and learning disabled, and drop out of high school at rates much higher than those of whites (Murphy, 1986). Too many children are relegated by tests and schools to inferior positions in the curriculum, and in low-income occupations because of early decisions about their talents (Scarr, 1981). Instead of accepting differences in test scores as a fact of life, schools must seek fairer and more comprehensive measures of achievement. Curricular and instructional changes are also in order.

Testing often has an adverse effect on school and college placements and subsequent life experiences for people of color and females. Authentic and fair ways of assessing children's academic progress are needed. Otherwise, the vicious test-placement-retest cycle will continue to debilitate the lives of many children from low income and minority groups.

Chapter Eight—The Workplace

Multicultural issues in many professions (e.g., business, law, education, medicine) will be discussed in this chapter. Both blue and white collar jobs are addressed. Civil rights, affirmative action, and other issues are covered. The intent of this chapter is to give educators a preview of what the futures of their students will be like and the role that education plays in this outcome.

The cultural and governmental systems of the United States have been established on the premise that some people were meant to rule and live in luxury and some were meant to serve and live in poverty and suffering (Sleeter, 1993). Although this notion contradicts the true creed of this country, institutional discrimination is prevalent in schools and in the workplace.

Women and people of color do not fare as well as white males in the workplace. They are generally paid less and often face "glass ceilings." Although there is opposition directed toward Affirmative Action, it still remains an effective mechanism for reducing discriminatory practices in the workplace. The fallacy that Affirmative Action results in hiring unqualified employees is not founded. This chapter demonstrates that white males still dominate many fields and almost all of the high executive offices. Additionally, people of color and women frequently report that they must work three times harder to receive even half of the recognition given to white males. As a nation, we have a long way to go to make the workplace inclusive and equitable.

Chapter Nine— Conclusions

The final chapter draws conclusions from the previous chapters and discusses implications. According to the Constitution of the United States, our country seeks to establish justice, promote the general welfare of all people, and ensure liberty for all. Educators, parents, and employers have a moral responsibility to create a country that meets these ideals. In a multicultural society, both individuals and groups must be empowered. Additionally, we must challenge oppressive tendencies of society (Hillis, 1996).

Multicultural education emerged from concerned individuals who observed that the injustices in society did not reflect the goals of democracy. Recently, multiculturalism has come under attack by the political right. The political right interprets the history of this nation as one of unsurpassed glory and progress. Multiculturalists, on the other hand, question whether there has truly been "liberty and justice for all." "The success of U. S. democracy should be judged not only by those who have the most, but by those who have the least" (Hillis, 1996, p. 143). Multiculturalists believe that they have a moral mandate to establish justice and to reconcile society's written ideals. As Hillis notes, multicultural education takes democracy at its word. The democratic ideal is to create a society that is moral and just.

"Respect for diversity is the hallmark of democracy" (Hilliard, 1992, p. 13). With any luck and effort, we can truly become a multicultural society that appreciates and values diversity. Then, we would finally live out the true creed of this country: One nation under god with liberty and justice for all.

❖ MAJOR ISSUES

One of the major political questions of our time has to do with the manner in which our nation deals with unity and diversity (Lubeck, 1994). While politics and multiculturalism are intricately interrelated, we would like to stress at the onset of this book that the necessity of becoming multicultural extends deeper than "political correctness." Instead, multiculturalism should be viewed as a moral conviction (Lubeck, 1994). Additionally, viewing multiculturalism as a political rather than a moral issue trivializes critical issues of bigotry, oppression, and racism (Grant, 1994). At the center of the multicultural debate is a profound ideological struggle over the values of American culture (Robeson, 1993). Many multiculturalists are interested in changing the knowledge and power equation in this country so that members of all races, classes, genders, and other historically marginalized groups will have equity and equality in all the structures of society (Grant, 1994). The basic premises of multiculturalism are built upon the very same tenets on which this country was established (Banks and Banks, 1993). Concepts such as fairness, equality, and pursuit of happiness are constitutional premises of our nation. These facts alone make the case for multiculturalism compelling. However, rapidly changing demographics also call our attention to the need for a more inclusive society. It is not unusual to read about the "browning" of America and the world. Fu (1993) notes that in the foreseeable future, demographers expect that current minority groups will become the new majority in this country. Demographers also predict that students of color will make up about forty-six percent of the nation's school-age population by the year 2020. Additionally, students of color are already majorities in the nation's twenty-five largest school districts as well as in California, our most populous state (Banks and Banks, 1993).

Nevertheless, the issue of diversity continues to be hotly debated at many levels of our society including schools, workplaces, and the political arena. Multicultural programs have been offered as a panacea for problems that have deeper roots and more profound implications; however, multicultural programs by themselves will not guarantee a more egalitarian society (Lubeck, 1994). Becoming an egalitarian society is a complex process as this book will illustrate.

In academic arenas, dialogue and literature about multiculturalism is profuse; however, in practice, authentic multicultural classrooms seem scarce (Boutte and McCormick, 1992). The scarcity of multicultural practices is the result of a number of factors. First, paradigm changes are slow—ethnocentrism has dominated schools for most of our lifetime. Locating information and changing one's orientation are time-consuming processes. Shifting to a multicultural paradigm will demand dividing and restructuring of power in this country. Relinquishing power is never an easy process. This point will be discussed in more detail later.

Second, many teachers, administrators, and staff at predominately white school districts do not think that multicultural education is needed. They mistakenly believe that only children of color benefit from multicultural education. Ayers (1993) points out that white students are handicapped by narrow curriculums which feature only European "greats." They miss out on valuable pieces about other worldviews and do not understand the ultimate connectedness that humans share. When white children are exposed to a curriculum that constantly validates their culture and invalidates other cultures (often subtly and unintentionally), superiority over other races is encouraged. When confronted with issues of diversity later in life, whites who have not learned to appreciate diversity may be less empathetic, respectful, and sensitive to the needs of other cultural groups. This hampers effective relationships with others and the opportunity to work and live together in harmony.

Third, there are a number of misconceptions about multicultural education. For example, many critics contend that it opposes the Western tradition (Banks, 1993). Multiculturalism does not reject the Western tradition and conceptualizations of Americans; however, it opposes the traditionalist way of constructing a common culture with over-simplified notions about achieving a common heritage through universalism and transcendence of people's differences (Grant, 1994). In contrast to traditionalists, multiculturists believe that common culture is not a given—it has to be created by engaging with cultural differences that are part of life in the United States (Grant, 1994). Banks (1991/1992) notes that it is important to realize that Western traditionalists and multiculturalists are entering the debate from different power positions. Presently, Western traditionalists hold the balance of power and financial resources and the top positions in mass media, schools, colleges and universities, government, and in the publishing industry (Banks, 1991/1992). Despite rhetoric about how Western tradition is threatened by the onslaught of women and writers of color into the curriculum, the reality is that the curriculum in the nation's largest schools and universities is largely Western in its concepts, paradigms, and content (Banks, 1991/1992). Banks points out how Euro-centric concepts such as the Middle Ages and the Renaissance are still used to organize the majority of the units in history, literature, and the arts. Furthermore, when African and Asian cultures are incorporated into the curriculum, it is typically viewed within the context of European concepts and paradigms. When a multicultural perspective is taken, Western traditions are still valued; however, other traditions will be *equally* valued and viewed from the perspective of non-Europeans. This approach does not diminish Western tradition; however, it does not make it superior to other cultures.

Many people also worry about the balkanization of the United States. They fear that our society will become fragmented and that the concept of "American" diminishes when multiculturalism is valued. These critics worry about trends which acknowledge the special needs of different ethnic groups because of possible intergroup tension. They argue that it is not the role of public schools to teach children the customs and folkways of their ethnic or racial group since this is the role of the family, church, and communities (Ravitch, 1991/1992). Ravitch argues that it is the role of public schools to open children's minds to new worlds, new ideas, and new possibilities. It is the role of schools to teach about commonalities (versus differences) in order to forge a national identity as Americans. Interestingly, this point of view does not acknowledge that schools have been and are currently teaching the customs of folkways of a particular ethnic group—European Americans. Moreover, multiculturalism does open children's minds to new ideas and, indeed, helps them to critically examine different perspectives. Finally, given the racial and social class cleavages in the United States, it is inaccurate to claim that the study of ethnic diversity will threaten national cohesion (Banks, 1991/1992). On the contrary, *ignoring* and *devaluing* differences has seemingly led to racial, social, religious, and other divisions (Schofield, 1997). Yet, many people believe that talking about and noticing cultural differences is a sign of prejudice. As the subsequent quotes (from students enrolled in a school where race was treated as an invisible and taboo characteristic) demonstrates, not discussing differences does not mean that they are not foremost in individual's minds.

> Howard, a white male, leaned over to me (*a white female observer*) and said, "You know, it just wasn't fair the way they set up this class. There are sixteen black kids and only nine white kids. I can't learn in here." I said, "Why is that?" Howard replied, "They copy and they pick on you. It just isn't fair." (Schofield, 1997, p. 258)

> Interviewer: "I have noticed . . . that [in the cafeteria] very often white kids sit with white kids and black kids sit with black kids. Why do you think that is?"

> Mary (white): "Cause the white kids have white friends and the black kids have black friends . . . I don't think integration is working . . . blacks still associate with blacks and whites still associate with whites . . .
>
> Interviewer: "Can you think of any white kids that have quite a few black friends or of any black kids who have quite a few white friends?"
>
> Mary: "Not really." (Schofield, 1997, p. 260)

Indeed the awareness of cultural differences permeates our schools, society, and homes even when we try to ignore them. Acknowledging that there is a cultural divide in this country seems to be the logical first step for moving beyond it.

Many educators also argue that multicultural education results in the watering down of the curriculum. Multicultural curricula and instruction can and should be as rigorous as traditional approaches. In fact, it can be argued that an ethnocentric curriculum that cannot be questioned and critiqued is not rigorous at all. That is, repressing different viewpoints or limiting books that make up the "canon" discourages intellectual development among both students and educators. Grant (1994) argues that most critics of multiculturalism apparently leave their research skills, scholarship, and willingness to conduct a thorough review of the educational literature at the academy door. Many such critics, Grant continues, criticize multiculturalism after reading (not studying) a few limited selections from the vast amount of multicultural literature. Admittedly, in an attempt to value diversity, some educators (with good intentions) emphasize respect for diversity and neglect teaching students the necessary skills. For example, some teachers who seek to respect the language of African American children who do not speak Standard English emphasize fluency, but do not ensure that students gain the necessary English skills that are needed to be successful in this country (Delpit, 1986; 1988). Obviously, this is not the intent of multiculturalism. The understanding and appreciation of children's cultures should be used as a bridge to mastery of school requirements. In other words, rather than framing this as a dichotomous issue (skills versus respect for diversity), multiculturalism should be viewed as a complement and asset to a rigorous curriculum, not as a liability.

A number of educators believe that multicultural education is not relevant to mathematics and science and is more appropriate for subjects like language arts, social studies, music, and art. Multiculturalism is relevant for all subjects and grade levels. Contrary to what some believe, science and mathematics are not purely objective disciplines. There is a widespread Eurocentric bias in the production, dissemination, and evaluation of scientific knowledge that mathematicians and scientists must address (Joseph, 1987). Valuing theories and processes from Greek culture versus other cultures or valuing linear versus circular thought processes is the result of a subjective decision that one way is "better" than another. For example, the traditional approach to science would not validate aspects of Native American cultures which have historically used folktales (versus a list of facts, hypotheses, and the like) to teach children about the night sky (astronomy) (Moody, 1996). From a multicultural viewpoint, alternate ways of studying science and math are valued and integrated into the curriculum rather than viewed as a less valid approach. This topic will be discussed further in Chapter Four.

Multiculturalism is also erroneously interpreted to mean that everything is relative (e.g., there are no universal wrongs and any decisions made by individuals are condoned). One of the most narrowly propagandized interpretations of this view asserts that multiculturalists accept any and all lifestyles and, therefore, homosexual lifestyles and "pagan" religions are condoned. While multiculturalists do respect differences in lifestyles, beliefs, and values (even when they conflict with our own), contrary to popular beliefs, multiculturalists do not believe that everything is relative. Without doubt, the basic tenets of life, liberty, and the pursuit of happiness, on which this country were founded are upheld by multiculturalists. From a multicultural point of view, there is room for opposing viewpoints; indeed, these are expected. However, certain behaviors such as hatred of other groups and murder (not for self-defense) are considered to be universally wrong and non-debatable.

Another misconception of multiculturalism is that it is an attack on whites. Ravitch (1991/1992) contends that most multiculturalists "demand that the curriculum teach contempt for the founders of the nation and for everything European or white" (p. 8). However, multiculturalism does not condone "race bashing" of any race. Whites are viewed as being just as "cultural" as people of color (Erickson, 1997). Some whites do feel criticized because the assumptions being questioned originated from European culture. Nevertheless, multiculturalism involves raising questions and reevaluating historical assumptions and issues that have been generally accepted for centuries. Additionally, multicultural education illuminates how whites (and others) contribute to racism every day—a notion that is often inconceivable and unanalyzed by many whites. Undoubtedly, some whites *and* members of other ethnic groups experience a high level of discomfort when the current power structure of the country is questioned. As the old adage "ignorance is bliss" suggests, it is easier to ignore racism and other "isms" than it is to confront them (Tatum, 1992).

Multiculturalism requires that all groups share power in a country where whites have historically held the majority of the privileges and white behavior has been considered the norm (Hewett, 1996). Questioning beliefs and values that are a deeply ingrained part of one's lives will evoke strong emotions (and perhaps resistance). However, a sense of disequilibrium (uncertainty and discomfort) is viewed as a part of the process of becoming multicultural. The issue of negotiating and sharing power will be discussed in detail later in the chapter. The tendency to dichotomize issues results in multiculturalism being viewed as an attack on whites rather than as an attempt to legitimize all voices and perspectives—including whites'. Racism and other forms of oppression hurts whites as much as they hurt other ethnicities (Tatum, 1992). For example, some whites may remember the pain of having lost black friends because they were not allowed to visit their homes. Thus, multiculturalism is not viewed as an attack, but rather as a mechanism for confronting the pain associated with racism, classism, and other "isms."

"We tend to fear and avoid conflict, rather than embrace it as a necessary element of growth that we can learn to manage and turn to our advantage." (Kennedy, 1996, p. 26) Currently, in this country, we tend to suppress conflict or turn it into emotional power struggles, leaving the differences that give rise to conflict intact and unexamined (Kennedy, 1996). This approach is a barrier to the fruitful dialogue necessary to move forward in a multicultural society. The book seeks to open up the dialogue.

❖ MAJOR CONCEPTS AND DEFINITIONS

Although a multitude of definitions exists for major concepts discussed throughout this book, the following definitions will be used.

Multiculturalism "is a worldview that rejects the global centrality of any single culture or historical perspective" (Madigan, 1993). It "is a principle, an approach, or a set of rules of conduct that guides the interactions and influences the perceptions, beliefs, attitudes, and behaviors of people from diverse cultural backgrounds" (Fu, 1993, p. 40).

Multicultural education is at least three things: A) an idea or concept, B) an education reform movement, and C) a process (Banks and Banks, 1993). The definition of multiculturalism extends beyond ethnicity and includes gender, socioeconomic status, religion, exceptionalities, and other qualities as well. Multicultural education embraces the idea that all students should have an equal opportunity to learn in school regardless of their gender, socioeconomic status, ethnicity, religion, physical or mental abilities, or other cultural characteristics.

The multicultural education movement grew out of the civil rights movement of the 1960s which was grounded in the Western democratic ideals of freedom, justice, and equality (Banks and Banks, 1993). A key tenet in American society is the idea expressed in the Declaration of Independence in 1776 that "all men are created equal, that they are endowed by their Creator with certain unalienable Rights, that among these are Life, Liberty, and the pursuit of Happiness" (Declaration of Independence, 1992, p. 76). Although the idea of equality expressed by the "founding fathers" in 1776 had very limited meaning at the time and referred to white men who owned property, the ideal remains an important part of United States culture and is still used by victimized groups to justify their struggles for human rights and equality (Banks and Banks, 1993). Multicultural education seeks to extend the ideals that were meant only for an elite few to all people. Essentially, then, multiculturalism encompasses the values and beliefs inherent in a democracy: the promotion of human rights and privileges, the sharing of power, and equal participation in all social contexts (Fu, 1993).

Multicultural education advocates maintain that knowledge is positional in that it relates to the knower's values and experiences. Furthermore, they contend that knowledge implies action (Banks, 1993). Although values such as equality and human dignity exist in United States society as ideals, they exist alongside institutionalized discriminatory treatment of numerous ethnic and cultural groups (Banks, 1993).

Culture refers to a totality of learned behaviors in the context of a social system (Slonim, 1991). Slonim adds that it is that complex whole which includes knowledge, belief, art, morals, law, custom, and any other capabilities and habits acquired by individuals as members of society.

Race is not a stable category and has changed over time (Apple, 1993). The terminology "race" is used frequently in our society (e.g., on school forms, birth certificates, death certificates, and the like) as if there were total agreement about its definition. However, nothing could be further from the truth. Depending on the source, race has been defined socially, biologically, and geographically.

Banks and Banks (1993) point out that race is a socially determined category that is related to physical characteristics in a complex way. For example, two individuals with nearly identical physical characteristics can be classified as members of different races in two different societies.

Race has also been used to refer to physical and inborn characteristics such as skin color, body build, or facial features (Berns, 1993; Slonim,1991). Slonim notes that unlike culture, race cannot be changed, learned, or acquired after birth. Other sources list four major human races: Negroid, Archaic White or Australoid, Caucasoid or White, and Mongoloid (Adams, 1995).

Race has also been defined geographically. Adams (1995) geographically outlined nine races: African, American Indian, Asian, Australian, European, Indian, Melanesian, Micronesian, and Polynesian (see Figure 1-1). Figure 1-2 provides the name of the continents and the percent of people in the world who live on each continent.

Although there are some genetically determined racial differences such as color blindness, sickle cell anemia, lactose deficiency, and the like (Adams, 1995), the interaction between the person's race, gender, culture, socioeconomic status, etc. often affects the type of life experiences that the person will have. When individuals from different races mate, the issues concerning race

FIGURE 1-1. Major Geographical Races

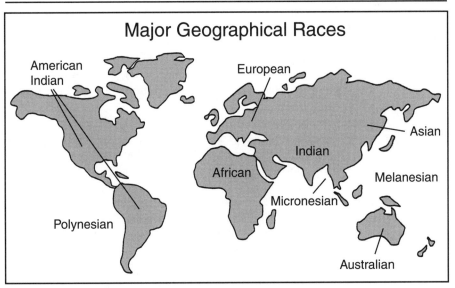

Courtesy of J.Q. Adams, *Dealing with Diversity. Teleclass Study Guide* (2nd. ed.) (Dubuque, IA: Kendall-Hunt, 1995).

FIGURE 1-2. 1990 World Population

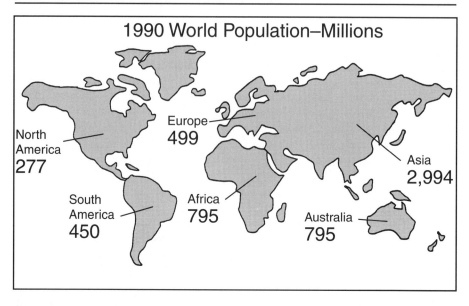

1990 World Population–Millions

North America
277

Europe
499

Asia
2,994

South America
450

Africa
795

Australia
795

Courtesy of J.Q. Adams, *Dealing with Diversity. Teleclass Study Guide* (2nd. ed.) (Dubuque, IA: Kendall-Hunt, 1995).

become even more complex. Therefore, the concept of race alone is often not a very useful one theoretically. Nevertheless, in the United States, race is an important social category in many aspects of life (Schofield, 1997). For example, individuals are routinely asked to designate their race when enrolling in school, applying for a job, and for numerous other purposes. Furthermore, statistics are often generated based on a person's race (e.g., test scores, income levels, census reports).

Although many argue that race does not matter, the emphasis that our society places on race contradicts the notion that race is unimportant. Indeed, many will claim that their race *affects* (not *determines*) the quality of their life experiences. People's ideas about race are developed within their everyday experiences which are socially organized and determined by social processes that extend into the broader society's treatment of race and race-related issues. For example, African American and Latino American men often report being unjustly harassed because of their race.

For many racial groups in this country, race carries such a heavy burden or conflict that they proclaim themselves to be *race-less* (Fordham, 1988). That is, they identify themselves as *human* or *American* to demonstrate their frustration with being classified. Fordham (1988) asserts that the desire of many people of color to be successful as defined by the mainstream society causes them to seek distance from the group with which they are racially or ethnically identified. However, she points out, efforts at dissociation or disindentification are often characterized by conflict and ambiguity about both the individual's identity and value. Since it is virtually impossible to eliminate all traces of the markers associated with one's indigenous cultural system, efforts at dissociation are often only marginally successful (Fordham, 1988).

In an attempt to appear non-biased, many people pretend to be "color-blind" and to not see color (Schofield, 1997). In the best of all worlds, race would not be an issue. However, denying that individuals' races are noticeable and making race incidental when it is not in this country is problematic. While the goal of effective multicultural relationships is to ultimately move beyond viewing racial differences as deficits, a person's race cannot and should not be overlooked. On the other hand, race should not be dwelled on. This issue will be discussed in more detail later in this chapter and in other chapters.

Tatum (1992) discusses three reasons why race is difficult to discuss in this country.

1. Race is considered a taboo topic for discussion, especially in racially mixed settings.
2. Many students, regardless of racial-group membership, have been socialized to think of the United States as a just society.
3. Many students, particularly white students, initially deny any personal prejudice, recognizing the impact of racism on other people's lives, but failing to acknowledge its impact on their own. (p. 5)

All three of these reasons are essential obstacles that must be overcome in order for discussions about race to begin (Tatum, 1992). Tatum (1992) recommends the following four strategies for reducing educators' resistance to discussing race.

1. The creation of a safe classroom atmosphere by establishing clear guidelines for discussion;
2. the creation of opportunities for self-generated knowledge;
3. the provision of an appropriate developmental model that students [and educators] can use as a framework for understanding their own process;
4. the exploration of strategies to empower students as change agents. (p. 18)

While this text is designed to provide many avenues for addressing strategies two, three, and four, it is important for the instructor who uses this book to create a safe classroom atmosphere in which educators feel comfortable discussing race and other multicultural issues (strategy 1). Tatum (1992) suggests that instructors ensure that classroom discussions are confidential and that educators demonstrate mutual respect for one another in the class. Additionally, attacks on another person are not permitted and everyone must speak from their own experiences. Educators should also refer to one another by name instead of "he," "she," or "that woman over there." When all of these ground rules are established the first day of class, educators can begin to get to the root of the issues (Tatum, 1992).

Because race is such a difficult and complex concept to employ in the United States (Herrnstein and Murray, 1994), it is often used interchangeably with *ethnicity*. In this book, we will use the terms interchangeably also.

Ethnicity deals with an individual's sense of identification and provides a sense of belonging to a reference group (Slonim, 1991). Table 1-1 provides the breakdown for ethnic "minority groups" in the U. S. which are derived from five major racial categories (black, red, yellow, brown, and white). The five ethnic groups listed on Table 1-1 are: African American, Native American, Asian American, Latino/a American, and European American. Mixing of ethnic groups is not uncommon; however, "interracial" groups are not included on this table because of the infinite number of possibilities. As Table 1-1 indicates, the United States is truly a polyethnic society. As with other ethnicities, there are many varieties of whiteness as well (Fine, 1997).

Non-white ethnic groups are often referred to as *people of color*. This term will be used throughout this text. Alternately, *students of color* may be used. While this terminology has shortcomings (e.g., it implies that whites are colorless), it is preferable to the term *minority*. Although the term minority is often used to refer to non-white groups who make up the numerical minority in the United States, it also connotes *less than* or *inferior*.

Ethnic groups are not assumed to be monolithic in nature and some individuals may cling closely to their ethnic identity while others denounce their ethnicity and attempt to assume a raceless persona (Fordham, 1988). Additionally, individuals may be at different stages of ethnic identity (Banks, 1997). Readers are encouraged to assess their stage of ethnic awareness using the the checklist on Table 1-2. The stages are intended to be fluid rather than mutually exclusive and individuals may exhibit characteristics of more than one stage (Powell, Zehm, and Garcia, 1996). Table 1-2 will also help readers assess their multicultural readiness. Higher stages indicate an individual's ability to understand and appreciate his or her ethnicity and view themselves from a global perspective as well. It is also helpful for educators to have some level of familiarity with their students' levels of ethnic awareness in order to better understand them.

TABLE 1-1. Ethnic Compositions in the United States

Ethnic Group	Inclusive Groups
African American (not limited to black)	African-Caribbean Native African
Native American/ Alaskan Native	Over 500 tribes; largest tribes include Cherokee, Navajo, Sioux, Chippewa/Aleut and Eskimo
Asian/Pacific American	Largest groups include Chinese, Japanese, Korean, Vietnamese, Cambodian, Thai, Filipino, Laotian, Lao-Hmong, Burmese, Samoan, Guamanian, Indonesian, East Indian, Pakistani, Saudi Arabian, Iranian, Iraqi, and other Arabic-speaking peoples
Latino/a American	Mexican, Puerto Rican, Cuban, Central and South American
European American	English, Welsh, Scottish, German, Dutch, Irish, French, Polish, Russian, Portuguese, Italian, Swiss, Danish, and other European groups

Courtesy of A.O. Harrison, M. N. Wilson, C. J. Pine, S. Q. Chan, and R. Buriel "Family Ecologies of Ethnic Minority Children", *Child Development* 61, 347-362. Copyright 1990 by the Society for Research in Child Development, Inc. Adapted by permission.

TABLE 1-2. Stages of Ethnicity

Directions: Examine the descriptors for each stage. Put a check mark next to those descriptors that you feel best align with your present stage of ethnic awareness. You might check descriptors in several stages. This indicates that you overlap these stages. Consider how the stage you most closely align with influences your role as an educator. You do not have to share your results with anyone else; this is a personal endeavor.

If you are at higher stages of ethnicity (Stage 5 or 6), you may have greater readiness for teaching/working in culturally diverse classrooms than if you are at lower stages. However, your potential for success is not based entirely on these stages. You may be able to demonstrate excellent technical skills for teaching (e.g., planning lessons) but still be at a lower stage of ethnicity. If you are at a lower stage, you need to broaden your awareness of other ethnic groups and deepen your understanding of your own ethnicity in order to respond appropriately to persons in groups other than your own. You also need to consider how your limited sensitivity for ethnic groups, if any, may cause you to have unintended cultural biases.

Stage 1. Ethnic Psychological Captivity

_____ hold negative ideologies about own ethnic group
_____ voice negative beliefs about own ethnic group
_____ demonstrate ethnic self-rejection
_____ demonstrate ethnic low self-esteem
_____ avoid contact with other ethnic groups purposely
_____ strive aggressively to become highly culturally assimilated
_____ have intrapsychic conflict about own ethnic group

Stage 2. Ethnic Encapsulation

_____ show ethnic exclusiveness
_____ live voluntarily around own ethnic group
_____ participate primarily in own ethnic community
_____ believe own ethnic group is superior
_____ show low tolerance for other ethnic groups
_____ prefer to live around own ethnic groups

Stage 3. Ethnic Identity Clarification

_____ clarify personal attitudes about own ethnicity
_____ hold low or no intrapsychic conflict about own ethnic group
_____ voice positive attitudes about own ethnic group
_____ accept self as member of a specific ethnic group

TABLE 1-2. Stages of Ethnicity (continued)

Stage 4. Ethnic Biethnicity

	hold a full and rich understanding of own ethnic identity
	demonstrate skills needed to participate positively and productively in own ethnic group
	demonstrate skills needed to participate positively and productively in another ethnic group
	desire to function effectively in two ethnic cultures

Stage 5. Multiethnicity

	demonstrate skills for functioning positively and productively in several ethnic sociocultural environments
	understand, appreciate, and share the values, symbols, and institutions of several ethnic cultures

Stage 6. Globalism and Global Competency

	hold skills, attitudes, and abilities needed to function in ethnic cultures within own and within other nations
	demonstrate a balance of ethnic, national, and global identifications
	internalize and act on the universalistic ethical values and principles of humankind

Courtesy of R.R. Powell, S. Zehm, and J. Garcia, *Field Experience: Strategies for Exploring Diversity in Schools.* (Englewood Cliffs, NJ: Merrill, 1996), p. 77. Powell, Zehm, and Garcia derived this table from J.A. Banks, *Teaching for Ethnic Studies* (Boston: Allyn and Bacon, 1991).

Throughout this book, the reader must realize the importance of understanding both between-group differences and within-group differences. It will be important for the reader to learn about the cultural practices of many ethnic groups and cultures without stereotyping or misinterpreting them. One problem in classrooms seeking to use multicultural practices is the overemphasis on visible (explicit) culture at the expense of the invisible and implicit aspects of culture (Erickson, 1997). Explicit aspects of culture include language, dress, food habits, religion, and aesthetic conventions. While important, these aspects of culture, which are taught deliberately and learned (to some extent) consciously, are only the tip of the iceberg of culture. Implicit (invisible) aspects of culture are equally important. As noted by Erickson (1997), our habits often become invisible to us for the most part. For example, how long in clock time can one be late before being impolite; how loud is too loud or not loud enough when speaking? Erickson (1997) points out that when we meet other people whose invisible cultural assumptions and patterns for actions differ from those we have learned, we usually do not realize that their behavior is cultural in origin. Rather, since we view their behaviors as personal rather than cultural, they are viewed as rude or uncooperative. Additionally, it is not unusual for clinical labels to be applied to people (e.g., students) when their behavior deviates from mainstream culture—low self-esteem, emotional disorders, and the like.

When educators treat cultural practices as sets of static facts, they trivialize them and make it seem as if culture is unchanging. For example, it is common for educators to teach that Mexicans have piñatas at parties. Erickson notes that if a piñata was not present at a Mexican party, the people would still be Mexican because culture is much more than things. A strategy for teaching about explicit culture without overgeneralizing is to emphasize the variability of culture within social groups. In every classroom, the cultural practices of students and teachers serve as resources for within-group and between-group diversity. Erickson notes that simply knowing that there are three Haitian students and four Cambodian students or seventeen girls and eleven boys in a classroom does not necessarily inform the teacher about specific cultural backgrounds of the students, their families, and the cultural assumptions that they make. "The teachers' tasks are to know not only about Haitians or Cambodians in general, or about girls and boys in general, but also about *these students in particular.*" (Erickson, 1997, p. 48) As this book will demonstrate, in order to be effective teachers, all aspects of culture must be considered: general, specific, explicit, and implicit.

❖ CONCEPTUAL FRAMEWORK OF THIS BOOK

The conceptual framework of this book is threefold. It will view multiculturalism from three perspectives: 1) a systemic and ecological perspective based on Bronfenbrenner's (1979) ecological theory, 2) a process point of view using the Reach Foundation's model, and 3) a developmental approach using Erik Erikson's (1963) psychosocial theory as a point of reference.

A Systemic And Ecological Perspective Of Multiculturalism

Conceptually, multiculturalism will be viewed systemically from an ecological perspective which emphasizes the complex interplay of interdependent parts that form a network. Recent literature has recognized that the process of becoming multicultural is a complex one which involves numerous social systems that are reciprocal and bidirectional in nature (Fu, 1993; Harrison, Wilson, Pine, Chan, and Buriel, 1990; Slaughter-Defoe, Nakagawa, Takanishi, and Johnson, 1990; Spencer and Markstrom-Adams, 1990). In other words home, school, society, the workplace, and numerous other factors must be considered when discussing multiculturalism since each of these continuously interacts with one another. None of the systems work in isolation. Using Bronfenbrenner's (1977, 1979) ecological model of the environment, this book will view multiculturalism as a series of nested structures. Urie Bronfenbrenner described four interlocking systems that affect development: microsystems, mesosystems, exosystems, and macrosystems (see Figure 1-3).

The innermost section on the ecological model (Figure 1-3) is the *microsystem*. This system refers to the activities, roles, and

Figure 1-3. An Ecological Model of Human Development

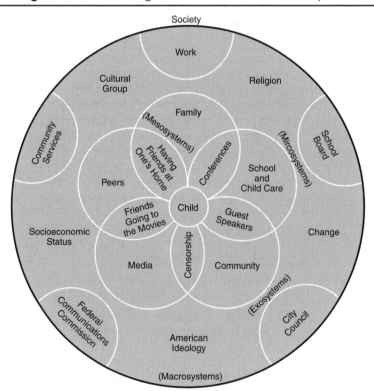

Source: R.M. Berns, *Child, Family, Community. (2nd ed.)* (New York: Holt, Rinehart, & Winston, 1989).

relationships in the child's immediate surroundings. For example, the child's home, child care center, family, peers, school, and so forth, interact and affect the individual's cultural orientation, experiences, actions, and attitudes.

A second level of Bronfenbrenner's model is the *mesosystem*. This system refers to the interrelationships or linkages between two or more settings such as the home and the school or between the community and the school. We propose that multicultural development is facilitated by interconnections among these systems. For example, a child's development of prejudice may depend not just on what is reinforced at home, but at school as well (and vice versa). A challenge that multicultural education faces is how to help students from diverse groups mediate between their home and school cultures (Banks and Banks, 1993).

The next level of the model is the *exosystem* which refers to social settings which do not directly involve the individual, but affect his/her experiences. Examples include parents' workplaces, health and welfare systems, or the Federal Communications Commission (FCC). Although children are typically not directly involved in the type of programs shown on television, they can be affected by harmful negative images of people from various social classes, religions, and ethnicities. Additionally, the gender roles shown on television will indirectly affect an individual's interactions. School boards that mandate the implementation of curriculum (which may be ethnocentric) are other examples of exosystems which affect children indirectly.

Finally, the *macrosystem* refers to the overarching ideology, values, laws, regulations, rules, and customs of a particular culture. For example, in a society where women are treated as inferior, the macrosystem will be crucial in determining a female's experiences, interactions, and outlook on life. However, history has repeatedly demonstrated that the macrosystem can and will change (Fu, 1993). Indeed, society shapes culture and is shaped by culture (Erickson, 1997).

We want to emphasize that all of these systems work together and affect multicultural development. Any problem in one of the systems inevitably affects the other ones. For example, the nature of parents' employment (exosystem) affects children's school work (microsystem). Hence, there are no simple solutions to the issues discussed in this book. Since humans are dynamic beings who are always changing, proposed "solutions" are not intended to be static or permanent resolutions. Our society often seeks one right way or solution to complex problems (Guild, 1994). If diversity is really valued, then we have to accept that 100 percent agreement among Americans is not a desired goal.

Different perspectives should be welcomed as opportunities for growth and development. Yet, as noted by James Banks (Brandt, 1994), in a democratic society views and opinions that violate the human rights of others cannot be sanctioned or tolerated. For example, the vast majority of the world would agree that the incidents surrounding the holocaust in Nazi Germany do not deserve to be respected in their own right.

When multiculturalism is approached from a systemic and ecological approach, issues are not polarized (e.g., melting pot versus cultural pluralism; black versus whites; males versus females; or rich versus poor). Instead, the focus is on a continuum of differences in opinions, lifestyles, attitudes, and cultures. Each individual is viewed as a member of multiple cultures such as race, ethnicity, gender, or religion (Fu, 1993).

A major goal of schools should be to help students acquire the knowledge, skills, and attitudes needed to function effectively within the national macroculture, their own microcultures, and within and across other microcultures (Banks and Banks, 1993). Ultimately, we must find a way to learn to respect, appreciate, and tolerate differences if we are to survive on this planet. Systemically thinking, each of us is affected by the actions and attitudes of others. In a multicultural society, we will come to the realization that we cannot hurt another person without ultimately harming ourselves. We are all prisoners of the same "isms;" the hater and hated bound up together in a web of lies that have shaped both of us (Elrich, 1994).

From an ecological perspective, schools alone cannot equalize the opportunities of children of color (Berns, 1993). "Band-aid" approaches to the deeply rooted problems addressed by multicultural education cannot heal wounds that have festered for decades (Berns, 1993). Schools are only one microsystem and cannot heal past and present social ills alone. Schools can lead the way, but there are no quick remedies.

Multiculturalism As A Process

Multicultural development is a process, and this book will use Reach Foundation's "Stages of Multicultural Growth" (Table 1-3) as a framework for subsequent discussions. The stages cover four dimensions (level of self-awareness, emotional response to differences, mode of cultural interaction, and approach to teaching) and illustrate how an individual develops from unidimensional to multidimensional perspectives. Frequently, teachers and preservice teachers do not view multiculturalism as being very important and courses or workshops on the topic may have little effect on their attitudes (McCall, 1995). Unless educators are willing to examine and change their attitudes, multicultural education will not be effective.

Multiculturalism is not a collection of activities or construct that exists outside the individual. Each individual plays a role in the process. Since self-assessment is an important aspect of multicultural growth, the reader should focus on where she/he is in terms of the stages. Additionally, throughout the book, the reader is encouraged to engage in deep personal reflection and analysis of issues. This book will be most helpful to educators who do not view themselves as "technotrons" who simply want a list of things to do in their schools. It will be most helpful for individuals who see themselves as the center of the process of becoming multicultural and who are open to continuous professional and personal development. The recommended activities at the end of each chapter are designed to intimately involve the reader. However, these activities cannot facilitate the process unless the individual makes an effort to be open-minded and committed to multiculturalism.

Level of Self Awareness. As indicated on Table 1-3, self-awareness progresses from being unidimensional to ultimately being multidimensional. That is, during Stage One, one might feel that there is only one way to do something. Since we are reared from a particular cultural orientation and primarily view our experiences from this perspective, it is not surprising that most of us have a unidimensional perspective. During Stage One, conformity to cultural norms is stressed and often one laughs at or ostracizes people whose perspectives are different. A prime example of this stage is an incident relating to my own development. As a child, my family ate certain foods and used certain phases that were unique to my community. Although I often read about other perspectives or viewed them on television, I thought that they were peculiar. It did not occur to me that my own idiosyncratic cultural perspectives were equally strange to others. Typically, people operate in cultural vacuums and only become acutely aware of their heritage when they encounter contrasting practices (Fu, 1993). While attending college in another state, I remember musing out loud that I had a taste for boiled peanuts. All my college friends laughed, and after some discussion each of them were somewhat shocked to discover that the unique cultural perspectives and behaviors that they knew so well were totally unfamiliar to others. For example, a friend from Florida mentioned eating mangoes, which everyone else thought was funny. Although many people refuse to accept other cultural lifestyles, these experiences prodded my friends and me to be a little more open-minded and helped us move to Stage Two. When (or if) people reach Stage Three, they realize that cultural perspectives are dynamic rather than static. They also learn to respect different perspectives.

Emotional Response to Differences. Many people deny that our differences are just as pronounced as our similarities. Educators (or others) in Stage One often make comments such as: "When I look at children I don't see any differences." The general idea expressed here is that all children are basically the same. Although the presumed intent of educators who recite this phrase is that they treat all children equally, it also implies that cultural differences can be disregarded and all children can be

TABLE 1-3. Stages of Multicultural Growth

	Stage I	Stage II	Stage III
Level of Self Awareness	My perspective is right (only one)	My perspective is *one* of many	My perspective is changing and being enhanced
Emotional Response to Differences	Fear/ Rejection/ Denial/ We're all alike	Interest Awareness Openness	Appreciation/ Respect/ Joy/ Enthusiasm Active seeking
Mode of Cultural Interaction	Isolation Avoidance Hostility	Integration Interaction Acceptance	Transforming Internalizing Rewarding
Approach to Teaching	Eurocentric/ Ethnocentric Curriculum	Learning *about* other cultures	Learning *from* other cultures
Approach to Management	Monocultural Autocratic Directive	Compliance Tolerance	Collaborative Valuing Diversity/ Maximizing Potential

Risk Taking ➤ Personal Gain ➤ Ongoing Process ➤

taught in the same manner. Typically, this translates into treating all children as though they are European Americans from mainstream culture. Such an attitude guides teachers to overlook cultural, racial, and other differences which may affect children's learning styles, development, perspectives, and behaviors. Educators who focus solely on similarities often fear that discussing differences indicates prejudice. Therefore, they deny that differences exist. However, when they reach Stage Three, they realize that differences, as well as similarities, should be celebrated. In fact, they recognize that differences can be assets which can be used to facilitate children's development.

Ultimately, teachers must be able to see *and* not see color (Valli, 1995). Seeking to find the right balance is a difficult challenge and is not an either/or proposition. When attempting to make their classrooms multicultural, educators in the early stage of development (Stage One) tend to overemphasize race differences and inadvertently reinforce stereotypes. In an effort to avoid overemphasis on race, many educators revert to a color-blind paradigm and focus only on individual differences; thus, culture is totally disregarded. Dealing in cross-cultural (multiracial) settings requires teachers to deal effectively with the issue of color (Valli, 1995).

Mode Of Cultural Interaction. In Stage One, people tend to interact primarily with people who are similar to them. In schools, it is not uncommon to see children playing or sitting together with others who share the same ethnic group, gender, socioeconomic status, or some other similarity. In our society, frequent, prolonged interactions do not occur cross-culturally in many settings. People often live, relax, and worship with people who are similar to themselves, so it is no wonder that people tend to isolate themselves culturally. Presently, cross-cultural hostility (e.g., racial, religious, gender) is on the rise in this country and others. As we develop and expand our attitudes and reach Stage Three, we are capable of transforming the nature of our cultural interactions and maintaining rewarding relationships with others who may be culturally different from ourselves. No longer will our relationships be restricted to intracultural interactions.

Teacher education students and professional educators are largely European American women from rural areas, small towns, or suburban communities with little experience or knowledge of diverse cultures. Because of their cultural orientation, they typically prefer to teach children similar to themselves (McCall, 1995). Likewise, other ethnic groups may prefer to teach students from their own cultural group. With the assistance of multicultural education, educators can transform their modes of interaction and become effective teaching most children. As Ladson-Billings (1994) aptly demonstrated in her research, educators from any race can effectively teach children whose race differs from their own if they understand the child's culture and if they hold high expectations of the child.

Approach To Teaching. As we progress from Stage One to Stage Three, we move from an ethnocentric/Eurocentric approach to teaching to an authentic multicultural approach. For example, educators no longer teach about events like Christopher Columbus from a Eurocentric perspective; rather, they research other perspectives and include them in their presentations as well. We learn about as well as from other cultures like Native Americans. Importantly, educators also remain open to new perspectives and actively seek information to deepen understanding of other cultures. Essentially, in Stage Three educators become culturally adept teachers. This involves a total transformation of the way educators think and teach. Without this transformation, educators are likely to view multiculturalism as an addendum to the core curriculum rather than as an integral part of the curriculum (Valli, 1995).

The process of growing multiculturally is an ongoing process which involves risk-taking since we have to move out of our comfort zones. Multiculturalism involves a give-and-take process for all cultures, but has the potential of benefiting all. As indicated later in this chapter, it also involves sharing power. However, the ultimate personal, professional, and humanitarian gain is worth the effort.

Multiculturalism From A Developmental Perspective. This book examines the development of individuals from the early childhood years through adulthood. We assume that educators are committed individuals who really care about the long-term welfare of the students they work with. Therefore, the ultimate goal of education at any level is to prepare individuals to be well-adjusted and contributing members of society who reach their fullest potential. A developmental perspective helps educators keep this long-term goal at the forefront of their minds. One stage of development is built upon another and must be integrated into the whole. Although educators typically work at one or more grade levels, their effectiveness is influenced by both prior and subsequent experiences of their students. An educators' attempts at teaching a child may be retarded or advanced depending on the student's prior experiences. Likewise, progress made at any grade level can be thwarted or lost at subsequent stages.

This book will loosely use Erik Erikson's (1963) psychosocial theory of development as a guide during the school years.

Table 1-4. Erikson's Eight Stages of Personality Development

AGE	BASIC STAGE	POLARITY	VIRTUE
Infancy	Trust	Mistrust	Hope
Toddlerhood	Autonomy	Shame and Doubt	Willpower
Preschool	Initiative	Guilt	Purpose
Middle Years	Industry	Inferiority	Competence
Adolescence	Identity	Isolation	Fidelity
Young Adolescence	Intimacy	Isolation	Love
Adulthood	Generativity	Stagnation	Care
Aged	Ego Integrity	Despair	Wisdom

Courtesy of C. Tribe, *Profile of Three Theories: Erikson, Maslow, Piaget.* (Dubuque, IA: Kendall/Hunt, 1982), p. 4.

Erikson proposed that individuals progress through eight stages of development. At each stage of development, the individual is confronted with a central problem or crisis that must be resolved in order to proceed with confidence to the next stage. One side of the pole results in the development of positive aspects of the personality; the other side results in negative aspects. Erikson's stages are listed on Table 1-4 and will be elaborated on in subsequent chapters.

❖ THE ROLE OF POWER

"Power concedes nothing without a demand. It never did and it never will."
—Frederick Douglass

One complex issue at the root of the multicultural movement is the sharing of power. Traditionally, in this society white males have been the executers and possessors of power. During the civil rights and women's movements, people of color and women demanded their rights. However, many segments of the white American population remain committed to their position of dominance (Howard, 1993). Howard notes that many whites are ready to defend and legitimize their positions of power even in the face of overwhelming evidence that the world is rapidly changing.

The implication of an authentically multicultural society is that no ethnic or cultural group will be in a dominant position. This will require considerable change in education and psychological shifts for many white Americans. Undoubtedly, many white Americans will feel uncomfortable with the changes that are occurring in society. Throughout most of American history, there has been no reason why white Americans have needed to be sensitive to the cultural perspectives of other ethnic groups for their (whites) own survival or success (Howard, 1993). In contrast, people of color have not had this luxury. The daily survival of African, Native, Asian, and Latino/a Americans depends on knowledge of white America. To be successful in mainstream institutions, people of color in the United States have to be bicultural at the very least—optimally, multicultural. That is, they must be familiar with the rules of their own cultural community, as well as that of the dominant culture. In order to be successful in schools, children of color must be bicultural (Hale-Benson, 1986). Delpit (1988) asserts that it is particularly important for children of color to be proficient at using the "language of power" (standard English).

The inclusion of race-related issues of power in university courses often generates emotional responses in students that range from guilt and shame to anger and despair (Tatum, 1992). Many people in Stage One of the Reach model (Table 1-2) deny that people of color do not have equal access to the power structure in this society (Howard, 1993). They often exclaim, "All the talk about multicultural education and revising history from different cultural perspectives is merely ethnic cheerleading. My people made it, and so can yours. It's an even playing field and everybody has the same opportunities, so let's get on with the game and quit complaining. We've heard enough of your victim's history." (Howard, 1993, p. 38) Additionally, many whites fear the loss of European and Western cultural supremacy in the school curriculum. Such fear, coupled with denial and hostility, threatens to destroy the nation's commitment to equality, freedom, and justice for all people. As Howard so aptly notes, it is not multiculturalism that threatens to destroy this nation's unity; rather it is an inability to embrace differences and unwillingness to honor the very ideals that we espouse.

Once we accept the fact that much educational information has been systematically omitted and misconstrued (Pine and Hilliard, 1990), we can collectively build our futures in a more constructive manner. Although consensus is not expected on diversity issues, the power structure in this country must be shared and we must become more tolerant of the views of other cultures. Relinquishing power is a formidable task, but history has clearly demonstrated power structures are also capable of changing (or at least restructuring).

Elrich (1994) suggests that confronting the effects of "isms" should begin with whites, not because they are guilty, but because they have the resources and political power to make change possible. Yet Howard (1993) cautions whites to be willing to share the power and work closely with other ethnic groups. He notes that the appropriate role for white Americans is to *participate* in this evolution rather than lead the way (Howard, 1993). It is crucial to note that there is much healing that must occur among all of us.

Recently, there has been an upsurge of objections raised by white men against people of color. These men express anger and feel discriminated against; hence, they have attacked affirmative action, single voting districts, and other social attempts to bring about equity in our society. Many of the white men who protest seem to realize that racism, sexism, classism, and the like permeate all facets of our lives from our homes to schools, workplaces, the media, and society at large. Yet, they deny that they have benefited from the privileges of being white in this society. They argue that multiculturalism results in attacks on white culture.

Multicultural education is not an attack on whites, as some would have us believe. However, as this chapter will note, becoming a truly multicultural country requires that whites acknowledge the power that our society awards them and learn to *share* this power with other groups. In this country, whiteness is both invisible and dominant (Fine, Weis, Powell, and Wong, 1997). However, "it is no longer possible to assume a 'normalized' whiteness, whose invisibility and relatively monolithic character signify immunity from political or cultural challenge." (Winant, 1997, p. 40). Most of the literature on diversity, multiculturalism, and equity has focused on discrimination and disadvantages targeted against persons of color to the neglect of advantages received by whites. What is missing from the literature and various interventions is a better understanding of the role that whiteness plays in school failure of students of color (Powell, 1997).

Privileges in this society are not limited to ethnic groups. The rich often enjoy certain privileges that are not available to the poor. Males are granted privileges not given to females (e.g., they are generally paid more on jobs). Most of us realize that racism, classism, sexism, and other "isms" place someone (or some group of people) at a disadvantage. However, many people from advantaged groups (e.g., whites, males, or financially advantaged individuals) fail to admit (or recognize) that it also *benefits* their group (McIntosh, 1995). That is, advantaged groups often deny that they have benefited from this country's racist, sexist, classist, etc. social structure. The following excerpt illustrates this point.

As a white person, I realized I had been taught about racism as something which puts others at a disadvantage, but had been taught not to see one of its corollary aspects, white privilege, which puts me at an advantage. . . . I was taught to see racism only in individual acts of meanness, not in invisible systems conferring dominance on my group. (McIntosh, 1989, p. 10)

Additionally, members of advantaged groups typically do not acknowledge that the privileges that accompany their group membership are generally not earned. McIntosh (1995), a white female, outlines forty-six ways that whites benefit everyday from such a system and eloquently demonstrates that whites have many advantages that other ethnic groups do not share. A list of numerous other benefits could easily be generated by members of oppressed groups. Even if a European American decides not to take advantage of these privileges, there are still options for whites that most people of color do not have the luxury of enjoying (e.g., living anywhere in this country without being discriminated against). They are deeply embedded in the fabric of our country. An honest acknowledgement of the state of affairs is an important first step toward multiculturalism. The boxed section (Figure 1–4) presents a white male student's candid reflections on the issue of sharing power in the United States. His response reflects a variety of emotions that are typically expressed by individuals seeking to make sense of the issues involved. While his concern for fairness and equity are readily apparent, he also expresses ambivalence about the possibility of sharing power, and concern for the welfare of his family and himself.

Figure 1-4. Education Graduate Student's Reactions to Howard (1993) and McIntosh (1995)

My reactions to "Whites in Multicultural Education" and "White Privilege and Male Privilege" are very mixed. In one sense, I completely agree with the fact that simply because I am white, I have been given some political and societal advantages. I can choose to use this advantage to try and make life easier for others, or I can just as easily choose to ignore it. However, I have found that despite the obvious advantages of being a white male, today's society is moving more and more towards the opposite end of the spectrum. Yes, I acknowledge the white male dominance, but we are walking on eggshells in the workplace. I cannot totally agree with McIntosh's statement that I did or did not get my job based on my performance, rather than on the color of my skin. If I voice any suspicions that I did not get a job because of affirmative action, there are immediate cries of racism. While I agree that "people of color" deserve an equal chance at the job, I too, deserve that equal chance. Ideally, shouldn't we ALL be judged for a job according to what we can DO, not because we do or do not have skin of color?

It is a hard thing to admit that we, as whites, have been taught that racism does not affect us directly because we are the "norm," and minorities are striving to come up to our level. We are given an unfair advantage that corresponds to minorities' unfair disadvantage. We should all be striving for a middle ground to meet. Selfishly and honestly, I admit that I, as a white male, have a place of privilege and find it hard to find good reasons, in my own interest, to give that up. There is an unequal trade-off, but a trade-off nonetheless, that lately I am more scrutinized and feel the effects of "reverse racism." But I am still more likely to get that promotion, and that promotion will more adequately provide the lifestyle I want to give my wife and my future children. My first priority is to provide for my family, and anyone else could and should say the same about themselves. Is there a way of living a less privileged lifestyle, but still a privileged lifestyle and still provide opportunities for everyone else? Probably not. But it will take a lot for the "dominant white" society to find reason to give up that power for the good of greater society. It is selfish, but true. We all take honest steps towards not being racist and sexist in our daily life. However, we have been unconsciously taught that we deserve our place of power and it will take generations, starting from preschool up, to consciously teach that we all deserve a place of power. There should be no place of power for one set of people, by color, religion, gender, anything. America, ideally, is founded on everyone being on equal footing, so we are all unbiasedly judged on our pure *ability* and intelligence. We have a very long way to go.

Mark Avery Jennings. University of South Carolina graduate student enrolled in a multicultural course in education (EDTE 779). July 24, 1996. Used by permission.

The United States continues to be sharply divided along racial, gender, and social class lines. These divisions are caused by political, social, and economic factors that prevent large segments of society from fully participating in society. Because power has not been shared, marginalized groups' quest for inclusion has been elusive (Banks and Banks, 1997). As Figure 1–5 conveys, the roles and attitudes of whites are an important part of transforming our society to a truly multicultural one.

Figure 1-5. The Roles and Attitudes of Whites in Multiculturalism (Reaction to three articles on whites)

My impression of the assigned articles for this week is that the authors are addressing what is really the key to improving race relations and to moving forward as a healthy, diverse society. This course has presented a good overview of the various populations that are affected by the dialogue of multiculturalism, but the bottom line—in terms of transformation of our communities—is in the attitudes and roles of white America.

The authors would probably point out that I can safely say this because I am white! Actually, that is exactly why I should say it. As a member of the dominant group, I presumably have no reason to call for greater equality in our society. My speaking out should cause others to stop and think about the possibility that this is a concern for all citizens.

Gary Howard honestly, courageously, and clearly depicts the complicated and explosive issue of rethinking the role white Americans have played in perpetuating racism and the role they should play in curing this disease. I wish there was a way to ensure that all white Americans over the age of eight could read this and similar articles.

Obviously, that would not solve the problems we are struggling with, but *awareness* must precede *action*. An incredible dose of faith and commitment must also go into the formula, for what is being called for on the part of white Americans is that we embark on a long and arduous journey, one for which many of my race see no need.

"What must take place in the minds and hearts of white Americans to convince them that now is the time to begin their journey from dominance to diversity?" This is the question Mr. Howard and so many others are asking. His question actually contains part of the solution: minds *and* hearts. These two elements must work together and we must be firmly committed to embracing diversity as the only viable solution for *all* of us. We will never truly deal with racism unless white Americans see that we must be part of the solution and that we all benefit from such a shift. Perhaps I have suggested this before, but I firmly believe that this personal transformation is tied to a recognition of the essential oneness of humanity.

. . . I wish more people could read the McIntosh article, particularly her list of forty-six observations about privilege. If so much of what we do in this dance of prejudice is unconscious or based on ignorance, an encounter with the candid observation of a "peer" could perhaps begin a productive dialogue. We cannot walk in another's shoes, but Ms. McIntosh provides a glimpse of the struggle of walking in black shoes in American society.

. . . I think we have discovered as a nation that it is not possible to legislate a change of heart. Perhaps now we are finally coming the realization that along with the laws must go grassroots efforts to connect with one another in our local communities and to begin to take responsibility for addressing the complex, interrelated problems we face.

Margaret Menking. University of South Carolina graduate student enrolled in a multicultural course in education (EDTE 779). Fall 1996. Used by permission.

The purpose of the multicultural movement is not to focus on blaming whites for the past. The focus is on closely examining the past and gaining understanding of past mistakes in order to avoid the same pitfalls. People who currently hold power in this country must work hand in hand with disenfranchised and marginalized groups to achieve democratic ideals.

If this country intends to live out the true meaning of its creed, then the "isms" must continue to be challenged and, hopefully, changed. Each of us must ask how we can address these issues in our professional and personal lives. The role that each of us plays will be unique but important. This book will make a number of suggestions for doing so, but they merely scratch the surface. As the graduate student in Figure 1-4 pointed out, we _must_ begin during the early childhood years and continue throughout an individual's life if humans are going to learn to live together peacefully on this planet.

As a result of technology, more people have access to knowledge and information. Access to more knowledge changes the traditional power structure in society because the more knowledgeable people become, the less likely it is for power to remain in the hands of a few individuals/groups (Berns, 1993). Recent changes in the way that countries operate provide evidence of changing power structures. In North American society, there is a move away from a representative democracy to a participatory democracy. On a global level, access to information gave people in communist countries the power to demand democratic reforms (Berns, 1993). Other examples which demonstrate that times can and do change is the shift in power from doctors to patients and from schools to parents. Indeed, change is the inevitable result of enlightenment and access to knowledge.

Educators are often uncomfortable discussing the issues surrounding power in society. Connell (1994) points out that

schools are powerful places. Schools exercise power in the decisions they make. For example, Connell continues, grades are not
just aids to teachers, but they are also judicial decisions with
legal status which cumulatively make authoritative decisions
about the lives of individuals including progression in school,
selection into higher education, and prospects for employment.

❖ SUMMARY

Multiculturalism does not develop in a vacuum; rather, it
involves numerous social systems such as the family, the community, and society at large. Becoming multicultural is a complex
task which requires time, experience, reflection, and effort. An
individual's development during one stage of life inevitably
affects subsequent or previous stages. In order to fully understand a person's multicultural growth, it is important to be aware
of the numerous influences and dynamics that are likely to occur
during various stages of the life cycle. As we grow multiculturally, we realize that everyone has unique cultural idiosyncrasies.
However, as we increase our global awareness, we learn to be
more accepting and appreciative of cultural differences. We do
not all have to be homogenized in order to get along. There is a
place for everyone in society. Our strength comes from our diversity as well as commonalities.

❖ RECOMMENDED ACTIVITIES

Reflective action and self-assessment are integral parts of the multicultural process. The following activities are recommended to
facilitate understanding of the concepts discussed in this chapter.

1. *Journal entry*—Start a journal with reflections on each chapter. Chronicle insights that you have gained. Be very intro-
   spective. For this chapter, candidly discuss your feelings
   about multiculturalism. Do you feel it is overemphasized? Is
   it applicable to you? If so, how? Do you feel that there is too
   much emphasis on multiculturalism? Discuss other issues or
   concerns that you have.

2. *Name Activity*—Names are closely related to one's self-
   esteem, and often, one's cultural heritage. The following
   activity can be used as an introductory activity at most levels
   and settings. We emphasize that educators and other professionals should strive to respect their students' name prefer-

ences. Often, in this society, as a matter of convenience, teachers and professors routinely abbreviate students' names—especially non- Eurocentric ones such as Luzviminda, Zhaopei, or Bashili. Many times, other students may query: "Your name is *what?*" Other times, teachers "Europeanize" names (e.g., Luzviminda becomes Lucy) without students' permission. It is important to realize that this may indicate disrespect of a person's culture and send subtle negative messages.

As Tatum (1992) noted, addressing classmates by their names makes the interactions less detached and more humane. In an effort to develop a safe classroom where highly sensitive multicultural issues will be discussed, it is imperative that students develop some level of personalization.

What's In A Name?

A. Divide into small groups.
B. One volunteer in each small group is asked to begin discussion of the following points:
   1. Give your full, complete name.
   2. Tell how you got your name. For example, who named you? Were you named for someone? (Did they hope Aunt Delores might leave her fortune to little Delores?) Is the name a family heritage? What is the nationality background?
   3. What nicknames do you have? Who calls you by them? Friends, relatives? Do you like the names?
   4. What do people do with your name? For example, do they change it in some way to tease you? Do you feel badly about that?
   5. Do you like your name? If not, what would you like to be called?
   6. In this group, what would you like to be called?
C. After the first person finishes, another person is chosen to follow.
D. After each person has had the opportunity to respond, ask one person in each small group to introduce the group members to the larger group.

Suggested Discussion Questions:

A. What areas did some participants have in common? What were some areas which were unique to specific individuals?
B. How do names give us impressions of people?

C. How does a name reflect one's identity?

D. What are some cultural differences among names?

Courtesy of *Human Rights Training Manual*. (1982) American School Counselor Association. Reprinted with permission from the American School Counselor Association.

3. *Four quads* Courtesy of Karen DeBord, Ph.D., Child Development Specialist, North Carolina Cooperative Extension Service, North Carolina State University, College of Agriculture & Life Sciences, F-3 Ricks Hall Annex, Box 7605, Raleigh, NC 276995-7605.

Ask participant to fold 5 X 7 cards into four sections. Using the sections however each person likes (front, back, whatever), ask participants to write the response to these questions in each quadrant. Then divide class into small groups to share. During sharing, each person will be given exactly four minutes to share any portion of what is on the card with the group without interruption. When time is called, it is someone else's turn. The questions are:

1st quad: List something about your own culture of which you are proud. What is something about your culture that embarrasses you? What other culture would you like to learn more about?

2nd quad: Remember a time when you could (and did) stop or interrupt an act of prejudice. Remember an occasion when you couldn't interrupt acts of prejudice. What are some prejudices you still have?

3rd quad: When was a time that you were the focus of another's discrimination? When was a time when you focused discrimination on someone else and hurt them? List an act of discrimination you learned growing up.

4th quad: How has your university, agency, or organization prepared you to celebrate/respect/appreciate human diversity? What practices does your organization need to stop or improve on to make multicultural awareness more of a celebration of differences? What can you as an individual do to become more aware of and appreciate human differences?

Follow-up to four quads — How did it go? How did it feel?

4. *Beauty Regimens, Adornments, and Physical Characteristics.* To examine some of the implicit cultural definitions of beauty that you have, reflect on how you view each item listed below.

Your Reaction (check one)

Favorable   Not Favorable   Neutral

a. unshaven armpits _____

b. long eyelashes _____

c. braids or corn rows _____

d. long hair _____

e. blond hair _____

f. blue eyes _____

g. brunette hair _____

h. thick lips _____

i. dark skin _____

j. light skin _____

k. broad nose _____

l. thin lips _____

m. hair on legs_____

n. lipstick _____

o. colored (dyed) hair _____

p. fingernail polish _____

q. numerous hair barrettes _____

r. slanted eyes _____

How did you develop these notions of beauty (family, books, television, movies, etc.)? How do/will your implicit definitions affect your view of the children/students that you teach or work with?

You can further this exercise by examining other behaviors as well (e.g., speaking softly or loudly, being animated when communicating, showing affection, crying when upset). Reflect on how each behavior affects your view of children/students.

5. Ask each person to write down the following information. Individuals may be real, make-believe, dead, or alive. Used with permission from Craig A. Bowman, 1992, American Association of University Students (AAUS), 3831 Walnut St., Philadelphia, PA 19104-6195. (215) 387-3100.

   A. Name 5 prominent Americans.

   B. Name 5 prominent female Americans.

   C. Name 5 prominent African Americans.

   D. Name 5 prominent Asian Americans.

   E. Name 5 prominent Latino Americans.

   F. Name 5 prominent Catholic Americans.

   G. Name 5 prominent gay/lesbian Americans.

   H. Name 5 prominent physically challenged Americans.

Which categories were more difficult to name? Why? How is our knowledge related to ethnocentrism? A follow up class project would be to research one or more of these categories.

6. Re-examine the map on Figure 1-2 which gives the continents and the percent of the world population that lives there. Many Americans are surprised to discover that the vast majority of the world's people live in Asia (56.1%) and the second largest population is in Africa (14.9%). Additionally, the revelation that Europe is third in terms of population (9.3 %) and North America is fifth (5.1%) is startling to many people in the U. S.

Reflect on how ethnocentric approaches to teaching geography and history in U.S. schools is related to why many Americans are surprised by these facts—especially by the populations of North America and Europe. Why do you think Asia and Africa are not given much attention in U. S. schools or in the media? International students often note that the U.S. only dedicates five minutes to world news events whereas other countries devote considerable more time to the U.S. news. Additionally, Africans are often surprised to discover that many U.S. citizens do not realize that Egypt (which is frequently studied) is located in Africa.

Does the economic viability of the U.S. affect the sense of ethnocentrism that many Americans have? How do ethnocentric approaches to teaching about other continents affect U. S. students' knowledge of world geography?

7. *Map Activity*—As noted in the discussion about the Reach Model (Table 1-3), traveling to and meeting with people from different places (states and countries) helps us to develop multiculturally.

Find a blank map of the United States (available at most educational supply stores). Fill in the names of as many states as you can without consulting an atlas or completed map. Next, write in the names of all the states using an atlas if necessary. Denote all the states that you have visited or lived in.

Reflect on how your travels within the United States will affect how you teach students about other regions in the United States. How can you gain additional insights about other states to enhance your knowledge and instruction about different customs?

8. *Cultural Pursuit*—Do the activity on Table 1-5. The purpose of this activity is to demonstrate that because of varied cultural backgrounds, each person brings different information and

perspectives. (It is likely that no one person will be able to answer all items). However, when we all work together, we each contribute to the whole. Numbers nineteen and twenty are blank. Students can write examples of information (e.g., words, phrases, foods, etc.) that are unique to their culture, but may be unfamiliar to others. Answers can be found in Appendix A.

Table 1-5. Cultural Pursuit*

Directions: Read your pursuit card and put your initials in those boxes which you can answer. Next, find others who know the answers for the boxes that remain. Be prepared to share what you know.

Find someone who . . .

1 Has had her/his name mispronounced.	2 Is from a mixed heritage background.	3 Is bilingual/ multilingual.	4 Listens to ethnic music.
5 Has been misunderstood by a person from a different culture.	6 Has had to overcome physical barriers in life.	7 Has experienced being stereotyped.	8 Knows what "Kwanzaa" is.
9 Knows who Rosa Parks is.	10 Has an "Abuela".	11 Has traced their family lineage or heritage.	12 Knows what "Hanukkah" is.
13 Knows what "nappy" hair is.	14 Knows the difference between the effect of a permanent on white versus black hair.	15 Knows what a "sari" is.	16 Knows what "oonu" means.
17 Knows what *Ebony* is.	18 Knows what "roti" is.	19 Suggestions from students	20 Suggestions from students

*Adapted with permission from Craig A. Bowman (1992). American Association of University Students (AAUS), 3831 Walnut St., Philadelphia, PA 19104-6195. (215) 387-3100.

9. In order to become more familiar with different cultural practices, readers should visit various places of worship (e.g., Jewish synagogue, Islamic temple, Catholic church, African American Baptist or African Methodist Episcopal Church {AME}, Jehovah Witness Kingdom Hall). After the visit, engage in a classroom discussion about commonalities and differences of each place. Reflect on your experiences in terms of the Reach Model of Stages of Multicultural Growth (Table 1-3).

10. *Analysis of television programs*—View several television programs and commercials for stereotypical messages. What do these programs imply about various cultures (ethnicities, genders, social classes, etc.)? What macroculture values are being conveyed?

11. Cite and discuss other examples of gross historical and contemporary injustices in the world such as the ones cited in the preface in the beginning of the book. What can be learned from these experiences?

12. View and discuss the video, *The Issue is Race*. (1992) This video discusses black-white racism in America. The panelists indicate the tremendous variety in backgrounds and viewpoints of people of the same racial group (e.g., Sister Souljah, Alan Keyes, Cornell West, Tony Brown). Hosted and moderated by Phil Donahue. (Approximately two hours long). Available from Films for the Humanities, Box 22053, Princeton, NJ 08543-2053. Telephone: (800) 828–9424.

13. View the classic video, *The Eye of The Storm*, which features a teacher purposely discriminating against children based on the color of their eyes (blue vs. brown eyes). A wonderful demonstration of how prejudice affects the psyche of children and individuals. (Available from Center for Humanities, Communications Park, Box 1000, Mt. Kisco, NY 10549 or the nearest public library).

❖ REFERENCES

American School Counselor Association. 1982. *Human rights training manual*. Compiled by Frances Monsees and Nancy Crosby. 801 North Fairfax Street, Suite 39. Alexandria, VA 22314. (703) 683-2722.

Apple, M. W. 1993. Introduction to *Race, identity, and representation in education*. ed. C. McCarthy and W. Crichlow. New York: Routledge.

Ayers, W. 1993. *To teach: The journey of a teacher*. New York: Teachers College Press.

Banks, J. A. 1993. Multicultural education: Development, dimensions, and challenges. *Phi Delta Kappan* 75(1): 22–28.

———.1991/1992. Multicultural education: For freedom's sake. *Educational Leadership* 49(4): 32–36.

———.1991. *Teaching strategies for ethnic studies.* 5th ed. Boston: Allyn and Bacon.

———.1997. *Teaching strategies for ethnic studies.* 6th ed. Boston: Allyn and Bacon.

Banks, J. A., and Banks, C. A. M. 1993. *Multicultural education: Issues and perspectives.* 2nd ed. Boston: Allyn and Bacon.

———.1997. *Multicultural education: Issues and perspectives,* 3rd ed. Boston: Allyn and Bacon.

Berns, R. M. 1993. *Child, family, community: Socialization and support.* 3rd ed. New York: Harcourt Brace.

Berns, R. M. 1994. *Topical child development.* Albany, NY: Delmar.

Boutte, G. S., and McCormick, C. B. 1992. Authentic multicultural activities: Avoiding pseudomulticulturalism. *Childhood Education,* 68(3): 140–144.

Brandt, R. 1994. On educating for diversity: A conversation with James A. Banks. *Educational Leadership* 51(8): 28–31.

Bronfenbrenner, U. 1977. Toward an experimental ecology of human development. *American Psychologist* 32: 513–531.

Bronfenbrenner, U. 1979. The *ecology of human development.* Cambridge, MA: Harvard University Press.

Connell, R. W. 1994. Poverty and education. *Harvard Educational Review,* 64(2): 125–149.

Declaration of Independence. 1992. In *World book encyclopedia, vol. 5* Chicago: World Book, Inc.

Delpit, L. D. 1988. The silenced dialogue: power and pedagogy in educating other people's children. *Harvard Educational Review* 58(3): 280–298.

Elrich, M. 1994. The stereotype within. *Educational Leadership,* 51(8): 12–15.

Erickson, F. 1997. Culture in society and in educational practices. In *Multicultural education: Issues and perspectives,* edited by J.A. Banks and C.A.M. Banks. Boston: Allyn and Bacon.

Erikson, E. H. 1963. *Childhood and society.* New York: W. W. Norton & Co.

Fine, M. 1997. Witnessing whiteness. In *Off white,* edited by M. Fine, L. Weis, L.C. Powell, and L.M. Wong New York: Routledge.

Fine, M., Weis, L., Powell, L. C., and Wong, L. M., eds. 1997. *Off white: Readings on race, power, and society.* New York: Routledge.

Fordham, S. 1988. Racelessness as a factor in black students' school success: Pragmatic strategy or Pyrrhic victory? *Harvard Educational Review* 58(1): 54–84.

Fu, V. R. 1993. *Culture, schooling and education in a democracy. Perspectives from ERIC/EECE: A Monograph Series, no. 3* Urbana, IL: ERIC Clearinghouse on Elementary and Early Childhood Education, 38–50.

Graff, G. 1992. *Beyond the culture wars: How teaching the conflicts can revitalize American education.* New York: W. W. Norton & Co.

Grant, C. A. 1994. Challenging the myths about multicultural education. *Multicultural education* 2(2): 4–9.

Hale-Benson, J. 1986. *Black children—Their roots, culture, and learning. Rev. ed.* Baltimore: John Hopkins University Press.

Harrison, A. O., Wilson, M. N., Pine, C. J., Chan, S. Q., and Buriel, R. 1990. Family ecologies of ethnic minority children. *Child Development* 61(2): 346–362.

Herrnstein, R. J., and C. Murray. 1994. *The bell curve: Intelligence and class structure in American life.* New York: The Free Press.

Hewett, K. A. 1996. Our culture/Your good intentions. *Primary Voices K-6,* 4(3): 38–41.

Hilliard, A. G. 1991/1992. Why we must pluralize the curriculum. *Educational Leadership:* 12–15.

Hillis, M. R. 1996. Multicultural education as a moral responsibility. *The Educational Forum,* 60(2): 142–148.

Howard, G. R. 1993. Whites in multicultural education: Rethinking our role. *Phi Delta Kappan* 75(1): 36–41.

Joseph, G. G. 1987. Foundations of Eurocentrism in mathematics. *Race and Class* 28(3): 13–28.

Kennedy, D. K. 1996. After Reggio Emilia: May the conversation begin! *Young Children* 51(5): 24–27.

Kozol, M. 1991. *Savage inequalities.* New York: Crown Publishers.

Kunjufu, J. 1990. *Countering the conspiracy to destroy black boys, vol. 2.* Chicago: African American Images.

Ladson-Billings, G. 1994. *Dreamkeepers: Successful teachers of African American children.* San Francisco: Jossey-Bass.

Lubeck, S. 1994. The politics of developmentally appropriate practice. In B. L. Mallory and R. S. New (eds.), *Diversity and developmentally appropriate practices (Challenges for early childhood education),* (pp. 17–43). New York: Teachers College Press.

Mackenzie, B. 1984. Explaining race differences in IQ. *American Psychologist* 39(11): 1214–1233.

Madigan, D. 1993. The politics of multicultural literature for children and adolescents: Combining perspectives and conversations. *Language Arts* 70(3): 168–176.

McCall, A. L. 1995. Constructing conceptions of multicultural teaching: Preservice teachers' life experiences and teacher education. *Journal of Teacher Education* 46(5): 340–350.

McIntosh, P. 1995. White privilege and male privilege: A personal account of coming to see correspondences through work in women's studies. In *Race, class,and gender: An anthology*, edited by M.L. Anderson and P.H. Collins. 2nd ed. Belmont, CA: Wadsworth.

McIntosh, P. 1989, July/August. White privilege: unpacking the invisible knapsack. *Peace and Freedom*, 10–12.

Moody, A. 1996. Connecting Native American stories and science. *Primary Voices K-6* 4(3): 11–17.

Murphy, D. 1986. Educational disadvantagement: Associated factors, current interventions, and implications. *Journal of Negro Education* 55(4): 495–507.

Oakes, J., and Lipton, M. 1990. Tracking and ability grouping: A structural barrier to access and achievement. In *Access to knowledge: An agenda for our nation's schools*, edited by J. I. Goodlad and P. Keating. New York: College Entrance Examination Board.

Pine, G. J., and Hilliard, A. G. 1990. Rx for racism: Imperatives for America's schools. *Phi Delta Kappan* 71(8): 593–600.

Powell, L. C. 1997. The achievement (K)not: Whiteness and "black underachievement." In *Off white*. edited by M. Fine, L. Weis, L. C. Powell, and L. M. Wong. New York: Routledge.

Powell, R. R., Zehm, S., and Garcia, J. 1996. *Field experience. Strategies for exploring diversity in schools*. Englewood Cliffs, NJ: Merrill.

Ratvitch, D. 1991/1992. A culture in common. *Educational Leadership* 49(4): 8– 11.

The Reach Foundation Curriculum. 1991. 180 Nickerson St., Suite 212, Seattle, WA, 98109. Phone (206)284–8384.

Robeson, P. Jr. 1993. *Paul Robeson, Jr. speaks to America*. New Brunswick, NJ: Rutgers University Press.

Scarr, S. 1981. Testing for children. *American Psychologist* 36(10): 1159–1166.

Schlesinger, A. M., Jr. 1994. The disuniting of America. In *Taking sides: Clashing views on controversial issues in race and ethnicity*, edited by R.C. Monk. Guilford, CT: Dushkin Publishing Group.

Schofield, J. W. 1997. Causes and consequences of the colorblind perspective. In *Multicultural education: Issues and perspectives*, edited by J. A. Banks and C. A. M. Banks. Boston: Allyn and Bacon.

Slaughter-Defoe, D. T., Nakagawa, K., Takanishi, R., and Johnson, D. J. 1990. Toward cultural/ecological perspectives on schooling and achievement in African- and Asian-American children. *Child Development* 61(2): 363–383.

Sleeter, C. E. 1993. How white teachers construct race. In *Race identity and representation in education*, edited by C. McCarthy & W. Crichlow. New York: Routledge.

Slonim, M. B. 1993. *Children, culture, and ethnicity: evaluating and understanding the impact.* New York: Garland.

Spencer, M. B., and Markstrom-Adams, C. 1990. Identity processes among racial and ethnic minority children in America. *Child Development* 61(2): 290–310.

Tatum, B. D. 1992. Talking about race, learning about racism: The application of racial identity development in the classroom. *Harvard Educational Review* 62(1): 1–24.

Tribe, C. 1982. *Profile of three theories: Erikson, Maslow, Piaget.* Dubuque, IA: Kendall/Hunt.

Valli, L. 1995. The dilemma of race: Learning to be color-blind and color-conscious. *Journal of Teacher Education* 120–129.

Winant, H. 1997. Behind blue eyes: Whiteness and contemporary U.S. racial politics. In *Off white,* edited by M. Fine, L. Weis, L. C. Powell, and L. M. Wong. New York: Routledge.

The Early Childhood Years

Young children are often more comfortable with racial differences than adults.

INTRODUCTION

Three-year old Malik's mother was concerned because he always referred to his classmates by their ethnicity (e.g., "the black boy," "the white boy," "the Chinese girl"). He never referred to his classmates by their name or gender only. One day when Malik referred to "a white boy," his mother seized the moment and responded, "Malik, all of you are just boys. All of you can walk, right? You can talk. You run and sing together." Throughout this discussion Malik agreed with his mother. When she finished talking, Malik said, "Boys are just boys, but white boys have hair that move. Black boys don't."

As the scenario illustrates, children develop an awareness of racial differences very early in life (Derman-Sparks, 1991). Moreover, young children often discuss racial and diversity issues with more comfort and "matter of factness" than do older children or adults. Because of young children's inquisitiveness, awareness, and comfort level, multicultural education should begin during infancy (Swick, Boutte, & Van Scoy, 1994). During the early childhood years (birth to eight years), children develop attitudes towards people who differ from themselves in ethnicity, socioeconomic status, gender, physical, mental, and social capabilities, and religion.

Swick (1991) outlined three reasons for addressing multicultural learning during the early childhood years: 1) the early childhood years are the most influential period for influencing children's development of cultural understanding, attitudes, and perspectives; 2) parents are the most powerful models, guides, and designers of children's social and cultural experiences; and 3) teachers' use of parent and family involvement strategies is highly influential in promoting multicultural learning.

Children's ethnic, racial, and cultural attitudes are more strongly influenced during the early childhood years than at any other point in their lives (Neugebauer, 1992). Moreover, children express understanding of racial identity as early as three years and describe cultural group attributes of others (usually modeled after their parents' descriptions) between the ages of three and five (Banks, 1993; Derman-Sparks, 1989). Therefore, the early childhood years are the best time to foster culturally sensitive and proactive children.

This chapter will be divided into two major sections: family and school issues. As illustrated in Chapter One, both topics are interrelated. The issues discussed in this chapter should be viewed from a developmental perspective. That is, they are relevant to all levels of schooling, but are introduced here because they originate during the early childhood years. In order to fully understand and implement a multicultural approach at any level of development, one must be cognizant of the cumulative effect of school- and family-related issues. Long before many poor children and children of color reach high school (and middle school in some cases), most of their academic options are foreclosed (Kozol, 1991). Therefore, early childhood educators do not have the luxury of focusing only on children's development at one point in time, but must always be aware of the role that they play in the total equation.

During the early childhood years, children struggle to develop a sense of trust and hope, autonomy and willpower, and initiative and purpose (Tribe, 1982). These traits can be nurtured in both the home and in the school. Toward the end of the early childhood years, around age six, if children have progressed successfully through the stages and have developed a sense of trust, autonomy, and initiative, then they will be ready to proceed to Erikson's fourth stage "Industry vs. Inferiority" (see Table 1-4 in Chapter One). During this stage they will seek to develop a sense of competence and industry.

❖ FAMILY ISSUES

As indicated in Chapter One, each of us is reared from a particular cultural orientation. In the home setting, the process of cultural transmission happens naturally and almost unconsciously. Children acquire cultural behavior patterns, beliefs, and perspectives which have a powerful influence on subsequent perceptions and behaviors (Comer, 1990). This does not suggest that children's destinies are determined entirely by the first few years of life (Comer, 1990). One's culture can be enhanced and changed throughout one's life as suggested in the Reach model in Chapter One.

In the United States, families typically assume the primary role in the enculturation process. Family structures, practices, and attitudes vary tremendously across and within cultures. These cultural differences are the result of numerous complex issues such as history and societal values. Nevertheless, by the time children enter school, they have mastered culturally specific behaviors, attitudes, survival techniques, values, and interaction strategies. Yet, most of us are blind to our own cultural heritage and only notice the role of culture when we compare our behavior to others who differ from ourselves (Fu, 1993). When we notice differences, we may view them as strange or peculiar (refer to the Reach Foundation model in Chapter One [Table 1-3]).

While the cultural patterns of families are effective within one's community, many schools and other social institutions are not culturally synchronized with children's home culture (Comer, 1990; Irvine, 1990). Historically, political and social institutions in the United States have evolved from a western European tradition and are based on mainstream cultural values (the macroculture) (Gollnick and Chinn, 1994). Therefore, children who are reared in a home environment that deviates from the mainstream culture often do not have much in common with the school setting. This does not imply that children from the mainstream culture do not encounter conflict in schools. However, many schools and classrooms are simply an extension of many white children's homes, and ethnic minorities are more likely to experience cultural dissonance. For instance, Erickson and Mohatt (1982) point out that the concept of individualism within a group setting is one that Native American children probably encounter for the first time when they enter school. Many Native American children are not accustomed to the idea that a single individual can be structurally set apart from others, in anything other than an observer role, and yet still be part of the group organization. In other words, Erickson and Mohatt (1982) found that the concept of people as independent and competitive (versus co-independent and supportive) beings was unfamiliar to many Native American children. There is a critical need for teachers to understand perspectives and childrearing practices of families who are not from mainstream homes.

All children do not begin life with an equal chance to succeed in this society (Gollnick and Chinn, 1994). Since family background accounts for a large part of the variation in educational and occupational attainment, other factors such as family income, gender, and ethnicity also influence children's outcomes in this society. The ability to give every child a chance to succeed in school depends upon a full understanding of culture and learning styles (Guild, 1994). Unfortunately, negative stereotypical views about low-income, Latino/a American (and African and Native American) parents' lack of value for education seem to characterize the thinking of many educators and researchers (Goldenberg, 1988). However, Goldenberg asserts that many Latino/a, African, and Native American parents want their children to succeed in school and to go as far as possible in their schooling. Ogbu (1974) found that African and Latino/a American parents often urged their children to do well in school and to aspire to high status occupations. However, at the same time parents warned their children that they were going to be victims of discrimination and that even when they put their best foot forward they might still be frustrated.

It is evident that there is a need to understand the perspectives of families of children from ethnic groups who do not traditionally fare well in schools. Ogbu's (1990) anthropological analysis of "minority" cultures explains why some ethnic groups adapt to school and other social settings better than others. Ogbu proposes that one's interpretations, perceptions, and responses to Eurocentrism varies depending on his/her status as a minority.

Based on extensive research, Ogbu discusses differences in groups of minority cultures in the United States and divides them into two groups: 1) immigrant minorities and 2) involuntary minorities. Immigrant minorities are people who came to America more or less voluntarily because they believed that it would lead to increased economic well-being, better opportunities, or greater political freedom. He cites the Chinese in Stockton, California and Punjabi Indians in Valleyside, California as examples. Many other groups also fit this description. Involuntary minorities, on the other hand, are people who were initially brought to the United States against their will or who were conquered by European Americans. For example, African Americans were brought as slaves from Africa; Native Americans, the original owners of this land, were conquered and forced onto reservations; Latino/a Americans in the southwestern U.S. were also conquered and displaced from power.

It is important to recognize that immigrant minorities typically bring a sense of who they are (identity)—at least the first generation. Their culture was not stripped away and they perceive their social identity as different but not oppositional to white social identity in the United States. Additionally, their cultural and language differences did not develop in opposition to white United States culture and language or as part of boundary-maintaining mechanisms between them and white United States citizens. Therefore, they view these differences as barriers that they have to overcome to achieve the goals of their emigration. Ogbu asserts that they tend to trust in or acquiesce to white people more than involuntary minorities do. They even tolerate prejudice and discrimination because they rationalize such treatment by saying that they expect this because they are "strangers" in a foreign country. It is important to note that immigrants insist that children adopt appropriate academic attitudes and study hard. Parents stress that they have suffered to come to the United States. All of these factors give immigrant minorities a promising cultural outlook on their future.

In contrast, involuntary minorities do not have a homeland from which to compare and contrast present selves and future possibilities; therefore, they use white residents of the United States as a basis for comparison, and usually end up with negative conclusions and resentments. Involuntary minorities wish that they could get ahead, but know that they cannot because of racial barriers which are part of their undeserved oppression. Their distrust of white people and public schools makes acceptance of school rules problematic. A contributing factor to their distrust is that they have experienced intellectual and cultural derogation, like not acknowledging intellectual abilities and other accomplishments, labeling them as genetically inferior (African Americans), and attributing undesirable personal traits and negative stereotypes to them. It is extremely important to note that such denigration serves important emotional functions for whites in the United States (Ogbu, 1990). That is, boasting about superiority facilitates ethnocentrism.

African Americans in particular have historically developed survival strategies which compete with or detract from schooling as a way to get ahead. Based on a study of African American males, Majors and Billson (1992) concluded that they often assume a "cool pose." Many black men who are left without the means to fulfill traditional roles have become angry and alienated. In order to cope, they develop a tough-guy image to obscure their anger and disappointment. Majors and Billson trace the history of black posturing back to Africa and the slave era and illustrate how blacks were forced to mask their true emotions in order to survive. In essence, playing it cool and other verbal strategies that are evident in many black male circles are learned cultural responses. These must be understood and respected in their own right in order to enhance future possibilities for black men. Educators must understand that African American males' coolness does not mean that they do not care. Ironically, they often behave in this manner because they view it as the only accepted and expected response that they can exhibit. Moreover, it gives them a sense of power and allows them to be accepted in their communities.

Although the cool pose is prominent among many African American male adolescents, elements of the cool pose can be seen even in young children. As young African American males master the intricacies of their home culture, they naturally begin to imitate acceptable male behaviors that they see. Once educators respect and understand the importance of these aspects of African American male culture, they can begin the complex process of broadening the definition of black maleness while respecting the need for coolness.

Ogbu (1990) outlines other coping strategies used by many African Americans in order to maintain a sense of dignity in a historically ethnocentric society. Some of these strategies are fruitful from a Eurocentric perspective changing the rules (e.g., making the system work through affirmative action); collective struggle (e.g., working together to achieve equal rights through civil rights protests); achieving success in fields that are open to blacks such as entertainment and sports; and "uncle tomming" (essentially "brownnosing" one's way to success). Other coping techniques which may not appear fruitful from a Eurocentric perspective include hustling and pimping. After careful analysis of institutionalized racism and classism, Liebow (1967) pointed out that often this is the only level of "success" that many black men are allowed to enjoy. Interestingly, Elrich (1994) noted that the same dismal outlook still exists for many African American students. He found that few of his students aspired to be doctors, scientists, or attorneys. He concluded that they accept their fate and their place. Essentially, Elrich's students found a way to be successful on their own terms outside the Eurocentric system.

Too often the family life of people of color is viewed through the lens of the dominant culture and is often regarded as deficient. (Neugebauer, 1992). When children are reared with limited cultural vision, their cultural growth is impeded (Swick, Boutte, and Van Scoy, 1994). Many children are raised in monocultural settings in which there is often little or no interaction with people who are culturally different. Therefore, many children rely on television or other forms of media for cross-cultural understandings. Unfortunately, television often depicts women, people of color, individuals with special needs, and people who practice non-Christian religions in distorted, debilitating, and demeaning ways (Banks and Banks, 1993). Additionally, television and movie images typically do not represent the diversity of people who live in the United States. These images often contribute to the development of negative stereotypes about people of color. Unless families make an effort to ensure that children are exposed to a variety of cultures and cultural orientations, it is likely that young children will form many inaccurate views about people of color and whites.

❖ SCHOOL ISSUES

Schools bring together children of diverse cultures and backgrounds. Teachers have the tremendous task of teaching these children. For many years the "melting pot" conception of the United States was widely accepted. People from all parts of the world were expected to give up their cultures and become "American." This has not happened. The realization that the United States is a multicultural society has prompted an appreciation of differences in social customs. Rather than a "melting pot," we actually have a "tossed salad" or "quilt" in which every person has maintained his/her own identity, but added a new flavor to the whole (Broman, 1982). Authentic multicultural teachers realize that each child possesses different strengths. One child may be verbally precocious, whereas another may be physically adept. The combination of all children's strengths results in the best possible environment where each person can make a valuable contribution (Boutte and McCormick, 1992).

The need for educators to grow and change is especially vital in today's society because the population of children served by public schools is changing. In reference to teachers' role in the change process, Hendrick (1992) asserts that "Everyone thinks of changing the world, but no one thinks of changing himself." (p. 275). Unless teachers work in a particularly isolated school setting, their classes are likely to be characterized by cultural and ethnic diversity (Cangelosi, 1992). Boutte and McCormick (1992) note that each person has unique cultural idiosyncrasies and teachers should realize that their own cultural differences seem equally as strange to others as cultural differences of others seem to them. Hendrick (1992) further notes that if differences in others are accepted without condemning them, then teachers can begin to develop a wider, more tolerant view of the world.

Infancy And the Early Years

Until recently, most of the research on child development has been done within the context of the dominant macroculture (Berns, 1993). Consequently, the development of white, middle-class children is generally considered to be the norm for all children regardless of their ethnic, cultural, or socioeconomic status. This chapter will discuss work which broadens the typically narrow definition of child development by considering diversity issues which relate to the ethnicity, religion, gender, and socioeconomic status of children.

Many educators erroneously believe that multicultural issues are only relevant for school-aged children. However, cultural differences must also be considered with infants and toddlers who attend child-care programs. Gonzalez-Mena (1992) notes that both caregivers and parents have very strong notions about how infants should be cared for (e.g., how the child is held, the type of communications used, frequency and method of feeding). She notes that many of these notions are implicit in one's culture and are typically not brought to the conscious level unless they are challenged. Gonzalez-Mena stresses the importance of culturally sensitive and consistent child care for infants and toddlers. She notes that when home and school cultures conflict, caregivers may inflict practices that may be culturally assaultive to the child. Dialogue between parents and caregivers can reduce such conflicts.

The National Association for the Education of Young Children (NAEYC) has been in the forefront addressing diversity issues in preschool and other early childhood settings. However, their guidelines, which describe developmentally appropriate practices (DAP), have been scrutinized for their lack of attention to cultural differences (Jipson, 1991; Mallory and New, 1994).

New (1994) cites several cultural concerns about the DAP guidelines. One problem with the guidelines is that they subtly (and unintentionally) imply a Eurocentric cultural orientation. For example, individualism is encouraged although this world-view is contrary to values held by many cultures which stress cooperation (e.g., some Native American tribes). Additionally, the child development norms that the guidelines use are not based on cross-cultural research. For example, the notion that young children have short attention spans is contradicted by observations in Japanese programs and Italian Reggio Emilia programs. Children in these programs are often involved in long-term projects. Another cultural issue criticized in the guidelines is the role that teachers play in guiding children's activities. A Eurocentric perspective suggests that the majority of the activities be child-led; other cultural orientations encourage more guidance from teachers.

If children's homes are viewed as culturally deprived or unstimulating, then many teachers feel their job is to provide what was "lacking" so that children can succeed. Although the "deprivation" doctrine is not openly adhered to in the guidelines, Lubeck uses the following four examples to illustrate how this doctrine manifests itself in a subtle manner in the NAEYC guidelines for developmentally appropriate practices.

1. The belief that some cultural practices are preferable; and that others, if not "deficient," are certainly less desirable.
2. The focus on individuals (children and family members) in an effort to rectify social ills.
3. The intent to provide children with experiences they are not likely to get at home.
4. The commitment to share with parents the knowledge that they ostensibly lack. (Lubeck, 1990, p. 20)

Bowman and Stott (1994) point out that educators must understand that their beliefs and behaviors are deeply rooted in their own past experiences. In order to accommodate new values and practices, they assert that teachers must restructure their own personal knowledge systems and clarify realities that have previously been obscured by their personal blind spots.

One way for teachers to find out more about different cultures is by conducting home visits (Backer, 1994; LaPoint, Boutte, Swick, and Brown, 1993). During home visits, teachers learn about interaction and communication patterns, routines, and other valuable information which can be integrated in the classroom setting. For example, teachers can discover children's favorite toys and books and provide similar materials in the classroom to ease the transition between school and home.

Many children of color, children from low income homes, children with special needs, or children whose religions differ from the mainstream experience their first contact with mainstream culture when they enter school. Unless school is a place that is supportive and respectful of differences, children may lose the feeling of security and trust that they had gained from their community. They may not be as independent as they are in their home setting or may hesitate to take the initiative, thus hindering their successful psychosocial development (Boutte, LaPoint, and and Davis, 1993; Tribe, 1982). This explains why many children of color are described as being quiet in schools, but behave just the opposite at home (Boutte, LaPoint, and Davis, 1993; Heath, 1982). Educators must be cognizant of the straddling of two cultures or "double consciousness" that children from nonmainstream cultures must endure (DuBois, 1961; Hale-Benson, 1986).

Teacher preparation programs need to encourage educators to reflect on the intensity and vigor that they give to the study of other cultural groups. Theories and practices must be examined continuously for their cultural sensitivity and appropriateness. The contributions and limitations of many different theories should be examined (Bowman and Stott, 1994). Both preservice and inservice educators must view learning about other cultures as a moral imperative. The following section outlines components of multicultural classrooms

Components Of Multicultural Classrooms

Multiculturalism is a process that encompasses content and attitudes. We emphasize that authentic multicultural classrooms provide ongoing informal and formal activities which are integrated throughout the curriculum on a daily basis (Boutte and McCormick, 1992). Multicultural activities should not be limited to isolated and discontinuous activities such as formal units on Native Americans around Thanksgiving time, discussions of African American achievements during Black History Month, or cooking ethnic foods. While these activities have merit, they are "pseudomulticultural" or unauthentic in nature since they only provide brief, "exotic," glimpses of other cultures. An authentic multicultural curriculum provides sustained and deep coverage of cultural content and issues rather than marginalization of diversity issues.

Two basic complementary concepts should guide multicultural classrooms (Lay-Dopyera and Dopyera, 1987): 1) people are similar in that they have the same basic needs such as water, food, shelter, respect, and love and 2) people are different and may fulfill these needs in different ways (different types of houses, diets, etc.). Children's books which complement this theme are *We Are All Alike...We Are All Different* (Cheltenham Elementary School Kindergartners, 1991); *Bread Bread Bread* (Morris, 1989); *Houses and Homes* (Morris, 1992a); *Tools* (Morris, 1992b); and *People* (Spier, 1980). Many educators feel comfortable discussing commonalities among people, but are uncomfortable discussing differences. Since America was originally built on the premise of a "melting pot" society in which people were supposed to shed their differences and become "Americans," many people still consider it rude to discuss ethnicity. As a result, Latino/a, Native, Asian, and African American children have been exposed to negative imagery and a sense of invisibility in school materials—mainstream images of Native American women provide a case in point (Medicine, 1988; Spencer and Markstrom-Adams, 1990). As noted by Boutte, LaPoint, and Davis (1993), it is actually rude not to discuss differences. Since each child is unique, multicultural teachers must discover specifics about children and their families that facilitate children's learning and development. Both similarities and differences must be emphasized.

The following components are recommended for multicultural classes:

- Modeling by Teachers,
- Curricular Inclusion of Multicultural Heritage,
- Multicultural Literature,
- Multilinguistic experiences ,
- Resource Persons from Different Cultures (Lay-Dopyera and Dopyera, 1987).

Modeling By Teachers. If teachers demonstrate that they value persons of differing characteristics and backgrounds, children will sense and emulate this attitude. Therefore, educators should model acceptance of people who look, dress, or speak differently. Educators should not tolerate children teasing others about their language or other cultural idiosyncrasies.

Curricular Inclusion Of Multicultural Heritage. The curriculum should include religious beliefs, music, art, science, and so forth representing many cultures. For example, if educators use holiday themes, they should be sensitive to the fact that not all children celebrate Christmas. Although some children may celebrate Kwanzaa, Hanukkah, Three Kings Day, or other holidays, school calendars include holidays based on Christian tradition and on national historical events (Locust, 1988). Modern Curriculum Press publishes a collection of books and other educational materials about many different holidays which may be useful for educators seeking more information about various holidays.

Adding different holidays to the curriculum is not as simple as it appears on the surface. While discussing numerous holidays certainly gives a broader perspective than the traditional approach, there are a number of problems associated with this approach (Ayers, 1993; Banks and Banks, 1997; Kostelnik, Soderman, and Whiren, 1993). First it is difficult to present the many faiths and orientations that are present in this society. Educators must ask what students who are not committed to a specific faith can gain from understanding the beliefs of others (Ayers, 1993).

A discriminatory issue related to celebration of school holidays is that they revolve around Christian holidays. (Locust 1988). Consequently, in some school systems, American Indians do not enjoy religious freedom and are penalized for being absent from classes while participating in traditional tribal ceremonies. The same holds true for Jewish, Islamic, and other non-Christian religions. While it is unlikely and unfeasible for the school calendars to change, educators must be cognizant of the roles they play in sending messages about non-Christian holidays. Teachers routinely make curricular decisions, such as whether or not to do a unit on holidays. Although many teachers do not realize that they are involved in politics and power, curricular decisions such as how or *if* holidays are celebrated are very political and powerful decisions. Discrimination against individuals because of their beliefs is the most insidious kind of injustice (Locust, 1988). Moreover, it flies in the face of a major tenet of this country—religious freedom. Importantly, such actions end up being unfair to children who for the most part do not choose their religion, but assume the religious preference of their families.

Second, holiday themes run the risk of being little more than a convenient backdrop for children's participation in numerous craft projects, with minimal attention to content. In these settings, children usually do not expand their conceptualizations of various religions or cultures (Kostelnik, Soderman, and Whiren, 1993).

Third, when children spend a significant amount of time on a holiday (e.g., St. Patrick's Day), it takes on a disproportionate importance in comparison to more relevant and real-life experiences that should be addressed. The criticism that multiculturalism "waters down" the curriculum likely is a result of the overuse of holiday themes in an effort to emphasize diversity. Using numerous holiday themes also reinforces the practice of viewing multiculturalism as an "add-on" instead of being an integral part of the regular curriculum. Since there is so little time in school to cover every important topic, it may be best to omit or spend less time on holidays since children get heavy exposure to these issues outside the classroom.

Fourth, there is a risk of inadvertently teaching cultural or religious stereotypes typical of the ethnocentric approach to teaching about Thanksgiving (Stage One of the Reach Model presented on Table 1-2 in Chapter One). All too often, Native Americans are stereotypically depicted as wearing feathers in their hair, dancing, and war whooping, while their real contributions toward helping the European settlers are overlooked. Additionally, students rarely learn that many Native Americans view Thanksgiving as a time of mourning and fast in remembrance of the many tragedies suffered by their people following the arrival of the first white settlers (Billman, 1992; Kostelnik, Soderman, and Whiren, 1993; Medicine, 1988; Ramsey, 1979).

Not using holidays as the basis for unit planning does not mean ignoring them (Kostelnik, Soderman, and Whiren, 1993). Instead they can be integrated into larger concepts such as "Celebrations" or "Family Traditions". This approach supports children's growing awareness and appreciation of similarities and differences by exploring and comparing rituals in the home such as Christmas, Kwanzaa, Three Kings Day, and Hanukkah. Billman (1992) and Ramsey (1979) offer ways to teach about Thanksgiving in a manner that is respectful to Native Americans. Such holidays can be discussed any time of the year and several times of the year as they arise during regular units on "families," "seasons," "homes," and so forth.

Other issues related to curricular inclusion of different cultures have to do with the selection and use of instructional materials. Instructional materials such as dolls, videos, puzzles, and dress-up clothes and props should reflect diversity (Boutte, Van Scoy, and Hendley, 1996). Bulletin boards and other pictures should be representative of many different cultures.

It is also important that different perspectives about historical and other events are continuously presented. Typically, we have only been presented with Eurocentric perspectives. For example, the first Thanksgiving could be discussed from many different cultural perspectives (e.g., Native Americans and European colonists). Teachers can encourage children to complement book reports and other assignments with culturally relevant information. Children researching their state, for example, may be encouraged to complement textbook information by including accomplishments of African, Native, Latino/a, or Asian Americans. A balanced and well-rounded approach should be taken. When such an approach is taken, teachers may be surprised to discover perspectives that differ from that presented in the textbook. For example, when the 1848 United States takeover (annexation) of Texas from Mexico is discussed in history or social studies books, Mexicans are frequently referred to as "bandidos" (bandits). Although they probably did steal from rich Anglos, many Mexican people view the bandido as a "Robin Hood" whose response to Anglos' taking over their land was justified (Martinez, 1997).

The contributions and heritage of many ethnic groups are frequently not included or glossed over in classes. As the comments by Asian American students interviewed by Oei and Lyons (1996) reveal, Asian American students often try to maintain their cultural connections by joining special interest clubs or even weekend schools (e.g., Chinese schools). They appreciate when others show an interest in Asian cultures. On the other hand, omission of this information sends strong negative messages about Asian culture. The same holds true for Latino/a American, Native American, and African American students.

June (Taiwanese American): "What we're required to learn in school is set around U. S. history and government. The only chance in the curriculum to learn about Asian history is one

---

Teachers should have a substantial collection of multicultural literature which reflects many different dimensions of diversity: gender, ethnic groups, socioeconomic statuses, religions, exceptionalities.

world history class in our sophomore year. That does not do a good job. They have to cover 6,000 years of history in one year, and it is mainly Western culture. I don't think that is enough." (Oei and Lyons. 1996, p. 58)

Villy (Laotian American): "When I hear something about Laos, I say,' Wow, they said something about Laos. I'm pretty proud of that.' Actually, it's getting to be known in the outside world. We're getting somewhere." (Oei and Lyons. 1996, p. 59)

Tomoko (Japanese American): "Some people ask me, 'Do you like sushi?' I don't think they know a lot about Japan. It would be really nice if I could teach them something about Japan. I'd like to teach them about Japanese poetry, like haiku and tanka." (Oei and Lyons. 1996, p. 57)

As noted by Oei and Lyons (1996), Asian Americans take pride in the accomplishments of their cultures. It is important to Asian Americans and other ethnic groups to preserve the values of their ancestors while learning about mainstream culture as well.

Multicultural Literature and Textbooks. In order to expand the existing canon, teachers should use literature and textbooks that feature children of differing racial characteristics, ethnic backgrounds, home circumstances, and physical and mental differences (Smolkin and Suina, in press).

A comprehensive multicultural book collection should include the following types of books.

1. Books representing various ethnic groups (African-, Asian-, European-, Latino-, Native American and biracial); religious groups, both genders, different socioeconomic statuses, exceptional individuals, different ages, lifestyles (e.g., single parents)

2. Books that present both historical views (e.g., folk tales) and contemporary depictions of people from different ethnic groups

3. Holidays representing many different cultures (e.g., Passover, Easter, Three Kings Day, Hanukkah, Kwanza)

4. Fairy tales from different cultures (e.g., Africancentric, Asian, Latino)

5. Books showing males and females in nontraditional roles

6. Books that show people from different cultures working together and similarities and differences among people

7. Multicultural books from various disciplines (e.g., art, music, science, math)

8. Books written in different languages and dialects.

Use of multicultural literature is especially important in homogeneous settings where children are segregated by race or socioeconomic status. Grade level book lists should be examined for their multicultural representation. Books which show cultures working together are recommended. *Chicken Sunday* (Polacco, 1992) shows a Jewish and African American family working together; *Everybody Cooks Rice* (Dooley, 1991) illustrates many different ethnic groups living cooperatively in one community. Literature which discusses interracial and interfaith relationships should also be included. We would like to emphasize that there are multicultural books in all subject areas: art, music, and the like. A comprehensive book list which presents books by ethnicity and grade levels can be found in *Through the Eyes of a Child: An introduction to Children's Literature* (Norton and Norton, 1995).

During storytelling or similar oral activities, teachers should use names representative of different cultures. Illustrations using the "token" approach where only one person who is not a majority group member is pictured should be avoided. Sadker, Sadker, and Long (1993) recommend examining materials for the following **six forms of bias**:

- linguistic bias
- stereotyping
- invisibility
- imbalance
- unreality
- fragmentation

Linguistic bias—The language used in books and conversations should be examined for linguistic biases. Sexist terminology should be avoided (e.g., forefathers, mankind, fireman). These should be discussed with children and replaced with more appropriate terms such as ancestors, humankind, firefighter, and the like. Culturally loaded terms which imply negative connotations of various races or ethnic groups need to be examined for their offensiveness as well (e.g., black sheep, jew down).

Stereotyping—Literature that promotes stereotypes should not be used. Even young children can learn to detect and analyze stereotypes. Illustrations as well as storylines should be examined for stereotypes. Many types of stereotypes need to be considered such as gender, religion, exceptionalities, ethnicities, and socioeconomic status. Are boys shown exhibiting one set of values, roles, and behaviors and girls depicted with a different set of characteristics? Two children's books that show boys in a non-sexist manner are *Ira Sleeps Over* (Waber, 1972) and *Willie's Not the Hugging Kind* (Barrett, 1989).

Are certain ethnic groups always shown in particular careers? Are people from certain cultures depicted as being simple–minded while others are depicted as intelligent? Are the heroes or heroines always of a particular ethnic persuasion? Books should represent both contemporary and historical perspectives so that children will not develop stereotypes. In many classrooms, a common approach is to read only folk tales about people of color. This severely limits children's views of different cultures.

A wide variety of images within various ethnic groups should be shown in books and the teacher's collection should include a wide range of intraracial differences. For example, African Americans with light, medium, and dark skins should be shown. Likewise, people within a particular ethnicity should be shown with different lengths and colors of hair, if applicable. Whites also are often depicted in a monocultural manner. Care should be taken to show whites in a wide variety of settings and roles. Whites from various ethnic groups should be shown as well.

One children's book that has been criticized for perpetuating the stereotype that all Asians look alike is *The Seven Chinese Brothers* (Mahy, 1990). The book is based on a historical tale which features seven Chinese brothers who are identical in appearance. Books such as this one should not necessarily be eliminated because they have stereotypes in them. Rather, educators should be sure to have a wide variety of books in the classroom and use the book as an opportunity to alert children to biases in the books. Children can be taught how to critique stereotypes in books.

An attempt should be made to show authentic and accurate images of various ethnicities. When reading books about unfamiliar cultures, it is a good idea to have persons from representative cultural groups evaluate the literature for stereotypes, accuracy, and authenticity of the storyline and illustrations. However, Smolkin and Suina (in press) caution against trying to determine a book's authenticity on the basis of a single cultural member's response. Cultural groups are not monolithic and there may be a tremendous amount of variation in the evaluations of any given book. Therefore, educators must be careful not to convey to children that a book is about *the* culture of any group (e.g., *the* Native American culture). This reiterates an important point noted in Chapter One: there are no simple solutions to making classrooms multicultural. Teachers who cannot find members of a particular group may talk to local librarians, read reviews of books, and/or use their own judgment when selecting books.

If only one person of a particular group is available, it is acceptable to ask for their input when selecting books. For example, I asked a Taiwanese graduate student to evaluate _Tikki Tikki Tembo_ (Mosel, 1968) and _The Seven Chinese Brothers_ (Mahy, 1990) both books that are commonly used as multicultural literature. The graduate student said that _The Seven Chinese Brothers_ seemed to be okay since the emperor mentioned was real and part of China's history. However, she said that she was not aware of the Chinese tradition (mentioned in _Tikki Tikki Tembo_) of giving first sons extremely long names. Furthermore, the graduate student said that the depictions looked _Japanese_ rather than _Chinese_ to her. Since many people in the United States fail to notice distinctions among various Asian cultures, the importance of having a person who shares the same culture review the book becomes obvious. Another implication is that educators must carefully review books rather than adding "multicultural" books to their collection without scrutinizing them. A list of common stereotypes and misconceptions about Native Americans and Asians in books is presented in Figure 2-1.

In order to prevent stereotyping, a balance of images should be included. The book _People_ (Spier, 1980) does a good job of presenting both contemporary and historical images of people from around the world. However, there are times when contemporary images of whites are coupled with historical images of other ethnic groups, thus promoting stereotypes. Also, when occupations are discussed , all of the "American" jobs depict whites. Although the book is intended to convey the positive message that humans share commonalities and differences, subtle and unintentional "exotic" depictions of some groups may inadvertently reinforce or teach stereotypes. Educators using such a book would need to be sure to balance the images presented with other books.

Invisibility—Although people of many cultures, genders, and religions have made significant contributions to the growth and development of the United States, only a few have appeared in books for young children (children's literature, social studies, science, math, and other textbooks). Illustrations and information have systematically been excluded from curricular materials; hence, students are deprived of information about half the nation's people. Sadker, Sadker, and Long (1993) indicate that studies show that significant improvements have been made; however, many cultures, women, people with disabilities, and so forth are still grossly underrepresented in textbooks.

Invisibility in the curriculum is a major problem faced by Mexicans and other Latino/as (Martinez, 1997). They are simply not considered seriously in history and social studies textbooks. This sense of invisibility for people of color begins during the

---

Figure 2-1. Common Stereotypes and Misconceptions in
Books about Native American and Asian Cultures

Native American Culture

1. Alphabet books that treat Native Americans as objects rather than
   as human beings., e.g., *I is for Indian; E is for Eskimo.*

2. Counting books that objectify Native Americans as things or objects
   to count and romanticize the genocidal destruction of Native
   Peoples., e.g., the counting rhyme *Ten little, nine little, eight little
   Indians.*

3. Children "playing Indian," as if "Indian" were a role one could assume
   and dress up as, like doctors or cowboys.

4. Animals dressed as "Indians," suggesting Native Peoples are not
   fully human.

5. Indians with ridiculous, demeaning names, such as "Little Two Feet."

6. Hat books portraying unauthentic representations of Indian head-
   dresses (for purely decorative purposes), rather than accurately
   depicting them worn either in religious ceremonies or by Native
   Peoples who have earned honor.

7. Artwork consisting of predominantly generic "Indian" designs, rather
   than symbols of the particular tribe depicted in the book.

8. Presentation of only one side of an event or issue, causing distorted views and misconceptions.

9. Depiction of males as being savage, hostile warriors; drunken
   thieves; evil medicine men; loyal, brave followers; lazy, unemployed
   loafers.

10. Depiction of females as being either heavyset, workhorse "squaws"
    or Indian princesses.

Asian Culture

1. Depiction of males as smiling, polite and bowing; squinty-eyed and
   bucktoothed; wise, inscrutable or mystical; sinister or sly; expert in
   martial arts; exotic foreigners; super students; model minorities who
   work hard and "make it."

2. Depiction of females as being sweet, well-behaved girls; sexy, sweet
   "China Dolls"; evil "Dragon Ladies"; overbearing, old-fashioned
   grandmothers.

Courtesy of Frances Smardo Dowd and The Association for Childhood
Education International, 11501 Georgia Ave., Suite 315, Wheaton, MD.
Copyright © 1997 by the Association.

early childhood years and continues (and magnifies) throughout high school.

Imbalance—Textbooks and literature perpetuate biases by presenting only one interpretation of an issue, situation, or group of people. Feminists have pointed out that history textbooks are/were dominated by political and military history—areas in which men had been the main participants; therefore, women were invisible (Banks and Banks, 1993). Many different perspectives should be included.

The depiction of Christopher Columbus is probably the only historical episode with which all students are familiar by the time they reach high school (Powell, Zehm, and Garcia, 1996). The account of his "discovery" is recounted throughout school, beginning in the early childhood years. One way to avoid presenting one perspective in this case would be to have students look critically and skeptically at this account. Powell, Zehm, and Garcia (1996) suggest helping students understand that *discovering a country* (which suggests heroism and successful achievement) may actually be interpreted as *invading other societies* from a different perspective. Likewise, *civilizing a nation* from one perspective may mean *genocide* from another perspective (Powell, Zehm, & Garcia, 1996).

Teachers must take care to balance the presentation of books. *The True Story of the Three Little Pigs* (Scieszka, 1989) and *The Blind Men and the Elephant* (Backstein, 1992) are good starter books to help children discuss different perspectives.

A number of fairy tales have been retold from different cultural perspectives. For instance, the familiar Cinderella story by the Brothers Grimm also has Chinese, Egyptian, and Zimbabwean versions (Ladson-Billings, 1994b). In fact, Cinderella stories can be found in more parts of the world, told in more languages, and in more different ways than any other fairytale or folktale (Sierra, 1992). There are over 1500 versions of the story (Martin, 1992). All of the Cinderella tales involve a younger girl *or boy* who is mistreated by her/his family, but receives magical help and is recognized for the good and beautiful person that she/he really is. The first complete Cinderella story to be written down (around 850 A.D.) was the Chinese tale of Yeh-hsien. Two thousand years earlier, a Greek historian also recorded a story told in Egypt that was a version of Cinderella. Figure 2-2 presents a list of some of the ethnic variations of *Cinderella.* Because of culturally imbalanced perspectives presented in school, most people are only familiar with the Grimm or Disney version of the story. If educators realize that all of the stories convey the universal yearning for justice, then

---

Figure 2-2. Ethnic Variations of Cinderella

Climo, S. (1989). *The Egyptian Cinderella.* New York: Harper Trophy. (This is based on the first recorded story and features a servant girl named "Rhodopis." The author/illustrator decided to give Rhodopis European features).

Cole, B. (1987). *Prince Cinders.* New York: G. P. Putnam's Sons. (A humorous male version).

Compton, J. (1994). *Ashpet. An Appalachian Tale.* New York: Holiday House. (A version based on the 1948 Appalachian variant).

Crump, F. (1991). *Cinderella.* Nashville, TN: (African American version).

Ehrlich, A. *Cinderella.* New York: Dial Books for Young Readers. (The version that most people are familiar with. Originally told by Charles Perrault).

Hooks, W. H. (1987). *Moss Gown.* New York: Clarion Books. (An "Old South" version).

Huck, C. (1989). *Princess Furball.* New York: (Probably the second most popular Cinderella story motif).

Jackson, E. (1994). *Cinder Edna.* New York: Lothdrop, Lee, & Sheppard. (A contemporary, humorous, and feminist version).

Louie, Ai-Ling. (1982). *Yeh-Shen. A Cinderella Story from China.* New York: Philomel Books. (A version of the first completely recorded story of Cinderella).

Martin, R., & Shannon, D. (1992). *The Rough–face Girl.* New York: G. P. Putnam's Sons. (An Algonquian Indian version).

Myers, B. (1985). *Sidney Rella and the Glass Sneaker.* New York: Macmillan. (A contemporary male football version).

Shorto, R. (1994). *The Untold Story of Cinderella.* New York: Carol Publishing Group. (One of the stepsister's version of Cinderella).

Steptoe, J. (1987). *Mufaro's Beautiful Daughters.* New York: Lothrop, Lee, & Sheppard. (An African tale).

---

they will view sharing many versions as a way of not only balancing the curriculum, but also as a way to demonstrate the commonalities of the human heart (Martin, 1992).

Unreality—Many textbooks and literatures have presented an unrealistic portrayal of American history and contemporary life experiences by glossing over controversial topics and avoiding discussion of discrimination and prejudice. When controversial issues are not presented, students are denied information needed to confront contemporary problems. Children need to be exposed to a wide spectrum of experiences. For example, instead of selecting books which only show two-parent homes, books dealing with single parenthood and homelessness should also be read.

When discussing slavery, educators can help children investigate slavery from a broader perspective that extends beyond enslavement of African Americans. Research will reveal that all ethnic groups have been enslaved at some point in history (even whites). While the atrocities associated with the enslavement of African Americans in this country should not be downplayed, taking an approach that examines all ethnic groups may reduce the sense of inferiority felt by some African Americans when discussing slavery. Educators must be prepared to deal with the sense of embarrassment, shame, and anger felt by all ethnic groups when slavery is discussed.

Another example of unreality is the typical omission and/or glossing over of the brutal manner in which Native Americans and Latino/a Americans were displaced and killed by European "settlers." "There is also little recognition of the fact that almost one-third of the present-day United States used to be part of Mexico, and before that, Native American lands," laments Chicana activist Elizabeth Martinez (1997, p. 13). The vast wealth created by Mexican and Chinese labor is also largely unrecognized. Martinez points out that the Southwest was essentially built by Mexican, Chinese, and Filipino workers—yet these groups are typically viewed as immigrants and not as "real" Americans. Additionally, the fact that thousands of Mexicans were lynched in the century following the 1848 United States takeover (or "annexation") is frequently omitted or glossed over in history classes (Martinez, 1997). Neither the suffering of Mexicans during this period nor their contributions are included in most U. S. history books.

Educators tend to romanticize "traditional" cultures by focusing on "native" dances, arts, clothing, and foods. Seldom do they deal with more sensitive issues like racism and poverty (Montgomery-Fate, 1997). Montgomery-Fate (1997) asserts that as a culture, we regularly "celebrate diversity" while ignoring how diversity relates to disparities between classes. Our society is often more interested in Native American pottery and rugs, for example, than the ongoing struggles over treaty rights, poverty, and alcoholism that plague many reservations. It is not surprising that similar attitudes pervade schools as well. Montgomery-Fate concludes that studying the exotic tribal life of another era is a lot more tolerable for many people than the realities of racism, classism, and other "isms."

Educators do not gloss over or omit sensitive multicultural issues because they are malicious people. They often do so because they feel that the issues are too strong for young children to deal with. However, it is important to realize that presenting half-truths, myths, or fabrications can also be devastating and confusing to children when the truth is revealed.

Fragmentation—Textbooks often fragment the contributions of many groups by treating these contributions as unique occurrences rather than integrating them into the main body of the text. Contributions of women, people with exceptionalities, and people of color are frequently highlighted in separate boxes or contained in separate chapters. This communicates that these groups are an interesting diversion, but that their contributions do not constitute the mainstream of history and literature.

Fragmentation is also illustrated when certain groups are depicted as having little or no influence on society as a whole. For example, the cultural traditions of groups such as Puerto Ricans and Native Americans have been severely neglected (Rodriguez, 1995). Rodriguez notes that the histories of both of these groups tend to begin with the official date of conquest. Literature written prior to this is not typically incorporated in books.

Rarely are children taught about how Native Americans were dispossessed by European settlers. Few children learn that Indians were relocated, that their languages and religions were forbidden, or that Native American's economies were restructured to fit European notions (Lomaawaima, 1995). The harsh reprisals for resisting assimilation are also typically not addressed.

After reviewing the **six forms of bias** in books (linguistic bias, stereotyping, invisibility, imbalance, unreality, and fragmentation), some educators may tend to shy away from multicultural books because of the fear of not selecting appropriate books. However, all books about people are "multicultural" in the sense that they convey messages about a particular lifestyle. Additionally, in order to ensure that high quality literature is used in the classroom, *all* books should be evaluated. If educators have a balanced collection which represents many cultures and if they are willing to be open to evaluating their collection on a continuous basis, there is little need to worry since there are no one hundred percent guarantees about any book being the best possible selection. For example, *Arrow to the Sun* (McDermott, 1974), a Caldecott Award Book, has received mixed reviews. It is supposedly a Pueblo Indian folktale. However, some Pueblo Indians are offended by it and question the authenticity of the story; others absolutely love the book (Smolkin & Suina, in press). Teachers who are aware of this controversy may still share the book with children and simply point out that some people do not believe that the story is real, while some do. While teachers are encouraged to use the guidelines presented in this chapter to select their books, they must not become overly anxious and paranoid about selecting books. If the guidelines presented are used, it is highly probable that teachers will end up with a good collection. One or two inappropriate books out of an otherwise wonderful collection should not be devastating to students.

Multilinguistic Experiences.   Children should learn different words that represent the same thing. By integrating both colloquial and non-English expressions into the curriculum, teachers can help children realize the value and enjoyment of knowing different ways to talk. Ask children to name all the ways they know to greet someone (Hi, Yo, Howdy, Hey, What's up? Bonjour!). Then list these greetings and discuss possible reactions to unfamiliar expressions. Discussion of differences in the terminology used to refer to parents is also a good beginning activity (e.g., Mama, Mother, M'dear, Ma).

Once while I was reading the story *Flossie and the Fox* (McKissack, 1986) to a group of third graders, several children laughed at the term, "Big Mama." We stopped and briefly discussed the many different names that were used to refer to grandmothers. It was amazing to see the differences. Incidentally, one of the children actually called her grandmother, "Big Mama." Without such a discussion which modeled appreciation of differences, the child may have received subtle messages about her cultural terminology.

DeFlorimonte (1993) suggests sharing books and poetry which demonstrate various dialects in early childhood and elementary classrooms (e.g., *Flossie and the Fox* includes southern Black English vernacular; *Possum come a Knockin'* (Van Lann, 1990) includes Appalachian dialect; *De Gullah Storybook* (Daise and Daise, 1986) is written in the Gullah dialect). Older children would enjoy Virginia Hamilton's *The People Could Fly* (1985) which is written in Black English dialect. Many of these books are accompanied by an audio cassette which can be used when teachers experience problems mastering the dialect. Books with sign language and braille are also recommended. Since many parents who speak nonstandard English worry about their children learning standard English, teachers should apprise parents beforehand of their intent. Parents are usually supportive once they realize the value of maintaining children's natural vernacular. Teachers can also use dialect books to explicitly compare and contrast the dialect with Standard English. Delpit (1995) recommends explicit comparisons of the *rules* for both language systems. Simply modeling Standard English or doing isolated English workbook activities is typically insufficient for helping children (who do not speak Standard English) master the language system. Unless children are highly motivated to learn Standard English, most will not. Evidence of this is that such children go through twelve years of schooling which includes language arts or English each year, but exit school without mastering Standard English.

Boutte, Davis, and McCoy (1995) emphasize the importance of extending children's communication styles, as well as showing appreciation of their natural vernaculars. As noted by Delpit (1986; 1988; 1991), we do children an injustice if they exit school without mastering Standard English. She emphasizes explicit instruction for children who do not already speak Standard English— the "language of power." Teachers should ensure that children speak both Standard English and in their natural communication style. Admittedly, this is a difficult and delicate task, but children must be prepared to be successful in both settings. Heath (1988; 1991) found that both teachers and parents needed to learn to encourage children to communicate cross-culturally. Heath emphasized the importance of teachers understanding children's communication styles as well.

Delpit (1986; 1988; 1995) raises questions about whether "process" approaches such as whole language are effective for teaching children of color Standard English. Some people have misinterpreted Delpit's argument for explicit instruction to mean that teachers should teach isolated skills. However, Delpit's main point is that when children do not come to school speaking primarily Standard English, teachers must be sure to teach them the rules of Standard English in order to ensure future success in life. Delpit argues that the skills must be taught within a relevant context. Delpit argues against the dichotomy of viewing the teaching of English as a dichotomy where either skill or fluency is encouraged. Both are important. Indeed, whole language and other process methods can be effective with children of color. Kasten (1992) effectively argues that whole language is congruent with most Native American cultures. Kasten points out that both whole language and Native American cultures emphasize process over product. Native American cultures are frequently characterized as process-oriented, emphasizing life as a journey, which is more important than the destination. Additionally, whole language encourages work that extends over several days or weeks, and includes redrafts, peer conferencing, peer editing, and teacher feedback. This approach is more congruent with Native American culture than the traditional classroom approach which confines assignments to a single period or day after which a product for evaluation is expected.

We do not intend to imply that language within ethnic groups is uniform by any means (not all black children speak Black English). For example, Carol Phillips (1994) noted three linguistic patterns exhibited by African American children. The first pattern is evidenced by children who resist acculturation attempts by schools and continue to operate in the African American style regardless of the setting. She noted that these children often experience difficulty in the classroom because they may be regarded as "uneducable" since their language is in direct contrast to "school language."

A second pattern is manifested when children capitulate to the school demands and completely abandon the African American communication style altogether in all settings. Schools typically regard these students as "successful" since they use Standard English. However, they may encounter anxiety in their community.

A third pattern is evidenced by children who operate in both styles, each in the appropriate setting. Although these styles are oversimplified and generalized in their description, Phillips concludes that the third pattern appears to be adaptive within the sociopolitical context in which we live. This pattern permits children to move through the two contexts of school and family-community. Phillips suggests that educators should support this strategy since it empowers children by helping them become proficient in both communication styles. However, we hasten to note that it is unfortunate that all communication styles are not embraced in our society and that it is not recognized that many dialects are structurally rich and rule-governed. Yet, Solomon and Winsboro (1993) assert that "educators must make their students aware that limited language skills mean limited possibilities" (p. 12).

Resource Persons From Different Cultures.   Teachers should involve people of many different characteristics and backgrounds in classroom activities. Representatives of various cultural groups within the classroom and the community, such as local merchants, can be invited to the classroom to share aspects of their culture. Parents may be encouraged to share a family recipe or other family traditions. It is important to avoid stereotypes by inviting only blue collar workers from one ethnic group and white collar workers from another. Balances and frequent representations are needed.

❖ AVOIDING PSEUDOMULTICULTURALISM

Many educators mistake the term "multicultural" to mean addressing only the needs of minority children (often limited to

African American children). This approach is pseudomulticultural: it does not consider the needs of all children and assumes that white children's needs are generally taken care of in the classroom. Variation among whites exists and should be illustrated in the classroom also. Multicultural educators invite white parents (as well as members of other cultures) to the classroom to share their specific cultural heritage. Most parents enjoy sharing aspects of their own childhoods with children. This is a wonderful way to personalize historical information as well as to present a variety of role models to children.

Multicultural educators familiarize themselves with the extensive body of research that reveals that children from typically oppressed ethnic groups (i.e., African, Latino/a, and Native American) are disproportionately placed in special classes for the mentally retarded and the learning disabled and drop out of high school at rates much higher than those of whites (Murphy, 1986). (These issues will be discussed in detail in the subsequent section). Educators are aware that these children tend to score lower than white children on measures of cognitive ability and academic success. Multicultural educators are not guided by such information; rather, they interpret the information to mean that the differences children bring to school must somehow be accommodated in the classroom. Hence, multicultural teachers seek to meet the needs of all children and expect them to reach their fullest potential.

Multicultural teachers are comfortable teaching children to be bicultural; however, they realize that modeling the behavior from the general culture may need to be accompanied by explanations of the underlying dynamics. Many children of color apparently do not readily assimilate certain behavioral characteristics of the "white culture" considered necessary for success in schools and society (Delpit, 1988). In a multicultural classroom, the expectations of the "white culture" need to be articulated in an overt as well as covert manner. Educators often discuss how some behaviors are acceptable at home but not in other settings. The teacher may point out that when students nod or shake their heads or say "Uh huh" instead of answering questions clearly with a "yes" or "no," listeners may assume that the children are not interested in the topic being discussed. The teacher may designate times for "relaxed" talk versus "school" talk.

Essentially, multicultural teachers avoid being pseudomulticultural because they have a sincere desire to treat all children with respect in as many ways as possible and as frequently as possible. Teachers who aim to do this will provide the best possible classroom experiences for children.

❖ CULTURAL LEARNING STYLES

Researchers have identified typical learning patterns among various ethnic and cultural groups (Guild, 1994). For example, the literature indicates that African American children often value oral experiences, physical activity, and loyalty in interpersonal relationships. These learning styles call for classroom activities like discussion, active projects, and collaborative work. Native American students generally value and develop acute visual discrimination and skills in the use of imagery, perceive facts globally, and have reflective thinking patterns. Thus, classrooms should establish a context for new information, provide quiet time for thinking, and emphasize visual stimuli. In contrast, mainstream white Americans are typically described as valuing independence, analytic thinking, objectivity, and accuracy. Mainstream learning styles translate into classroom experiences that focus on competition, information, tests, grades, and linear logic. Mainstream patterns are prevalent in most schools.

Although information about cultural learning styles may be helpful to teachers who seek to provide inclusive classrooms, the concept of learning styles is often oversimplified, misunderstood, or misinterpreted. Often, educators assume that all children from these ethnic groups learn the same way. Hence, individual differences are forgotten and students are stereotyped or labeled. In multicultural classrooms, these learning styles are not intended to be prescriptions for students' destinies. Educators should not automatically attribute a particular learning style to all individuals within a group (Guild, 1994). Educators need to be aware of information about cultural learning styles, observe individual children's learning styles carefully, utilize a variety of teaching approaches, and assist children in becoming bicultural and/or multicultural. Cultural learning styles will be covered in more detail in Chapter Three.

❖ OVERT AND COVERT MULTICULTURAL ISSUES

Educational outcomes are vastly different for different racial, language, economic, and gender groups in this nation (Pine & Hilliard, 1990). Children from different social classes are likely to attend different types of schools, to receive different types of instruction, to study different curricula, and to leave school at different rates and times. As a result, children end their school careers more different from each other than they were when they entered (Persell, 1993; Wilcox, 1982). Differences in dropout rates, suspensions, expulsions, academic achievement indices, patterns of coursework, and instructional strategies are a few of numerous indicators of institutionalized discrimination in America's school system. *Institutional discrimination* is manifested through established laws, customs, and practices that reflect and produce inequalities in society (Nieto, 1992). It may be overt, covert, intentional, or unintentional. However, regardless of its form or intention, discrimination is unwarranted and detrimental to the recipients and to society at large. It is important to note that there are no simple solutions. Clark (1983) analyzed more than twelve hundred studies of urban schools and concluded that additional resources and upgrades in facilities alone are insufficient to affect school or program outcomes. Other factors such as curriculum and staff development must also be included.

Generally speaking, children from poor families are the least successful and hardest to teach by traditional methods (Connell, 1994). They are the least powerful of the schools' clients because they are the least able to insist that their needs be met. Yet, they must depend more on schools for their educational resources than any other cultural group (Connell, 1994).

In this section, both overt and covert multicultural issues that should be considered for educators' professional development will be discussed. Issues identified as overt are well documented and discussed in the literature. Covert issues, on the other hand, are often very subtle and not always clear. In fact, many people argue that covert issues are harmless and insignificant and should be ignored or overlooked (Boutte, LaPoint, and Davis, 1993). All of the issues discussed deal with familiar concepts that are often seemingly forgotten in practice.

The discussion of multicultural issues often causes discomfort for many people (see Table 1-3 in Chapter One). Louise Derman-Sparks, author of the *Anti-Bias Curriculum,* frequently remarks that such issues are handled like the "emperor's new clothes." In the classic children's book, *The Emperor's New Clothes,"* everybody knew that the emperor did not have any clothes on, but no one told him because it was not polite to do so. Similarly, in our society we have been taught that it is not polite to discuss sensitive issues—especially in certain geographic regions. For example, when children ask questions about the way a person speaks or their color, they are often told that it is impolite. Likewise, when children innocently inquire about a person's disabilities or religion, they are discouraged from asking questions. A more appropriate and informative response would be to answer children's questions and help them to see why they feel uncomfortable, if necessary (Derman-Sparks, 1989).

Overt Issues

Most will agree that the five issues discussed here (testing, placement, tracking, dropout rates, and quality of schools) are ones which often illustrate apparent differences based on race, gender, and socioeconomic status. Although race, gender and social class are often referred to separately, they are interrelated.

Testing. Since the early 1960s, researchers have reported that children from typically economically depressed ethnic groups such as African, Latino/a, and Native Americans tend to score lower than white and Asian children on various measures of cognitive ability and academic success. Many people accept these differences as an inevitable fact of life. However, the inequities surrounding differential performance need to be addressed. Asa Hilliard (1991) points out that our schools are so caught up in testing children that we have seemingly forgotten about *teaching them*. He adds that schools would rather blame and embarrass school children for low test scores than teach and nourish them.

Ogbu (1974) discovered that Latino/a and African American students do not attempt to maximize their scores on school tests or try to get the highest grades possible because they do not feel as if there is a reason to do so. School and test failure is an adaptation to the limited opportunities for social and economic mobility available to African, Latino, and Native Americans (Ogbu, 1974).

As early childhood educators, we know that standardized testing does not provide much insight into *how* children learn. Yet schools continue to use test results which relegate a disproportionate number of children to inferior positions in schools and in later occupations (Scarr, 1981). Alternative authentic assessment methods must be considered as a strategy for overcoming biases.

Placement (Remedial/Gifted Classes). Another overt issue closely related to testing is student placement. Children's placements are also often divided among racial lines; children of color are more likely to be placed in remedial classes and white children are more likely to be placed in gifted classes. The literature on these findings is extensive and reveals that children of color are placed in special classes for the mentally retarded and the learning disabled at rates much higher than those of their white counterparts (Murphy, 1986). Social class also affects placement decisions (Persell, 1993).

Jacqueline Irvine discusses how many schools use testing under the guise of providing objectivity and accountability. It is not uncommon to find that persistent parents often (subjectively) influence children's placement (Irvine, 1990). In her research,

Irvine found a number of students in advanced classes whose transcripts did not warrant their placement. Hence, if parents do not know how to play the placement "game," their children may end up in remedial classes throughout their school career. Moreover, children who are placed in remedial classes often receive low-level, skill-based instruction, score poorly on subsequent tests and remain in remedial or low ability classes. "Gifted" children, on the other hand, often receive higher level instruction, do well on tests and remain in classes that stress critical skills and thinking.

Negative testing experiences and subsequent placements can have a direct effect on a child's feelings of competence, trust, and initiative. Children who do not feel competent at school may develop a sense of inferiority (Tribe, 1982) or seek to find avenues for being competent outside the classroom and/or school (Hale-Benson, 1986). When children consistently experience non-success in school, they also began to distrust the school system and hesitate about taking the initiative in classes (Hale-Benson, 1986).

Tracking. It is evident that the test–placement–test sequence frequently becomes self-perpetuating and students often are placed in a high ability (gifted) or low ability (remedial) track during the early childhood years and remain there throughout their school careers. For this reason, tracking and ability grouping are generally not recommended in early childhood classes. Additionally, although students of all races, classes, and genders are publicly identified as of "low" or "average" ability, it is poor, African American, Native American and Latino/a American children who are disproportionately assigned to these categories (Kasten, 1992; Oakes and Lipton, 1990). Native American students have the highest likelihood of being labeled as handicapped or learning disabled of any ethnic group in the United States (Kasten, 1992). Oakes and Lipton point out that there is extensive data which indicate that schools serving predominantly children of color and poor populations offer fewer advanced and more remedial courses, and that they have smaller academic tracks and larger vocational programs. They conclude that "it is increasingly clear that children are consistently and systematically disadvantaged by a practice that is widely and firmly embedded in school traditions and culture" (Oakes and Lipton, p. 189). Schools are only recently beginning to search for appropriate alternatives to tracking.

Tracking originated when schools were pressured to provide an emerging industrial society with a trained work forced already sorted by ability levels. Today workplaces and colleges require a minimum level of competency and skill development for all workers and students. Yet Oakes and Lipton note that tracking continues to unfairly sort students for subsequent social and economic roles.

Typically, there are serious inequities in gifted and average classes. Gifted children often get the best teachers, have smaller class sizes, boast a superior academic mission, and high levels of parent involvement. Such classes are also more likely to encourage critical thinking, independence, and questioning. These classes spend more time on learning activities and less time on discipline, socializing, class routines, and homework. Paradoxically, "low" and "average" students who would benefit from such instruction rarely receive the same treatment. Interestingly, Oakes and Lipton noted that "high ability" students learn equally well in mixed classes. As we will demonstrate later, teacher expectations are closely related to tracking (Oakes & Lipton, 1990).

Dropout Rates. There is a wealth of data that points out unequivocal differences in dropout rates by race and social class. They are consistently higher for children of color. Although there are a number of exceptions, students from higher social classes tend to receive better grades and stay in school longer than do students from lower class backgrounds (Persell, 1993). The long and heartbreaking history of educating Native American students in the United States demonstrates that schools have not met their needs. Native American students have the highest dropout rates of all students of color (Kasten, 1992). Additionally, only 55 out of 100 Latino/as who enter kindergarten will graduate from high school (Garcia, 1997; Martinez, 1997). The exceptionally high dropout rates for Latino/a students are often a result of a number of complex problems. Without doubt, the cumulative effect of cultural denigration contributes to this problem. The first thing that typically happens when a child from a Spanish-speaking family goes to school is that his or her name gets Anglicized ("Roberto" becomes "Bobby"; "Estevan" becomes "Steve") (Martinez, 1997). Martinez notes that the identities and language of Latino/a children are also frequently attacked. Indeed, for many students of color and/or poor students, schools become hostile environments (Irvine, 1990; Martinez, 1997). From this point of view Martinez concludes that rather than "drop out," the process should be called "push out" for many Latino/as and other students of color.

In a multicultural school, such trends can and must be reversed. The importance of viewing this issue developmentally cannot be overstated. In the early grades, the academic achievement of students of color (African Americans, Latino/a Americans, and Native Americans) is close to parity with white mainstream students (Banks and Banks, 1997). Moreover, they are eager to learn and generally trust their teachers to know what is best for them (Kozol, 1991; Kunjufu, 1990). If one were to observe most children of color in kindergarten, they would seem content when participating in class activities (e.g., listening to stories, singing, dancing, and generally being joyful). If one was not familiar with the host of negative statistics and trends for many of these children, the moment may seem auspicious (Kozol, 1991). But if one knows the future that awaits most of the children, "it is terrible to see their eyes look up at you with friendliness and trust—to see this and to know what is in store for them." (Kozol, 1991, p. 45) The longer most students of color remain in school, the more their achievement lags behind that of white mainstream students. On the other hand, when students are treated with dignity and taught skillfully, they will affiliate with the school and achieve (Erickson, 1997; Ladson-Billings, 1994a). Multicultural education aims to give all children a fair and equal chance of learning and completing high school (Banks & Banks, 1997).

Quality of Schools. Another overt issue is discrepancies in the quality of schools. Kozol (1991) aptly and graphically demonstrates that schools for students of color and poor children are grossly substandard in terms of physical facilities and resources. Because funding for most public schools is based in part on local

---

When reading books about unfamiliar cultures, it is a good idea to have persons from representative cultural groups evaluate the literature for stereotypes, accuracy, and authenticity of the storyline and illustrations.

property taxes, "inner city" schools are typically grossly under-funded in comparison to suburban schools. Such inequities must be addressed if all children are to have access to a high quality education. Class inequality is a problem for the school system as a whole. The problem of poor quality schools is not unique to poor children; however, they face the worst effects of a larger pattern (Connell, 1994). Schools that earnestly seek change will need to mobilize parents, teachers, the community, legislators, and other interested parties in order to change laws and practices that not only adversely affect poor children but also hurt society at large in the long run.

Covert Issues

Despite the abundance of data by Brophy and Good (1970), Good and Brophy (1987), Irvine (1990), and others, many educators do not fully acknowledge the significant role that covert issues play in testing, placement decisions, ability grouping, and dropout rates. The literature indicates six covert issues that are closely related to the overt ones:

- teacher attitudes
- teacher expectations
- teacher-child interactions
- curriculum relevance/inclusion
- sensitivity to racial issues
- parent-school interactions

Most people would probably agree that these "covert" issues are important; however, many doubt that they are as powerful as we suggest. Educators in stage one on the Reach multi-cultural chart (Table 1-3, Chapter One) often believe that all children have an equal chance at success in school. They postulate that most of the racial issues suggested are "imagined," "blown way out of proportion," or easily overcome. I disagree. The results of covert actions and attitudes are powerful and have a cumulative effect on a child's future.

Teacher Attitudes (Societal attitudes). Societal attitudes (from the media, communities, etc.) and images (e.g., African American criminals or welfare recipients) undoubtedly affect educators' attitudes about various racial groups. The prevailing attitudes and images are mind-boggling. Unless we make a conscious effort to become multicultural, it is difficult to do because many of our attitudes have not been challenged. Additionally, since most teachers enter the teaching profession to help children, they often feel that they do not have any biases which may be damaging to students. Yet, we all have biases that need to be acknowledged and reflected upon. Most educators believe that they provide all children with equal chances for success. However, careful examination of attitudes and actions reveals that biases have crept into classrooms unbeknownst to the teachers. Jones and Derman-Sparks (1989) note that whether educators' biases damage children's self-esteem intentionally or not, the negative effect is still the same. Therefore, educators must engage in the continuous process of examining their behaviors and attitudes.

Teachers often hold negative attitudes about children of color (Steele, 1992). Incidentally, these negative teacher attitudes are not unique to white teachers. Because our society has traditionally been viewed from a Eurocentric perspective, teachers of color are equally as likely to hold negative attitudes about children of color. Again, it is emphasized that for the most part, the attitudes are not intentional and may not be recognized by teachers.

Often when teachers' and school officials' awareness levels progress to stage two on Table 1-3 (Chapter One), curricula materials and activities are sought to make classrooms more inclusive and less biased. However, in addition to curricular materials, it is equally as important (but certainly more difficult) to examine one's own attitudes and biases. Asa Hilliard often notes that it is easier for educators to blame the curriculum for its shortcomings than to examine themselves. Nevertheless, it is important to emphasize that actions speak louder than anything that is said—certainly louder than any curricular materials. Actions are closely tied to belief systems and attitudes and children are very adept at detecting hidden messages.

Teacher Expectations. Teacher expectations have a subtle but powerful effect on students. Although it is readily acknowledged that children's success in school is due to a number of complex factors (e.g., home environments, personalities), teachers must recognize the power they have over their students' destinies. The notion of a self-fulfilling prophecy is frequently discussed in educational circles; however, it is seemingly easily forgotten in practice. Negative self-fulfilling prophecies are often initially false, but a series of events causes them to be true. Children learn that teachers expect little from them and, hence, provide expected responses. Teacher expectations are closely related to differences in overt issues such as ability grouping. Lindfors (1989) notes that "What one sees depends on how one looks" (p. 65). If we view children's cultures as assets, then we build on them and recognize their strengths. If, on the other hand, we see their cultures as deficits, then we fail to recognize and acknowledge positive attributes.

After a comprehensive evaluation of schools, Claude Steele (1992) concluded that the cause of school failure among African American children is the devaluation that the children face. Steele found that the effect of years of low teacher expectations are still evident when students reach college. Hundreds of studies on teacher expectations have been conducted. The literature from these studies indicates that, in addition to race, a number of factors influence teacher expectations (Brophy and Good, 1970; Irvine, 1990). The subsequent section discusses many of these factors that are based on comprehensive studies by Brophy and Good, 1970; Clifford and Walster, 1973; Good and Brophy, 1987; Irvine, 1990; and Mason, 1973. The list is not intended to be exhaustive.

Some of the factors which influence teacher expectations are: ethnicity, gender, socioeconomic status, student achievement, personality, seating location, physical attractiveness, writing neatness, speech characteristics, body odor or other physical characteristics, and a combination of these factors. Many of the factors are connected and it is difficult to separate them.

Ethnicity—The literature indicates that teachers frequently hold lower expectations for children of color (presumably because of what they know about children's ethnic groups from society). Paradoxically, many teachers in stage one (Table 1-3, Chapter One) adhere to a "colorblind theory" and maintain that race does not affect their expectations. For some teachers this is true; for many others, the literature informs us otherwise. Negative attitudes toward students of color lower expectations for achievement, which in turn lowers achievement (Ladson-Billings, 1994b).

Gender—Teachers and schools are typically more willing to examine gender differences than racial differences since they are somewhat less threatening. Recently, many teachers have become familiar with the American Association of University Women's (AAUW) research findings on gender bias by way of television documentaries and talk shows. Many teachers, who found the data hard to believe, agreed to be videotaped in their classrooms. They were surprised to discover that they had indeed called on boys more frequently or that they held different expectations based on the gender of the students. In fact, many teachers even explained why they held different expectations (e.g., boys are more active; they are better in math) without giving much thought to the cumulative effect of differential treatment of students.

Socioeconomic status (SES)—As with gender issues, many people feel more comfortable dealing with socioeconomic status than with race. Certainly, both are interrelated and affect teacher expectations. Lower expectations are generally held for children from a low socioeconomic status. Kathleen Wilcox's (1982) ethnographic study demonstrated how teachers channel children into different vocational paths (blue collar vs. white collar) based on children's socioeconomic statuses without being aware of it. This study is discussed in more detail in Chapter Eight. Interestingly, the channeling process begins during the early childhood years.

Ladson-Billings (1994b) notes that teachers often perceive African American students from working class or lower socioeconomic status backgrounds as incapable of high quality academic work.

Student Achievement—Using students' past achievement as a basis for teacher expectations has merit, but is not always founded. It is often recounted that more children fail in the teachers' lounge than anywhere else. The meaning of this statement is that a teacher often discovers information about students' past performance long before the students enter the teacher's classroom. Instead of relying solely on students' past achievement patterns, it is incumbent upon educators to continuously examine and reassess the amount of effort put forth by all children and realize that achievement is dynamic. Since young children are continuously developing and changing, tracking is not recommended.

Personality—Teachers tend to hold higher expectations for students with *outgoing* personalities; whereas quiet children are often overlooked or not expected to make valuable contributions in class. As noted by Heath (1982), whether or not a child feels free to talk in classrooms may be related to cultural issues such as communication styles.

Seating Location—When classes are organized in a "traditional" seating arrangement with the teacher in the front, he or she may hold higher expectations for children in the front of the class since they are in the "action zone" and encounter more frequent interactions. Seating patterns should be examined for their effectiveness in facilitating the involvement of all children.

Physical Attractiveness—When the macro society shows us what beauty is, it is easy to figure out what beauty is not. If beauty is long, blonde hair, then it is not short, black, kinky hair.

The following statements made by a Vietnamese American illustrates this point.

Khanh (Vietnamese American): "The media is propagating its depiction of the beautiful people, and everybody is white and has wavy long hair and blue eyes, and that's what beauty is. So when you look at yourself and you're not that model, you say, 'Oh I'm so ugly!' no matter what else you've achieved in your life." (Oei and Lyon, 1996. p. 54)

Khanh (Vietnamese American): Each one of us is different. Every single time I look in the mirror, I know that I'm Asian and I know that I'm Vietnamese. I have my own understanding that it's what you think and what you believe in that's important. But on the other hand, I know I feel deep down inside that I can never be physically as beautiful as somebody who is white. No matter how much I say, 'I am my own person. I'm very strong about my ideas,' and all that I would think that my life would be so much better if I was white. And I thought that for so, so long, and it's hard to try to undo all those things and all those images from the past." (Oei and Lyon, 1996. p. 54)

Teachers hold higher expectations for children who are physically attractive based on societal descriptions of beauty. Types of clothing also influence teachers' beliefs. In fact, teacher expectations are more influenced by negative information about students' physical characteristics than by positive data (Clifford and Walster, 1973; Mason, 1973). Educators must examine if or how their attitudes about children who are disabled influence their expectations. For example, can educators look beyond children's physical handicaps or disabilities and see the true beauty of the children? Teachers must carefully evaluate what their views are toward children in wheelchairs, children missing limbs, or children whose physical handicaps cause them to drool or to lack control of bodily functions. Although some children will undoubtedly have disabilities that prevent them from achieving the same level of success as many other children, educators must expect all children to reach the highest level of achievement possible for them. Activity #4 in Chapter One will help educators reflect on how physical attractiveness affects teacher expectations.

Writing Neatness—Teachers who value neat penmanship hold higher expectations for children who write neatly. Interestingly, in a number of studies, when teachers who valued neat handwriting were shown identical content written in different levels of neatness, teachers judged the papers with neater handwriting higher and expected the children to be "smarter."

Speech Characteristics—The vast majority of people use dialects at some time or other. Teachers often mistakenly equate speech characteristics to intelligence. Therefore, higher expectations are often held for children who speak Standard English. Lisa Delpit (1986; 1988; 1991) makes the case for teaching children to speak Standard English as well as their dialect so that they will have a better chance at being successful in school.

Body Odor and Other Physical Characteristics—In "Teddy's Story," an anecdotal account of the effect of low teacher expectations, the description of Teddy's odor was a salient factor in the teachers' feelings about him. Without a concerted effort to treat children fairly, it is easy to treat such children inequitably.

Educators should examine their biases about all physical characteristics including dirty clothes, messy hair, outdated glasses, and physical size.

Combination of any of the above factors—As we noted earlier, many of these factors are interrelated. Based on what we know about teacher expectations, envision the treatment of a black female (from a low socioeconomic status, who has a poor achievement record, is quiet, sits in the back, is not physically attractive, writes poorly, and speaks Black English vernacular) in many classrooms. How would these factors affect teacher expectations and interactions with the child?

Teacher-Child Interactions. Teacher expectations and interactions are inevitably related. Although teacher-student interactions can be directly observed, interaction patterns are often more difficult to detect. Without careful observation, the quality of teacher interactions is often not brought to the surface. Six considerations that teachers can use to examine the nature of their interactions with children will be briefly discussed: 1) positive vs. negative reactions, 2) frequency of interactions, 3) nonverbal communication, 4) differences in grouping patterns, 5) labeling, and 6) reaction time.

Teachers are encouraged to videotape themselves since most educators think that they treat all children fairly. A favorite example of the effectiveness of videotaping involved a mature preservice teacher who had received consistent feedback about her lack of enthusiasm from her cooperating teacher and college supervisor. However, the student continued to view herself as an enthusiastic person. When she was finally videotaped during her student teaching experience, she exclaimed, "Am I really that boring?" Seeing is believing!

Making small changes in everyday classroom participation structures may be one strategy by which more culturally relevant pedagogy can be developed (Erickson & Mohatt, 1982). I hasten to point out that there are many positive things that teachers do in their classrooms; however, the following section focuses on issues that teachers can examine in order to more effectively give all children an equal chance of success in school regardless of their ethnicity, gender, socioeconomic status, or religious persuasions.

Positive vs. Negative Reactions—When examining treatment of children from various races, genders, and classes, teachers should routinely make mental notes or keep written records on the frequency of their positive vs. negative reactions to children. Many teachers are surprised to discover that some children consistently receive positive or negative responses from them. The nature of these interactions are often related to cultural beliefs.

Frequency of Interactions—Closely related to the quality of responses is the quantity of responses that children receive from their teachers. Because it is so easy to unconsciously interact with children differentially (due to a number of factors such as differences in student personalities), many teachers find it helpful to devise methods to ensure that they interact with all children each day regardless of race, socioeconomic status, gender, etc. Sheila Hanley, a fourth-grade teacher in South Carolina, says that she routinely places all children's names in a box and makes sure that every child is called on at least once daily by randomly selecting names from the box throughout the day. Another teacher shared that she assigns students to serve as classroom monitors. The classroom monitors are in charge of alerting the teacher to students who have not been called on during the day. These examples emphasize the necessity of making a conscious effort to overcome interaction biases.

Nonverbal Communication—Often, our nonverbal communication sends powerful, subtle (covert) messages to children. Teachers smile more at some students and demonstrate impatience more with others. When nonverbal communication conflicts with verbal responses, students often read the nonverbal responses as well as what the teacher says. For example, a teacher who exclaims, "Very Good!" while frowning with her arms crossed tightly may convey mixed messages to students.

Differences in Grouping Patterns—Teachers are encouraged to closely examine the composition of their low ability groups (if applicable). If they are comprised mostly of children of color, there may be a problem. Additionally, teachers may reflect on whether children in high ability groups receive more or less positive responses. It is interesting that teachers often take credit for children's progress in high ability groups. For example, when children do well, teachers often proudly state, " *I* taught her. " On the other hand, when they do poorly, the blame is shifted to the child and we say, "*She* can't learn." It is not uncommon for children's cultural patterns of behavior (speech and other culturally idiosyncratic responses) to interfere with grouping patterns. As Heath (1982) and Irvine (1990) pointed out, when teachers and students lack cultural synchronization, behaviors that are encouraged and reinforced at home are frowned upon at school. In other words, a child who is regarded as precocious at home may be considered "below average" in school. Teachers need to examine to what degree cultural styles affect their grouping of children. Classrooms should be inclusive and show respect for many different cultural styles while extending children's orientations. Interestingly, when cultural chasms exist between teachers and students, teachers often view students' behaviors as atypical (Boutte and McCormick, 1992; Heath, 1992).

Labeling—Often children of color are negatively labeled as "low ability," "slow," or "quiet" (Boutte, LaPoint, and Davis, 1993; Heath, 1982). Heath (1982) discovered that African American children who were labeled as quiet at school were definitely not quiet at home. It would behoove teachers to examine their use of labels for all children—not just children of color. Being familiar with children's home settings adds insight into a holistic understanding of children. Instead of focusing on weaknesses, teachers can instead focus on strengths that children possess. The behavior of children of color should be examined and appreciated in terms of what is typical for their culture rather than in comparison to the majority culture.

Reaction Time—Another way that teachers respond differently to children in classrooms is the amount of reaction time allowed for children. The AAUW's study illuminated this issue. When teachers consistently wait longer for certain children to respond and provide more prompting and cues to particular children, children infer the type of expectations that teachers hold. Typically, they respond according to what they conclude that expectation is, and it becomes a self-fulfilling prophecy. African American children learn very early that if they pause a minute, the teacher will go to the next child. Consequently, around fourth grade many African American children stop putting forth effort and seek appreciation of their natural gifts outside the classroom (Hale-Benson, 1986; Kunjufu, 1985, 1986, 1990).

Curriculum Relevance/Inclusion. This section amplifies points made earlier regarding curricular inclusion of multicultural heritage. Although schools are rapidly changing to address diversity, most schools operate from a Eurocentric paradigm which does not validate the accomplishments of people of color. Subtle messages are sent which indicate whether one's social class, religion, exceptionality, gender, and ethnicity are valued in society. Transforming curricula into a multicultural focus requires numerous changes in attitudes, perspectives, and curricula. We do not recommend a few additions to the curriculum; rather, we advocate holistic transformation of the curriculum so that it is inclusive and integrated throughout the year (Boutte and McCormick, 1992). We cannot expect change overnight since it took five-hundred years to evolve our present curriculum (Howard, 1993). Suggestions for increasing curriculum relevance are made below.

- All aspects of the curriculum need to be considered such as books, videos, plays, holidays, field trips (e.g., African American museums as well as general museums). Regardless of whether the setting is homogeneous or heterogeneous, schools should show appreciation of all cultures. There is a proliferation of multicultural materials available; however, many teachers lament that it is exceedingly time-consuming to locate and obtain these materials. The sole responsibility of seeking multicultural curricula materials should not lie only with teachers. School districts that are serious about multiculturalism will select textbooks and other materials that reflect diversity so that teachers will not be overwhelmed and discouraged when trying to locate information. Additionally, parents and other community members can be excellent resources for providing materials and references. Contributions of many ethnic groups such as Latino/a artists, African American poets, African scholars and inventors, etc. need to be integrated into the curriculum. Again, it is emphasized that such information should not be presented in isolated units as if it were merely unique, add-on tidbits of information. It should be thoroughly integrated throughout the curriculum as is other relevant content.
- Presently, many children of color encounter a sense of invisibility in the classroom. It is imperative that children of color see themselves in books and in the curriculum. They need to know that role models exist and that they (children of color) can be politicians, teachers, writers, inventors, or anything that they aspire to be. Eurocentric curriculum subtly, but powerfully, teaches European American children that they are superior. Reinforcing

false information about a race is damaging in the long run for all children—white or otherwise (Howard, 1993). Curricula should help children seek the truth about their history as well as the history of others. Such information may not always be positive and easy to digest; however, all cultural groups will have some history worthy of celebration and some that is unfavorable.

- Bulletin boards and classroom displays should be examined to determine if they represent diversity (racial, gender, physical abilities, etc.). One common technique used is the "token" approach where one person of color is displayed amidst a large group of whites (Derman-Sparks, 1989). Although negative racial *attitudes* are probably more damaging and sustaining than negative visual images and depictions, care should be given to include images of people of color as well as whites. Additionally, bulletin boards should be examined for stereotypical depictions of racial groups. Authentic depictions and real photos of people provide a more realistic image of people than do caricatures or cartoon pictures.

- Cultural artifacts can also be displayed in the classroom such as African sculptures, Chinese vases, Mexican blankets, and so forth (Boutte, Van Scoy, and Hendley, 1996). A wide range of artifacts should be used to avoid presenting a narrow view of various cultural groups.

- Omission, distortion, and reduction of content information are other covert ways of excluding various racial and cultural groups. It is imperative that curricula include multiple perspectives rather than a purely Eurocentric perspective (Stage One on Table 1-3, Chapter One). Phrases like "The New World" and "The Westward Movement" reveal covert and implicit assumptions about the Americas before the Europeans arrived. Banks and Banks (1993) noted that these phrases fail to recognize Native Americans and their cultures which existed in the Americas 40,000 years before the fifteenth century. The "westward movement" suggests the perspective of the European Americans rather than the Lakota Sioux who were already in the west. Resource persons from respective racial and cultural groups who are knowledgeable about historical and current perspectives should be invited into classrooms. The intent is not to pit one perspective against the other. In the quest for a more authentic curriculum, students should be made aware that there are multiple and/or contrasting viewpoints and interpretations. A close examination of the numerous myths and stereotypes that are perpetrated in classrooms point to the necessity of presenting multiple perspectives in classrooms. We must seek balance and accuracy in the curriculum.

- Frequently, schools reinforce stereotypes—racial and otherwise. While we all hold stereotypes, teachers must be aware of subtle ways negative stereotypes are reinforced in the classroom. For example, it is not uncommon for students to make stereotypical remarks about a particular racial group during everyday conversation (i.e., Chinese people do well in math; African Americans are good athletes). Teachers must be careful not to condone such remarks and must be prepared to discuss these issues in a nonthreatening manner. Many teachers ignore such remarks because of their own discomfort (Boutte, LaPoint, and Davis, 1993). Admittedly, it is sometimes best to ignore inappropriate remarks; however, teachers cannot allow stereotypes to be perpetuated in classrooms. Native Americans are frequently stereotyped in classrooms and young children learn little authentic information about the multifaceted nature of Native American cultures (Billman, 1992; Ramsey, 1979). A number of historical events have been romanticized and contain more myths than facts (e.g., The First Thanksgiving). Many children erroneously are led to believe that all Indians live in teepees, and students have little, if any, conception of contemporary Native Americans. When Indian cultures are studied in school, students often learn stereotypical information and gain a superficial view of Native Americans. The typical focus is on physical elements and tangible cultural information which are by no means the most essential aspects of Indian culture (Banks and Banks, 1997). Indeed, we often limit the range of information presented about many groups including European Americans. Seldom do children see images of poor whites. Another common example of the effects of misinformation or incomplete information is seen when students exit schools thinking that all Africans live in villages. When schools limit the information that they present, they reinforce stereotypes such as the beliefs that African Americans tend to be on welfare, are drug users, and live in single parent homes.

Sensitivity to Racial Issues. As noted in Chapter One, discussing racial issues can evoke strong emotional responses that range from guilt and shame to anger and despair (Tatum, 1992). The discomfort associated with these emotions can cause educators to resist becoming multicultural. However, it is difficult to discuss multicultural issues without also reflecting on racism and other "isms" (Tatum, 1992). In order to be aware of racial issues in their schools and classrooms, educators will need to examine their own state of ethnic awareness (refer to Table 1-2 in Chapter One).

As noted by Boutte, LaPoint, and Davis, (1993), racial issues will undoubtedly emerge in classrooms. Teachers must become more cognizant of overt and covert racial slurs and defamations. In light of the racial disharmony in this country, teachers(who have a tremendous influence on young children's racial attitudes) must bring racial issues to the forefront and confront them. Teachers need to be sensitive to racial issues that affect children of color's response patterns in integrated classrooms. For example, if children are in the minority, they may try to shed any of their natural cultural overtones in an effort to "fit in" and not call undue attention to themselves. If children of color do not see themselves represented in classrooms, they may infer that there is something shameful about who they are. Additionally, teachers need to be prepared to address situations when racial defamations or jokes are used in their classrooms (e.g., nigger or Polack) (Boutte, LaPoint, and Davis, 1993).

Other racial issues that need to be examined are selections of children for school plays, speeches, awards, etc. How does race play a part in these? What messages are children being taught if all of the children of color are consistently placed on the back row during a performance? The intent here is for teachers to be more aware of such issues that send powerful messages. For example, teachers must consider how they determine which students receive major speaking roles? Who gets selected for class queens and kings? Student of the week? Many teachers are reluctant to include race as a consideration when making such selections because they delude themselves that they will choose the best students. Little thought is given to the fact that all students need to be provided with an opportunity to succeed, and that with practice, most children can excel and be excellent students. Moreover, the influence that factors like students' speech and cultural patterns have on the selection process are often not systematically considered. While we are certainly not suggesting a token approach, we definitely think that the role that race (as well as gender, socioeconomic status, and exceptionality) plays in these issues should be considered. There are many qualified students of color; however, a Eurocentric-driven "system" often excludes their access to many school activities. As with

Affirmative Action issues, when equity does not exist, a mechanism for achieving it must be devised. As Afrocentric schools demonstrate, when given a chance and high expectations, children of color rise to the expectations.

Kunjufu (1986) states that teachers cannot teach children they do not love; they cannot teach children they do not respect; they cannot teach children they are afraid of; and they cannot teach children if their political baggage (i.e., sexism and racism) is brought into the classroom. These statements imply that teachers must understand and respect all children. Moreover, they must be aware of their cultural learning styles and ways of viewing the world. Unless teachers are sensitive to such issues, all children will not reach their fullest potential and have a reasonable chance at success in society.

Parent-School Interactions. Finally, the importance of involving all parents in school activities cannot be overstated. The quality of parent-school interactions are crucial to students' success in school. Yet, schools often react differentially to parents depending on a number of factors like race and socioeconomic status (Boutte, 1992). Schools must examine how they welcome or "un" welcome parents. How do secretaries, teachers, administrators, and other school staff greet and interact with parents? Is correspondence written in a respectful versus a derogatory manner? Why do parents not attend PTA (Parent Teacher Association) meetings? We contend that the current structure of PTA meetings are largely ineffective for dealing with parents' individual needs.

Some parents work and are unavailable during the day. Activities that parents can do at home might be more appealing to working parents. Schools should seek input from parents as to what works best for them. In a society where exosystems such as the workplace and the school are closely connected (e.g., Reggio Emilia programs in Italy), employers gladly allow parents to routinely visit their children's schools. While our society has a long way to go before reaching high quality school–work–home connections, it is certainly worth it for schools to try to work towards convincing local employers to release their employees for school visitations. In the long run, parent involvement can certainly pay off for the entire community and society at large since schools will have a better chance at producing highly educated and productive students when parents are involved. Finally, home visits are also recommended to assist teachers in understanding and appreciating children's home environments (LaPoint, Boutte, Swick, and Brown, 1993). Chapter Six discusses parent-school interactions in more detail.

❖ SUMMARY

The discussion of multicultural issues remains a difficult topic, but is necessary in order to move beyond a single perspective approach that is obviously not beneficial to children of color or European American children. Demographers predict that by the year 2020, children of color will make up approximately forty-six percent of the nation's school-age population (Banks and Banks, 1993). As the section on overt factors indicates, schools are currently not meeting the needs of children of color, poor children, and children of other groups. Children's school experiences will inevitably affect their future success (or failure) in life.

Arciniega (1977) mused that too often schools shift the burden of responsibility onto the shoulders of those whom they purport to serve: children and their families. This is the "perfect crime," since educators can never truly be held accountable for their failure to educate children from "culturally deprived" homes. The reasons for their school failure are said to be the fault of poor homes, cultural handicaps, linguistic deficiencies, and deprived neighborhoods (Arciniega, 1977). The fact that schools are geared primarily to serve monolingual, white, middle-class clients is never questioned.

Because of the complexity of the issues discussed in this chapter, many children are at risk for not developing healthy personality from an Eriksonian perspective (refer to Table 1-4 in Chapter One). Many children of color may exit the early childhood years with a sense of cynicism, guilt, and/or inferiority. These devastating traits can be overcome in multicultural classrooms where teachers nurture and respect children's home culture(s) while extending the culture(s)

Schools have the obligation to educate all children—not just a select few. To do so effectively, attitude adjustments are required in terms of how we view children's culture. In sum, it is incumbent upon all educators to become "multiculturally literate" and to educate all children.

Joanne Hendrick (1990) asserts that everybody thinks of changing the world, but no one thinks of changing themselves. As educators who have a tremendous influence over our students lives, we must make a conscious and continuous effort to equitably educate all children regardless of their race. When we teach European American children that they are superior to other groups, we cripple all of us since we ultimately must all learn to live on this earth together. Children can be *different* from each other without being inferior or superior.

The evidence that clearly indicates discrepancies in children's school treatment is compelling and sends powerful messages about current perspectives on equity issues. Unless teachers are able to recognize (without overreacting to) subtle detrimental attitudes, teachers (regardless of race) will unwittingly engage in a powerful form of systematic racism, classism, sexism, and the like. Depending on one's perspective, the issues discussed here may seem unreal or contrived. You are encouraged to use the lenses provided to decide for yourself if the issues are real or imagined.

❖ RECOMMENDED ACTIVITIES

1. *Journal entry*—If you are an early childhood teacher (prekindergarten to third grade), reflect on how your instruction and guidance will affect children's development throughout their school experiences and later employment (or nonemployment). Be very reflective and examine whether or not you have done all you can to help children reach their fullest potential. Examine the type of teacher expectations that you hold for all children, instructional strategies that you use, and other aspects of teaching outlined in this chapter. If you are not a teacher, answer on the basis of what you plan to do or on what you have done during practicum experiences. If you teach at another level or plan to teach at another level, reflect on how the students that you teach (or plan to teach) are affected by the early childhood years. Also, reflect on what your challenges will be if the student leaves the early childhood years without requisite skills, motivational levels, or self-esteem.

2. Critique children's literature and textbooks. Examine several children's textbooks for biases listed in this chapter. Be alert for subtle messages. Compare books written before 1970 with current books.

3. Examine a classroom's literature collection. Are all ethnic groups represented? Is there a good balance of contemporary and historical books? Are there books which address gender issues and which show nonsexist viewpoints? Are exceptionalities addressed? Are people with exceptionalities shown as "typical" or "atypical"? Is there a collection of books that represents different religions and socioeconomic statuses? Are the storylines and illustrations of these books positive? How can the collection be enhanced?

4. Locate some of the versions of Cinderella from Table 2-2 (or find other versions). Compare and contrast the various versions in terms of publication dates, storylines, etc.

5. Ask a group of children between the ages of five through eight to draw pictures of Cinderella without providing any prompts regarding her description. Then, question them about what they know about Cinderella. Listen closely to their descriptions of Cinderella. You may have to probe by asking, "How did Cinderella look? What color was her hair?" Also, find out how the children think princesses should look. Are their answers or illustrations based on European definitions of beauty espoused in popular fairy tales? This will give you an indication of whether children's images of Cinderella and beauty needs to be broadened.

6. Share one of the other versions of Cinderella (preferably one with a non-European person or a male). What were the children's reactions to the story? Is it easy to extend their definitions of princes and princesses? Why or why not?

7. Compose an annotated list of children's books and/or videos that depict both historical and contemporary images of a particular ethnic group.

8. School observations—Visit a local elementary school. Observe for instances of overt and covert discrimination. Are boys and girls treated equitably? Count the number of times each child is called on during your observations. Note differences by subject areas such as math, science, and language arts. Write a summary of your findings and the implications for teaching children about gender.

9. Videotape yourself teaching or interacting with a group of children. Be as natural and typical as possible. Review the videotape and write down comments that were made to students and observe nonverbal messages (e.g., rolling your eyes, smirking, crossing your arms). Carefully, analyze the comments and nonverbal messages in order to determine the covert messages and tone. For example, try to determine if you may have unintentionally conveyed high expectations or doubt about a child's ability. Do you generally convey the message that you value and respect the children that you teach? Provide evidence to support your answer.

10. Visit a predominantly white and black (or other ethnicity) school. Compare differences in instructional and curricular issues. For example, do children at both schools engage in higher order thinking activities? Look for evidence of differential teacher expectations by listening carefully to the types of comments made to children. Examine the amount of time children are given to respond to questions..

11. Cultural research—Go to the library and research information about the learning and cultural styles of the five major eth-

nic groups: African, Asian, European, Latino/a, and Native Americans. Also, research any information that you can find on the cultural learning styles of interracial children. (This works well as a small group activity. Each group could research a different ethnic group).

To get a better understanding of contemporary issues that are important to people of color, go to the library and read a few issues of magazines such as *Ebony* (African American magazine) or contemporary magazines targeted at other people of color (e.g., *Hispanic Magazine, Hispanic Business, Hispanic American, Korean Focus, Koreana, Look Japan*). Compare and contrast the perspectives presented in these magazines with those presented in contemporary magazines. What are the educational implications of such differences?

If you are currently teaching or doing a practicum in a school, either check out copies of these magazines from your school library (if possible) or purchase some of them. Be sure to censor all magazines for their appropriateness. Parents may also donate magazines. Place these in your classroom and allow children (all ethnicities) to peruse them. Listen to informal and unsolicited comments made by the students. Reflect on what you learned from this experience.

12. Call your local state education department and request information on gifted and remedial (special education) classes. Try to obtain information by ethnicity and income (free lunch recipient information is usually available as an indication of family income level).

13. Read Howard Gardner's *Frames of Mind* (1983) which discusses other intelligences that children may have (other than linguistic and logico-mathematical which are usually emphasized in schools).

14. Read Vivian Paley's book, *White Teacher* (1989). It is an anecdotal account of a white teacher's multicultural development in a kindergarten class. It is a short book (142 pages) that reads easily. Provides much insight into racial issues that early childhood teachers confront in classrooms.

15. Read Stacey York's *Roots and Wings* (1991). It contains over sixty multicultural activities that teachers can use in early childhood education classrooms. York relates the activities to typical units that are covered.

16. Read *The Antibias Curriculum* by Derman-Sparks (1989). It does a wonderful job of explaining multicultural issues for early childhood education teachers.

❖ REFERENCES

Arciniega, T. A. 1977. The challenge of multicultural education for teacher educators. *Journal of Research and Development in Education* 11(1): 52–69.

Ayers, W. 1993. *To teach: The journey of a teacher.* New York: Teachers College Press.

Backer, B. F. 1994. Home visits. *First Teacher* 15(5): 6–7.

Backstein, K. 1992. *The blind men and the elephant.* New York: Scholastic.

Banks, J. 1993. Multicultural education for young children: Racial and ethnic attitudes and their modification. In *Handbook of research on the education of young children,* edited by B. Spodek. New York: Macmillan.

Banks, J. A. 1997. *Teaching strategies for ethnic studies.* 5th ed. New York: Allyn and Bacon.

Banks, J. A., and C. A. M. Banks, 1993. *Multicultural education: Issues and perspectives.* 2nd. ed. Boston: Allyn and Bacon.

————.1997. *Multicultural education: Issues and perspectives.* 3rd. ed. Boston: Allyn and Bacon.

Barrett, J. D. 1991. *Willie's not the hugging kind.* New York: Harper Trophy.

Berns, R. M. 1994. *Topical child development.* Albany, NY: Delmar.

Billman, J. 1992. The Native American curriculum: Attempting alternatives to tepees and headbands. *Young Children* 47(6): 22–25.

Boutte, G. S. 1992. Frustrations of an African American parent: A personal and professional account. *Phi Delta Kappan* 73(10): 786–788.

Boutte, G. S., B. Davis, and B. McCoy. 1995. Helping African American students maintain *and* adapt their communication styles: A challenge for educators. *The Negro Education Review* 46(2):1–2.

Boutte, G. S., S. LaPoint, and B. Davis. 1993. Racial issues in education: Real or imagined? *Young Children* 49(1): 19–23.

Boutte, G. S., and C. B. McCormick. 1992. Authentic multicultural activities: Avoiding pseudomulticulturalism. *Childhood Education* 68(3):140–144.

Boutte, G. S. , I. Van Scoy, and S. Hendley 1996. Multicultural and non-sexist prop boxes. *Young Children* 52(1): 34–39.

Bowman, B. T., and F. M. Stott 1994. Understanding development in a cultural context. In *Diversity and developmentally appropriate practices: Challenges for early childhood education,* New York: Teachers College.

Broman, B. 1982. *The early years in childhood education.* Boston: Houghton Mifflin.

Brophy, J., and T. Good 1970. *Teacher-student relationships: Causes and consequences.* New York: Holt, Rinehart, and Winston.

Cangelosi, J. S. 1992. *Systematic teaching strategies.* New York: Longman.

Cheltenham Elementary School Kindergartners. 1991. *We are all alike... We are all different.* New York: Scholastic.

Clark, R. 1983. *Family life and school achievement: Why poor black children succeed or fail.* Chicago: The University of Chicago Press.

Clifford, M., and E. Walster. 1973. The effect of physical attractiveness on teacher expectation. *Sociology of Education* 46(2): 248–258.

Climo, S. 1989. *The Egyptian Cinderella.* New York: Harper Trophy.

Cole, B. 1987. *Prince Cinders.* New York: G. P. Putnam's Sons.

Comer, J. P. 1990. Home, school, and academic learning. In *Access to knowledge: An agenda for our nation's schools,* edited by J.J. Goodland and P. Keating. New York: College Entrance Examination Board.

Compton, J. 1994. *Ashpet. An Appalachian Tale.* New York: Holiday House.

Connell, R. W. 1994. Poverty and education. *Harvard Education Review,* 64(2): 125–149.

Crump, F. 1991. *Cinderella.* Nashville, TN: Winston-Derek (African American version).

Daise, R. 1986. *De Gullah storybook.* Beaufort, SC: G. O. G. Press.

DeFlorimonte, D. Y. 1993. Bridging the language differences gap through poetry: Children's background as language users. *Reading: Exploration and Discovery* 15(1): 8–16.

Delpit, L. 1991. A conversation with Lisa Delpit. *Language Arts* 68: 541–547.

———.1995. *Other people's children. Cultural conflicts in the classroom.* New York: The New Press.

———.1986. Skills and other dilemmas of a progressive black educator. *Harvard Education Review* 56(4): 379–385.

———.1988. The silenced dialogue: Power and pedagogy in educating other people's children. *Harvard Education Review* 58(3): 280–298.

Derman-Sparks, L. and the A. B. C. Task Force. 1989. *The Anti-Bias Curriculum.* Washington, D. C.: National Association for the Education of Young Children.

Dooley, N. 1991. *Everybody cooks rice.* New York: Scholastic.

Dubois, W. E. B. 1961. *The souls of black folk.* Greenwich, Conn.: Fawcett Publications.

Ehrlich, A. 1985. *Cinderella.* New York: Dial Books for Young Readers.

Elrich, M. 1994. The stereotype within. *Educational Leadership* 51(8): 12–15.

Erickson, F. 1997. Culture in society and in educational practices. In *Multicultural education: Issues and perspectives,* edited by J. A. Banks and C. A. M. Banks. Boston: Allyn and Bacon.

Erickson, F., and G. Mohatt. 1982. Cultural organization of participation structures in two classrooms of Indian students. In *Doing the ethnography of schooling,* edited by G. Spindler. Prospect Heights, Illinois: Waveland.

Fu, V. R. 1993. Culture, schooling and education in a democracy. _Perspectives from ERIC/EECE: A monograph series, No. 3._ Urbana, IL:ERIC Clearinghouse on Elementary and Early Childhood Education, 38–50.

Garcia, E. E. 1997. The education of Hispanics in early childhood: Of roots and wings. _Young Children_ 52(3): 5–14.

Gardner, H. 1983. _Frames of mind._ New York: Basic Books.

Goldenberg, C. N. 1988. Methods, early literacy, and home-school compatibilities: A response to Sledge et al. _Anthropology and Education Quarterly_ 19(4): 425–432.

Gollnick, D. M., and P. C. Chinn, 1994. _Multicultural education in a pluralistic society._ 4th ed. New York: Merrill.

Gonzalez-Mena, J. 1992. Taking a culturally sensitive approach in infant-toddler programs. _Young Children_ 47(2): 4–9.

Good, T. L., and J. E. Brophy 1987. _Looking in classrooms._ New York: Harper & Row.

Guild, P. 1994. The culture/learning style connection. _Educational Leadership_ 51(8): 16–21.

Hale-Benson, J. 1986. _Black children—Their roots, culture, and learning._ 2nd ed. Baltimore: John Hopkins University Press.

Hamilton, V. 1985. _The people could fly._ New York: Scholastic.

Heath, S. 1982. Questioning at home and at school: A comparative study. In _Doing the ethnography of schooling,_ edited by G. Spindler. Prospect Heights, Illinois: Waveland.

Heath, S. B. 1992. _Ways with words._ New York: Cambridge University Press.

Hendrick, J. 1990. _Total learning._ 3rd ed. Columbus: Merrill.

Hilliard, A. G. 1991. _Testing African American students._ Morristown, NJ: Aaron Press.

Hooks, W. H. 1987. _Moss Gown._ New York: Clarion Books.

Howard, G. R. 1993. Whites in multicultural education: Rethinking our role. _Phi Delta Kappan_ 75(1): 36–41.

Huck, C. 1989. _Princess Furball._ New York: Scholastic.

Irvine, J. J. 1990. _Black students and school failure: Policies, practices and prescriptions._ New York: Greenwood Press.

Jackson, E. 1994. _Cinder Edna._ New York: Lothdrop, Lee, and Sheppard.

Jipson, J. 1991. Developmentally appropriate practice: Culture, curriculum, connections. _Early Education and Development_ 2: 120–135.

Jones, E., and L. Derman-Sparks. 1992. Meeting the challenge of diversity. _Young Children_ 47(2): 12–17.

Kasten, W. C. 1992. Bridging the horizon: American Indian beliefs and whole language learning. _Anthropology and Education Quarterly_ 23(2): 108–199.

Kostelnik, M. J., A. K. Soderman, and A. P. Whiren. 1993. _Developmentally appropriate programs in early childhood education._ New York: Merrill.

Kozol, J. 1991. *Savage inequalities.* New York: Crown Publishers.

Kunjufu, J. 1985. *Countering the conspiracy to destroy black boys.* Vol. I. Chicago: African American Images.

Kunjufu, J. (1986). *Countering the conspiracy to destroy black boys.* Vol. II. Chicago: African American Images.

Kunjufu, J. (1990). *Countering the conspiracy to destroy black boys.* Vol. III. Chicago: African American Images.

Ladson-Billings, G. 1994a. *The dreamkeepers: Successful teachers of African American children.* San Francisco: Jossey-Bass.

———.1994b. What we can learn from multicultural education research. *Educational Leadership* 51(8): 22–26.

LaPoint, S. A., G. S. Boutte, K.J. Swick, and M.H. Brown. 1993. Cultural sensitivity: How important is it for effective home visits? *Daycare and Early Education* 20(4): 11–4.

Lay-Dopyera, M., and J. Dopyera. 1987. *Becoming a teacher of young children.* 3rd ed. New York: Random House.

Liebow, E. 1967 *Tally's corner: A study of Negro streetcorner men.* Boston: Little Brown.

Linfords, J. 1987. *Children's language and learning.* 2nd ed. Englewood, Cliffs, New Jersey: Prentice-Hall.

Locust, C. 1988. Wounding the spirit: Discrimination and traditional American Indian belief systems. *Harvard Educational Review* 58(3): 315–330.

Lomaawaima, K. T. 1995. Educating Native Americans. In *Handbook of research on multicultural education,* edited by J. A. Banks and C. A. M. Banks. New York: Macmillan.

Louie, Ai-Ling. 1982. *Yeh-Shen. A Cinderella Story from China.* New York: Philomel Books.

Lubeck, S. 1994. In *Diversity and developmentally appropriate practices: challenges for early childhood education,* edited by B. L. Mallory and R. S. New. New York: Teachers College Press.

Madigan, D. 1993. The politics of multicultural literature for children and adolescents: Combining perspectives and conversations. *Language Arts* 70(3): 168–176.

Mahy, M. 1990. *The Seven Chinese Brothers.* New York: Scholastic.

Majors, R., and J. M. Billson. 1992. *Cool pose: The dilemmas of black manhood in America.* New York: Touchstone.

Mallory, B. L., and R. S. New, 1994. *Diversity and developmentally appropriate practices: Challenges for early childhood education.* New York: Teachers College.

Martin, R., and D. Shannon. 1992. *The roughface girl.* New York: G. P. Putnam's Sons.

Martinez, E. 1997. Unite and overcome! *Teaching Tolerance* 6(1): 11–15.

Mason, E. J. 1973. Teachers' observations and expectations of boys and girls as influenced by biased psychological reports and knowledge of the effects of bias. *Journal of Educational Psychology* 65(2): 238–243.

McDermott, G. 1974. *Arrow to the sun.* New York: Penguin Group.

McKissack, P. 1986. *Flossie and the fox.* New York: Dial Books for Young Readers.

Medicine, B. 1988. Native American (Indian) women: A call for research. *Anthropology and Education Quarterly* 19(2): 86–92.

Modern Curriculum Press. *Multicultural Celebrations:* Cleveland, OH: Paramount Publishing.

Montgomery-Fate, T. 1997. Beyond the multi-culture. *The Other Side* 33(2): 16–20.

Morris, A. 1989. *Bread bread bread.* New York: Mulberry.

———.1992a. *Houses and homes.* New York: Lothrop, Lee, & Sheppard Books.

———.1992b. *Tools.* New York: Lothrop, Lee, & Sheppard Books.

Mosel, A. 1968. *Tikki Tikki Tembo.* New York: Henry Holt and Co.

Murphy, D. 1986. Educational disadvantagement: Associated factors, current interventions, and implications. *Journal of Negro Education* 55(4): 495–507.

Myers, B. 1985. *Sidney Rella and the glass sneaker.* New York: Macmillan.

Neugebauer, B., ed. 1992. *Alike and different: Exploring our humanity with young children.* Washington, D. C.: National Association for the Education of Young Children.

New, R. S. 1994. Culture, child development, and developmentally appropriate practices: Teachers as collaborative researchers. In *Diversity and developmentally appropriate practices: Challenges for early childhood education,* edited by B. L. Mallory and R. S. New. New York: Teachers College Press.

Nieto, S. 1992. *Affirming diversity: The sociopolitical context of multicultural education.* New York: Longman.

Norton, D. E., and S. E. Norton. 1995. *Through the eyes of a child: An introduction to children's literature.* Englewood Cliffs: NJ: Merrill.

Oakes, J., and M. Lipton. 1990. Tracking and ability grouping: A structural barrier to access and achievement. In *Access to knowledge: An agenda for our nation's schools,* edited by J. I. Goodlad and P. Keating. New York: College Entrance Examination Board.

Oei, T., and G. Lyon. 1996. In our own words: Asian American students give voice to the challenges of living in two cultures. *Teaching Tolerance* 5(2): 48–59.

Ogbu, J. U. 1974. *The next generation: An ethnography of education in an urban neighborhood.* New York: Academic Press.

———.1990. Overcoming racial barriers to equal access. In *Access to knowledge: An agenda for our nation's schools,* edited by J. I. Goodlad and P. Keating. New York: College Entrance Examination Board.

Paley, V. G. 1989. *White teacher.* Cambridge, Mass: Harvard University Press.

Persell, C. H. 1993. Social class and educational equality. In *Multicultural education: Issues and perspectives*, edited by A. Banks and C. A. M. Banks. Boston: Allyn and Bacon.

Phillips, C. B. 1994. The movement of African American children through sociocultural contexts: A case of conflict resolution. In *Diversity and developmentally appropriate practices: Challenges for early childhood education*, edited by B. L. Mallory and R. S. New. New York: Teachers College Press.

Pine, G. J., and A. G. Hilliard. 1990. Rx for racism: Imperatives for America's schools. *Phi Delta Kappan* 71 (8): 593–600.

Powell, R. R., S. Zehm, and J. Garcia. 1996. *Field experience: Strategies for exploring diversity in schools*. Englewood Cliffs, NJ: Merrill.

Polacco, P. 1992. *Chicken Sunday*. New York: Scholastic.

Ramsey, P. G. 1979. Beyond "ten little Indians" and turkeys: Alternative approaches to Thanksgiving. *Young Children*, 28–50.

Sadker, M., D. Sadker, and L. Long. 1993. Gender and educational equality. In *Multicultural education: Issues and perspectives*, edited by J. A. Banks and C. A. M. Banks. Boston: Allyn and Bacon.

Scarr, S. 1981. Testing for children: Assessment and the many determinants of intellectual competence. *American Psychologist* 36(10): 1159–1166.

Scieszka, J. 1989. *The true story of the three little pigs*. New York: Scholastic.

Shorto, R. 1994. *The untold story of Cinderella*. New York: Carol Publishing Group.

Sierra, J. 1992. *Cinderella*. Phoenix, AR: The Oryx Press.

Smolkin, L. B. and J. H. Suina. In press. Exploring a "multicultural" award-winning book: Multiple traditions, multiple perspectives, multiple pedagogies. *The New Advocate*.

Solomon, I. D. and B. L. Winsboro. 1993. Black English in the classroom: The implication of rhetoric vs. reality. *The Negro Educational Review* 44(1-2): 12—22.

Spencer, M. B., and C. Markstrom-Adams. 1990. Identity processes among racial and ethnic minority children in America. *Child Development* 61(2): 290–310.

Spier, P. 1980. *People*. New York: Doubleday.

Steele, C.M. 1992. Race and schooling of Black Americans. *The Atlantic Monthly* 269(4): 68–78.

Steptoe, J. 1987. *Mufaro's beautiful daughters*. New York: Lothrop, Lee, & Sheppard.

Swick, K. 1991. *Perspectives on understanding and working with families*. Champaign, IL: Stipes.

Swick, K. J., G. Boutte, and I. Van Scoy. 1994. Multicultural learning through family involvement. *Dimensions of Early Childhood* 22(4): 17–21.

Tatum, B. D. 1992. Talking about race, learning about racism: The application of racial identity development theory in the classroom. *Harvard Educational Review* 62(1): 1–24.

Tribe, C. 1982. *Profile of three theories: Erikson, Maslow, Piaget.* Dubuque, IA: Kendall/Hunt.

Van Laan, N. 1990. *Possum come a knockin'.* New York: Alfred A. Knopf, Inc.

Waber, B. 1972. *Ira sleeps over.* New York: Scholastic.

Wilcox, K. 1982. Differential socialization in the classroom: Implications for equal opportunity. In *Doing the ethnography of schooling edited* by G. Spindler Prospect Heights, Illinois: Waveland.

York, S. 1991. *Roots and wings.* St. Paul, MN: Redleaf.

The Elementary Years

Most children remain eager to learn during the early childhood years. However, by fourth grade, many students of color and poor children lose their enthusiasm.

INTRODUCTION

Hakim, a sixth grade student, strutted into the classroom on the first day of the new school year. He was abruptly stopped by the teacher and asked if he was in the right class. As he glanced around the room, Hakim observed that he was the only African American person present. He realized that the teacher perceived there had been a mistake in placement since this was an advanced math class. His class schedule verified the correct placement but the teacher then asked, "Are you certain you want to be in this class?" When Hakim answered yes, his teacher warned that she would not tolerate any misbehavior in her class. Several weeks later, the teacher admitted to Hakim, "You're a terrific young man and not what I expected you to be." His response took the form of a question, "Why did you prejudge me?" to which the teacher had no answer.

The above scenario clearly portrays the way some teachers make generalizations and do not believe in the abilities and propensity for appropriate conduct of elementary school children who belong to minority ethnic groups (Hixson, 1990; Ogbu, 1990). As noted in Chapter Two, a teacher's attitude and behavior in the classroom is a significant factor which helps children to reach their potential. However, teachers often unknowingly transmit biased or stereotypical messages to students.

Elementary school students bring into classrooms different histories and cultural perspectives about how school and the world in general works. They bring diverse learning styles and personal experiences. However, many educators are not sensitive to the needs of culturally and ethnically diverse students, nor do most teachers hold similar points of view as their students (Gay, 1993). The disparities and socio-cultural gap between teachers and many elementary school children continues to increase. In her discussion of the disparities, Gay points out that even though the percentage of elementary school children who are African American, Latino/a American, Asian American, Native American, poor, and limited English speaking is increasing significantly, the number of teachers with similar backgrounds to these children is declining. It is critical that teachers examine and change their basic assumptions and beliefs. They must believe that all children can learn regardless of their ethnic group, gender, or social class (Banks, 1992). A long-term commitment to implementing multicultural education programs will increase educational equality for elementary school children of diverse ethnic and cultural groups, exceptional children, and both gender groups (Gay, Cole-Slaughter, and Barber, 1995). Therefore, an important goal for elementary school students and their teachers is to transform their thinking and make paradigm shifts in order to view this nation and the world from the perspectives of different racial, cultural, ethnic, and gender groups.

In this chapter, the elementary years will refer to grades three through eight. The effect of a child's foundation during the early childhood years are apparent during the elementary years. Obviously, children with a strong early childhood foundation have a better chance of succeeding than children who do not. As children progress from grades one through six, the achievement gap between advantaged and disadvantaged children grows larger and is almost never overcome (Hirsch, 1993). For example, despite their socioeconomic disadvantages as a group, African Americans begin school with test scores that are fairly close to the test scores of whites their age. However, the longer they stay in school, the further they fall behind. By the sixth grade, African Americans in many school districts are *two* full grades behind whites in achievement. This pattern holds true for children from both middle and lower income homes. The record does not improve during the high school years (Steele, 1992).

Several significant changes occur during the elementary school years. The peer group becomes increasingly important. As children get older, they tend to play with peers who are similar to themselves in terms of race, gender, and socioeconomic status. Elementary school children are expected to become more independent during these years; thus, many teachers are not as nurturing as they were during the early childhood years. Typically, a decline in parent involvement is also seen as children progress to higher grades. Another change during the elementary years is that virtually all children change classes (or regroup) during the school day. Unlike the early childhood years, most elementary school children have two or more teachers. This implies that children are now exposed to more personalities and perspectives. Because children remain with a teacher for only one or two periods per day, there is a tendency for teachers to focus primarily on content as opposed to children's social and emotional development. However, we urge elementary teachers to give full consideration to all areas of development (social, emotional, physical, and intellectual) in order for them to take full advantage of the numerous opportunities for multicultural growth for their students. We emphasize that teachers should not only focus on multicultural *content*, but also on diversity issues as well.

According to Erikson, most elementary school children are struggling to be industrious and competent (refer to Table 1-4 in Chapter One). Ideally, during this stage, children will be focusing on learning the value of work, cooperation, and responsibility (Tribe, 1982). Therefore, the role of the school is very important, since competence comes from having the necessary skills to be successful.

A key issue addressed in this chapter is the ways in which elementary schools build competence (or incompetence) in students from all walks of life. It is important that all students be empowered to succeed in the future. As the subsequent discussion will demonstrate, many children of color, females, poor children, and children with exceptionalities encounter barriers in many elementary schools. However, as this chapter will illustrate, schools which emphasize multiculturalism can do a better job of effectively developing children who are competent and prepared for the future. Congruent with the developmental nature of the book, this chapter will contain issues that relate to other levels of schooling as well. When examining issues from a developmental standpoint, there will undoubtedly be overlap of various issues since development is continuous rather than isolated in one particular stage or level. Thus, several issues that were presented in Chapter Two will be revisited in this and later chapters.

Hermendez (1989) offers eight basic assumptions that help to define a multicultural-based approach to education. These premises serve as a framework for which this chapter is presented. Each of these premises has implications for elementary schools interested in helping students develop into competent individuals later in life.

1. It is increasingly important for political, social, educational, and economic reasons to recognize that the United States is a culturally diverse society.
2. Multicultural education is for ALL students.
3. Multicultural education is synonymous with effective teaching.
4. Teaching is a cross-cultural encounter.
5. The educational system has not served all students equally well.
6. Multicultural education is synonymous with educational innovation and reform.
7. Next to parents, teachers are the single most important people in children's lives.
8. Classroom interactions between teachers and students constitute the major part of the educational process for most students.

❖ PREMISE ONE

It is increasingly important for political, social, educational, and economic reasons to recognize that the United States is a culturally diverse society.

During the last two decades, there has been an increasing awareness of and research on the permanent changes in the student population. Students of color compose forty percent of all elementary schools (Gay, 1993). In 1990, the population of the United States was primarily Anglo, (seventy-six percent). However, by the year 2050, the statistics project that the Anglo group will decrease to fifty-two percent, while other ethnic groups will continue to grow (see Table 3-1). These realities require that we recognize and accept that diversity is an essential part of our society.

Table 3-1. U. S. Bureau of Census Projections
for Ethnic Groups in the U. S.

Ethnic Group	1990	2050
Anglo American	76%	52%
African American	12%	16%
Latino/a American	9%	22%
Asian American	3%	10%

Courtesy of U. S. Bureau of the Census (1992).

Social and economic satisfaction are integral to school life. Schools presently exist in a society in which it is imperative to understand their sociopolitical contexts. Hence, schools often perpetuate the social structure of society and the early labeling, biased curricula, standardized testing, low teacher expectations, and inequality of instructional time which occurs during the elementary years often have ramifications for a lifetime (Nieto, 1992). As the United States continues to become more culturally diverse, individuals from various ethnic, racial, religious, and gender groups will assume different roles in society. Educators must take responsibility for understanding and appreciating the many diverse students and individuals who make up our school and society.

The political and international standing of the United States currently ranks below that of several industrialized nations.

Multicultural education is for *all* children.

Multicultural education provides children with a solid base of knowledge, skills, and confidence needed to meet global standards and challenges in the new millennium (Banks, 1994; Gay, 1993).

In elementary schools, it is important to set high expectations, inspire self-confidence, and instill strong cultural values in students so that they exit elementary school as competent individuals. Since elementary students who are achieving academically will also later contribute to the economic, social, and political well-being of society, successful educational results will impact homes, the community, and the society.

❖ PREMISE TWO Multicultural education is for *ALL* children.

> Martin Luther King Jr. once explained that "we are all caught in an inescapable network of mutuality tied into a single garment of destiny. Whatever affects one directly, affects all indirectly. We are made to live together because of the interrelated structure of reality" (Washington, 1986, p. 254).

One misconception about multicultural education is that it focuses only on students of color. Curriculum transformations in multicultural education classrooms are designed to increase the academic achievement of students of color as well as white students. Therefore, all students, including white mainstream students, benefit academically and socially as they develop the appropriate skills and attitudes for living in a pluralistic society (Banks, 1994). All students must be prepared to function in our highly technological society and world. Multicultural education is necessary to help all of the nation's future citizens acquire the knowledge, attitudes, and skills needed to survive in the twenty-first century (Banks, 1992).

Not teaching white children about multiculturalism leads one to the erroneous assumption that whites are not part of the multicultural equation. As Howard (1993) advises, the issue of cultural diversity in this nation is a human problem—not an African American, Native American, or Latino/a American problem. As the demographics of society continue to change, all students will need to know how to effectively work with other ethnicities. Our histories are so intricately interwoven that we cannot fully understand our own history without studying a myriad of other perspectives.

When white children are denied the richness of music, literature, lifestyles, values, and perspectives of other ethnic groups, their potential understandings are limited. Additionally, such an approach (intentionally or unintentionally) gives white children a false sense of superiority which may later lead to prejudice and racism. Holding negative biases against other ethnic groups is potentially damaging to the goal of teaching white children to ultimately view themselves as contributors to societal development rather than *the leaders to improvement* of society. Racism and other "isms" are not only damaging to people of color or other recipients, they hurt everyone. The pain and guilt that results when white children realize the role that their ethnicity contributes to disadvantage in this country could be avoided (Howard, 1993; McIntosh, 1995).

It is typically assumed that teachers of color automatically know how to teach *white* children. Teaching children, even white students, as if they are from middle-class families without regard for socioeconomic status or other differences is not the best practice. Multiculturalism also helps all teachers appreciate the diversity among white students.

Although the prevalent tenet of some school systems is the "innate ability paradigm" (Edwards, 1986), teachers can successfully educate *ALL* students. Unless students' diversity is perceived as an instructional resource and as the foundation on which educational principles are built, schools as they are currently structured cannot fulfill the nation's goals of becoming a world class society. In order to thrive in our rapidly changing

---

Educators cannot effectively teach a child who they do not love, respect, or understand.

diverse world, all students need the skills a multicultural education can provide them in order to understand and work with others. It is only through the reform of curriculum to reflect the reality of students, changing the structure of schools, and changing instructional strategies that all students will benefit (Nieto, 1992).

❖ PREMISE THREE Multicultural education is synonymous with effective teaching.

"You cannot teach a child who you do not love.

You cannot teach a child who you do not respect.

You cannot teach a child who you do not understand.

You cannot teach a child whom you are afraid of.

You cannot teach a child if your 'political baggage' i.e. sexism and racism, is brought into the classroom.

You cannot teach a child without bonding first, which results from love, respect, and understanding." (Kunjufu, 1986, p. 32)

Many elementary teachers erroneously assume that the goals of multicultural education are met by simply adding on a few units or making minor changes in their curriculum. Multicultural education extends far beyond "add-on" approaches and should be an integral part of the educational process. Authentic multiculturalism requires that teachers understand and respect the children that they teach. Furthermore, it requires that teachers understand themselves as well as the greater society in which they live. Effective teachers also seek to reduce prejudices that often emerge in the classroom (Pate 1992). Early in teacher education programs, preservice teachers should be exposed to effective teaching strategies and techniques which emphasize appreciation of diversity. Effective teacher preparation programs will inevitably result in a reduction in prejudice and substantial changes in prospective teachers' attitudes toward children. In teacher education programs, teachers should be encouraged to reflect on their own cultural experiences and prejudices they bring to an instructional environment. For example, had Hakim's teacher (in the scenario at the beginning of this chapter) been trained in effective multicultural teaching practices, she would have been more sensitive and she would have exhibited high expectations for him and all students. Additionally, effective teacher preparation would have increased her knowledge and experiences so that she understood the needs of culturally diverse students, various learning styles, and the importance of attending to individual differences and treating all children equitably and fairly.

Culturally Diverse Students

The shifts in school demographics indicate the rapid increases in the number of students who are from culturally diverse groups. It is only when teachers become sensitive to the cultural diversity in their classrooms and provide effective instruction for all students that educational equity will exist in elementary schools (Banks, 1988; Gay, 1993). Schools should reflect the perspective that diversity is a strength and that it provides an opportunity for teachers and students to respect and understand the cultures of others.

A substantial body of research indicates that there is a relationship between children's culture and their academic, social, and emotional success in school (Guild, 1994). These data point out that not all children from a particular cultural group will exhibit these cultural patterns. However, educators need to be familiar with the research in order to consider the influence of children's culture on their learning. Moreover, ignoring the effects of culture and learning styles might depress learning among nonmainstream children. When cultural styles and patterns are ignored, the children will either adjust to the teacher's style or continue to have difficulty in school (which happens frequently). Yet, cultural learning styles may easily be oversimplified, misunderstood, or misinterpreted. As Guild (1994) notes, this can lead to stereotyping and labeling rather that the identification of educationally meaningful cultural differences. However, Hilliard (1989) encourages educators not to avoid addressing cultural styles for fear of stereotyping students. He points out that empirical observations about typical cultural differences are not the same as stereotyping and that the observations must be empirical and must be interpreted properly for each student. As emphasized in Chapters One and Two, it is important for educators to familiarize themselves with differences between and within cultures.

*We emphasize that culture should be used as a **guide** rather than as a road map to a particular destination. That is, there are always exceptions.* There is no way that one can possibly learn everything about every culture, nor is this an attainable or desirable goal since most cultures are always in a state of flux. However, some knowledge of cultural styles is important. Otherwise, educators may misread or ignore significant verbal and nonverbal cues from their students. They may also be unaware of how their students are interpreting and perhaps misreading their behavior. As educators struggle to become more multicultural, they must also begin to examine issues of cultural representation in their curriculum (Tatum, 1992). *We stress that cultures are not static and are subject to change as one's experiences and horizons are broadened through interaction with other cultures.* Cultures frequently borrow behaviors and attitudes from other cultures, and revise and/or discard behaviors and attitudes when deemed necessary. Individuals consciously or unconsciously choose to change their cultural behavior and attitudes for a number of reasons (e.g., to fit in, to expand horizons, to avoid being shamed or embarrassed). Yet, it is not uncommon for cultural attributes to re-emerge when individuals are comfortable, relaxed, fatigued, frustrated, angry, or inebriated. Therefore, we question whether one's cultural roots are ever truly erased or whether they should be.

Research on cultural styles and patterns typically contrasts European American students' ways of learning with those of children of color. The research reveals that Latino/a Americans, Native Americans, and African Americans tend to have high regard for family and personal relationships and are comfortable with cognitive generalizations and patterns (Guild, 1994). Hence, these children tend to perform better when they have a personal relationship with the teacher and when they work in cooperative groups.

Research about African American culture indicates that they often value oral experiences, physical activities, and loyalty in personal relationships (Hilliard, 1992; Hale–Benson, 1986). Therefore, teachers are encouraged to use approaches such as discussion, active projects, and collaborative work to complement children's cultural learning styles (Guild, 1994).

Guild (1994) notes that Native Americans generally value and develop acute visual discrimination and skills in the use of imagery, perceive globally, and have reflective thinking patterns. Therefore, teachers of Native American children may want to establish a context for new information, provide quiet times for thinking, and emphasize visual stimuli.

Asian American children also tend to value family and to respect adults. Therefore, they may not speak up as much as Euro-American children. They also tend to do well in science and math. Teachers can use these subjects as a starting point for involving Asian children in other subjects.

The literature indicates that European Americans tend to prefer competitive, objective, independent activities. Information, tests, grades, and linear logic are also commonly cited. These patterns are prevalent in most schools in the United States; therefore, white children and children who prefer this cultural style are at an advantage for succeeding in school.

Generally, in order to be effective, teachers should use a variety of approaches to meet children's needs. Although the aforementioned approaches tend to work well with children of color, many Euro-American children prefer these approaches as well. Effective teachers must meet the needs of *ALL* children. They must also help children be bicultural. That is, children must be proficient in their culture as well as mainstream culture.

Misunderstanding of cultural behaviors has been shown to lead to errors about children's intellectual potential, which results in mislabeling, misplacement, and mistreatment of children (Hilliard, 1992). Teachers often perceive African American students from working or low income backgrounds as incapable of high quality academic work (Ladson-Billings, 1994). In addition to African American children, the harmful consequences of ability grouping falls heavily on Latino/a, immigrant, and poor children (Wheelock and Hawley, 1992). Therefore, these children are subjected to low-quality educational experiences. Interestingly, teachers rarely attribute their problems with children of color to ineffective teaching approaches. The overall implication of the research on cultural learning patterns is that if teachers are to be effective, they need to be prepared to teach children who are not white as well as white children (Ladson-Billings, 1994). Providing children with an equitable and effective pedagogy demands that teachers use the language and understandings that children bring to school to bridge the gap between what students know and what they need to learn (Ladson-Billings, 1994).

In addition to cultural learning styles and patterns, subconscious patterns of gender bias can influence the behavior of teachers and affect the child's self image (Kaplan and Aronson, 1994). Study after study has shown that male students consistently demand and receive more attention than females (Sadker, Sadker, and Long, 1993). When giving feedback about children's work, teachers often tell boys that they have not tried hard enough and encourage the boys to keep working. On the other hand, girls are merely told that their answers are wrong (with no additional feedback) (Sadker, Sadker, and Long, 1993). After years of this type of feedback, boys become persistent, and girls give up (Streitmatter, 1994). Teachers must work to overcome such biases.

Effective teachers must address children's gender, socioeconomic status, religion, and the interaction of these factors. For example, poor children are typically not shown much respect by school officials. Theoretically, being poor and female means that children have two strikes against them in school. How do teachers treat poor females? To add more complexity to this issue, consider how Latino/a females from low-income families are treated by schools. Add exceptionality to this example and question how Latina females with attention deficit disorder from low-income homes might be treated. It becomes obvious that teachers have the complex task of considering all facets of children's culture.

Learning Styles

Multicultural education recognizes that children perceive and learn in a variety of ways and demonstrate their understanding in unique ways. Teachers must provide multicultural classrooms where positive student/teacher interactions are based on respect for personal, cultural, and social strengths, and the skills students bring to the classroom. Effective teachers provide more experiences, perspectives and multicultural principles (Diaz, 1992).

Although diversity within each culture or ethnic group exists, it is crucial that teachers also be aware of learning styles. Teaching styles will frequently have to be adapted and varied in order to accommodate all students. Teachers who want all children to succeed use varied teaching methods that treat children fairly. For example, teachers may want to balance their use of individual and collaborative methods. Since cooperative learning has been shown to facilitate the learning of children from various groups, it should be integrated into instruction (Nieto, 1992).

Another strategy for accommodating a variety of student needs is to balance the amount of visual, auditory, and tactile-kinesthetic approaches used. A promising approach for assessing a fuller range of student abilities is Howard Gardner's theory of multiple intelligences (Powell, Zehm, and Garcia, 1996). His theory has important implications for making learning experiences more culturally compatible, since the theory asserts that each individual is capable of several relatively independent forms of intelligence. Rather than relying solely on the typical linguistic and logical mathematical intelligences, teachers should utilize and encourage children to use other intelligences. There are *at least* five other intelligences that teachers can address: musical, spatial, bodily kinesthetic, interpersonal, and intrapersonal (Gardner and Hatch, 1990). Since integrated or interdisciplinary units lend themselves to addressing many different intelligences, more children's needs will be met when these methods are used. Put simply, teachers have to move away from using linguistic and logical mathematical approaches as the center of their curriculum if they want ALL children to succeed.

Attending To Individual Differences and Treating All Children Equitably and Fairly

Teachers must realize that although members of various ethnic, socioeconomic status, and gender groups share commonalities, there are also considerable individual differences. Guild (1994) emphasizes that the task of considering cultural and individual differences as well as equity in classrooms will not be an easy one. Indeed, the complexity of balancing so many variables requires teachers to continuously reflect on their treatment of children. Effective teachers realize that they may have to experiment with several strategies before finding ones that are effective.

One of the most challenging tasks faced by educators will be to determine how to use information about children's cultural groups as a guide while also focusing on each child's individual and family circumstances. We reiterate the assertion made in Chapter One that there are no simple solutions for doing this. Educators must hold several variables constant simultaneously when trying to meet the needs of children from diverse backgrounds. Educators must determine the degree of influence that culture has on the children they teach. Not only must literature on cultural learning styles be examined for its usefulness for a particular child, but educators must examine students' records to find information about the child's family background, the profession of the parents, the child's socioeconomic status, and so forth. This information is not intended to be used in a way that biases the teacher against the child; rather, it should be used to provide more insight about individual family circumstances. Because information is not always easily discerned, educators may find it useful to request information about the "culture" of the family from parents at the beginning of the year. For example, a friendly letter like the one outlined in Figure 3-1 may help start the process of gathering information about cultural and individual learning styles. A letter such as this one also conveys the expectation that parent interaction is needed and expected in order for the child to be successful in school. Alternately, educators could also gather such information at parent-teacher conferences. Most parents enjoy talking about their children, especially in a non-threatening way. The information that parents provide should help the teacher determine if the child prefers analytical versus global activities. It may also reveal whether the child has a particular intelligence that can be used as a basis for instruction. Inferences drawn based on the nature of activities done at home will inform the teacher about values held by the parent. Even the types of television shows or movies watched can shed light on cultural values.

FIGURE 3-1. Sample Letter Requesting Information from Parents About Children's Individual and Cultural Learning Styles.

Dear Ms. Benita:

I am excited about having the opportunity to teach Kaleef this year. In order for me to learn as much as possible about how Kaleef learns best, I would appreciate your answering the questions listed below. Feel free to provide any additional information that you think would help me get to know Kaleef better. Thank you. I look forward to working with you and Kaleef this year!

Sincerely,

Gretta McKay

(Please cut and return the bottom portion of this letter.)

1. What is your child's favorite subject(s)?_____
2. What is your child's least favorite subject(s)? _____
3. What type of activities do you or other family members do at home to help your child with these subjects?
   A. Science _____
   B. Math _____
   C. Reading _____
   D. Geography/History/Social Studies _____
   E. Art _____
   F. Music _____
   G. Physical Activity _____
4. List any hobbies your child has _____
5. Does your child enjoy watching television?_____ If so, what are his/her favorite television shows?_____
6. Does your child enjoy going to the movies?_____ If so, what are his/her favorite movies or type of movies?_____
7. List any extracurricular activities (such as dance) that your child paticipates in.

   _____

8. List other things that you think would be helpful for me to know about your child.

   _____

9. Are you willing to come to the classroom to share information that may relate to units of study with us?_____Check all of the following that you feel comfortable sharing with the class.
   _____ cultural information
   _____ religious information
   _____ family historical information
   _____ family recipes
   _____ other

The complexity of balancing knowledge of children as individuals as well as children who are influenced by their culture can be illustrated by a detailed examination of both cultural and individual differences among Asian American students. The implications for educators is that while Asian American students share many common attributes, effective teachers would be remiss if they did not look deeper to explore individual differences as well.

Many educators tend to view Asian Americans as a homogeneous group and fail to see within-group differences. There is also a tendency to view Asian American students as if they are "foreigners." Additionally, Asian Americans are generally viewed by some as the "model minority" (Bell, 1994). However, educators teaching Asian American students must seek to avoid the pitfall of relying only on general information about Asian American culture and must regard individual differences as well. There is a tremendous amount of variation within every cultural group. Among Asian American students, some are recent immigrants, some speak only English, some speak the language of their ancestors, some are from middle income families, and some are from refugee families who live in poverty (Oei and Lyon, 1996). Yet, as June, a Taiwanese American student laments,

> White people cannot tell Asian people apart. It's kind of funny because we can tell white people apart, but sometimes some whites think we're the same person. We're completely different people! But they just see the yellow skin and the black hair and the brown eyes. (Oei and Lyon, 1996, p. 51).

Failure to look closely at distinctions between Asian students and other students of color is not unique to European Americans however. Because of the long history of ethnocentrism in this country, other individuals from non-Asian groups also tend to group all Asians together.

Asian Americans are the fastest growing minority group in the country and in schools (Oei and Lyon, 1996). They come from more than twenty countries, speak more than two dozen different languages, practice a variety of religions, including Hinduism, Buddhism, Islam, and Christianity (Oei and Lyon, 1996). Table 1-1 in Chapter One presented some of the ethnic backgrounds of Asian Americans.

Educators must be cognizant of the challenges faced by many students of color who seek to balance two cultures (Oei and Lyon, 1996). To illustrate this point, we will specifically examine some of the conflicts that Asian American and African American students face. The way Asian Americans identify themselves has a lot to do with how long they have been in this country, the language they are most comfortable with, who their friends are, and how closely they feel connected to their heritage. Even then, their perceptions of who they are can change over time.

The quotes below from Asian American students demonstrate the tremendous amount of individual differences among them (based on interviews by Oei and Lyon (1996) of ten Asian students). As the diversity of student viewpoints show, it is helpful for teachers to have a general understanding and respect for the culture; however, getting to know each individual is a requirement for effective teaching of all children.

Khanh (Vietnamese American): I'm more Western than a lot of the Asian people in my school, but I'm a lot more Eastern than American people I associate with. I don't have a lot of Asian friends. . . . The Vietnamese group and the ESL (English as a Second Language) kids . . . always spoke to me in English. I would say something back in Vietnamese, but they would speak to me in English. It was like, "You don't really understand about the Asian culture because you're so Americanized." (p. 52)

Clifford (Korean American): Some Asian people consider me sort of whitewashed because I've been here so long they don't identify me as Asian. Sometimes I don't identify with Koreans as well as I'd like—sometimes I'm intimidated by Koreans because I lack so much of what real Koreans have—the tradition, the history they know. I've forgotten a lot of history and Korean folklore, things I was taught as a little kid. (p. 53)

Marisa (Japanese American): I realized after a while that I really didn't know anything about the Asian half of me. Where I grew up, all of my friends were white, and that was what I identified with more. I felt that I was missing something. (p. 53)

Khanh (Vietnamese American): Growing up, I always felt a void in my life, like there's something out there and I know I need to go out and find it. I had an opportunity to visit Vietnam, and being able to walk on the land and see its people and taste its food helped me to get a greater sense of who I am. It's not necessarily that I had to go on the outside to find that, but it made me realize that it was always within me." (p. 53)

Villy (Laotian American): ESL kids get left out. Other people say, "They're ESL kids, they can't speak any English." . . . Sometimes I feel bad that there are some kids who feel they are much better than other kids and look down on them. (p. 53)

Clifford (Korean American): I think expectations of me are different because I'm Asian. My friends used to say to me, "Oh, Cliff, you must have it worse," because stereotypically Asian parents are harder on their kids. A lot of teachers said I wasn't the typical Asian student. I was sort of rambunctious in class. I was never the quiet one. (p. 53)

Tomoko (Japanese American): When I speak in class, they get quiet and try to listen to me. They are trying to understand and that's really nice, but it makes me nervous when they get quiet. Why don't you treat me just like an American in class?(p. 54–55)

Khanh (Vietnamese American): The media is propagating its depiction of the beautiful people, and everybody is white and has wavy long hair and blue eyes, and that's what beauty is. So when you look at yourself and you're not that model, you say "Oh I'm ugly!" no matter what else you've achieved in your life. (p. 54)

Khanh (Vietnamese American): Each one of us is different. Every single time I look in the mirror, I know that I'm Asian and I know that I'm Vietnamese. I have my own understanding that it's what you think and what you believe in that's important. But on the other hand, I know I feel deep down inside that I can never be physically as beautiful as somebody who is white. No matter how much I say, "I am my own person. I'm very strong about ideas", and all that, I would think that my life would be so much better if I were white. And I thought that for so, so long, and it's hard to try to undo all those things and all those images from the past. (p. 54)

Genevieve (Laotian American): Some people will always see us as foreigners. (p. 54)

Dhayal (Indian American): My name is supposed to be pronounced Dah-YAHL, but it wasn't easy to pronounce for most people. I remember around 2nd grade, some people started making fun and I started crying. It made me feel kind of inferior to the others. So when I came to high school I just told everybody to pronounce my name Dial. It's a lot easier to say, so that's what most people call me now. (p. 55)

Khanh (Vietnamese American): I realized I was different and that I didn't have a lot of the things other kids had. Not only was it a question of being Asian, but a lot of it had to (do) with economics, with not knowing the language, with my mom not being able to get a good job, and the place that we lived. I started noticing those differences and looking at other people. I wanted really badly when I was young, in 6th, 7th, 8th, and 9th grades, I wanted to be more white, I wanted to be American and lose my Asian-ness and my yellowness. (p. 55)

Marisa (Japanese American): Most people think of Asians as being introverted and very oriented towards their studies. I think a lot of it comes from what people know about schools in the East, where they stress school very much, and they think that gets transferred—and in some instances it probably does. (p. 56)

Khanh (Vietnamese American): Everybody in America said, "Oh, well we can all be the same, it doesn't matter who you are or where your background is; just come here and assimilate." Part of that is good, but part of it is telling you you must leave behind all your culture and become one of us. I realized when I visited Vietnam that I wouldn't have to do that. I can still live in America and be an American and be appreciative of my roots. (p. 59)

Hmong teen (cited in Trueba, Jacobs, and Kirton, 1990): Some Hmong kids are shy and all they hang around with are Hmong people. They are shy to speak up in classes and stuff. Maybe they should get in there like American kids and start talking in class and stuff. I think that when they get older they will be less scared and shy. Sometimes I think to myself that I wish I didn't know my language and just knew English so I wouldn't be so confused. But on the other side I think about my culture and keeping it. (p. 74).

As the poignant comments from these students indicate, having a sense of individualism is important. Yet, the connectedness to culture is powerful and ultimately escapable. The myth of the "model minority," based on the economic and academic success of many Asian Americans combines both truth and fiction (Oei and Lyon, 1996).

The Asian students' comments reflect deep cultural conflicts associated with being bicultural in the United States. Like Asian Americans, many African American students struggle with ambivalence and ambiguities that result from trying to negotiate dual cultures (Fordham, 1988).

Gray (as cited in Fordham, 1985): During my pompous period, I dealt with my insecurities by wearing a veil of superiority. Except around my family and neighbors, I played the role—the un-Black . . . To whites, I tried to appear perfect—I earned good grades and spoke impeccable English, was well-mannered and well-groomed. Poor whites, however, made me nervous. They seldom concealed their contempt for blacks, especially 'uppity' ones like me . . . To blacks, I was all of the above and extremely stuck up. I pretended not to see them on the street, spoke to them only when spoken to and cringed in the presence of blacks being loud in front of whites. The more integrated my Catholic grammar school became, the more uncomfortable I was there. I had heard white parents on TV grumbling about blacks ruining their schools; I didn't want anyone to think that I, too, might bring down Sacred Heart Academy. So I behaved, hoping that no one would associate me with "them" (other Black Americans). (p. 62–63)

Ellis(Fordham, 1988): Last year, the student council president, who was black, wanted to set aside a day to honor [Dr.] Martin

Luther King. A lot of blacks said it was a good thing to do, but a lot of whites said it was a waste of time and was not fair. ... I felt hurt that they (my white friends) would accept me as a black person but would not accept the idea of honoring a black person . . . One of my white friends said, "I don't see you as a black friend, but as a friend." But I want them to look at me for what I am. *I am a black person* [emphasis added]." (p. 62)

Sylvester Monroe (cited in Fordham, 1988): Looking back on it, I was pleased to show what black boys were capable of. Yet, there was a faint disquiet. What bothered me was that some people found it easier to pretend I was something else. "We're colorblind here [at St. George's]," a well-meaning faculty member once told me. "We don't see *black* students or *white* students, we just see students." But black was what I was; I wasn't sure he saw me at all. (p. 61)

As these examples indicate, educators must couple their knowledge of cultural differences with information about each individual child in order to arrive at the most complete understanding of their students. Adopting either a "color-blind" approach or a cultural difference approach will not suffice. It is crucial that educators understand the dilemmas that students of color encounter when they feel as if their cultures are not valued in school and society. As evidenced by these students' comments, many students have internalized the negative messages associated with their ethnicity. In a society that sends many overt and covert messages about white superiority, some students of color exhibit forms of self-hatred for their blackness, redness, brownness, and yellowness (Woodson, 1933). Many choose to subordinate their identity as an African American (for example) to their identity as an American in the hopes that a raceless persona will mitigate the harsh treatment and severe limitations in the opportunity structure that are likely to confront them as African Americans (and other people of color) (Fordham, 1988).

Children are often unaware of the long-term implications of how changes in culture and language influence their self-perception of ability and self-confidence (Trueba, Jacobs, and Kirton, 1990). Many find it impossible to integrate contrasting home and school values. In a study by Trueba, Jacobs, and Kirton (1990), Hmong children found it frustrating and traumatic when trying to participate fully in classroom learning activities.

They became increasingly aware of their collective and individual cultural differences and values as seen through the eyes of their teachers and peers. Feeling unusually high levels of anxiety and stress, they sought alternatives to cope with classroom activities. Their teachers, although well meaning, remained securely attached to their own cultural norms of per-

In order to teach effectively, educators must be adept at cross-cultural communication.

formance, which they communicated to the children in English language. When the teachers' expectations were not met, they passed judgments on the children's ability to learn and determined collectively with other resource staff that these children had learning disabilities. School personnel viewed these students as having low potential, performing at low levels of achievement, and giving clear signs of suffering learning disabilities, but neither teachers, nor principal, nor psychologist could explain the nature of the presumed disability. The Hmong children under study showed deep frustration and an attitude of hopelessness as they failed to engage meaningfully in learning activities. (Trueba, Jacobs, and Kirton, 1990, pp. 75–76).

Effective teaching requires balancing many pieces of information about children. As the subsequent section will illustrate, it is important for teachers to develop cross-cultural competence.

❖ PREMISE FOUR Teaching is a cross-cultural encounter.

An important goal of multicultural education is to help students develop cross-cultural competencies (Banks, 1994). It is imperative that teachers assist students in understanding the interconnectedness of all people in the United States and the world. Yet, while all people are inextricably tied to one another, each person is a unique cultural entity. When comparing teacher and student's cross-cultural encounters, each brings to the classroom a distinct combination of beliefs, values and experiences (Hermendez, 1989). These differences influence actions, perceptions, attitudes, and performance. Because of the infinite number of cultural possibilities that humans possess, students should have opportunities on a regular basis to practice necessary skills and to discover what it takes to get along cross-culturally (Gay, Cole-Slaughter, and Barber 1995). Cross-cultural competence can be accomplished successfully but requires a comprehensive approach to include relevant curriculum content, learning skills, and instructional strategies.

In order to demonstrate and model effective cross-cultural communication to students, teachers must be proficient at communicating cross-culturally. Cross-cultural competence assumes an even more important role as the teaching population in the United States becomes increasingly white while the student population is becoming increasingly diverse (Sleeter, 1993). White teachers commonly insist that they are "color blind" and that they see children and do not see race (Boutte, LaPoint, and Davis, 1993; Sleeter, 1993; Schofield, 1997). The denial of the importance of race in this society often results in teachers trying to teach all children in the same manner—typically from a Eurocentric perspective (Boutte, LaPoint, and Davis, 1993). Teaching from a monocultural perspective keeps teachers from communicating effectively cross-culturally, and they often fail to correctly interpret the messages that children are sending. Furthermore, many white teachers do not respect children's communication styles and tend to view African Americans and Latino/a Americans (in particular) in a pathological manner (Heath, 1983). That is, children of color and poor children's homes and communities tend to be viewed as dysfunctional, and teachers believe that the children lack ability and motivation (Sleeter, 1993). Culturally idiosyncratic communication styles that may be praised in the child's home and community may be looked upon with disdain by teachers and school personnel.

Subtle differences in people's ways of behaving may seem trivial at first; however, these have profound effects on people's reactions and interactions—especially in face-to-face encounters between people of differing ethnic and cultural backgrounds (Erickson and Mohatt, 1982). Feelings about situations or inferences about intent vary widely among cultures. When people experience cultural shock from going from one society to another, it is probably not obvious differences that cause the greatest sense of cognitive dissonance. In other words, it is not the overt differences in dress, religion, or even food which bring on the strongest sense of confusion. Rather, it is often the assumptions underlying everyday life, shared by members of a cultural group by virtue of constant interaction from birth, and assumptions that are so much a part of the culture that they are not even consciously held. Because implicit cultural differences have such a powerful effect on cross-cultural interactions, it is important for teachers to at least have some knowledge of typical cultural behavior, with the understanding that exceptions do exist. Erickson and Mohatt (1982) advise that discovering small differences in social relations may make a big difference in understanding how children of color engage with the content of the school curriculum. For example, Erickson and Mohatt found that many Native American children preferred to be seated in a group at a table versus sitting individually. In their ethnographic study, Erickson and Mohatt observed that teaching reading through individual tutoring versus large group instruction and using a narrative versus phonic approach were more effective ways of teaching some Native American students. Understanding *how* to communicate with children from different cultures is indeed important for effective teaching. Likewise, understanding a particular culture may also provide insight into appropriate disciplinary methods. For example, praise that is overdone in public is thought of as a negative form of individual attention in some Native American cultures (Erickson and Mohatt, 1982; Hewett, 1996). Although the intent of teachers' public praise is to provide positive feedback to children, giving extreme praise may cause embarrassment and discomfort among some Native American children.

Figure 3-2 highlights some of the possible verbal and nonverbal sources of miscommunication between cultural groups. We emphasize that the communication styles listed on this table are based on the literature and on anecdotal reports (1986). Additionally, these styles are based on individuals from the working class and may not apply to students from families where parents hold professional positions and may be more likely to exhibit mainstream behavior and attitudes. *As with other information on cultures, we recommend that the table be interpreted as one possible explanation which may assist in understanding the complex dynamics surrounding cultural learning styles.* While we do not agree with everything in Figure 3-2, we have found some of the information to be useful. The table compares the communication styles of African Americans, Asian Americans, and Latino/a

Americans to that of European Americans (since mainstream culture is based on Euro-American communication styles). Taylor (1986) did not include communication styles of Native Americans on this chart.

Figure 3-2 demonstrates that behavior condoned by one culture may be offensive in others. The macroculture in this society tends to condone European behavior while viewing other communication styles as inappropriate. Therefore, some of the cultural communication styles outlined in Figure 3-2 have taken on a negative connotation in larger society, thus causing some members of these cultural groups to disassociate themselves from the behaviors—especially individuals who consider themselves raceless (Fordham, 1988). In a multicultural society, there is room for many different communication styles. As the differences outlined in Table 3-2 imply, it is wise for educators who teach children from cultural groups that differ from their own (including differences in class and gender) to take time to carefully observe both verbal and nonverbal communication styles of the students they teach.

As educators attempt to digest information about communication styles of different cultures, they must remember the caveat that norms may not apply to all students. For example, Medicine (1988) contends that many general "truths" about Native American people could be challenged. Medicine presents evidence of this by citing recent work with the Menominee Indians indicating that eye contact between an elder and a child was necessary for informal teaching to proceed. Likewise, she noted that Lakota (Sioux) parents may state, "look me in the eyes!" when addressing children and grandchildren (Medicine, 1988). Yet, because of overgeneralizations, the pervasive belief that Indians avoid contact is frequently cited in the educational and psychological literature without the acknowledgement that cultural norms are only intended as a guide. It is also important to remember that cultural behaviors typical to one particular ethnic group may be evident in other groups as well.

Children who speak two or more languages are also often misunderstood in classrooms—particularly when the child is just learning to speak English and the teacher speaks only English. There are approximately eleven million school children who are not fluent in English or speak a language other than English at home (Trueba, Jacobs, and Kirton, 1990). Additionally, potential cuts and/or the elimination of bilingual education programs threaten to make it harder for more recent Asian immigrants to succeed in schools (Huang and Oei, 1996).

Table 3-2. Possible Verbal and Nonverbal Sources of
Miscommunication Between Cultural Groups

African Americans	European Americans
Hats and sunglasses are sometimes considered adornments much like jewelry, to be worn inside.	Hats and sunglasses are considered utilitarian, as outer wear, and are to be removed indoors.
Agreement and approval are given through gestures such as "giving five" (slapping hands).	No gestural counterpart for agreement or approval exists.
Touching one's hair by another person is often considered offensive.	Touching of one's hair by another person is a sign of affection.
Direct eye contact in conversation may not occur although the individual is being attentive.	Direct eye contact is considered a sign of attentiveness and respect.
Public behavior (e.g., at a play or concert) is emotionally intense, dynamic, and demonstrative, as in laughter, shouts, and so forth.	Public behavior is modest and emotionally restrained; outward displays are seen as irresponsible or in bad taste.
"Signifying" as a form of verbal insults is common among men.	No engagement in verbal insults as an extended activity.
Asking personal questions of someone one has met for the first time is seen as improper and intrusive.	Inquiring about jobs, family, and so forth of someone one has met for the first time is seen as friendly.
Use of direct questions is sometimes seen as harassment (e.g., asking when something will be finished is seen as rushing that person to finish).	Use of direct questions for personal information is permissible.
"Breaking in" during conversation is usually tolerated. Competition for the floor is granted to the person who is most assertive.	Rules on turn-taking in conversation dictate that one person has the floor at a time until all of his or her points are made.

Table 3-2. Continued

African Americans	European Americans
Conversations are regarded as private between the recognized participants; "butting in" is seen as eavesdropping and is not tolerated.	Adding points of information or insights to a conversation in which one is not engaged is sometimes seen as being helpful.
Use of "you people" is seen as pejorative and racist.	Use of "you people" is tolerated.

Hispanic Americans	European Americans
Hissing to gain attention is acceptable.	Hissing is considered impolite and indicates contempt.
Booing and hissing at a play or concert indicate extreme approval.	Booing and hissing at a concert are signs of disapproval and bad manners.
Touching is often observed between and two people in conversation.	Touching is usually unacceptable and often carries sexual over tones.
Avoidance of direct eye contact is a sign of attentiveness and respect; direct eye contact is regarded as an insult.	Direct eye contact is a sign of attentiveness and respect.
Relative distance between two speakers in conversation is close.	Relative distance between two speakers in conversation is farther apart.
Telling a woman that she is getting fat is considered as a compliment.	Commenting about a person's weight is considered an insult.

Asian Americans	European Americans
Touching or hand-holding between members of the same sex is acceptable.	Touching or hand-holding between members of the same sex may be considered a sign of homosexuality.
Hand-holding, hugging, kissing between men and women in public looks ridiculous.	Hand-holding, hugging, kissing between men and women in public is acceptable to some groups.

Table 3-2. Continued

Asian Americans	European Americans
A slap on the back is insulting.	A slap on the back denotes friendliness.
It is not customary to shake hands with persons of the opposite sex.	It is customary to shake hands with persons of the opposite sex.
Waving motions are used only by adults to call little children and not vice-versa.	Waving motions are often used to call people.

European Americans	Other Ethnic Groups
Symbols of the old South, such as confederate flags, Black lamppost lawn ornaments are acceptable to some groups.	African Americans view confederate flags and Black lamppost ornaments as offensive and racist.
Using cultural in-group gestures such as "giving five" and bowing is seen as patronizing.	Using cultural in-group gestures is seen as patronizing.
Including a "minority" person in group activities is seen as democratic.	Purposely including a minority person in group activities is seen as tokenism.
Adopting the dance pattern or music styles of other cultural groups is seen as free exchange.	Adopting the dance patterns or music styles of other cultural groups is offensive.
Maintaining eye contact in conversation is regarded as respectful or as a sign of sincerity.	Maintaining eye contact in conversation is regarded as staring or a sign of condescension.

Courtesy of: O. L. Taylor. *Nature of Communication Disorders in Culturally and Linguistically Diverse Populations.* San Diego, CA: College-Hill Press, 1986, pp. 36–37.

Gender differences also interfere with effective cross-cultural communication. The majority of the elementary teaching profession is female and female-oriented. Therefore, the culture of the school often reflects a female perspective. The disproportionate number of males who are subjected to disciplinary actions—especially African and Latino males (McCoy and Boutte, 1995; Sleeter, 1993)—may often be the result of males trying to thrive in a female-oriented environment. Children are expected to sit for long periods of time, speak softly, raise their hands before speaking, etc. Such behavior tends to be more difficult for males since they have typically been socialized to be active and independent. In schools across the nation, boys are more likely to be scolded and reprimanded in classrooms even when the observed conduct of boys and girls does not differ (Sadker, Sadker, and Long, 1993). Additionally, boys are far more likely to be identified as exhibiting learning disabilities, reading problems, and mental retardation. They also receive lower grades, are more likely to repeat grades, and are less likely to complete high school. They also perform significantly below females in writing achievement.

Unfortunately, most females do not understand the "male" culture and cannot "speak their language." For example, when boys engage in rough-and-tumble play on the playground, female teachers may misinterpret it as fighting, although it is commonplace among boys.

The manner in which female teachers treat males may be influenced by how they (female teachers) feel about the males in their lives (e.g., their husbands, brothers, fathers, sons, uncles, nephews, etc.) (Kunjufu, 1986). Kunjufu notes that the sexism issue becomes even more complex with white teachers who teach black males, since many of the white female teachers may have never had direct contact with a black male. Kunjufu questions who white female teachers see when they look at black males. Do they see a Jesse Jackson or a drug addict? The way teachers view and treat black males depends on prior experiences and societal perspectives about black males.

Credence is added to the claims that elementary schools are more female-oriented when we observe honor rolls at many middle schools. Recently, one of the authors attended an honor roll program for sixth, seventh, and eighth graders. Approximately eighty percent of the honorees were white females. Only a few males were presented with awards and even fewer African American children. All of the Asian children at the school received awards. The point is that the honorees basically looked just like the teachers—white females! Teachers typically note that the reason middle school boys do not earn good grades is that it is "uncool" for them to do well in school. Nevertheless, educators have the responsibility of teaching all children. Whenever a particular segment of the school population is not succeeding, the implication is that it is worth examining the way things are done instead of continuing with business as usual.

The racial and sexism issues highlight the need for a more diverse and male teaching staff (Kunjufu, 1986; Sleeter, 1993). Unless schools and teacher education programs emphasize effective cross-cultural communication, it is likely that teachers will continue to communicate ineffectively cross-culturally. Problems surrounding cross-cultural communication are compounded by the frequent hiring of new teachers in diverse and often demanding schools. Typically, most of these new teachers are white and female and become frustrated when children do not respond or learn according to typical theories about how children learn (Chen and Goldring, 1992). Consequently, teachers may be faced with significant personal conflict since their perspectives and communication styles differ from those of their students. These

---

Many children communicate cross-culturally
with less difficulty than adults.

The educational system has not served all students equally well.

differences must be overcome if the goal of cross-cultural communication is to be met. Teachers must familiarize themselves with literature about communication styles of different cultures and genders. They also need actual experiences working with diverse populations (Chen and Goldring, 1992). Additionally, they must carefully observe and value differences in communication styles. Finally, students and the teachers must learn to be bicultural and master Standard English and at least one other communication style.

❖ **PREMISE FIVE The educational system has not served all students equally well.**

Several multicultural education/anti-racist researchers have revealed that prejudice, classism, sexism, and racism are major problems in our nation's schools (Donaldson, 1994; Murray and Clark, 1990; Pate 1992; Pine and Hilliard, 1992). We have learned from these researchers that students who are poor, are members of certain ethnic groups, and are linguistically, culturally, or socially different from the mainstream population are generally the targets of unequal treatment (Hermendez, 1989). Schools' approaches to educating some students have been found wanting because of negative and counterproductive attitudes and beliefs about students. Elementary school teachers who believe that only some children are intelligent enough to become well-educated undermine their pedagogy and engender lack of confidence in youngsters rather than a sense of competence. The conventional assumption that not all children can learn has become the paradigm or theory for tracking and evaluating elementary students. Schools continue to be heavily segregated racially and economically despite decades of integration efforts. Tracking is one mechanism which has the potential for fostering and perpetuating negative expectations and self-fulfilling prophecies for many children.

Heightened attention currently expressed by parents, educators, business leaders, and politicians reveals the breadth and seriousness of the national concern over educating all children. In order to transform our educational system, elementary school teachers must examine current assumptions about children and find new and more effective pedagogical techniques that will serve all children equally well. As Hixson points out, "Teachers' sense of efficacy must be tied to a belief system founded not only on the reality that 'all students can learn,' but also, that the differentiating factor is the appropriateness and effectiveness of the instructional experiences to which they (students) are exposed, rather than the characteristics of the families and communities from which they come, or the 'learning credentials,' they bring to the classrooms" (Hixson, 1990, p. 4).

The problems that many children face inside and outside classrooms (racism, poverty, language differences, and cultural barriers) are not adequately acknowledged and addressed in most schools. Consequently, schools continue to face low achievement and high drop out rates among certain groups. In addition to these challenges, elementary schools must confront the following issues: culturally biased tests, tracking/placement inequities, peer pressure, the fourth grade syndrome, language dilemmas, curriculum biases, and teacher biases.

Culturally Biased Tests

A test is considered to be biased if equally abled individuals from different groups do not have equal probabilities of success. Conceptually, test bias involves the issue of differential validity. That is, a test may be valid for one group, but not another (Shepard, Camilli, and Averill, 1981). The basic validity question is whether a test measures what it purports to do for all groups. Students are required to take standardized tests which are primarily normed on white middle class students and which may not be the best indicator of the achievement levels of children of color. Additionally, test results often relegate a disproportionate number of children to inferior positions in the curriculum and in later occupations (Scarr, 1981). As Hilliard (1991) concluded, in the final analysis, test results are merely mirrors that reflect the socioeconomic milieu which have conditioned the test-taker's lives.

Tracking/Placement

Many districts place students in special education classes to avoid the high-stakes consequences of test results of low-performing students (Powell, Zehm, and Garcia, 1996). Powell, Zehm, and Garcia add that the majority of these special education students are low-income students, students of color, and students for whom English is the second language. For example, approximately sixteen percent of elementary classrooms are comprised of African American students. Yet, according to Hacker (1992) almost forty percent of these students are placed in special education classrooms or labeled as disabled or mentally retarded.

Many times tracking is based on teachers' perceptions and low expectations of students' behavior patterns, learning styles and cultural differences. Howard (1992) reports that children of color are even more severely underrepresented in the upper end of the placement hierarchy (in the "advanced placement" or "gifted and talented" classes). In reference to ability grouping, Howard further asserts that these groups dictate curricular, academic, or vocational tracks which lead to very different destinations in United States society. Ability group placements represent powerful expectancies. When children are grouped according to teacher assessment of their intelligence, then teachers communicate clearly what they think of kids. Teachers then shape conceptions about students' places in the world. Research has shown that self-assessments based on scores and ability group placement become permanent features of the child's self concept, and shape attitude and behavior toward academic work. (Hilliard, 1976; Oakes, 1985; Steele, 1992; Wigdor and Garner, 1982).

Most experts will agree that ability grouping has proved harmful for the most vulnerable children, has contributed to within-school segregation, has lowered expectations for most students, and has denied access to higher levels of learning to many (Wheelock and Hawley, 1992). Many educational leaders and advocates actively oppose ability grouping and tracking (e.g., the National Middle Schools Association, the National Education Association, the Carnegie Endowment for Children, National Association for the Education of Young Children) (Wheelock and Hawley, 1992). New instructional practices and ways of organizing curriculum make ability grouping increasingly unnecessary.

Wheelock and Hawley emphasize that the implementation of alternatives to ability grouping includes more than the regrouping of students from homogeneous to heterogeneous groups. It is not something that teachers can do alone. Instead, whole school reform is needed that requires educators to investigate and adapt a variety of new approaches to curriculum and instruction in the classroom. Curriculum and instruction developed expressly for heterogeneous groups should emphasize thinking skills, cultural perspectives, and high expectations for all students.

Wheelock and Hawley add that successful school reform depends on demonstrating to different interest groups that children will not be harmed and will benefit from alternatives to ability grouping without diluting the curriculum. They note that schools do not operate apart from a broader political context. Like other organizations, schools are subject to a variety of formal and informal laws and regulations. Furthermore, organizational arrangements often reflect a long history of compromises and accommodations to different interest groups. Constituencies representing children labeled as "gifted and talented" exist in every community and are often the most outspoken. Any changes that schools make should be done in phases and involve interested constituencies.

Peer Pressure

Often peers play a more significant role in academic achievement than teachers or parents. Students may be opposed to their classmates' commitment to academic excellence and display this opposition by name-calling or referring to achievers as "nerds," for example. Achievers are sometimes excluded from social activities in and outside of the classroom. Many children of color refer to high achievement as "acting white" (Fordham, 1988). They may also refer to using Standard English as "talking white." Since many children of color must identify with their own culture in order to survive, they tend to reject school-related behaviors such as performing well in class and speaking Standard English (Majors and Billson, 1992). Teachers must help children learn to balance both their home culture and the mainstream culture so that they will have a better chance at being successful in school (Boutte, McCoy, and Davis, 1995; Delpit, 1988; Hale-Benson, 1986).

Fourth Grade Syndrome

Jawanza Kunjufu (1990) in his book *Countering the Conspiracy to Destroy Black Boys* discusses the high interest level that young African American males exhibit in the early years of elementary school. Although teachers view the high energy level of these children as aggressive, negative behavior and equate it with behavioral problems, most black males and other children of color fare relatively well until around fourth grade. However, during and immediately after fourth grade, a consistent decline in academic success is seen. Factors that contribute to the decline achievement are:

- a decline in parental involvement
- an increase in peer pressure
- a decline in nurturance and an increase in discipline problems
- a decline in teacher expectations
- a lack of understanding of learning styles
- a lack of male teachers

Elementary teachers must work closely with early childhood teachers to derive solutions for preventing the classic fourth grade decline.

Language Dilemmas

We have found that more often than not, children in elementary classrooms who speak a different language or dialect are viewed as being deficient. Teachers need to perceive language diversity as a positive rather than a negative condition (Nieto, 1992). Dialects are not deficits; rather, they are assets. According to DeFlorimonte (1993), "It is crucial that teachers learn to accept the rich and unique abilities of students. Every attempt must be made to provide a supportive environment which expands and accommodates the diverse language capabilities of our children." (p. 9-10)

Curriculum Biases

An authentic rather than a pseudo-multicultural curriculum is imperative if we are to infuse the voices and experiences of a range of cultural and ethnic groups (Banks, 1992; Boutte and McCormick, 1992). An important aim of multicultural education in elementary schools must be that it is inclusive and reflects the histories and experiences of the diverse cultures and groups that make up the American society. Experts maintain that multicultural education must be infused into the learning experiences of many cultures, in all areas of the curriculum and at every grade level (Banks, 1992; Boutte, La Point, and Davis, 1993; Gay, 1993; Nieto, 1992).

Teacher Biases

Students from different ethnic groups have notably different experiences in school (Berns, 1993). For instance, Chinese, Japanese, and some Southeast Asian students have typically succeeded in schools; whereas other Asian, Pacific, and Native American children have been less successful (Berns, 1993). Because most teachers are from the majority culture and tend to invoke the ways of the majority culture, educational underachievement by other ethnic groups is usually blamed on incompatibilities between the students' cultures and that of the school. However, teachers often unknowingly and unintentionally contribute to the underachievement and school failure of students of color. As noted in Chapter Two, teachers must examine biases about children that are based on ethnicity, socioeconomic status, disability, gender, and religion in order to ensure the success of all children.

Teacher bias may manifest itself in a number of ways. For example, differences have been noted in the time that teachers wait for students to respond to a question before talking again (White and Tharp, 1988). In one study, the response time of a Navajo and a white teacher of the same group of third graders was compared. The Navajo teacher waited considerably longer than the white teacher after the children responded before talking again. What was perceived by the white teacher as a completed response was often intended by the child as a pause, which the white teacher interrupted. Since the culture of most American Indians encourages deliberate thought, short "wait times," tend to be disadvantageous to them (Nieto, 1992). As noted in Chapter Two, the amount of reaction time provided for students may be based upon teachers' expectations for children. When teachers think that students know the answer, they tend to give students adequate time to respond. On the other hand, when teachers do not expect students to respond, they tend to forge ahead, apparently in an effort to avoid prolonging student embarrassment.

White and Tharp (1988) found that while Navajo students preferred long wait times between responses, Native Hawaiian students preferred waiting times during which the listener spoke without waiting for the speaker to finish. Teachers from other ethnic groups often interpreted such interruptions as being rude, though in Hawaiian society it demonstrates involvement and relationship (Berns, 1993). Teachers who have carefully observed the communication styles of their students are less likely to make such cultural *faux pas* which limit the possibilities for students' responses.

❖ **PREMISE SIX Multicultural education is synonymous with educational innovation and reform.**

Banks and Banks (1983) noted that reform of the total school is imperative, if educational equality is to become a reality. Innovative efforts to promote education reform across the nation have been commendable, albeit disjointed at times. However, a more comprehensive approach to the development of a serious multicultural education movement that seeks to change the entire school environment is needed. This process will never be totally completed but we must constantly strive for the improvement of the goals and objectives of multiculturalism. Erickson and Mohatt (1982) suggest that making small changes in everyday classroom participation structures may be one strategy for developing a culturally responsive pedagogy. Changes in the following areas are an essential part of this process.

Assessment And Testing

Authentic strategies for assessing children's progress are needed. Instead of relying only on standardized tests, schools must gather information from a number of sources. Additionally, assessment should be ongoing rather than once a year, and should be tied to curriculum and instruction.

Instructional Delivery

Teachers need to use a wide variety of instructional delivery methods to increase the likelihood of meeting the needs of all children. One instructional strategy that has been shown to improve social relations among children, particularly in the area of ethnic relations and acceptance of other-abled students who have been "mainstreamed," is cooperative learning. This approach may be particularly useful during the elementary years when students depend on their peers for approval. The use of peers in a cooperative learning setting (to solve academic tasks and to prepare reports) has been shown to increase student achievement more than in a teacher-directed setting (Berns, 1993). Although cooperative learning strategies may work for some students, it may be ineffective for others who have different learning styles. Therefore, educators should use a balance of teaching methods such as lecture, discussion, inquiry, learning centers, cooperative groups, individualized instruction, computerized instruction, and the like.

Respect for Different Languages and Dialects

Bilingual education should be provided for all children when possible. The United States is one of the only technologically advanced countries that does not teach children more than one language. Cross-cultural communication is a must for the twenty-first century. Bilingual instruction should also be emphasized with children who speak a dialect other than Standard English. In other words, Standard English may have to be taught as their second language. For example, the Los Angeles Unified School District uses this approach for African American children whose first language is not mainstream English (Standard English) (LeMoine, 1996).

Instructional Materials

Classrooms must have nonbiased instructional materials which present different perspectives. Children and teachers can learn to critique all instructional materials.

The Formalized Curriculum

As discussed in Chapter Two, the curriculum at most schools must become more multicultural. This might mean changing the content of subjects that have been taught the same way since the inception of public school. For example, the typical over-emphasis on white males needs to be replaced for a more balanced approach. Contrary to what opponents of multicultural education suggest, changing the content and focus of the curriculum does not result in a "watered down" curriculum. In fact, since a multicultural curriculum includes scholarly debate about the content, it may be more rigorous than using a traditional curriculum without questioning its validity. An important area for school reform is addressing the manner in which European scholarship has represented the history and potentialities of non-white societies (Joseph, 1987). Additionally, the contributions of women mathematicians have also been neglected.

Most subject areas are beginning to make reforms in instructional materials; however, many educators do not see the relevance of reforming their curriculum and perspectives in math and science. Educators must become aware that a substantial body of research evidence points to significant development in mathematics in Mesopotamia, Egypt, China, and pre-Columbus America. However, this information is typically omitted in math and credit for many math theories are given to Greeks. Advanced sixth, seventh, and eighth grade students could research variations of topics that they are studying. For example, the Pythagorean theorem is found in varying degrees of detail all over the world. There is evidence that Pythagoras (one of the earliest and greatest Greek mathematicians) and Thales (legendary founder of Greek mathematics) traveled widely in Egypt and Babylonia and learned much of their mathematics from these areas (Joseph, 1987).

Joseph further points out that the first clear statement of evolution and the underlying rationale for the scientific method has been traced to Arabian science. Yet, most books cling to the erroneous portrayal of the Greeks as having created the most impressive civilization of ancient time.

True educational reform will require that educators seriously reconsider and change what and how we teach. No longer can we continue to convey to children that Europe was the center of the world. Practically all topics taught in mathematics today are directly derived from the work of mathematicians from Western Europe before the twelfth century A. D. Therefore, there is a widespread acceptance of the view that mathematical discovery can only follow from a rigorous application of deductive axiomatic logic (which is perceived as a unique product of Greek mathematics). Consequently, intuitive or empirical methods are dismissed as of little relevance in mathematics. However, the most recent edition of the math standards published by the National Council of Teachers in Mathematics (NCTM) are congruent with multicultural goals since nontraditional strategies for teaching mathematics are encouraged (versus only "Eurocentric" strategies). Reformed math and science classes must also be tailored to children's experience of their social and physical environments.

When this is done, mathematics can easily be integrated with other subject areas such as art and design, history, and social studies, which are currently ignored in mathematics curricula. Taking a more holistic and less Eurocentric approach to math and science instruction is a wonderful (albeit momentous) entrance to true reform (Joseph, 1987).

The Attitudes/Perceptions of School Employees

Attitudinal changes are most difficult to bring about. However, an authentic multicultural approach cannot be utilized unless the professionals involved believe in the basic tenets of multiculturalism. All school personnel, including secretaries, cafeteria employees, and so forth, would benefit from diversity sensitivity workshops which focus on treating all families with respect. Indeed, multiculturalism extends much beyond providing instructional materials and activities that stress diversity. The activities in this book should be helpful for addressing the attitudinal issues necessary for a successful multicultural classroom.

School Culture and the Hidden Curriculum

Educators must realize that the covert factors mentioned in Chapter Two of this book are prevalent and have a strong impact on students' educational experiences. Educators must learn to assess the "hidden messages" that they send to children. For example, if teachers fail to call on females, girls will soon get the message that the teacher does not expect them to respond. Likewise, if teachers allow little or no reaction time for some students to respond and extended response time for others, children will pick up on these trends. Indeed, children are very adept at detecting who is valued in the classroom and society (and who is not).

Teachers' Expectations for Students

Teachers and other educators must seriously examine their own beliefs about children from various cultural, religious, ethnic, gender, socioeconomic status, and ability groups. As noted in Chapter Two, these expectations and beliefs inevitably guide teaching practices and interactions.

❖ PREMISE SEVEN Next to parents, teachers are the single most important people in children's lives.

In elementary classrooms, teachers' attitudes, personality, values and skills all play important role in the lives of young children. As a teacher of elementary school children, how one interacts with students, and the kind of environment and program the teacher provides make a lasting impact on children, families, and society (Feeney, Christenson, and Moravcik, 1991). The capacity to support children's development, caring, and compassion are qualities needed by teachers to be effective with children, especially as the dynamics of childhood in the United States are changing. Teachers can serve as socializing agents and provide a nurturing environment where day-to-day interactions can help children to develop positive self-identities (Hale-Benson, 1991).

Multicultural innovation can be incorporated effectively into the education of young children. The fundamentals of self-concept and cooperation should both be embraced by the elementary school teacher. The role of the adult is central to a child's acceptance of appropriate behaviors related to cultural appreciation (Graves, Garginla, and Sluder 1991). Next to parents, teachers are an important key to promoting a positive multicultural environment and modeling cultural awareness in the classroom. Educators must realize that when they make denigrating comments about children's families and home environments, they are essentially condemning the children and have decided that the children are beyond help. Therefore, we recommend that negative comments and attitudes be substituted with attitudes which demonstrate respect for the strengths that children bring to schools. Table 3-3 demonstrates how negative comments can be replaced with more positive ones.

Table 3-3. Substituting Negative Comments With Positive Ones

Negative Comments	Positive Comments
1. These children come from the projects and their parents don't care about them.	1. Most parents care about their children—even poor parents. I need to find a way to show parents that education may be a way to a better life for their children. It will be difficult for me to be successful without the parents' assistance.
2. The language these students use is weird and not good.	2. My high expectations and respect for children who speak a different language will affect positively their performance. I can help them keep the beauty of their natural vernacular while extending it to include Standard English.
3. Most of the children in my class are from single parent homes, and their parents don't care about them.	3. Just because a child is from a single-parent home does not mean that his mom or dad do not care about him or her. Some children from two-parent families may be no better off than this child. How can I help the child be successful in my classroom?
4. These children don't do well because they have "low self-esteem."	4. The children's self-esteem will be supported by successful experiences in my classroom.

In addition to examining comments, teachers also need to carefully reflect on their culture and how it relates to their view of the children that they teach. Figure 3-2 provides issues and questions which will help teachers examine their beliefs and attitudes about the children they teach.

Figure 3-2. Understand Your Culture in Relation to the Children You Teach

In the first two columns, write brief answers for each of the items below. Then compare you and your students on each of the items and check whether they are the same or different.

	YOU	YOUR STUDENTS	SAME	DIFFERENT
Ethnicity	_____	_____	_____	_____
Religion	_____	_____	_____	_____
Preferred language or dialect	_____	_____	_____	_____
Nationality	_____	_____	_____	_____
Geographic region of your home (originally)	_____	_____	_____	_____
Social economic status (social class)	_____	_____	_____	_____
Gender	_____	_____	_____	_____
Things you value	_____	_____	_____	_____
Type of neighborhood you currently live in (e.g., suburban, city)	_____	_____	_____	_____
Type of music you prefer	_____	_____	_____	_____
Favorite foods	_____	_____	_____	_____
Type of movies you like	_____	_____	_____	_____

After answering the items, respond to the following questions.

1. Do you and your students have more in common or more differences?
2. How do you view the differences? In other words, what connotations do you attach to the differences? Is one choice more positive than the other?
3. Are your instructional goals aimed at changing the students and making them more like you? Do you want your students to become bicultural? Multicultural?
4. How do you really feel about aspects of your students' culture as compared to yours?

Since teachers are very important persons in their students' lives, it is important for them to be "culturally relevant teachers." Ladson-Billings (1994) asserts that teachers who practice culturally relevant methods help their students make connections between their local, national, racial, cultural, and global identities. Additionally, culturally relevant teachers:

- have high expectations for all children.
- do not blame children and families.
- believe that all of their students can succeed rather than that failure of some is inevitable.
- demonstrate a connectedness to children beyond the boundaries of the classroom.
- challenge children.
- assume responsibility for children's learning.
- encourage a community of learners with and among students.
- view knowledge as something that is continuously recreated, recycled, and shared.
- are passionate about knowledge.
- help students develop necessary skills.
- help students develop knowledge and skills by building bridges and scaffolding for learning.

Ladson-Billings (1994) believes that teachers from any ethnic background can be culturally relevant teachers. Teachers have the capability for creating a positive learning environment in their classes. In the hectic day-to-day routine, it is easy for teachers to forget the tremendous influence they have on their students. Even when they carry out seemingly noninstructional actions, such as smiling at students or showing disapproval, they are engaged in pedagogy. It becomes obvious that although elementary school children are influenced by a large array of factors (e.g., families, peers, their communities, and society at large), the teacher's role is an important part of the equation for success.

❖ PREMISE EIGHT Classroom interactions between teachers and students constitute the major part of the educational process for most students.

All classrooms are social environments and the strong interaction between teachers and students is of significant importance. The attitude of teachers and the way they relate to students are critical factors in the quality of instruction children receive. When teachers are cognizant of the cultural differences, learning styles, and language differences of students, their personal interactions will result in a positive and equitable manner. However, if the teachers are not aware of their own insensitivities they create barriers to communication. Research by Good and Brophy (1987) addressed the personal interactions between teachers and high- versus low-achieving students. Their study confirms the differential treatment received by low achieving students. Interactions with high achieving students were usually more frequent, public, friendly, and rewarding. On the other hand, teachers demanded less, were less friendly, had less eye contact with and criticized low-achieving students more often than high-achieving students.

Teachers must examine the nature of their interactions with students as well as students' interactions with each other. It is important for the teacher to model working together across gender, class, ability, and ethnic groups.

❖ SUMMARY

Elementary schools build on the educational experiences provided during the early childhood years and set the stage for the high school years. Unfortunately, in most places, there is little cross-communication and efforts to ensure continuity throughout children's school careers. Transitions from one level to the next are often not smooth.

This chapter outlined eight assumptions and principles that elementary teachers (and indeed teachers from other levels) should utilize if they want to provide multicultural classrooms which encourage all children to exit schools as competent individuals. Multiculturalism should be a school-wide effort and requires that teachers closely examine their teaching strategies as well as their attitudes. All children deserve the right to a high quality and equitable elementary school experience regardless of their gender, ethnicity, exceptionality, religion, or class. Teachers can use the strategies and suggestions provided in this chapter to ensure that all children will reach their highest potential. The future of the children affects all of us.

As the reader continues to reflect on multicultural issues presented in this book, it will be helpful to examine her or his readiness for teaching or working with culturally diverse children (including white children). Figure 3-3 can be used to evaluate the reader's readiness for implementing aspects of a multicultural classroom.

Figure 3-3. Evaluating Your Readiness for Teaching Culturally
Diverse Children

Directions: Each of the following statements provides a basis for fostering your
awareness, knowledge, and understanding of diversity issues. For each statement,
put a check in the space that best reflects your degree of alignment. For each item
that you mark "no" or "unsure," develop an action plan for enhancing your awareness
and understanding of this area. For items marked "yes," summarize how you developed this quality. Remember that the purpose of this activity is to enhance your
readiness for teaching culturally diverse children by pinpointing areas that may constrain your effectiveness with students. Therefore, be honest and open with yourself
as you respond to each statement.

Response			Item
Yes	No	Unsure	
____	____	____	1. I am comfortable teaching in culturally diverse classrooms with students who share different value systems.
____	____	____	2. I am comfortable conferencing with parents of diverse cultures.
____	____	____	3. I accept and affirm students' usage of dialects or other languages.
____	____	____	4. I can explain how culture enhances students' learning of academic content.
____	____	____	5. I know how to design and implement lessons that are instructionally appropriate and academically challenging for all students.
____	____	____	6. I can develop strategies that engage all students in instruction and that help them express themselves confidently at school.
____	____	____	7. I can describe the historical antecedents to the marginalization of African Americans Latino/a Americans, and Native Americans.
____	____	____	8. I can identify subtle forms of racism, includ-ing unintended cultural bias, that might influence my own teaching.
____	____	____	9. I can explain how my personal life influences the values and beliefs I hold for making classroom decisions about curriculum and instruction.
____	____	____	10. I am able to tailor instruction to the needs of all my students.

Figure 3-3. Evaluating Your Readiness for Teaching Culturally Diverse Children (continued)

Response			Item
Yes	**No**	**Unsure**	

____ ____ ____ 11. I am able to describe the relationship between local communities and schools and in all economic and social areas, especially schools where students are likely to be economically disadvantaged.

Factors That Constrain Readiness to Work With Culturally Diverse Children

____ ____ ____ 1. I prefer teaching students who share my social class and cultural background.

____ ____ ____ 2. I believe that limited-English proficiency (LEP) students need lower-level work.

____ ____ ____ 3. I have limited cross-cultural experiences.

____ ____ ____ 4. I believe that students of color, such as African Americans, Latino/a Americans, and Native Americans, may not be as capable of learning as other students of color, such as Asians.

____ ____ ____ 5. I'm unsure about the cultural qualities of social groups other than my own.

____ ____ ____ 6. I believe that more problems than assets surround cultural diversity at school.

____ ____ ____ 7. I have a limited understanding of the complex relationship between society, schools, and ethnicity.

____ ____ ____ 8. I'm unsure how biases and stereotypes that I might have for other cultural groups could unintentionally influence my classroom instruction.

____ ____ ____ 9. I would rather teach in monocultural school settings.

____ ____ ____ 10. I have a limited understanding of how sociocultural and/or cognitive factors related to student diversity could influence my personal and academic relationship with students.

Field Experience: Strategies for Exploring Diversity in Schools. By Powell & Garcia, © 1995. Reprinted by permission of Prentice-Hall, Inc., Upper Saddle River, NJ

❖ RECOMMENDED ACTIVITIES

1. *Journal entry*—To continue your focus on the developmental effects of schooling, reflect on strategies that elementary school teachers need to use in a multicultural society. Can an elementary teacher reverse negative learning trends and attitudes about different cultures that students enter elementary school (fourth through eighth grades) with? If so, what strategies would be used? If not, why not? If you answered "no," are you assuming that schooling is ineffective for children who did not come to fourth through eighth grades prepared? In other words, why bother to teach? How will teacher expectations affect what students learn?

2. Before we can begin to understand and appreciate the cultures of the children we teach, we must first understand and appreciate our own culture and background. All of us, regardless of the number of generation of "Americans" we have behind us, still carry certain traditions, values, and customs that are part of our individual or family culture (Williams & DeGaetana, 1995). In small groups (or alone), do the following. 1) Discuss or list things that are part of your culture (e.g., music, food, concepts of beauty, celebrations, clothing, styles, child-rearing practices, etc.). 2) Discuss or list family traditions and customs. 3) Discuss or list values that you and your family hold.

4. Visit a setting where you are in the minority in terms of ethnicity, gender, socioeconomic status, ability, and/or religion. It is best if you can spend an extended period of time in this setting. Note similarities and differences between you and the group. Try to see the world through their lens. You may ask questions of the group to get further clarification of the culture. Write a brief summary of your observations.

5. Identify any classrooms or schools in your district (or similar districts) that are successfully implementing alternatives to ability grouping. Summarize their efforts. What problems have they encountered?

6. Interview a teacher (or several teachers) who advocate ability grouping. Also, interview a teacher (or teachers) who do not. Which do you agree with? Why? Summarize pros and cons of each side of the argument.

7. Interview two elementary school children. Find out who their best friends are. Find out if their friendships extend beyond ethnic and gender lines.

8. Visit an elementary school where you can observe a child whose is different from you in terms of ethnicity, gender, or socioeconomic status. Observe the child for an hour or more (Ideally, do this for several days in order to get a fuller understanding of the child). Write a summary of what you learned. Answer the following questions in your summary. How did you pick the child? Be aware of your own preferences for children of a particular gender, personality type, language characteristics, intellectual level, and so forth. Think about your initial impression of the child. Did the child behave in the way that you expected him or her to behave? What commonalities did you and the child share? Note behavior observed that defied stereotypical descriptions about the child's ethnicity, socioeconomic status, gender, and/or exceptionality.

9. Re-read Table 3-3 and other general information about the cultural learning styles of students that was presented in this chapter. Which items do you agree or disagree with? Why?

10. This activity is designed for the entire class. Using adhesive mailing labels, the instructor makes labels with the names of different ethnic groups (national and international) (e.g., Russian, Taiwanese, Swedish, Jamaican). Place one label on each students' back (college students) without letting them see the actual label. Students move around the room for five to ten minutes talking to other classmates to figure out what their label says. Classmates are encouraged to use stereotypical descriptions which will help individuals figure out what their labels say. After trying to figure out what their labels say, the instructor and students discuss some of the stereotypes that were given. An in-depth discussion of how these stereotypes have influenced what students know about different ethnic groups should follow. This activity can also be done using epithets if students feel comfortable exploring these highly sensitive issues.

11. *Community Plunge*—This activity is designed to help educators become familiar with aspects of the community's social, economic, and cultural organization. Specifically, this activity allows educators the opportunity to gain insight about the places in which the students live, play, worship, shop, secure social services, "hang out," or "cruise." For the purposes of this book, this activity is designed to be used to become more familiar with schools which enroll predominantly low-income, rural, urban, and/or children of color. It should also

be carried out in schools that enroll children who live in the same community as the school (versus in a school where children are bused from another community).

While this activity is designed to help readers view neighborhoods from the perspectives of the children and families who live there everyday, some safety precautions may have to be taken depending on the neighborhood. Before starting the community plunge, readers are advised to talk to teachers and administrators who work at the school to find out current information about the safety of certain areas. It should be noted that many of the readers may already work in schools in similar neighborhoods or are likely to be employed in such schools. Therefore, this experience will be particularly beneficial to these educators. Educators who do not work in such schools or who are unlikely to work in such schools will also benefit since this experience may help them better understand all children and prompt them to be advocates for all children. **Respect for the lifestyles of the families and children is important (versus feeling sorry for the families). Seek to view the community through the lens of the children and their families.**

As a safety precaution, this activity should be carried out in small groups. If the area is a high crime area, either find another safer neighborhood and/or notify the local police department of your plans as an additional caution. This activity may be carried out on Saturday mornings when stores and shops are likely to be open (and when streets are less likely to be isolated). Additionally, readers are not advised to carry a lot of money with them.

Four hours should be allotted for the community plunge. One faculty member is advised to always be near a telephone (at the school if possible) during the morning of exploration. Another faculty member should travel in a vehicle to check periodically on the groups' progress. A completely charged cellular telephone should be carried by each group.

Readers are expected to eat at a restaurant, visit a place of worship, a park, store and/or shopping center, a person's home (which may be arranged by the school), housing projects, trailer parks, and the like.

Additional guidelines are provided on Figure 3-4. The instructor may adapt the guidelines as needed.

Figure 3-4. Community Plunge

Objectives: This activity, a type of cultural scavenger hunt, is intended to provide interns with an introductory experience in the community served by the schools in which they will student teach. Through this activity, the interns will have the opportunity to identify and explore, in a limited fashion, several aspects of the community's socioeconomic and cultural organization. Additionally, the activity is intended to help interns begin to develop a spirit of camaraderie, which will be a useful support to them during their student teaching experience.

Activity Format: The interns will be divided into groups (four or five students per group). Each group will receive a map of the area, bus schedule, distinct route description, and a cultural questionnaire to be completed during the exploration of the particular route. Each group is to travel together on foot and by public transportation. Each group will have approximately three to four hours in which to conduct the community exploration.

Prior to departure, group members will select one person for each of the following responsibilities:

1. Tour Guide: knowing where all group members are at all times, helping group to decide which community elements to explore, keeping track of time
2. Travel Agent: responsible for route directions, bus schedule, map, and helping group to decide where to explore
3. Recorder: ensuring that data collected by group members is recorded on questionnaire
4. Reporter: responsible for reporting salient findings/observations to entire group during debriefing

(NOTE: If the group has five members, then two Recorders may be selected.)

All groups will reassemble together to debrief the community plunge experience.

YOU ARE ENCOURAGED TO UNDERTAKE THIS PLUNGE WITH SENSITIVITY, CREATIVITY, AND JOY TO GATHER INFORMATION AND INSIGHTS ABOUT YOUR NEW COMMUNITY.

HAVE FUN AND BE SAFE!

Community Plunge Debriefing Protocol

1. What problems did you encounter with your assigned route?
2. What city services, such as parks, did you observe?
3. What standards of beauty or taste did you experience (in terms of home adornment, clothing, cars, etc.)?
4. What evidence of social conflict did you see? (e.g., gang graffiti wars)
5. What evidence of wheelchair accessibility did you find on the sidewalks? restaurants? business?

6. What evidence of lack of code enforcement did you note?
7. What evidence of languages other than English did you find?
8. What types of social services did you investigate?
9. What types of business seemed to be predominant in the area?
10. What interesting places, not on the group questionnaire, did your group investigate?
11. How does this area compare to the area where you now live? What does it have that you do not and vice versa?
12. What was your most impressive or surprising finding or experience?
13. How did this experience alter your perception of the community?
14. What generalizations could you make about this community based on your immersion experience?
15. What else could you do now to further explore your student's life and culture?
16. As a teacher of students who live in this area, how would you determine what prior knowledge or schema you must build so that your students can be successful in your class?
17. What is one thing you experienced or saw that you could use in the classroom?

ROUTE #1 QUESTIONNAIRE

From Cowart Elementary, proceed north on Ravinia one block to Sharon. Go east on Sharon two blocks to Superior.

As you walk attend to the following aspects of the neighborhood:
How would you describe the dominant architecture?

Are most of the houses wood frame or brick?

What types of adornments or decorations are visible in the yards or houses?

What patriotic or religious symbols did you see in the yards or houses?

What is your assessment of the physical condition of most of the homes?

Approximately how many homes were vacant? For Rent? For Sale?

Were the sidewalks wheelchair accessible at the corners?

Based on the houses you observed, how would you classify the average standard of living in the neighborhood?

What type of economic activity, if any, did you notice in the neighborhood?
What evidence of social problems did you see?

When you reach Superior, take the DART bus No. 510 "Sunset" (destination 8th & Corinth Station). Be certain to notice the houses and businesses along the route. Converse with other riders about where they are going or how often they ride the bus.

How does the neighborhood north of Clarendon compare to the one you walked through?

Get off the bus just past Sunset High School at Marlborough. Walk east on Jefferson Blvd. to Catholic Charities.

What services does this organization offer to people in this area? **Continue east on Jefferson to the Salvation Army center at Rosemont.**

What services does this organization offer to people in this area? **Continue east to the small triangular shaped park between Jefferson and Tenth and Montclair and Windomere.**

What information does the historical marker in the park contain about the Winnetka Heights neighborhood? **From the park, walk north on Windomere four blocks to Davis.**

What differences do you notice between this neighborhood and the one near Cowart Elementary?

Explore the following businesses in the area from Windomere east four blocks to Wilomett:

1. De La Fuente Produce and Elvie's Party Supplies (1424 W. Davis): How much are the piñatas? Who makes them? How long does it take to make one?
2. Changó Botánica (1405 W. Davis): Look at the saints, herbs, powders, and candles. Ask about the history of a saint you select. How much is the statue?
3. Lilly Bridal Shop (1325 W. Davis) and Pretty Lady (La Dama Bonita) Bridal Salon (1324 W. Davis): How much is a quinceañera gown? How much does a family pay for a typical quinceañera celebration?
4. The Antique Shop (502 N. Edgefield, same building as Pretty Lady/LaDama Bonita Bridal Salon): What was the most interesting item you discovered? Do items come from homes in the area?
5. Super Mercado Monterrey (1314 W. Davis): What meats or fresh produce do you find here that you do not have in your local market? How do prices compare with those in your market?
6. Ngoma Mkristo African Dance School (606 N. Edgefield): What types of dances, drumming, costuming classes are offered here? Does the school have a performing group that will come to schools? Who can enroll in the classes? How much do classes cost?

For lunch you might select one of the following restaurants in this area:

1. El Pulpo Azul (1227 W. Davis)
2. La Cabaña Restaurant (1417 W. Davis)
3. Norma's Cafe (1123 W. Davis)
4. El Rinconcito Norteño (1009 W. Davis)

After lunch, return to Jefferson Blvd. via Winnetka. Attend to the architecture of the homes along the route. On Jefferson take the No. 510 "Sunset" (destination Hampton Station) bus back to the Cowart neighborhood. Get off at Bentley and walk west two blocks to Cowart Elementary.

Courtesy of Dr. Ronald Wilhelm, University of North Texas, P.O. Box 13857, Denton, TX 76203

❖ REFERENCES

Banks, J. A. 1992. *Multicultural education: Nature, challenges and opportunities in multicultural education for the 21st century.* Edited by Carlos Diaz, Service Editor Robert McClure, NEA National Center for Innovation. Washington D.C.88.

————.1994. *An introduction to multicultural education.* Boston: Allyn and Bacon

Banks, J. A. and C. A. M. Banks. 1989. *Multicultural education: Issues and perspectives.* Needham Heights, MA: Simon & Schuster.

Bell, D. A. 1994. Are Asian Americans a "model minority"? In *Taking sides: Clashing views on controversial issues in race and ethnicity.* Edited by R.C. Monk. Guilford, CT: Dushkin.

Berns, R. M. 1993. *Child, family, community.* 3rd edition. New York: Harcourt Brace.

Boutte, G. S., B. McCoy, and B. D. Davis. 1995. Helping African American students maintain and adopt their communication styles: A challenge for educators. *The Negro Education Review* 46(1-2):10–21.

Brophy, J., and T. Good. 1970. Teachers' communication of differential expectations for children's classroom performance: Some behavioral data. *Journal of Educational Psychology* 61(3):365–374.

Chen, M., and E. Goldring. 1992. The impact of classroom diversity on teachers' perspectives of their schools as workplaces. *EDRS.* ED 354 615.

Crawford, L. W. 1993. *Language and literacy Learning in multicultural classrooms.* Needham Heights, MA: Allyn and Bacon.

DeFlorimonte, D. 1993. Bridging the language differences gap through poetry: Children's background as language users. *Reading: Exploration and Discovery* 15(1): 8–16.

Delpit, L. 1988. The silenced dialogue: Power and pedagogy in educating other people's children. *Harvard Educational Review* 58(3): 280–298.

Derman-Sparks, L., C. Tanaka Higa, and B. Sparks. 1980. Children, race and racism: How race awareness develops. *Bulletin* 11(3 & 4): 3–9.

Diaz, C. ed. 1992. *The next millennium: A multicultural imperative for education for the twenty-first century.* Robert McClure NEA Mastery In Learning Consortium, NEA National Center for Innovation Series Editor. Washington D.C.

Donaldson, K. B. 1994. *Racism in U.S. schools: Assessing the impact of an antiracist multicultural arts curriculum on high school students in a peer education program.* University of Massachusetts, Amherst: unpublished dissertation.

Edwards, R. 1986. Characteristics of effective schools. In *The School Achievement of Minority Children: News Perspectives.* Edited by Elrich Neisser. Hillsdale, NJ: Erlbaum.

Erickson, F. E., and G. Mohatt. 1982. Cultural organization of participation structures in two classrooms of Indian students. In *Doing the ethnography of schooling.* Edited by G. Spindler. Prospect Heights, Illinois: Waveland.

Feeney, S., D. Christensen, and E. Maravick. 1991. *Who am I in the lives of children.* Macmillan Publishing Company, New York, 1991.

Fordham, S. 1988. Racelessness as a factor in black students' school success: Pragmatic strategy or Pyrrhic victory? *Harvard Educational Review* 58(1): 54–84.

Garibaldi, A. 1989. *Educating black male youth.* New Orleans: Public Schools.

Gardner, H., and T. Hatch. 1990. Multiple intelligences go to school: Educational implications of the theory of multiple intelligences. *Educational Researcher* 18(8): 4–10.

Gay, G. 1993. Building cultural bridges. *Education and Urban Society* 25(3): 285–299.

Gay, G., B. Cole-Slaughter, and C.R. Baber. 1995. Why aren't we getting along? *Holistic Education Review* 8(2): 30–39.

Gay, G., 1992. Effective teaching practices for multicultural classrooms. In *Multicultural education for the twenty-first century,* Edited by Carlos Diaz. Washington D.C. NEA National Center for Innovation.

Gibbs, J.T., ed. 1988. *Young, black and male in America: An endangered species.* Dover, MA: Auburn House.

Good, T.L., and J. E. Brophy. 1987. *Looking in Classrooms.* New York: Harper & Row.

Graves, S., R. Gargiula, and L. Sluder. 1996. *Young children: An introduction to early childhood education.* St. Paul, Minnesota: West Publishing Company.

Guild, P. 1994. The culture/learning style connection. *Educational Leadership* 51(8): 16–21.

Hacker, A. 1992 *Two nations: Black and white, separate, hostile, unequal.* NY: Charles Scribner's Sons.

Hale-Benson, J. 1986. *Black children: Their roots, culture and learning styles,* 2nd ed. Baltimore: John Hopkins University Press.

———.1991. The transmission of cultural values to young African American children. *Young Children* 46(6): 7–15.

Heath, S. B. 1983. *Ways with words: Language, life and work in communities and classrooms.* New York: Cambridge University Press.

Hermendez, H. 1989. *Multicultural education.* Columbus, Ohio: Merrill Publishing Company.

Hewett, K. A. 1996. Our culture, your good intentions. *Primary Voices K-6* 4(3): 38–41.

Hilliard, A. 1976. *Alternatives to IQ testing: An approach to the identification of gifted minority children.* Report to the California State Department of Education.

Hilliard, A. G., III. 1992. Behavioral style, culture, and teaching and learning. *Journal of Negro Education* 61(3): 370–377.

———.1989. Teachers and cultural styles in a pluralistic society. *NEA Today* 65–69.

Hilliard, A. G. 1991. *Testing African American students.* Morristown, N.J. : Aaron Press.

Hirsch, E. D. Jr., 1993. The core knowledge curriculum—What's behind its success? *Educational Leadership* 23–30.

Hixson, J. 1990. Multicultural issues in teacher education: Preparing teachers for new realities and challenges. Paper presented at the American Association of Colleges of Teacher Education Annual Conference, Chicago, Illinois.

Hodgkinson, H. L. 1985. *All one system: demographics in education, kindergarten through graduate school.* Washington D.C. The Institute for Educational Leadership.

Howard, G. R. 1993. Whites in multicultural education: Rethinking our role. *Phi Delta Kappan* 75(1): 36–41.

Howard, J. 1992. The third movement: Developing black children for the 21st century. Paper presented by The Efficacy Institute, Inc.

Huang, A., and T. Oei. 1996. Behind the myth. *Teaching Tolerance* 5(2): 57.

Irvine, J. J. 1990. *Black students and school failure: Policies, practices, and prescriptions.* New York: Praeger.

Joseph, G. G. 1987. Foundations of Eurocentrism in mathematics. *Race and class* 28 (3): 13–28.

Kaplan, J., and D. Aronson. 1994. The numbers gap. *Teaching Tolerance* 21–27.

Kunjufu, J. 1986. *Countering the conspiracy to destroy black boys.* Vol. II. Chicago, Illinois: African American Images.

Kunjufu, J. 1990. *Countering the conspiracy to destroy black boys.* Vol. III. Chicago, Illinois: African American Images.

Kyle, R. A. 1987. Reaching for excellence: An effective school source book. In *Prejudice reduction and the schools.* Edited by J. Lynch. New York: Nichols Publishing Co.

Ladson-Billings, G. 1994a. *The dreamkeepers: Successful teachers of African American children.* San Francisco: Jossey-Bass.

———.1994b. What we can learn from multicultural education research. *Educational Research* 51 (9): 22–26.

LeMoine, N. 1996. Personal communication with author, 30 July.

Majors, R., and J. M. Billson, 1992. *Cool pose: The dilemmas of black manhood in America.* New York: Touchstone.

McCoy, B., and G. S. Boutte. 1995. Excluding black males in school. *Kappa Delta Pi Record.* 31(4): 172–176.

McIntosh, P. 1995. White privilege and male privilege: A personal account of coming to see correspondences through work in women's studies. In *Race, class, and gender: An anthology 2nd ed.* Edited by M. L. Anderson and P. H. Collins. Belmont, CA: Wadsworth.

Medicine, B. 1982. Native American (Indian) women: A call for research. *Anthropology & Education Quarterly* 19(2): 86–92.

Minami, M. and B. P. Kennedy, eds. 1992. Language Issues in literacy and bilingual/multicultural education. Cambridge, MA: *Harvard Educational Review* Reprint Series #22.

Murray, C. B. and R. M. Clark. 1990. Targets of racism. *The American School Board Journal* 177(6): 22–24.

Nieto, S. 1992. *Affirming diversity: The sociopolitical context of multicultural education.* New York: Longman Publishers.

Oakes, J. 1985. *Keeping track: How schools structure inequality.* Yale University Press.

Oei, T., and G. Lyon. 1996. In our own words: Asian American students give voice to the challenges of living in two cultures. *Teaching Tolerance* 5(2): 48–59.

Ogbu, J. 1990. "Overcoming racial barriers to equal access." In *Access to knowledge: An agenda for our nation's schools.* Edited by John Goodlad and Pamela Keating. New York: The College Board.

Pate, G.S., 1992. Reducing prejudice in society: The role of schools. In *Multicultural Education for the 21st. Century.* Edited by Carlos Diaz. Washington, D.C.: NEA School Restructuring Series.

Perez, S. A. 1994. Responding differently to diversity. *Childhood Education* 70(3): 151–153.

Phillips, C. 1992. Forward. In *Alike and different.* Edited by B. Neugebauer. Washington D.C.: National Association for the Education of Young Children.

Pine, G. J., and A. G. Hilliard, III. 1990. Rx for racism: Imperatives for America's schools. *Phi Delta Kappan* 71(8): 593–600.

Powell, R. R., Zehm, S., and J. Garcia. 1996. *Field experience: Strategies for exploring diversity in schools.* Englewood Cliffs, NJ: Merrill.

Reschly, D. J. 1988. Minority MMR overrepresentation and special education reform. *Exceptional Children* 54: 316–323.

Rosenthal, R., and L. Jacobson. 1968. *Pygmalion in the classroom: Teacher expectations and pupils' intellectual development.* New York: Holt, Rinehart & Winston.

Sadker, M., D. Sadker, and L. Long. 1993. Gender and educational equality. In *Multicultural education: Issues and perspectives.* Edited by J. A. Banks & C. A. M. Banks. Boston: Allyn and Bacon.

Scarr, S. 1981. Testing for children: Assessment of the many determinants of intellectual competence. *American Psychologist* 36(10): 1159–1106.

Schofield, J. W. 1997. Causes and consequences of the colorblind perspective. In *Multicultural education: Issues and perspectives,* edited by J. A. Banks and C. A. M. Banks. Boston: Allyn and Bacon.

Shepard, L., G. Camilli, and M. Averill. 1981. Comparison of procedures for detecting test-item bias with both internal and external ability criteria. *Journal of Educational Statistics* 6(4): 317–375.

Shipman, V. 1976. *Young children and their first school experiences.* Education Testing Service.

Slavin, R. E. 1983. *Cooperative learning.* New York: Longman.

Sleeter, C. 1993. How white teachers construct race. In *Race identity and representation in education.* Edited by C. McCarthy and W. Crichlow. New York: Routledge.

Steele, C. M. 1992. Race and schooling of black Americans. *The Atlantic Monthly* 269(4): 68–78.

Streitmatter, J. 1994. *Toward gender equity in the classroom: Everyday teachers' beliefs and practices.* Albany: State University of New York Press.

Tatum, B. D. 1992. Talking about race, learning about racism: The application of racial identity development theory in the classroom. *Harvard Educational Review* 62(1): 1–24.

Taylor, O. L. 1986. *Nature of communication disorders in culturally and linguistically diverse populations.* San Diego, CA: College-Hill Press.

Tharp, R. G. 1987. Psychocultural variables and constraints: Effects on teaching and learning in schools. *American Psychologist* 44(2): 349–359.

Tribe, C. 1982. *Profile of three theories/Erikson/Maslow/Piaget.* Dubuque, IA: Kendall/Hunt.

Trueba, H. T., L. Jacobs, and E. Kirton. 1990. *Cultural conflict and adaptation: The case of Hmong children in American society.* New York: The Falmer Press.

U.S. Bureau of the Census. 1992. *Statistical Abstract of States.* 112th ed. Washington D.C.: U.S. Government Printing Office.

Washington, J.M., ed. 1986. *A testament of hope: The essential writings and speeches of Martin Luther King, Jr.* San Francisco: Harper.

Wheelock, A., and W. D. Hawley. 1992. What next? Promoting alternatives to ability grouping. *EDRS.* ED 353 220.

White, S. and R. G. Tharp. 1988. "Questioning and wait time: A cross-cultural analysis." Paper presented at the American Educational Research Association. New Orleans, LA.

Wigdor, A. and R. W. Garner, eds. 1982. *Ability testing: Uses, consequences and controversies.* Washington D.C.: National Academy Press.

Williams, L. R. and Y. D. Gaetano. 1985. *Alerta: A multicultural, bilingual approach to teaching young children.* Menlo Park, CA: Addison-Wesley.

Woodson, C. G. 1933. *The miseducation of the Negro.* Washington, DC: Associated Press.

The High School Years

Adolescents from various ethnic groups, genders, and socioeconomic status groups levels dress similarly. Does youth culture supersede race at times?

INTRODUCTION

A group of high school boys are standing outside the school building. They are garbed in clothes that are three sizes too large for them (popularly referred to as "sagging" or "grunge" style). Their expressive haircuts are equally unconventional and are representative of many others who share the youth culture. Although the group is made up of African, Asian, Latino/a, and European American teenagers, the similarity of their dress is more prominent than their race.

I leave you finally a responsibility to our young people. The world around us really belongs to youth, for youth will take over its future management. Our children must never lose their zeal for building a better world. They must not be discouraged from aspiring toward greatness, for they are to be the leaders of tomorrow.

—Mary McLeod Bethune

Clearly our concept of education comes from our image of what the future will be like for our children. If our image is shortsighted, and it sometimes is, then the plan for the education of our children will not meet their needs or the needs of the society in which they will live and work. Often in the past when we have planned education for the future, it was done with the belief that society, as the planners knew it, would perpetuate itself. Projections made in the past about how schools would look in 1996 were often inaccurate. The last quarter of the century has been filled with changes in technology, lifestyles, demographics, international relations, and family and labor patterns which demand that we plan education with the anticipation of change.

Nowhere is the limited acuity with which we have imagined the future more clearly visible than in the high schools of the United States. A visit to many of them will reveal that we know little about how students learn, how life in the world in which we teach is changing, how the composition of whom we teach has changed, and how we have made school decisions that have not impacted significantly enough on the structure of high schools and what students are taught.

Much clamor abounds about curriculum changes at the collegiate level; however, it should be noted that secondary school programs reach far more students at a time when their thoughts can be impacted upon. Curricular changes at the high school level are urgently needed.

In this chapter, high school will refer to grades nine through twelve. During the high school years, most children exhibit distinct behaviors that are commonly referred to as "youth culture." According to Erik Erikson's theory of psychosocial development, high school is the period during which adolescents develop a sense of identity (Tribe, 1982). That is, they are struggling to find out who they are and what their preferences are. Since an identity can be found only through interaction with other people, the adolescent may go through a period of compulsive peer group conformity as a means of testing roles to see how they fit him/her. Eventually, adolescents have to free themselves from the peer group orientation in order to become themselves. However, a teen's trajectory toward maturity and individuality has many implications for effectively educating students from diverse backgrounds.

In high schools, the criteria of effectiveness have broadened to include better attendance, fewer dropouts, improved relationships among students of different ethnic groups, fewer teen pregnancies, and less violence and drugs (Firestone, 1989). This chapter will address each of these issues and how high schools need to be restructured in order to address them.

❖ DROPOUT RATES

By high school, the cumulative effects of educational experiences are pronounced. Elementary school ability groups and tracks have solidified. Consequently, many high school students do not possess even basic academic skills. In 1980, for example, 25,500 students of color, largely African American and Latino/a, entered high school in Chicago (Steele, 1992). Steele notes that "Four years later only 9,500 graduated, and of those only 2,000 could read at grade level. The situation in other cities is comparable." (1992, p. 68)

As noted in Chapter Two, more children of color drop out of school than do white children—with the exception of Asian Americans as a group. Students of color frequently complain that teachers, counselors, and other school personnel do not care whether students are learning (Delgado-Gaitan, 1988).

Native Americans have the highest dropout rates of any students of color (Barba, 1995; Kasten, 1992). Drop out rates of Latino/a Americans are also high (Delgado-Gaitan, 1988; Martinez, 1997). However, Delgado-Gaitan found that Chicano (self-identifying label used by participants in this study) students who remain in school typically had consistent, systematic support from their families throughout their elementary and high school careers. Approximately twenty percent of Asian Americans and European Americans do not have a high school diploma (Huang and Oie, 1996).

As Hamby remarks, "Any dropout rate represents an incalculable loss of human potential and a staggering cost to society" (Hamby, 1989, p. 22). Students must have good reasons to attend and remain in school. Students who reach high school and are unable to read at a functional level and who have already been retained once or twice are prime candidates for dropping out (Shepard and Smith, 1989). One of the most effective strategies for keeping students in school is to keep them continuously learning something relevant (Hamby, 1989). Hamby asserts that students do not drop out because they do not want to learn. Rather, they leave school because they are failing to learn. Hamby outlines eight A's necessary to keep students in school: achievement, attitude, awareness, attendance, atmosphere, adaptation, alternatives, and advocacy. Table 4-1 presents some of the recommendations made by Hamby for each.

Table 4-1. Seven A's For Keeping Students in School

Strategy	Suggestions For Achieving Strategy
1. Achievement	Develop continuous progress mastery approaches to instruction in basic skills.
	Develop Tech-Prep 2+2 programs which allow students to take two years of specific courses during junior and senior years of high school in preparation for a two-year associate degree at a college or junior college.
	Recognize improvements as well as absolute achievement.
	Involve parents in their children's learning.
	Provide classes for parents on how to help children learn.
	Develop peer tutoring programs in which at-risk students can serve as tutors or be tutored.
	Use volunteer tutors including parents, senior citizens, high school students, college students, business persons, and anyone else with an interest and skills to help.
2. Attitude	Develop and communicate a philosophy that each student is a worthwhile individual who deserves the best the school has to offer.
	Establish a regular series of informal discussions during which all school constituents (students, parents, school staff) can engage in nonthreatening dialogue.
	Involve students, particularly those at risk for dropping out, in extracurricular activities.
	Provide staff development on building positive interpersonal relations for all school personnel, including clerical staff, cafeteria workers, and others.
	Enlist adult and peer mentors for students at risk of dropping out.

Table 4-1. Seven A's For Keeping Students
in School (continued)

Strategy	Suggestions For Achieving Strategy
3. Awareness	Increase the awareness of the dropout problem among students, parents, and community leaders. Use the school newspaper and other media to inform people of the problem. Involve individual students and clubs as much as possible. Make videotapes from successful people in the community discussing the value of a high school diploma.
4. Attendance	Develop a systematic accounting system for early identification. Notify parents immediately when their child is absent by writing, using volunteers, automatic calling machines, or other methods. Develop incentives for good attendance. Organize peer calling groups. When removing students from classrooms for disciplinary reasons, use in-school rather than out-of-school suspension.
5. Atmosphere	Provide adequate, safe, and well-maintained facilities. Develop a proactive student management plan. Conduct staff development on how to create positive interpersonal relations for all school personnel.
6. Adaptation	Stay abreast of issues that affect students. Provide frequent group and individual counseling for students with personal problems. Create a library of videotapes and other media about jobs and careers.
7. Alternatives	Provide alternative means for meeting the same goal. Provide after-school tutoring classes. Hold Saturday classes for make up or advanced work. Provide summer school programs.
8. Advocacy	Speak on behalf of potential drop-outs. Form networks of community agency resources.

Courtesy of J. V. Hamby. 1989. How to get an "A" on your dropout prevention report card. *Educational Leadership* 46(5): 21–27.

❖ TRACKING

Few educational practices point to the need for schools to address the issue of diversity as much as the practice of ability grouping and tracking. Tracking began in the 1920s at a time when schools were pressed to provide a trained work force already sorted by ability levels (Oakes and Lipton, 1990). Despite an abundance of current literature which indicates that tracking is typically not sound practice, it is so deeply entrenched in the education system that it is difficult to eliminate. Many schools have no idea of what to do in lieu of tracking (Oakes and Lipton, 1990).

Schools often represent a metaphor for society. The tracking system that exists in schools, particularly high schools, makes the same distinctions that society makes between those who have and those who have not. Using a variety of variables, most frequently test scores, students are grouped according to ability. The result is that many students have been tracked to either succeed or fail. Tracks are used to separate the academically gifted from those considered average or below average. Students are herded into either college preparatory or vocational tracks depending on test scores. As noted in previous chapters, a close examination of race, socioeconomic status, and to a lesser extent, gender composition of many high school classes will reveal whether the class is one with high academic expectations or one with low expectations.

At one time test scores were used as a signal that more needed to be done to help students, but that is no longer the case. Increasingly, test scores are used to justify the notion that some students can learn while others cannot. Consequently, the message that educators receive is that effort is not worth much when pitted against test-measured ability. Students in lower tracks learn that they are different and not equal to their counterparts in the classroom. Designations of average, below average, and above average are divisive and indicate either superiority or inferiority.

Early determinations that teachers make about children's abilities are often permanent (Oakes, 1995). These early assessments follow children throughout their lives and as they progress through school. More and more of their classes are tracked with the effect that by high school eighty to ninety percent of students are in classes labeled with an assortment of ability descriptors. Native Americans have the highest likelihood of being labeled as handicapped or learning disabled than any other students of color (Kasten, 1989). Overcoming the educational deficiencies of high school students in the lower tracks can be a formidable task for schools. Without intensive remediation or intervention, it is likely that students in the lower tracks will remain there. The solution is to *prevent* inequities in education during the elementary years before they accumulate.

When schools are asked to defend tracking policies, the most frequent answer involves academic excellence. Officials will point to motives related to renewed emphasis on student achievement and public confidence that testing is the proper means of gauging student performance. Motives that involve teacher preference for ability-grouped classes and subtle attempts by some school districts to resegregate schools are rarely discussed (Oakes, 1985).

Whatever the motives, the result is that secondary schools are denying many students equal access to education. Tracked students in the lower levels or vocational tracks often receive an education at a less than acceptable level of instruction. Students in lower tracks are infrequently exposed to higher level thinking skills, great works of literature, or information needed to be successful in a higher education environment. Often in English and math classes, lower tracked students study "functional-skills-watered-down literature," grammar usage, completion of forms, basic computation, and simple measurement. School counselors must examine their rationales and policies for advising students into tracks. They must also be cognizant of the future implications of tracking for students. High expectations for students from different ethnic, cultural, and gender groups are required if all students are to realize their career goals and aspirations.

Peterson (1989) studied three Utah school districts and found that ability grouping actually hurt the remedial students that it was designed to help. In fact, he found that high school remedial students learned more in mathematical programs designed for the higher ability student levels. Not only does tracking raise educational questions, but it also raises ethical and other issues as well (e.g., issues regarding equity and access to knowledge). Nevertheless, schools continue with tracked courses and students may find themselves tested out of the opportunity to obtain a quality education.

Cone (1994) notes that descriptors given to these classes often reflect the expectations that teachers have for students. Teachers who speak of their first period "practical," "low," or "basic" class have done more than identify the class, they have listed their expectations for that class. Teachers have to be taught to teach students of all ability levels and to believe that all students can succeed. Teachers must be trained with a pedagogy that enables them to select materials and vary teaching strategies. Cone believes that this process begins with the establishment of classrooms with "safe environments." In such classes, students can feel free to ask questions, share, make mistakes, and take and challenge stands. Only in such classrooms will students grow as thinkers. Among the expectations that teachers should have for all students are making students responsible for meeting deadlines, making up missed work, attending school regularly, and contributing to the safe environment of the classroom. Having established these as expectations for all students in a heterogeneously grouped class, the level of student performance can be raised significantly (Cone, 1994).

The time for tracking as a means of preparing students for society's expectations is over (Slavin and Braddock, 1994). If the United States is to maintain its standard of living for all citizens, then the workers of tomorrow must be thinkers who are capable of learning, making decisions, and solving problems. To track students is to write off a large percentage of students, thus diminishing their chances of becoming economically successful. The largest portion of students who experience the negative aspects of tracking are students of color; therefore, schools should be concerned because these students, particularly African Americans and Latino/as, represent the fastest-growing segment of the population. To fail to educate these groups with the skills needed for living in a technologically advanced society is to jeopardize the well-being of this country. In addition, as the country grows more culturally diverse, the need for appreciation of cultural diversity becomes imperative (Slavin and Braddock, 1994).

When Schools Present Information in a Relevant Manner, Learning and Motivation Flourish.

The decline of the United States and public education cannot be separated from the fate of United States cities, which day by day are becoming poorer, less socially cohesive, more violent, and more isolated. Racism and other "isms" must be taken seriously. Otherwise, they may yet destroy our society.

Most schools reflect a composite of many ethnic and socioeconomic status groups. Both students and teachers must learn to be comfortable with that fact. Schools must also accept the fact that some ethnic groups have endured hundreds of years of systematic defamation that has distorted and denied historical reality (Hilliard, 1991/1992). Having accepted this truth, schools can embark on the task of making school a place where every person is respected as an individual.

❖ SCHOOL RESTRUCTURING

The last quarter century has seen the call for many far reaching changes in schools. These reforms grew out of the fear that accompanied reports declaring that United States children trailed those of other countries and that students were unprepared to become productive in workplaces or in colleges. Schools have been urged to restructure and reform the way they do business. During the last two decades, the rather limited, century-old goal which calls for "education for all" has been refined to make the "all" more universal (Goodlad, 1990). The past two decades have seen the nation awaken to the realization that the delivery of education to diverse student populations will not be easy.

Such are the challenges faced by secondary schools across the United States today. Over the years there has been a gradual national awakening to the realization that our schools do not do a very good job educating young people. Schools are now faced with an urgent agenda that begins with far-reaching reforms in the way we educate teachers. As citizens we should expect teachers to be among the most educated citizens of the community. Teachers must possess humility enough to recognize failures and be willing to try new and innovative alternatives, and they must believe that all of their students are capable of learning (Goodlad, 1990).

Despite the drastic changes in schools, teachers have not altered their instructional methods or content. Furthermore, teachers still leave colleges and universities ill-prepared for what they will have to do to succeed as teachers in high schools. The process of school restructuring begins with the school's mission statement (O'Neil, 1993). Mission statements should reflect norms and practices that are supportive of the value of diversity to the whole school program. However, simply providing lip service to the mission is insufficient. Unless educators are truly committed to the school's mission, diversity will not be appreciated.

Once schools have decided on a mission statement which better meets the needs of all students, the curriculum and other activities should be examined to determine if they complement the mission.

Revisiting High School Curriculum, Classes, and Activities

High schools are often the most rigid institutions in school districts with strict time structures and state requirements for graduation (Jacobs, 1989). Therefore, most high schools, more than any other level, would probably benefit from a total reconceptualization of school organization and practices. A number of structural aspects common in most high schools conflict with current research on effective pedagogy and multiculturalism. For example, in most high schools subjects are typically taught in an isolated fashion within short fifty-minute time constraints. Alternative methods of instruction that focus on the knowledge, skills, and abilities that students possess need to be examined (Means and Knapp, 1991).

One of the key reasons that students drop out of school is because they do not see the relevance of their course work to their lives (Firestone, 1989; Hamby, 1989; Jacobs, 1989). Recent legislation ("School to Work") which mandates that schools show students how schoolwork relates to later employment is an attempt to address this issue.

During high school when students begin to develop new patterns of social and sexual relations that absorb a great deal of their energy and attention, they are more likely to disengage themselves from school work unless they see its relevance (Newmann, 1989). When students perceive that academic achievement will lead to rewards that they value, they will become engaged in school work. Learning has to be personalized in response to different learning styles, intelligences, and cultural styles similar to the ones addressed in Chapter Three (Newmann, 1989). As the comments that follow illustrate, students need personal reasons to meet the standards (Firestone, 1989).

> I don't see the purpose of algebra. All you need is English and math. The rest just fills time. (p. 43)

> In English you need to learn to speak and read right, but reading stories is pointless. (p. 43)

Curriculum relevance is a must for students experiencing the greatest amount of difficulty in school. The clearest way to show at-risk (for dropping out) students the relevance of school-work is to provide a short-term direct connection to future employability (Firestone, 1989).

The challenge for educators, then, is to find ways of making the curriculum more relevant and engaging to students' minds. High schools have to design curricula and instructional methods that build on prior learning and complement rather than contradict students' experiences. When possible, information should be related to students' every day experiences. Because it is virtually impossible to avoid teaching in a fragmented manner given the typical time constraints, some schools have extended their class periods (block scheduling) in an effort to engage students in prolonged and meaningful study of curricular issues (Jacobs, 1989). Schools that offer block schedules typically offer subjects for half a year (versus the entire year). However, classes for each subject last twice as long (e.g., 1 hr., 40 min. versus 50 minutes) so that more time is available for student engagement of content. Additionally, many schools are engaging in interdisciplinary curricular design in order to make information more relevant. Interdisciplinary instruction requires collaborative planning and teaching, but it allows students to see natural linkages between disciplines. Table 4-2 provides a sample topic and related issues that may be covered on an interdisciplinary unit on "Man and Interdependence: People and Environment." Multicultural issues

Many students learn better when group activities and hands-on experience are used.

Table 4-2. Sample Interdisciplinary Unit on "Man and Nature Co-Existing"

English

- Write letters to legislators about enacting and advocating laws regarding the environment.
- Write editorials to the school and local newspapers regarding the importance of protecting the environment.
- Read *Brothers and Sisters* by Bebe Moore Campbell*.
- *Grapes of Wrath* (Steinbeck)
- *Future Shock* (Tofler)

Biology

- Investigate the role of racism and classism in environmental issues (e.g., Are hazardous waste materials more likely to be dumped in poor neighborhoods or in communities where people of color reside?)*
- Ecology
- Populations*
- Human Ecology
- Energy: Energy/living cells, cell respiration
- Photosynthesis
- IQ—the role of genetics and the environment*

Math

- Study and calculate the amount of waste materials generated by each student during a one week period. Have students bring in items to recycle and calculate the weight using the metric and English systems. Graph the information. Introduce statistics by making predictions about the amount of aluminum, plastic, glass, and so forth that would be generated in a year, five years, etc.

International Studies

- Negotiation/Conflict resolution*
- Population*
- Movement/Migration*
- Resource Problems*
- Food/Agriculture*

Teens do not always succumb to peer pressure. Parents tend to have more influence over adolescents' basic life values and educational plans, while peers have more influence over short-term matters such as type of dress, taste in music, and choice of friends.

are easily integrated into the unit of study. Asterisks are placed after activities that lend themselves to multicultural discussions.

As high schools reconceptualize instructional delivery and other aspects of schools, they would be remiss if they do not rethink the role of parents and families in teens' lives. High school is the level when parents typically become less involved. However, in order to strengthen the likelihood of success, the school-home partnership must be vitalized. High schools face the challenge of figuring out how to involve parents from all walks of life in a manner that will not infringe on the independence of the students.

Restructuring Classes

An integral part of school restructuring is the offering of relevant courses in relevant ways. The subsequent sections will examine additional strategies (other than interdisciplinary units) for restructuring English, math, and science classes. Other subject areas, while not specified in this chapter, would also benefit from reexamination within a multicultural context. Information presented about English, math, and science classes should be helpful for revising and restructuring other content areas.

Rethinking English Literature Classes. Careful examination of the materials selected for use in the classroom is needed. Although English naturally relates to other disciplines and an interdisciplinary approach is recommended, there are times when English teachers will not use this approach. Nevertheless, all literature will need to be examined from a multicultural perspective.

Pace (1992) examined five of the most commonly used anthologies from major publishers. Examining the American literature of each series, Pace compiled a textbook canon of authors whose names appeared in at least three of the books. She found that the books did not represent what might properly be called multicultural texts. Of the ninety-six authors on the list, there were sixty-five white males, sixteen White females, ten African American women, two Native Americans, and one Latino/a American. Broken down by genre, most of the women were poets. Only one short story was written by an African American, and no women were included in the essay section. While not devaluing any literary form, Pace makes an observation that very often reflects what happens in the high school literature/English class. Poetry, she notes, very often appears near the end of the text. Hence, even the most well-intentioned teacher is typically unable to reach that section of the text. High school English courses in schools traditionally involve the study of literature composition, vocabulary, and speaking and listening skills. Add to the hours spent on these skills the other distractions associated with high school, and teachers have little time to cover everything in the text. Feeling compelled to study the major writers, the ones to be omitted are frequently women and writers of color. Writers of color and women must be better represented in the curriculum, and that representation must be balanced to reflect both the positives and the negatives of their experiences.

Some scholars object to the proposal of adding multicultural literature to the curriculum. Hirsch (cited in O'Neil, 1988) suggests that all students be required to read a common set of "literary classics." Hirsch believes that the primary culprit for decline in student scores on the National Assessment of Education Progress and the verbal portion of the Scholastic Aptitude Test (SAT) is the fragmentation of a traditionally common school curriculum (O'Neil, 1988). However, opponents of Hirsch's approach refute his claims and note that students in most high school English classes still frequently read the "classics" of fiction: *The Scarlet Letter, Of Mice and Men,* and *Macbeth* (Hillis, 1996). Moreover, they point out that there is no convincing evidence that the "classical model" ever worked well. Hillis adds that most marginalized groups would likely admit that the classics never

adequately served their needs. Yet, Hirsch and other conservatives insist on romanticizing a mythical past which glorifies a traditional education system (Hillis, 1996).

Other critics of Hirsch's classics note that the content of the
curriculum should be flexible enough to account for differences
in student ability and interests. Past instruction in the "great
books" did not accomplish this. A significant aspect of the resistance to Hirsch's conception of content is the view that white
male-dominated literature should not replace multicultural literary offerings (O'Neil, 1988). Hirsch's list of great books is very
Anglocentric, very male, and very elitist. In the past two decades,
efforts to include more people of color and female authors helped
nudge the "great books" out of some classrooms. The question of
who decides on the content is crucial, O'Neil notes. Without a
plurality of voices in the literature that students read, the curriculum will be very narrow indeed. A wealth of multidiscipli-
nary, international, and multiracial literature exists that will
allow authentic stories of the roles of all groups in human history to be included in the curriculum (Hilliard, 1991/1992).
However, multicultural books (as with all books) should undergo scrutiny to ensure that they are of high quality.

Guidelines for reviewing literature that were presented in
Chapter Two can be used for evaluating books. Additionally,
Stotsky (1994) adds the following advice.

1. Introduce literature by/and about members of all ethnic and
    other socially-defined groups in this country over the course
    of students' school years.
2. Offer some literature each year about a few different ethnic
    groups—including religious groups such as the Amish, the
    Shakers, or the Chasidim.
3. Show how indigenous cultures differ now and historically.
    Avoid romanticizing Native Americans or engaging in
    overemphasis on the topic.
4. Cover a range of groups, some religious, some secular, some
    based on gender, and so forth.
5. Include literary works about the immigrant experience in
    this country that, across works, show a variety of responses
    to their experiences.
6. Feature literary works with male or female characters
    (regardless of race and ethnicity) who demonstrate a variety
    of positive and negative qualities. Neither gender has a cor-
    ner on virtue or vice.
7. Include literary works that feature, across works, both nega-
    tive and positive characters who are members of particular
    ethnic, racial, or religious groups, not just one type of char-

acter. For example, *Maggie's American Dream*, a story about a strong-willed African American mother in a two-parent family whose four children all became successful professionals despite racial discrimination, counterbalances *The Women of Brewster Place*, a novel about mainly single mothers and their children in a housing project; while the biography of Colin Powell counterbalances the negative image of black males in *The Color Purple*.

8. Include literary works in which "white" America is portrayed as containing decent, civic-minded people as well as prejudiced or mean-spirited individuals. An overdose of "white guilt" literature like *The Bluest Eye* may cause students to associate multicultural literature with "white guilt" literature.

9. Include literary works about members of ethnic or social groups that feature a range of themes, not just those focusing chiefly on contemporary political and social issues. Include books that show members of ethnic groups coping with the kinds of situations or problems that may arise in the lives of many human beings and have little to do with their ethnicity.

10. Eliminate some books to make room for newer works from time to time. Replace more contemporary works (published since the 1970s) than older works, since there seem to be fewer pre-twentieth-century works than twentieth century works. A reasonable balance of the two is necessary for encouraging interdisciplinary curricula with history departments, for familiarizing students with our literary past, and for helping them understand the evolution of contemporary literature.

11. Reduce the number of works about those groups that may be overrepresented in the curriculum to reflect a broader range of groups.

As Stotsky's list of suggestions indicate, literature selections should be well thought out from pre-kindergraten through twelfth grade to ensure well rounded, multicultural coverage. It is wise at the K-12 level for educators to solicit the advice of a committee representing a broad spectrum of parents, teachers, and community members (Stotsky, 1994). Decisions about the ethnic and cross-cultural composition of school literature programs are likely to be more widely accepted if they reflect a broad consensus among committee members. However, selection of specific books should remain in the hands of the literature teacher. It is important to keep in mind that selecting works automatically excludes as well as includes. Thus, criteria for selecting books need to be applied judiciously and can, with care, be modified (Stotsky, 1994).

Rethinking Mathematics And Science Classes. It is especially important for math and science teachers to rethink their approaches for teaching math and science since these are subjects that many students consider irrelevant (Barba, 1995). Additionally, females and students of color (with the exception of most Asian Americans as a group) tend to do less well than white males in these subjects. Contrary to popular belief, math classes are not bias-free (see discussion in Chapter Three). Joseph concludes that "there exists a widespread Eurocentric bias in the production and evaluation of scientific knowledge" (Joseph, 1987, p. 13). For numerous reasons, females and some minority groups do not fare well in math or do not have the opportunity to take high level math courses in high school. Only one out of three students in high school calculus and advanced physics is a female. Few females emerge from high school believing that math is a subject that they can achieve (Kaplan and Aronson, 1994). Furthermore, they do not take the requisite high school courses which will prepare them for future careers in math—or science-related areas.

Although girls begin school ahead of boys in speaking, reading, and counting, their achievement test scores show significant decline as they progress through the early grades (Sadker, Sadker, and Long, 1993). Conversely, the scores of boys continue to rise and eventually reach and surpass those of their female counterparts, particularly in the areas of math and science. As Sadker, Sadker, and Long/note "Females are the only group in our society that begins school ahead and ends up behind" (Sadker, Sadker, and Long 1993, p. 119). Gender differences in mathematics become apparent at the junior high level. Male superiority increases as the level of mathematics becomes more difficult and is evident even when the number of mathematics courses taken by both males and females is the same.

Males substantially outperform females on all subsections of the Scholastic Aptitude Test (SAT) and the American College Testing Program Examination (ACT) (Sadker, Sadker, and Long, 1993). The largest gap is in the math section of the SAT, followed by the ACT natural science reading, and the ACT math usage.

Despite lower standardized achievement test performance, girls frequently receive better grades in school. Sadker, Sadker, and Long suggest that better grades may be one of the rewards that females receive for being more quiet and docile in classrooms. However, the authors point out that female's silence may be at the cost of achievement, independence, and self-reliance.

Although the high school years seem to favor males, males experience their own set of problems (Kaplan and Aronson, 1994). Males test lower in some academic areas, are more likely to drop out of school, and are more likely to be victims of violence—especially African American, Latino American, and Native American males.

To combat gender differences in math performance Sadker Sadker, and Long (1993) recommended the implementation of a bias-free curriculum and gender-equitable career counseling. Peer tutoring and cooperative learning strategies may be used by teachers as supplements to teacher-led instruction to de-emphasize competition between boys and girls in math and science. Sadker, Sadker, and Long also recommend that teachers evaluate their questioning patterns to determine if they are biased toward males or females. Specifically, teachers should examine the number of questions that they pose to males, females, and various ethnic groups. Teachers can learn to wait longer before calling on students since boys tend to raise their hands faster than girls—even when girls know the answer (Kaplan and Aronson, 1994).

Like math, the study of science and related technology has also traditionally required students to adapt to a Eurocentric/androcentric worldview (Barba, 1995). That is, the basic assumptions of science, as taught in United States textbooks, focus on male and European ways of viewing the world versus female or Eastern, African, or South American worldviews. The value system of modern science instruction in the United States is based on principles of realism which hold that there are ultimate truths that humans can discover in their natural world. Emphasis in science classes is typically on famous men of science (and their discoveries, methods, formulas, etc.), while contributions by women and people of color are generally ignored. In order to be successful in math, science, and technology classes, students must assimilate to a Eurocentric instructional model of learning "facts" or, in other words, accept an Anglo/European, male-dominated instructional style and value system. As mentioned in Chapters Two and Three, this style of learning is often contradictory to that of many children of color. In addition, many white females, although they are linguistically assimilated in mainstream American culture, **are not** culturally assimilated to male ways of learning science and often find it unappealing (Barba, 1995). On the other hand, many white male students find it relatively easy to engage in science activities since they are presented in a familiar language and in a culturally familiar manner. While eliminating all of the current strategies for teaching science is not necessary, changes are needed if more females, children of color, and children from low socioeconomic standing backgrounds are to achieve. Changing the ways that science, math, and related technology courses are taught involves changing the ways that knowledge, teaching, and learning in these disciplines are viewed (Barba, 1995). One of the most important steps in this process is the recognition by educators that females, culturally diverse students, and poor students are not from culturally deficient backgrounds. Although these students often view the world from a decidedly different perspective than the mainstream culture, their perspectives can be used as assets rather than deficits. Finally, it should be noted that white males also benefit from learning to view the world from different perspectives.

To further illustrate the Eurocentric nature of science, Barba (1995) discusses "the scientific method." In most textbooks and instructional materials (which are written by people trained in the Eurocentric scientific method), the scientific method is presented as a five-step method for investigating the natural world: 1) stating the problem, 2) collecting information, 3) forming a hypothesis, 4) testing the hypothesis, and 5) drawing a conclusion. Barba points out that "Within this tradition, Jean Lamarck is credited with discovering a theory of evolution, Watson and Crick discovered the structure of the DNA molecule, and Boyle discovered the gas laws" (1995, p. 56).

Science is frequently presented to students as a single way of investigating the world rather than as a multifaceted construct. According to this line of reasoning, if a scientist or group of people does not follow this formula the result is typically not considered to be "scientific." For thousands of years, Native Americans of the Southwestern United States and Central America have cultivated corn. Each year, the biggest and best ears of corn were saved by the harvesters and used as seed the following year. The tradition of sowing only genetically superior seeds resulted in the improvement of corn from stubby little weeds into the well-formed ears of corn that we currently know.

In this example, Native Americans followed the scientific method (identified the problem, collected information about which ears of corn were the best, formed the hypothesis that planting the biggest seeds would result in an improved plant, conducted experiments in plant growth for thousands of years, and passed on the findings orally to their children). However, Native Americans are not viewed as the founders of genetics research because they did not keep written records of their research or present their findings for peer review in the "scientific" community. Credit for the discovery of genetics research is given to Gregor Mendel in science textbooks. The pressing question is whether or not Gregor Mendel alone discovered genetics research or were there others who walked down the same path before Mendel? A

Eurocentric view of science which insists that the scientific method must be used (keeping copious notes, writing reports of findings, and reporting findings to scientific societies) excludes the research of generations of Native Americans (Barba, 1995).

Science as it is currently taught in most classrooms is not only dominated by the scientific method, but also by discoveries attributed to white males. Sammons reports that in 1721, Onesimus, an African American slave, explained to his master, Cotton Mather, how he had been inoculated against smallpox when he was a child. Onesimus' tribe knew that it was common sense to transmit a less virulent form of smallpox to children to keep them from getting a deadly form of the disease. African parents routinely taught their children this simple inoculation procedure through a tradition of oral history and learning. Cotton Mather wrote a letter to Dr. Boylston explaining the smallpox inoculation procedure which Onesimus had shown him. In turn, Boylston tried the procedure on his son and two slaves and subsequently reported his findings in a letter to a colleague. Boylston was called to London for his discovery and honored in the scientific community and made a fellow of the Royal Society. Onesimus, the slave responsible for bridging the knowledge gap between the oral medical practices of his homeland and the European world, received no credit. Again, the question is, who discovered the smallpox vaccination (Barba, 1995)?

Some may argue that the genetics research of Native Americans and the discovery of a smallpox vaccination by the Banyoro tribe in Africa were pre-Scientific Revolution discoveries that fall into a category of quasi-science. However, even when people of color and women made scientific discoveries using the scientific method, their discoveries were frequently claimed by white male colleagues (Barba, 1995). For example, discoveries regarding the functions of the honeybee's antennae, the expulsion of drones from the beehive, and the fertilization flight of the queen bee made by Maria Aimee Lullin (1750–1831) were published under the name of her husband, Francois Huber (Barba, 1995).

During many points in history, discoveries made by women and people of color were not acknowledged to be as credible as those made by white men. Many women resorted to publishing under male names. Countless other examples exist which demonstrate how scientific contributions of women and people of color were deliberately omitted from scientific records and false information conveyed to generations of students. In sum, Barba concludes that there is a need for a broader definition of science to include the oral tradition of recording historical information, group versus individual discoveries, and alternate conceptions of the scientific method. Bias in reporting the discoveries of people of color and women (attributing discoveries to the wrong author or ignoring the contributions of everyone) needs to be eliminated from curricular materials.

Barba suggests using culturally syntonic variables for increasing the interest and achievement levels of students of color, females, and students from low socioeconomic status environments. Culturally syntonic variables are those factors or influences which are in harmony with normative behaviors, values, and attitudes of particular ethnic or cultural groups. Research has demonstrated that culturally syntonic variables impact not only learning, but also the teaching and testing of students (Barba, 1995).

In the science classroom, culturally syntonic variables for diverse learners include variables such as:

1. the format of printed materials
2. instructional language
3. level of peer interaction
4. the use of culturally familiar role models
5. culturally familiar elaboration and context
6. the level of interactivity with manipulative materials (Barba, 1995).

As in previous chapters, it should be noted that various ethnic groups are not monolithic and, therefore, may differ individually in their beliefs, values, attitudes, and cultural histories.

1. *Format of printed materials*—Photonovels (a highly visual storybook format) have been shown to be the most effective means for conveying verbal information to most "unassimilated" Latino/a and certain Southeast-Asian learners. These students are likely to learn more declarative knowledge (knowledge we can state) from textual materials printed in photonovel content than from traditional textbooks. Additionally, these students have been shown to *prefer* this format over textbooks.

2. *Instructional language*—For students who are not fully assimilated linguistically into mainstream culture, access to instruction in their "home language" is beneficial. Allowing students to use their home language in small group settings for the purposes of cued recall should be encouraged. Culturally syntonic classrooms allow students to bring their home learning to class and combine it with school learning.

3. *Level of peer interactivity*—Peer tutoring, especially when new concepts or vocabulary are introduced in a class, improves

students' acquisition of concepts. When students of color are allowed to work together, their attitudes toward science and school in general and self-esteem have been shown to improve.

4. *Role models*—The presence of culturally familiar role models, both in person and in printed materials or textbooks, impacts on the cognitive learning of all students. For example, females who read about Marie Curie may aspire to be scientists. Studies (reported in Barba, 1995) have shown that the presence of culturally familiar role models in textual materials significantly increased students' self-esteem, concept acquisition, and motivation to pursue science careers.

5. *Elaboration and context*—Culturally familiar elaborations, which use culturally familiar objects, environments or contexts, examples, and analogies are powerful variables in terms of culturally diverse students' concept acquisition. Educators often use examples and analogies from their own mainstream United States experience. However, many students do not share this frame of reference and students may not understand teachers' explanations. When familiar examples are used, students can connect their home learning to school learning.

6. *Interactivity with manipulative materials*—Interaction with laboratory equipment and manipulative materials have been shown to increase the learning of conceptual and declarative knowledge among students. Additionally, interaction with materials positively impacts on students' attitudes toward science. Although there is adequate research which indicates that multiple means of knowledge representation benefits all learners, most teachers rarely hold hands-on activities in the same regard that they view textbook-based activities.

Barba concludes that most math and science classes are seen as hostile environments for many students of color, females, and low socioeconomic status students. Making these classes user-friendly requires changes in teacher/student interactions, instructional methods, and curriculum content. To improve teacher/student interactions, teachers must become familiar with the way(s) in which students learn. Information presented in this and previous chapters of this book should be helpful in this regard. The instructional methods used in these classrooms need to be models in which students are free to interact with others in ways that are culturally familiar and comfortable. Generally speaking, long periods of large group interactions in which students are expected to receive information are ineffective pedagogical strategies. Barba suggests that "personalization of instruction, small group interactions, and opportunities for hands-on experiences are vitally needed in science classrooms" (1995, p. 19).

A frequent objection made by educators regarding utilizing instructional strategies such as the ones suggested in this and previous chapters is that the methods are too time-consuming. They assert that they simply do not have time. Viewed from a different perspective, numerous indicators show that teachers are currently wasting time. That is, students of color and females are not performing well on tests and in classrooms. Since teachers currently spend large amounts of time teaching and are still ineffective, it would seem that attempting alternative instructional methods would be a more productive use of time. In other words, it seems as if many educators are currently spinning their wheels and wasting countless hours, days, and years in science and math classrooms. From this perspective, educators cannot afford not to take the time to try alternative methods that have been shown to be more effective for all students. For educators who desire information about the contributions of people of color, Barba (1995) provides quite an extensive list which includes the names of the individuals, dates, fields (e.g., math, chemistry, botany, geology, physics, medicine, astronomy, engineering), country of origin, and contribution made (pp. 64–67).

Developing Positive Identities

In order to develop positive self-concepts, high school students need to feel respected. High school students expect to receive respect from teachers and other school personnel (Firestone, 1989). In fact, respect is one of the attributes that high school students say that effective teachers possess (Firestone, 1989). Respect is particularly important for males of color who often feel the brunt of racism in this country (Kunjufu, 1990; Majors and Billson, 1992). As the subsequent student comments illustrate, high school students are particularly resentful of teachers who are disrespectful to them (Firestone, 1989).

"Some teachers talk down to you like you're stupid when you ask questions." (p. 42)

"Some teachers embarrass you in front of the class. They make jokes about failed tests, poor grades, and things." (p. 42)

If students feel disrespected in high school, it is unlikely that they will put their best foot forward. Coupled with curriculum relevance, showing respect for all students provides many students with a reason for staying in school, minimizes the forces that often encourage students to drop out, and fosters an environment where students' needs for belonging and recognition are met (Firestone, 1989).

Teachers may also consider the nature their instructional and evaluation methods. Using methods that allow students to have input communicates respect for their competence. For example, allowing students to engage in cooperative learning groups and to present information versus using a primarily didactic approach communicates respect for students' ability. Likewise, using open-ended versus multiple choice tests allows students to produce knowledge in their own words (Newmann, 1988). Using a portfolio to assess student learning versus relying only on a standardized test allows students to have input into the evaluation process and to select exemplary work which best represents their performance and competence levels.

Another way of building positive identities in high school students is to bridge the gap between school and home cultures so that children do not experience cultural dissonance when they attend school (Erickson and Mohatt, 1982). Many children from low socioeconomic status homes and children of color experience cultural dissonance between their homes and schools. Native American students are particularly prone to cultural dissonance because their culture differs drastically from mainstream culture (Kasten, 1988; Erickson and Mohatt, 1982). This does not suggest that all Native American students share the same culture, even if they share membership in the same tribe, but that their beliefs and values need to be understood by their teachers. Not only does the culture of the school differ from the culture of many Native American students' homes, but it is also diametrically opposed to the values that many Native American children learn at home (Kasten, 1988). As emphasized in previous chapters, strong school-home partnerships are imperative.

Students from low income homes may need extra assistance from schools. Programs such as the federally-funded Upward Bound program which is structured to improve the academic performance and motivational levels of low-income high school students, are needed. Participants in the Upward Bound program receive tutoring, counseling, and basic skills instruction. The intent is to encourage students to finish high school and get admitted to college (McNergney and Herbert, 1995).

Nonacademic Activities. For most high school students, there is more to life than doing school work. Teens display a wide range of interests that occupy their leisure hours. Destructive activities such as drug abuse, teenage pregnancy, and gang membership receive the most attention (these will be discussed later).

However, there is a brighter side to high school students' lives outside of school. Teens' interests range from athletics to music, from cars to computers. In order to better understand adolescents' lives and to explore possibilities for integrating these interests into students' overall education experience, these activities will be examined. Additionally, these activities provide an alternative path to achievement and self-esteem for many teens who are not high achievers in school (Murtaugh, 1988).

Students enrolled in regular education classes will more likely tend to be seriously involved in activities outside of school than special education students. Males seem more likely to have outside interests than females (Murtaugh, 1988); however, females tend to value popularity while males tend to value athletic ability (Berns, 1993). Students who are physically more attractive tend to be more popular than those who are not (Berns, 1993). The definition of beauty is often guided by societal images of beauty. Although these images are continuously being broadened to include people of color, European notions of beauty still abound. Even in racially segregated schools attended by people of color, students who resemble European Americans are considered to be more attractive physically (e.g., lighter skin, silkier hair, less prominent facial features) (see Morrison, 1992; and Pieterse, 1992 for a deeper discussion on these issues). Educators can help broaden the traditional, European definition of beauty by ensuring that positive images of all ethnicities are prominent in their classrooms.

Many males—especially males of color—seek self-esteem through sports (Kunjufu, 1985). High schools generally have pep rallies which glorify athletic participation. However, they often neglect to do the same for academic achievement. Many males judge their competency physically rather than by their academic proficiency. While involvement in athletics can help students develop leadership skills necessary for future success, schools need to make the academic curriculum more attractive so that students (especially boys) learn to view mental development positively. Coaches of athletic teams are powerful role models for males—especially when no male is present in the home (Kunjufu, 1985). They have the opportunity and obligation to teach students the importance of academics. Currently, too many males of color see professional athletics as the only avenue to a better life. However, they seem oblivious to the tremendous odds against becoming a professional athlete, and need guidance to realize that education is a more probable way to a better lifestyle.

The Role Of Race in Positive Identity Development. As noted at the beginning of this chapter, one of the key challenges faced by adolescents is the development of a positive self-identity. Race plays an integral role in the development of identity (Fordham, 1988). African American and other students of color often struggle between choosing the individualistic ethos of the school—which generally reflects the ethos of the dominant society—and the collective ethos of their community (Fordham, 1988; Oei and Lyon, 1988). As a result, many adolescents choose to become "raceless," in an effort to achieve success in high school (Fordham, 1988; Oei and Lyon, 1988). That is, the desire to succeed as defined by the dominant culture causes subordinated peoples to seek social distance from the group with which they are ethnically or racially identified. However, efforts to disassociate or disidentify with one's culture often causes conflict and ambiguity about the individual's value and identity (Fordham, 1988). Since it is virtually impossible to eliminate all traces of the markers associated with one's indigenous cultural system, disassociation efforts are only marginally successful (if at all).

For African American and other cultures who value a collective identity, there is a sense of "fictive kinship" (Fordham, 1988). Among African Americans, for example, there is a connection that extends beyond social and economic welfare, to include political function as well. There is a sense of "sisterhood" or "brotherhood" of *all* African Americans. This sense of fictive kinship is evident in various kinship terms used by African Americans such as "brother," "sister," or "blood" to refer to one another. This reiterates an important notion about culture mentioned in previous chapters: although no culture is monolithic, one's culture cannot be denied in this society. Fictive kinship also implies a particular mind-set or worldview of African Americans (Fordham, 1988).

The collective fictive kin ethos is challenged by the individual ethos of the dominant culture when children of color enter school and experience competition between the two cultures for their loyalty. (This is also the case with many Asian and Native American cultures [Erickson and Mohatt, 1982; Oei and Lyon, 1996]). Therefore, for many African American adolescents, the mere act of attending school is evidence of either a conscious or semiconscious rejection of indigenous black American culture (Fordham, 1988). Hence, many African American students who choose to assimilate into the school culture to improve their chances of succeeding in school develop a raceless persona in order to succeed in school and life.

In a country that professes to value diversity, children should not have to endure the severe, and often detrimental, mental anguish of trying to choose one culture over the other.

There is room for both in a multicultural society. Schools must find relevant ways of using students' indigenous cultures as a bridge to mainstream culture and to biculturality. When students feel that they have to choose mainstream culture, they often internalize the subtle message that their culture is inferior. Students become raceless to circumvent the stigma attached to being black, and to achieve vertical mobility. Unfortunately, they tend to become alienated from their indigenous culture.

Teachers may be unaware of the cultural conflicts that students of color face. To teachers, the students may seem well-adjusted since they are succeeding in school. High achieving students of color firmly believe in the American dream and probably do not need to be shown the value of education. However, educational success should not cause students of color to divorce their culture which has potentially devastating results as this quote from an African American suggests.

> "I am burdened daily with showing whites that blacks are people. I am, in the old vernacular, a credit to my race . . . my brothers' keeper, and my sisters', though many of them have abandoned me because they think that I have abandoned them. . . . I assuage white guilt. I disprove black inadequacy and prove to my parents' generation that their patience was indeed a virtue." (Fordham, 1988, p. 60)

High school teachers who use multicultural approaches such as the ones suggested in the previous section on curriculum (math, science, English, interdisciplinary) will likely support the development of both cultures. The message (overt or covert) given by schools should not be "choose to keep your culture **or** choose to be educated." Indeed, as Ogbu's (1974; 1990) work has shown, racism has discouraged some of the best and brightest students from succeeding in school and developing positive identities (Hawkins, 1988).

❖ OTHER RELATED HIGH SCHOOL PROBLEMS

In many ways, youth culture transcends ethnicities, genders, socioeconomic status, exceptionalities, and religions. Once formed, cliques (which typically consist of five to seven members) often develop dress codes, ways of speaking, and behaviors that separate them from other cliques and from the adult world. However, since these members are usually close friends, they are likely to be similar in terms of age, ethnicity, and social class (Berk, 1994). During early adolescence, cliques are limited to same-sex members; however, by mid-adolescence, mixed-sex groups are common. High school cliques can generally be identified by their interests (Berk, 1994).

Adolescents tend to view older people such as teachers and parents as "uncool." Hence, it is not surprising that parent involvement typically declines during the high school years. Being cool is especially important for some groups such as African American males. Although "coolness" may have survival value in some communities, it often manifests itself in ways that are not complementary to school success (Majors and Billson, 1992).

Peer pressure to conform is great during the high school years (Berk, 1994). Even positive peer pressure to engage in pro-adult behavior such as getting good grades and cooperating with parents is strong. Teens do not always succumb to peer pressure. Parents tend to have more influence over adolescents' basic life values and educational plans while peers have more influence over short-term matters such as type of dress, taste in music, and choice of friends.

Peer pressure can also be positive in other ways. Close friendships promote good school adjustment both in middle- and low–income students. Youth with satisfying friendships tend to do well in school. When teenagers enjoy interacting with friends at school, they seemingly view all aspects of school life more positively (Berk, 1994). As children get older, the peer group becomes less influential and individual decisions dominate (Berns, 1993).

In addition to curricular concerns, high school educators typically address a host of other related problems. Teenage pregnancy, sexuality, violence, and drug usage are common in high school and can adversely affect students' educational experiences.

Teenage Pregnancy And Sexuality

Teenage pregnancy is now a common problem among high school students. The burden of teenage parenting often falls on females and can interfere with schooling. Although many schools do not prohibit pregnant teenagers from attending school, many pregnant teenagers drop out of school (Berns, 1994).

If viewed within the larger cultural context of society, the influence of the macroculture is obvious. Sexuality is a selling mechanism commonly employed on television commercials and programs. Additionally, sexuality pervades contemporary movies and music. Teens need to be taught to critically critique images and messages presented in the media.

Although teenagers are bombarded with sexual imagery in the media, they remain ignorant and uninformed about scientific facts of reproduction and sexually transmitted diseases (STDs) (Berns, 1994). Prevailing myths among teens that pregnancy cannot occur during the first intercourse is often due to the developmental levels and maturity of high schoolers. Teenagers typically create a "personal fable" in which they believe that bad things cannot happen to them (Berns, 1994; Berk, 1994). Additionally, contraception is viewed as being uncool and unromantic.

The role of schools in teaching sexual responsibility is hotly debated by many groups. However, schools *can* teach decision-making skills (Berns, 1994). Although adolescents are becoming independent from their parents, they have little experience in making decisions. When examining problems such as teenage pregnancy and sexuality, the influence of all levels of the ecological model (Figure 1-2, Chapter One) are apparent: the home and school (microculture); the laws pertaining to sex education in schools (exosystem); the influence of society (macrosystem); and the communication between homes and schools (mesosystem). Interaction and dialogue about sexual issues between the schools and the home is critical. While it is not the role of schools to tell parents how to deal with such issues, the lines of communication must remain open.

Violence And Drugs

At one time, violence and drugs in high schools were virtually nonexistent. This is no longer the case. High school students who are developing their own identity typically have an inflated image of themselves and believe that everyone is observing them (Berk, 1994). It is more important than ever to be "cool." Unfortunately, for some teens, coolness manifests itself in drug usage and violent behavior.

Gang membership is not uncommon in high schools. Gangs exist not only in urban areas, but in rural and suburban areas as well. Furthermore, gang members can be found in all races, socioeconomic statuses, and genders. No groups are exempt. Huang and Oei, (1996) note that behaviors that lead Asian American youth into depression, drugs, gangs, and violence are sometimes overlooked because of "model minority" myths.

Teens (and preteens) join gangs for a number of reasons. Adams (1995) notes that some teens join groups for a sense of identity and recognition. Others are intimidated into joining a gang. Still others join for protection, fellowship, brotherhood, or money. Since adolescents are in the process of figuring out their identity, they are often easily influenced by the attitudes of others—particularly the peer group (Tribe, 1982). Children who do not find satisfaction in their home or school environment may likely turn to gangs for acceptance. This realization should underscore the need to ensure that all children feel successful in school settings regardless of gender, socioeconomic status, ethnicity, religion, or exceptionality. If they do not find satisfaction in socially condoned ways, they are likely to find it elsewhere.

Children from low socioeconomic status groups particularly may need to be convinced that education is valuable in the long run. The appeal of having money in a materialistic society is sometimes too great for even the most well-intentioned students. It is not uncommon to hear stories of one teen shooting another one for the $100 shoes that the victim is wearing. Students are willing to do almost anything to acquire expensive attire that they feel will indicate that they are "with it." Students in middle and high school frequently tease others about their attire. The following chant exemplifies how students taunt each other and, thus, increase their sensitivity about what they wear. The chant teases children about wearing generic brand shoes versus popular and more expensive name brands (e.g., Nike).

> Bo-bos—they make your feet feel fine. Bo-bos—they cost a dollar, ninety-nine. . . .

Many schools have implemented dress codes and uniforms in order to discourage violent crimes that are related to apparel. Low income students, particularly, need to learn about success stories of people who were once poor. Hearing or reading about success stories of famous people who grew up poor, but who used their education to get ahead, may deter young people from joining gangs to get money. Inviting successful people to schools as speakers or mentors may also motivate students to perform well in school.

Regardless of the reasons for joining, gangs are generally unproductive in terms of societal norms. Gang members are likely to engage in criminal acts and drop out of school. Schools must take preventative measures and work with families during the early childhood and elementary years in an effort to help children find more positive ways of belonging than gang membership. Elementary and high schools should coordinate their efforts on this endeavor. Schools and families need to focus on teaching children independence and decision making skills.

Violence. The incidence of violence is increasing among the youth culture. One out of five students carry a weapon at some time (Adams, 1995). Fifty-five percent of students have carried knives and razors; twenty-four percent, clubs; and twenty-one percent, guns (Adams, 1995). Such statistics are alarming. Educators and society at large must realize that efforts to deter violence should begin early in life. Such efforts benefit not only the children and families involved, but all of society. Even students who are trying to achieve academically in school may be harassed by violent students and gang members. Moreover, criminal activity is not confined to any one area. Often criminals burglarize homes outside of their neighborhoods or commit violent crimes against innocent victims in communities other than their own. Many historically oppressed groups are angry at society and the power structure of this country. Hence, they might express their anger against the social system through violent acts.

Violence affects everyone; hence, we all must work toward solving it. A number of professional organizations and child advocates are seeking to curb the amount of violence that is viewed on television and in movies. However, the process is a slow one. In order to curb violence, schools must have consistent disciplinary practices. However, a balance between safety and self-respect must be sought, since overemphasis of "get tough" approaches tend to compromise students' personal freedom and self-respect (Firestone, 1989). Addressing violence in school is a complex issue, as are most of the issues discussed in this book. However, given that the tempers of many teens are extremely volatile, whatever the school's policy, it should be well thought out and be non-discriminatory against students from different ethnic, socioeconomic status, genders, and religious groups.

Violence against oneself and suicide are also issues that high school educators must confront. Some ethnic groups tend to have a higher incidence of suicide. For example, Native Americans have the highest suicide rate of any students of color (Kasten, 1992). In 1988, the suicide rate for Native Americans was nearly twice that of European Americans (McNergney and Herbert, 1995). Homosexual adolescents are two to three times more likely to attempt suicide than their heterosexual peers. Suicide rates for Latino/a, African, and Asian Americans tend to be lower than those for European American (McNergney and Herbert, 1995). As mentioned earlier in the discussion about drop out, it is imperative that schools have effective counselors who can help students work through their school–related and personal problems which lead to suicide.

Alcohol and drug use. Teenage alcohol and drug use in the United States is more pervasive and higher than any other industrialized nation (Berk, 1994). By age fourteen, forty-two percent of teens have already tried cigarette smoking, fifty percent have tried drinking, and twenty-three percent have tried at least one illegal drug (usually marijuana) (Berk, 1994). Although these figures represent a decline since 1985, they are still high. Television shows, movies, and music videos continue to glamorize drug and alcohol use. School-based programs which seek to discourage alcohol and drug use must go beyond conveying information. They must also teach skills for resisting peer pressure and offer substitute activities such as dances and sports events (Berk, 1994). Communities can get involved by offering free video arcades or teen clubs.

Noteworthy is the fact that teens who feel competent and worthwhile are less likely to follow peers who engage in undesirable behavior such as early sexual activity, delinquency, and frequent drug use. Many schools have implemented conflict management programs to teach students strategies for handling conflict in nonviolent ways. Stressing cooperation across ethnic, gender, and socioeconomic status groups through the school years (early childhood through high school) may lead to decreasing violent acts in schools. This is especially important since many adolescents do not know how to express their anger in socially appropriate ways. They tend to be intolerant of even petty differences in aspects of language, gestures, hairstyles, and dress (Tribe, 1982). Consequently, many fights result from this intolerance.

❖ SUMMARY

Desegregation laws have mandated that students attend schools with other students from various ethnic and socioeconomic backgrounds. This has had both positive and negative effects. On the positive side, more students than ever report having friends of ethnic backgrounds different from their own. On the negative side, schools have not done enough to help students see the importance of respecting and appreciating other cultural groups. It is that failure on the part of the education system that may, in part, account for the 1990 Harris Poll which found that more high school students said that they would join in or silently support a racial confrontation rather than condemn it. Ironically, the public school is perhaps the most ethnically diverse place in which most students will ever find themselves. If students fail to acquire the skills for tolerance and respect for all cultures in schools, they may never learn to appreciate differences.

The problems associated with tracking and the diversity will change little without a new interest in the way that teachers are prepared. Teacher education programs will have to address hard issues and look at themselves in terms of their three essential elements: how students are placed, how teachers are trained, and how the school day is utilized.

When working with high school students, educators must possess an understanding of the many dynamics that contribute to students' behavior. In order to understand the youth culture, the larger cultural context in which drugs, materialism, and sexuality are glorified must also be examined. While it is never too late to alter behavior, attitudes and actions of adolescents are extremely difficult to change.

High schools, elementary schools, families, and communities must work together to prevent some of the typical problems from occurring. When students enter high school unprepared because of systematic discrimination that exists in schools, educators will have to contend with negative behavior which adolescents turn to when they cannot find satisfaction through socially appropriate avenues. Teen's social and emotional development affects their academic performance; therefore, high schools must emphasize social and emotional development as well as academics.

❖ RECOMMENDED ACTIVITIES

1. *Journal entry*—Reflect on your own high school experiences. Was most of the information that you learned ethnocentric or multicultural? Give examples. How did these experiences influence your worldview or way of thinking? Give examples.

   Reflect on how your school experience from pre-kindergarten through twelfth grades prepared you for college. Do you personally know people who graduated from high school with you who are not faring well today? If yes, how did their school experiences (pre-kindergarten to twelfth grade) influence their current standing in life?

   If you are a high school teacher, how can you ensure that children are prepared to succeed in adult life (that is, be employed in a position that is at least reasonably satisfying to them, as opposed to being involved in nonproductive or criminal activities)?

2. View music videos on Music Television (MTV) and Black Entertainment Television. Count the number of violent and sexual acts and innuendoes in a video. What messages and

values are being conveyed? Discuss how music influences adolescent behavior.

3. Interview high school students to find out if gangs exist in your community. Try to find out the names and characteristics of the gang(s).

4. Find out as much as you can about the youth culture. Interview adolescents to find out their favorite television shows, songs, and movies. Watch the shows and listen to the songs to determine how inappropriate behavior is encouraged or discouraged. Find out what are teen's favorite foods. What style of dress do they like? What are their least and most favorite school subjects? Why? How are these things influenced by the macroculture?

5. Reflect back to your teenage years. What classes did you find least useful and interesting? Why? In small groups, share this information with others. What implications does this have for teachers? Based on your teen experiences, how can schools better educate youth?

6. View one or all of the following movies: 1) *Lean on Me* (based on a true story of an African American principal's success story with an urban school which enrolled Latino/a and African American high school students); 2) *Stand and Deliver* (based on a Latino American's teacher's success teaching Latino/a American students high level math courses); 3) *Dangerous Minds* (a fictitious story about female, ex-marine who is successful teaching Latino/a and African American high school students). All of these movies should be available at local movie rental stores. Discuss the movie(s) in reference to concepts discussed in this and previous chapters (e.g., tracking, teacher expectations, cultural learning styles, relevance of school, the effects of the microsystem, mesosystem, exosystem, and macrosystem). Refer to Chapter One for a review of Bronfenbrenner's theory.

7. Since high school students are developing their identities, interview students to explore what role they feel race plays in defining who they are. Also, find out what racial terminology they prefer (e.g., white, Anglo American, Caucasian).

8. As a small group research project, devise a list of books for either ninth, tenth, eleventh, or twelfth grade that meets the criteria set forth in this chapter (and in Chapter Two). Write a summary of issues that you considered when selecting your collection of books. Discuss how diversity issues have been considered.

9. Compare a current edition of a high school science textbook with one that was published before 1980. How are they different in terms of information presented about scientific contributions? Are people of color and women's contributions thoroughly integrated throughout the book or presented in a fragmented manner (see book critiquing information in Chapter Two)? How can the book be changed to make it more appealing to students from many different walks of life?

❖ REFERENCES

Adams, J. Q. 1995. *Dealing with diversity: Teleclass study guide.* Dubuque, IA: Kendall/Hunt.

Barba, R. H. 1995. *Science in the multicultural classroom: A guide to teaching and learning.* Boston: Allyn and Bacon.

Berns, R. M. 1994. *Topical child development.* Albany, NY: Delmar.

Berk, L. E. 1994. *Child Development.* 3rd ed. Boston: Allyn and Bacon.

Cone, J. K. 1994. Learning to teach in an untracked class. In *Access to knowledge: The continuing agenda for our nations's schools,* edited by J. I. Goodlad and P. Keating. New York: College Entrance Examination Board.

Delgado-Gaitan, C. 1988. The value of conformity: Learning to stay in school. *Anthropology and Education* 19(4): 354–381.

Erickson, F. E., and G. Mohatt. 1982. Cultural organization of participation structures in two classrooms of Indian students. In *Doing the ethnography of schooling,* edited by G. Spindler. Prospect Heights, Illinois: Waveland.

Firestone, W. A. 1989. Beyond order and expectations in high schools: Serving at-risk youth. *Educational Leadership* 46(5): 41–45.

Fordham, S. 1988. Racelessness as a factor in black students' school success: Pragmatic strategy or Pyrrhic victory? *Harvard Educational Review* 58(1): 54–84.

Goodlad, J. 1990. *Teachers for our nation's schools.* San Francisco: Jossey Bass.

Hamby, J. V. 1989. How to get an "A" on your dropout prevention report card. *Educational Leadership* 46(5): 21–27.

Hawkins, J. 1988. Racelessness, collectivity, and individuality in the black community. *Harvard Educational Review* 58(3): 420–422.

Hilliard, A. G., III. 1991/1992. Why we must pluralize the curriculum. *Educational Leadership* 49(4): 12–15.

Hillis, M. R. 1996. Multicultural education as a moral responsibility. *The Educational Forum* 60(2): 142–148.

Huang, A., and T. Oei. 1996. Behind the myth. *Teaching Tolerance* 5(2): 56–57.

Jacobs, H. H. 1989. *Interdisciplinary curriculum: Design and implementation.* Alexandria, VA: Association for Supervision and Curriculum Development.

Joseph, G. G. 1987. Foundations of Eurocentrism in mathematics. *Race and Class* 28(3): 13–28.

Kaplan, J., and D. Aronson. 1994. The numbers gap. *Teaching Tolerance,* 3(1): 21–27.

Kasten, W. C. 1992. Bridging the horizon: American Indian beliefs and whole language learning. *Anthropology and Education Quarterly* 23(2): 108–119.

Kunjufu, J. 1990. *Countering the conspiracy to destroy black boys.* Vol. III. Chicago: African American Images.

Kunjufu, J. 1985. *Countering the conspiracy to destroy black boys.* Chicago: African American Images.

Majors, R., and J. M. Billson. 1992. *Cool pose: The dilemmas of black manhood in America.* New York: Touchstone.

Martinez, E. 1997. Unite and Overcome! *Teaching Tolerances* 6(1): 11–15.

McNergney, R. F., and J. M. Herbert. 1995. *Foundations of education: The challenge of professional practice.* Needham, Heights, MA: Allyn and Bacon.

Means, B., and M. Knapp. 1991. Cognitive approaches to teaching advanced skills to educationally disadvantaged students. *Phi Delta Kappan* 73(4): 282–288.

Morrison, T. 1992. *Playing in the dark: Whiteness and the literary imagination.* New York: Vintage Books.

Murtaugh, M. 1988. Achievement outside the classroom: The role of nonacademic activities in the lives of high school students. *Anthropology and Education Quarterly* 19(4): 382–395.

Newmann, F. M. 1989. Student engagement and high school reform. *Educational Leadership* 46(5): 34–36.

Oakes, J. 1985. *Keeping track: How schools structure inequality.* New Haven, CT: Yale University Press.

————.1988. Tracking: Can schools take a different route? *NEA Today* 6:41–42.

Oakes, J., and M. Lipton. 1990. Tracking and ability grouping: A structural barrier to access and achievement. In *Access to knowledge: An agenda for our nations's schools,* edited by J. I. Goodlad and P. Keating. New York: College Entrance Examination Board.

Ogbu, J. U. 1990. Overcoming racial barriers to equal access. In *Access to knowledge: An agenda for our nation's schools,* edited by J. I. Goodlad and P. Keating. New York: College Entrance Examination Board.

————.1974. The next generation: An ethnography of education in an urban neighborhood. New York: Academic Press.

O'Neil, J. 1993. A new generation confronts racism. *Educational Leadership* 75: 60–63.

O'Neil, J. 1988. Cultural literacy: Common sense or misguided broadside? *ASCD Curriculum Update* 5–8.

Pace, B. G. 1992. The textbook canon: Genre, gender, and race in U.S. literature. *English Journal* 8(5): 33–38.

Peterson, J. 1989. Remediation is no remedy. *Educational Leadership* 71: 24–25.

Pieterse, J. N. 1992. *White on black: Images of Africa and blacks in western popular culture*. New Haven: Yale University Press.

Sadker, M., D. Sadker, and L. Long. 1993. In *Multicultural education: Issues and perspectives*, Needham Heights, MA: Allyn and Bacon.

Shepard, L. A., and M. L. Smith. 1989. *Flunking grades: Research and policies on retention*. New York: Falmer Press.

Slavin, R. E., and J. Bradock, III., 1994. Ability grouping: On the wrong track. In *Access to knowledge: The continuing agenda for our nation's schools*, edited by J. I. Goodlad and P. Keating. New York: College Entrance Examination Board.

Steele, C. M. 1992. Race and the schooling of black Americans. *The Atlantic Monthly* 269(4): 68–78.

Stotsky, S. 1994. Academic guidelines for selecting multiethnic and multicultural literature. *English Journal* 83(2): 27–33.

Tribe, C. 1982. *Profile of three theories: Erikson, Maslow, Piaget*. Dubuque, IA: Kendall/Hunt.

Higher Education

Faculty of color are grossly underrepresented at institutions of higher education. Having a diverse faculty benefits all students—not only students of color.

INTRODUCTION

An African American Professor of Education at a predominantly white university frequently shares information pertaining to African American children with prospective teachers. As a result, many white prospective teachers accuse the professor of being biased. The professor informs the students that they are always exposed to the biases of the professor who teaches the course. She adds that it just happens that the students are more comfortable with biased presentations that tend to focus primarily on white children. Although the professor was hired for the diversity that she would add to the program, she often feels that her ideas are unwelcomed by both students and faculty.

The futility of examining one stage of development in isolation becomes more evident in this chapter. Because of life circumstances, cultural differences, opportunities, school experiences, and/or family values, many adults never make it to college. Although college is not a goal for many individuals, it should be an opportunity for all. Yet, as this and previous chapters point out, many students of color and children from low-income homes never attend college because they are either unprepared or do not see college as an option.

Diversity issues introduced in the previous chapters are also relevant in higher education. This chapter will discuss how diversity issues relate to college students, professors, and administrators. Curriculum, recruitment, and retention issues will be discussed.

Each of the following excerpts is either meaningful or meaningless to individuals in this country.

- E pluribus unum . . .
- We hold these truths to be self evident that all men are created equal . . .
- . . . one nation under God, indivisible, with liberty and justice for all
- . . . not . . . judged by the color of their skin but by the content of their character
- An Equal Opportunity/Equal Employment/Affirmative Action
- A racially unidentifiable student body . . .
- My country tis of thee, sweet land of liberty, to thee I sing.

Society and higher education greatly influence how members of diverse populations interpret the above statements. The fact is that it is, fundamentally, business as usual, education as usual, and perceptions as usual in most institutions of higher education. Questioning what has been considered "the norm" for too long is still life-threatening to many members of mainstream society.

It is . . . significant that although many teachers and scholars profess to admire and try to emulate the Socratic method of teaching, most conveniently forget that Socrates was put to death for "corrupting the youth of Athens." One who questions not as an intellectual game, not as a kind of conceptual muscle-building, but in order to make evident and open to serious reconsideration the deepest presuppositions and behaviors of the culture and state, is going to arouse discomfort and anger . . . [and cause everyone to realize that] the Emperor [really] is naked! (Minnich, 1990, pp. 81, 186).

Just as the child in the children's book, *The Emperor's New Clothes*, spoke truthfully about the emperor's nakedness, the truth must be spoken about the state of multicultural education in higher education.

Some academic environments are exhibiting genuine sensitivity to the plight of previously ignored cultures; however, many still view the state of diverse cultures through foggy lenses believing that little was ever wrong, little is now wrong, and changes in attitudes, behavior, personnel or procedures are unwarranted.

Realizing and acknowledging how far we must travel to reach the goal of multiculturalism is essential in mapping out a plan to achieve it. So where is higher education in this multicultural education maze? Has there been a united, committed effort to reach the goal? Upon close examination, has this concept been embraced and nurtured to facilitate its move farther along on the continuum? Or like the story of the emperor's new clothes, is the facade continuing? What is needed or must occur in academe in order to help this nation realize the multiple gains the fabric of multiculturalism will provide?

As with previous chapters, this chapter invites those concerned about the present conditions of education and this society to examine the ostensibly monocultural position. To ensure better conditions for all United States residents, a thorough look at the effects of the limitations and restrictions of a monocultural worldview for all cultures past and present is necessary, as well as an understanding of how a monoculturalistic view is shortsighted in an evolving global multicultural economy.

This discussion in this chapter is not an attempt to prove that only white males are privileged, for even within this select group, some individual members are disenchanted. Additionally, for those white males who appear privileged today, the future is more uncertain than it is for other groups who have been subjected to the effects of "monoculturalism" over an extended period of time (Wilson, 1995). Therefore, every group has issues to deal with, which is why a concerted move to promote multicultural education in this multicultural society is gaining momentum (P. McRaven, personal communication, 1995). Since institutions of higher learning should propagate new knowledge, they must take the lead in discussing diversity issues and facilitating respectful debate of conflicts (Graff, 1992). During this process it will be especially important for white academics to talk among themselves about their own racism and how white racism works (Scheurich, 1993).

Throughout this chapter, members of institutions of higher education are admonished to move beyond superficial programs, administrative placebos, and ineffective panaceas. The assertion that "something is better than nothing" is no longer sufficient, especially when many of the recipients and providers of the "something" assess it to be tokenism or lip service. Promoting an egalitarian society where each and every citizen has unrestricted privileges and opportunities to be productive contributors should be the charge of institutions of higher education (IHEs). Society, for the most part, is still cloaked in a role of complacency covering its nakedness toward multicultural issues. Therefore, IHEs are encouraged to engage in some disrobing and like the child truthfully exposing the naked Emperor, expose society's nakedness toward diversity issues and then teach it how to dress.

Inroads are being made to facilitate the progress of multicultural education, but the key is to promote acceptance and development while preventing relapses from occurring. Relapses or cursory attention to multicultural education are often rooted in unnecessary fears, prejudice, and discrimination. When the principles and practices of individual IHEs are examined in relation to multicultural education, the institutions can be classified as facilitators, detractors, or simply spectators. As detractors or even spectators, institutions of higher learning ". . . project the unspoken message: [to both students and faculty of color that] 'We are not sure we want you here, but we had to recruit you'" (Logan, 1990, p. 12). Reyes and Halcon charge that "[M]inorities . . . know from personal experience that racism [a detractor] in education is vigorous and pointed" (Reyes and Halcon, 1990, p. 70).

Banks (1993) notes that the highly publicized controversies surrounding the "literary and historical canon" basically distracted attention away from recent advances in multicultural education. To hear some academic, community, or national leaders debate that multicultural efforts are overzealous or will result in a sacrifice of quality and standards to the canon kindles old arguments and revives unpleasant memories (Banks, 1993; Diaz, 1994; Minnich, 1990; Obiakor, 1992). Progress (change) of any kind has met similar obstacles. Comparable charges and protests of reverse discrimination evolved after decisions in the women's suffrage movement, the Brown versus Board of Education case, the Civil Rights Act, and Affirmative Action were implemented. Minnich (1990) remarks, and most people of color would agree, that "the idea of reverse discrimination is, in a hierarchical system, every bit as absurd as its suppressed premise—that we are all alike" (p. 70). Yet, these objections to progress and inclusivity serve to perpetuate the status quo and are, in effect, scare tactics which result in divisive outcomes. Objections to multicultural education, especially, have ". . . heightened racial and ethnic tension and trivialized the field's remarkable accomplishments in theory, research, and curriculum development" (Banks, 1993, p. 22).

❖ COMMITMENT OR COMPROMISE?

Mattai (1992) notes that the commitment to infusing multicultural education into what was known as American education evolved around 1972 when the American Association of Colleges for Teacher Education (AACTE) adopted and published the following statement:

> Multicultural education is education which values cultural pluralism. Multicultural education rejects the view that schools should seek to melt away cultural differences or the view that schools should merely tolerate cultural pluralism . . . . It affirms that major education institutions should strive to preserve and enhance cultural pluralism. To endorse cultural pluralism is to endorse the principle that there is no one model American (p. 67).

The tenets of multiculturalism, espoused through the above statement, were lofty and thought provoking. The notion that accepting cultural pluralism equated to confirming that there was no one model American may have been disquieting to many. It appears, almost a quarter of a century later, that the "one model American" concept cannot be dispelled. For example, in trying to address some of the prevalent myths about multicultural education, Banks (1993) discusses the fallacy that "multicultural education is for the others" (p. 22). He further notes that:

> Despite all that has been written and spoken about multicultural education being for all students, the image of multicultural education as an entitlement program for the "others" remains strong and vivid in the public imagination, as well as in the hearts and minds of many teachers and administrators . . . [Therefore], when educators view multicultural education as the study of the "others," it is marginalized and held apart from mainstream education reform (p. 23).

If programs that encourage cultural pluralism still have to "fight for academic legitimacy," academe may need to revisit its commitment to this cause (Hu-DeHart, 1993, p. 50). Clearly, the ideals set forth in the original commitment recognized the benefits of inclusivity for everyone regardless of gender, ethnicity, or circumstances. Therefore, the myths and misconceptions plaguing this commitment simply affirm what people of color and the disenfranchised already know—that race really does matter as well as gender, physical ability, socioeconomic status, sexual orientation, religious beliefs, and nationality (Bernstein and Cock, 1994; Reyes and Halcon, 1990; West, 1993).

❖ STATISTICS AND STATIC

While multicultural education has made some progress (Banks, 1993), accelerated action is required to avoid stagnation, or worse yet, regression. It is evident through observation of daily realities and from an examination of the literature that enrollment, recruitment, retention, promotion, instruction, programming, policies, equal access, and inclusivity still present unnecessary obstacles for certain members of this society. Obiakor asserts that "The widespread notion that America is a 'color-blind, [inclusive] society' is a myth" (1992, p. 16). While some figures for people of color increase (Evangelauf, 1992; Evangelauf, 1993; Leatherman, 1994; Shea, 1994), others decrease (Feagin, 1992; Gose, 1995; Magner, 1993; McMillen, 1991). Further, in-depth analyses of some reported numbers even reveal disproportionate representations which could lead to distorted perceptions (Bernstein and Cock, 1994; Drummond, 1995; Wharton, 1986). As shown on Table 5-1, whites dominate the leadership positions in higher education. The only instance where people of color hold more leadership roles are as Directors of Affirmative Action—a role which typically has little power. In fact, many of the Affirmative Action positions may soon be eliminated if other IHEs follow the University of California (one of the nation's most racially diverse systems) and end racial preferences in their hiring and admissions policies (Chronicle of Higher Education Almanac, 1995).

❖ FACULTY

Although many IHEs are making efforts toward incorporating multiculturalism in many aspects of higher education, the absence of diversity among faculty members at historically white IHEs contributes to slow progress toward appreciating diversity. It is especially important for higher education institutions to increase their efforts to hire, promote, and retain faculty of color since they form the vital links to people of color in the general population for all professions (regardless of whether it is business, economics, education, medicine, law, and so forth).

Patai writes that "[A]fter decades of soul-searching reform and affirmative action, women are still underrepresented on

TABLE 5-1. Percentage of Minorities in
Leadership Roles 1986-93

	1986		1993	
Position Title	**White**	**Minority**	**White**	**Minority**
Chief Executive Off.	93.1%	6.9%	93.5%	6.5%
Chief Academic Off.	93.1	6.9	93.2	6.8
Chief Business Off.	93.8	6.2	94.5	5.5
Chief Stud. Affairs	87.4	12.6	84.4	15.6
Chief of Development	95.3	4.7	96.0	4.0
Chief of Public Rel.	96.0	4.0	94.9	5.1
Chief of Personnel	87.7	12.2	84.8	15.2
Chief of Budgeting Oil.	93.6	6.4	90.9	9.1
Learning Resources Dir.	88.6	11.4	90.8	9.2
Grant/Contracts Admin.	91.3	8.7	91.1	8.9
Affirmative Action Dir.	46.3	53.7	31.4	68.6
Chief Physical Plant	93.8	6.2	94.2	5.8
Student Activities Dir.	86.8	13.2	89.1	10.9
Campus Security Dir.	84.4	15.6	87.6	12.4
Information Systems Dir.	96.1	3.9	95.8	4.2
News Bureau Dir.	97.9	2.1	94.9	5.1
Financial Aid Dir.	85.1	14.9	85.9	14.1
Student Placement Dir.	90.3	9.7	89.2	10.9
Student Counseling Dir.	87.2	12.8	86.4	13.6
Athletic Dir.	94.2	5.8	91.1	8.9
Alumni Affairs Dir.	94.4	5.6	93.8	6.2
Arts/Sciences Dean	92.0	8.0	91.5	8.5
Business Dean	92.9	7.1	90.8	9.2
Continuing Education Dean	92.2	7.8	91.6	8.4
Education Dean	87.7	12.3	87.2	12.8
Engineering Dean	94.2	5.8	91.4	8.6
Fine Arts Dean	95.6	4.6	92.6	7.4
Graduate Programs Dean	94.8	5.2	88.4	11.6
Nursing Dean	90.0	10.0	93.7	6.3
Social Work Dean	71.0	29.0	70.4	29.6

Courtesy of Dr. Marshall Drummond, President's office, Eastern Washington
University 526 Fifth Street, Cheney, WA 99004 (509) 359-2371.

American faculties . . . As for African Americans, their scant
presence on university faculties is a national disgrace" (1992, p.
A52). Similarly, Reyes and Halcon note that "the racism experienced by Chicanos in academia is not new. . . . Hispanics believe

that for the first time there exists a noticeable number of over-qualified, under-employed Hispanic Ph.D.s unable to gain access to faculty positions in IHEs" (1990, p. 70). In Welch's (1992) *Perspectives On Minority Women In Higher Education*, Nieves-Squires' discussion of Hispanic women in faculty positions revealed that they are "clustered at the lower end of the academic ladder." Examples were employment in lower-status institutions or in areas outside their disciplines, as well as in part-time, non-tenured, lecturer positions.

Table 5-2 outlines the number of faculty and administrators at IHEs by ethnicity. As the table indicates, people of color collectively comprise only a small percent of faculty and administrators at IHEs. Moving into the twenty-first century, faculty members of color still too often represent the "only" or the "first" in various positions at institutes of higher education. Patai (1991) reported that ". . . in the early 1960s, I did not study with, or even know of one black professor. . . . There were some white women on the faculty, but not many. . . . In four years I studied with only one" (A52). In 1996, the situation is much the same as it was in the 1960s. Faculty of color are still somewhat of an anomaly on university campuses. Many white students at predominantly white IHEs experience some level of discomfort with faculty of color especially when the faculty's instructional style differs from that of white faculty members. Faculty of color at predominantly white IHEs frequently question whether their ethnicity influences student evaluations.

At this writing, many IHEs must increase "minority" hiring because of federal lawsuits. The fact that IHEs must be bound by laws to provide equal employment opportunities gives some

TABLE 5-2. Full-Time Faculty and Administrators in Colleges and Universities By Ethnic Groups, 1991-92

	Total	Native America	Asian	African American	Latino/a	White
Faculty	520,551	1,655	26,545	24,611	11,424	456,316
Executive, Administrative, Managerial	136,908	503	2,163	11,886	3,453	118,903

Courtesy of: U. S. Equal Employment Opportunity Commission, cited in *Chronicle of Higher Education Almanac*, (September 1, 1995, p. 22.

indication of the degree to which exclusiveness is being protected and perpetuated in this arena.

"We cannot find qualified . . ." or "there aren't any minority candidates out there" is the prevalent rationalization for the under-representation of different cultures in academia (Light, 1994, p. 166). This position is met with frustration, disdain, and disbelief from members of those cultures whose members have successfully prepared themselves for academic positions. They believed that preparation would provide admission to "an egalitarian status with mutual respect among professional colleagues, where the new rules of competition would be truly based on [objectivity, fairness, and] merit" (Reyes and Halcon, 1990, p. 70).

> Despite the minimal gains for minorities in tenure-track positions, we continue to be plagued with the assumption that we are mere tokens and have been hired without the appropriate credentials, experience, or qualifications. The legacy of tokenism and its negative implications has led to a current situation, in which unspoken pressure is put on minority academics to continually prove that they are as good as White [sic] academics (p. 73).

If Reyes and Halcon (1990) are correct that many people of color believe this attitude is prevalent in many historically white IHEs, the creeds, mottoes, policies, and verbal exhortations affirming diversity by those institutions are reduced to lip service; and disillusionment, distrust, and discord are the consequences.

Higher education institutions may have sent and may be continuing to send the message to people of different cultures that whatever they ". . . have isn't needed, and whatever they [don't] have is exactly what is needed" (Dual, 1992, p. 5). Even when people of color are hired, they often experience difficulty when applying for tenure. Disclosing the inequities in recruitment, retention, research, evaluation, research acceptance and publication, and tenure decisions is difficult. While the demographics are changing, this change is slow. White males still hold the majority and top positions in IHEs (See Tables 5-1 and 5-2) as well as on editorial boards of journals in which faculty members must publish. Many people of color and women tend to be interested in scholarship relating to diversity and gender issues which may not be valued or considered to be legitimate by some academicians. Moreover, tenure committees at historically white IHEs also tend to be comprised mainly of white males. It continues to be much easier to accept the "traditional assumption that 'it's too bad the minorities have failed' rather than admit that IHEs have 'failed the minorities'" (Cibik and Chambers, 1991, p. 129). There is considerable belief among people of color that both overt and covert discrimination as well as unknowing and willful indifference permeates academic environments (Cibik and Chambers, 1991; Reyes and Halcon, 1990). An example of this is the discrepancies that exist between the salaries of white men, and people of color and women.

❖ ADMINISTRATION

"The senior level administration at historically white, four-year institutions of higher education consists overwhelmingly of European American males. . . . Women who hold such positions are few and African American women are even more scarce," (writes Ramey, 1995, p. 113). Haro concurs: "Many search committees still do business as if talented people of color do not exist or are a 'minor' part of our population" (Haro, 1991, p. B2). Thus, academic hiring and placement practices reflect the larger society.

Like tenured faculty positions, top-level administrative positions are positions of power. Presently, that power largely eludes people of color and the diverse populous. (In his article "Minorities in Higher Education Leadership Positions: A Report of Eight Years of Disappointment, 1986-1993," Drummond (1995) describes the disheartening progress of people of color in key administrative positions during this time period. And while many IHEs are currently under federal mandates and lawsuits to diversify the educational environment, there have always been ways to sidestep directives and laws by finding the proverbial loophole or escape hatch. Non-compliance, therefore, is easily justified and disguised.

Recently, an African American professor relayed a story about a white disabled student who enrolled in her class. The student approached the professor with a list of considerations for the professor to comply with in order to accommodate the student's learning experience. When the professor objected to certain accommodations which appeared inconsequential to the learning experience, the student adamantly told the professor what the law required and what the professor had to do or face legal repercussions. In addition, the student remarked that he thought the professor would show more empathy and realize the legal ramifications since they were both members of a protected group. The professor empathized and was familiar with the student's plight. However, she (the professor) stressed that just because laws exist, being a member of a "protected" group does not guarantee equality or freedom from covert and sometimes overt discrimination. People know how to bend and break the law. And legal repercussions are generally bound in bureaucracy, heavy burdens of proof, and lengthy waiting periods which usually end in technical dismissals.

This scenario illustrates two major points. First, forced compliance to laws may temporarily alter behavior but do little to change attitudes. Second, people of color, females, and disabled individuals do not generally expect any extra or preferential treatment; however, they are entitled to be treated fairly.

A candid statement by Antonia Hernandez (as cited in Rodriguez, 1994) also summarizes the above situation. Hernandez said that "because of the racist character of judges in Texas and other Southern judges, both African Americans and Latinos must consider alternatives to legal action, or at minimum, political pressure to support those legal challenges" (p. 9). An even greater consideration is that while this statement may appear to be characteristically true of Southern judges, it may not be limited to Southern judges. In *New Voices* by Denise Hawkins (1993) Okianer Dark, a law professor at the University of Richmond, was quoted as saying, "the law does not exist in tablet form like Moses coming down from the mountaintop. It comes from people in power positions, so you can't always count on it to be objective and reasonable although we would like to think that it is" (p. 14).

Additionally, forced compliance could fuel anti-Affirmative Action attitudes. Those attitudes, as Hayes (1995) suggests when manifested in resistance to Affirmative Action guidelines to increase faculty of color, provide no incentives for recruits to subject themselves ". . . to an environment that will undoubtedly be insensitive, cold and unwelcome" (p. 35).

Drummond (1995) quotes from a study by Smith (1980) that:

> Black administrators were hired to pacify the Black community and/or to demonstrate that the hiring institution is an "equal opportunity employer," neither of which is legitimate; the leadership which they could provide based on their knowledge of given issues is neither accepted nor respected by those who must be influenced (p. 45).

Similar to Moses' (1993) findings, many administrators of color, like faculty and students of color "are hired [or admitted] as tokens and then isolated" in an environment which is "predominantly white and unfriendly or hostile" (Logan, 1990, B1–B2). Their credentials are often discredited, abilities dismissed, and behavior scrutinized. This happens not only as a result of the white academic population's reaction to people of color, but the principle of "divide and conquer" may prevail on college and university campuses also. Therefore, people of color may be afraid to talk with and support each other because socializing among themselves (which is frequently done among whites) is typically viewed negatively as caucusing. Other minorities (out of fear for their own job security) may even mimic white personnel in questioning the talents and abilities of their colleagues of color during issues of performance reviews and evaluations (Fordham, 1988).

Additionally, the authority of administrators or faculty members of color is oftentimes challenged or undermined. A particularly classic case is one where an African American male, the *only* African American in the college of a predominantly white state university in the south, chairs a remedial transitional program for probationary students who wish to attend the university. The African American male has a master's degree and holds a senior lecturer's position within the college. All the other faculty members in the department are white and have doctoral degrees. The evaluation system of the college is structured so that faculty members on any level can only be reviewed by faculty members on a higher level. Therefore, while this African American male chairs the program and faculty members supposedly report to him, he has no legitimate power to evaluate any faculty member and no job security by definition of his position. The unwritten and unspoken message is for him to stay in his place, which most minorities would view disdainfully as "Uncle Tomming," but which he probably considers a survival tactic.

Yet this institution gives the appearance of being receptive to diversity issues of hiring, promotion, and retention. Similar to the outrage of many people of color to the Clarence Thomas appointment to the Supreme Court, people of color pose the question of why the university did not hire a person of color with a doctoral degree who would have had legitimate power to fulfill all the duties and responsibilities. On the other hand, few whites would question whether such a decision was a coincidence or orchestrated. As pointed out in Chapter One, people of color do not have the luxury of *not* questioning such decisions. In sum, simply fulfilling minimum Affirmative Action standards (hiring a person of color) does little to promote multiculturalism.

Also, the pressure to do well and succeed for administrators, faculty, and students of color comes with a high premium. The stress and pressure experienced at historically white IHEs sometimes manifests itself in physical and mental exhaustion. As Logan (1990) indicates regarding African American students, which applies to administrators and faculty as well, "several have observed that too much anxiety, stress and tension can lead to severe emotional and physical disturbances (depression, schizophrenia, ulcers, migraine headaches)" (p. 13).

While there have been some gains made in improving the visibility of people of color at historically white IHEs, the concern for sufficiency and effectiveness is amplified (Hayes, 1995). Role modeling and mentoring are important factors in students' success (Astone and Nunez-Wormack, 1990; Drummond, 1995); therefore, diversifying administration is especially crucial in contributing to the success as well as retention rate of students of color (Hayes, 1995, p. 35).

❖ STUDENTS

Diaz writes, "An ideal academic environment is one where all students are treated with dignity and accorded equal attention. Research has indicated that classrooms in higher education do not always measure up to this standard" (Diaz, 1994, p. 10). With population shifts and considerable changes in the country's demographics, disregard and inattentiveness to the needs of students of color will result in dire consequences (Astone and Nunez-Wormack, 1990; Cibik and Chambers, 1991; Wilkerson, 1992;

At Many Institutions of Higher Learning, Students of Color are Steered Away from Some Career Fields and Often Dismissed to Others.

Table 5-3. Student Enrollment At IHEs by Ethnicity and Gender

Ethnicity	Enrollment	Social Group	Percent of Students Enrolled
African American	1,410,300	Women	55.1%
Native American	121,681	Minorities	23.4%
Asian American	724,124	International Students	3.2%
European American	10,603,746		
Latino American	988,960		
International Students	456,847		
Total	14,305,658		

Courtesy of: U. S. Department of Education, cited in *Chronicle of Higher Education Almanac* September 1, 1995, p. 5.

Smith, 1995). As Table 5-3 shows, minority enrollment at IHEs is approximately twenty-three percent; international student enrollment is three percent. IHEs can ill afford to ignore the needs of over a quarter of its student body. Yet, these figures reflect that many Native American students have not attended IHEs at rates close to the national norms (Lomawaima, 1995). For example, in 1980, eight percent of Native Americans completed four years of college compared to the national rate of sixteen percent (Lomawaima, 1995). Moreover, Native Americans have concentrated their studies in a few fields and disciplines—mainly education.

In a few years, 40 percent of the 18-to-24 year-old population in the United States will be Chicano/Latino, African-American, Native American, and Asian-American. Institutions of higher learning must prepare an increasingly diverse population for full participation in and contribution to the life of this nation and world. We must now educate a population that has historically been poorly served by our institutions (Wilkerson, 1992, p. 59).

The challenge for higher education is simply to provide diverse cultures with the same opportunities that have been available to whites. The initial requirement to address the challenge, however, is the realization that our current educational programs are not serving all of our students (Dual, 1992). In many IHEs students of color are steered away from some career fields and relegated to others. They get the subtle message that they either are not welcome in the field or that their intellectual abilities are discounted. Students of color confided to Chira (1992 p. A12) that school personnel "blinded by the color of [students'] skin" often ignored, discouraged, and deterred them from pursuing their intellectual goals. Not surprisingly, these students are often subjected to having their culture, language, and experiences devalued. Many students of color also question whether inequities in grading exist at predominantly white institutions.

Many programs in academic institutions designed to improve the educational environment and contribute to all students' success result in an extension of the same camouflaged stereotyping, tracking, and biased treatment present in elementary and secondary schools (Logan, 1990). For example, remedial or developmental study programs are often perceived (erroneously) to serve mostly students of color. Honors programs in IHEs are perceived to (and often do) serve white students. At historically white IHEs, white students are more likely to receive the assistance, encouragement, and counseling necessary to prepare them to pursue graduate degrees or obtain significant job offers upon graduation. Students of color, on the other hand, are often left floundering in an effort to figure it out for themselves, both at the undergraduate and graduate levels. This continuous exclusion and lack of a receptive, cultural pluralistic environment for students of color erects formidable hurdles throughout their educational experience.

While students of color have historically experienced this type of disparate treatment, white students are also adversely affected. A recent study by Nora and Cabrera (1996) pertaining to student persistence rates indicated that while students of color perceived more prejudice and discrimination than white students, these perceptions exerted "an indirect effect on their decisions to persist; yet, perceptions of prejudice and discrimination were found to have both total and indirect effects among the nonminority student population" (141). Being subjected to continuous discriminatory acts in academe, students of color may have become callous to its effects and developed survival techniques. White students, on the other hand, may be so unaccustomed to these experiences that they succumb, resulting in a noticeable effect on persistence decisions (Nora and Cabrera, 1996).

Both cumulative exclusion and discrimination have far-reaching effects (Feagin, 1992). Students of color's experiences of disparate treatment are often dismissed as paranoia unless whites validate it (this is true for faculty, staff, and administrators as well as students).

Recently in a university class of twelve students, the only international student (Russian) was absent from my class for several days. None of the other students ever inquired about the student or even seemed to notice that the student was absent. Yet, on the third day that the Russian student was absent, one of the American students was also absent for the first time. The entire class either asked about her whereabouts or provided information about her absence (she was sick). When the professor asked the students if they knew what was going on with the Russian student, they all shook their heads in disinterest. The professor realized that the challenge with this class was to encourage the students to practice inclusivity.

Since most students of color have been historically, politically, socially, economically, and psychologically subjected to this type of overt and covert exclusion continuously and over extended periods of time, the number of racial/ethnic and intergroup clashes which erupt are predictable. The literature supports the fact that students of color receive constant dosages of disparate treatment; therefore, they quickly realize that the exclusion and discrimination is institutionalized. Whites, on the other hand, tend to refute the fact that racism exists since they often recognize instances of racism as normal treatment (McIntosh, 1995).

I recall that during my early experience in a predominantly white institution (where I was the "only" African American professor in the department), an African American student became very distraught and dismayed. The student had gone to her assigned (white) advisor for information on graduate schools, but the advisor told the student that she should not bother with graduate school because there would be plenty of jobs available in the field when she graduated. The student reported that she was ushered out of the office without any information or encouragement. My impression of the student was that she was quite capable in initiative, drive, and academics to pursue graduate studies and should have at least been provided the information, if not offered encouragement.

In many historically white IHEs, there is the tendency to "lump" all students of color together and administer collective programs and services which do not serve the specific needs of individual ethnic groups nor individual members within groups. This may account for much of the strife and tension that erupts between minority groups and that the media sensationalizes and unnecessarily emphasizes. Astone and Nunez-Wormack (1990) report that:

> As campus presence of students from the larger minority groups increases, their desire to be recognized separately

intensifies. In turn, the cultural identity of different nationalities within each group emerges to claim its place in the collectivity. The desire of Hispanics to be acknowledged separately from African-Americans or Asian-Americans is the same desire Chicanos feel in wanting to be acknowledged separately from Cubans, Dominicans, and Colombians. . . . In addition to differences stemming from cultural identity, other important factors affect the quality of a student's experience at the institution and directly affect persistence and graduation (p. 44).

Other factors which affect students of color within and between groups are social class (e.g., upper, middle, lower socioeconomic status), cultural values (e.g., attitudes toward family and gender issues) and learning styles (Astone and Nunez-Wormack; Sleeter and Grant, 1990).

Diaz (1994) notes that "Whether the variable is race, gender, or ethnicity, research on classroom climate suggests that . . . students [in IHEs] often do not experience similar levels of support and receptivity even when attending the same class" (p. 11). This also holds true for other aspects of IHEs regarding students of color. A stark realization, however, is that "minorities are [or soon will be] the majority" (Hayes-Bautista, 1992, p. B1; Hu-DeHart, 1993). And there is a perilous need to "create a sense of community on . . . college campuses conducive to the education, retention and success of all students" (Dual, 1992, p. 3). Presently, however, many historically white university campuses have special organizations for students of color or religious groups (e.g., International or African American organizations) which provide additional support and solidarity for the students.

African American students attending historically black colleges and universities (HBCUs) have significantly higher graduation rates than those attending predominantly white IHEs. Additionally, the graduate's ability to function successfully both in the workplace and at predominantly white graduate and professional schools is not compromised by having attended a HBCU for undergraduate study (Ladson-Billings, 1994).

❖ THE CURRICULUM

Wilkerson (1992) characterizes the essence of perceptions regarding academic curriculums. She wrote that "what we require, recommend, or have available for students to study tells them what we consider worthy of consideration in this world" (p. 59). When the comprehensive histories and contributions of diverse populations are not acknowledged or recognized, it sends a clear signal about their past, present, and future worth. For the most part, students of color have learned and continue to learn from, about, and according to the European American perspective.

The development of ethnic studies programs made progress in addressing this curriculum deficiency but these courses, to a great extent, heightened the divide between what *were* considered required, "significant" courses and "trivial," elective courses. Further, ethnic study courses inadvertently promote separatist behavior since only those students interested in the courses will enroll.

Many accrediting agencies require programs to include diversity in their curriculums. Some institutions address this standard by simply adding courses to the curriculum or infusing information about diverse groups into course contents. Many times this information is presented as a deviation from the norm and in such an inconsequential manner that students do not benefit from it. It further damages the self-esteem and self-confidence of students of color and prevents white students from acquiring knowledge of and information about the contributions and cultures of people of color.

While some academicians have staunchly refused to address diversity issues in their course content, other more conscientious have tried to revise course content to promote inclusion. But as Minnich (1990) details, those conscientious academicians may be unduly charged with overemphasizing or being obsessed with diverse group concerns. The opening scenario in this chapter is an example of this. The underlying issue is that students are not accustomed to objectively examining information about diverse groups and are therefore understandably uncomfortable doing so. Moreover, white students often view themselves as monocultural and do not recognize the need to study their own culture as well as the culture of others (Howard, 1992). However, as Minnich (1990) indicates, "their discomfort is but one more indication that such courses are very badly needed, not that 'the students don't want them'" (p. 79).

In an effort to prepare students for a global society, some IHEs such as Iowa State University have made multiculturalism part of their general education requirements. However, such a decision has not been without hot debates among proponents and opponents of multiculturalism.

Because the demographics of this country are changing so rapidly (Cibik and Chambers, 1991; Diaz, 1994; Hayes-Bautista, 1992; Smith, 1995; Treadwell, 1992; Wilkerson, 1992) and there is a definite move toward a global economy (Diaz, 1994; Wilkerson, 1992), past practices in academia will not address impending needs. Furthermore, Eurocentrism does not make sense economically (Diaz, 1994).

Students themselves are imploring IHEs to make the changes which will bind people from all walks of life (Hayes-Bautista, 1992; Wilkerson, 1992). Students in IHEs understand that ". . . all students, and particularly white students, are disadvantaged by a narrow, exclusive education—and that, without curricular change, this generation will be ill-prepared to work, live, and make decisions in this diverse society and interdependent global community" (Wilkerson, 1992, p. 59).

❖ ASSESSING THE SITUATION

The fact that [historically] non-represented groups are now under-represented groups in IHEs indicates that some progress has occurred. However, many IHEs are still striving to achieve total inclusivity. There has been little progress over the years in eliminating those factors (discriminatory policies, racism, etc.) which promote exclusivity and hamper the development of a cultural pluralistic environment (Reyes & Halcon, 1990).

Ironically, after 30 years of heightened attention to the task of improving the participation of minority students and the hiring of increased numbers of minority faculty and staff, the proportion of minority students, faculty and staff in today's colleges and universities is less than it was at the turn of the century (Drummond, 1995, p. 43).

Perhaps at issue is the feeling that academe is simply *tolerating* the inclusion of some minority faculty, administrators, and students. Many well-intentioned supporters of multiculturalism advocate the need for tolerance. In reality, tolerance can be offensive when acceptance is preferred. Many white students and faculty, as well as administrators, are under the false assumption that Affirmative Action is code for "underprepared" in the case of students, "not equally talented" in the case of faculty, and "not qualified enough" in the case of administrators (Nieves-Squires, 1992).

In reality, United States culture has always been multicultural (Fishkin, 1995). It should not suddenly appear that people of color are "taking over." The problem appears to be ". . . that our predecessors generalized too far from too few. . . . It is, simply, that while the majority of humankind was excluded from education and the making of what has been called knowledge, the dominant few not only defined themselves as the inclusive kind of human but also as the norm and the ideal" (Munnich, 1990, pp.184; 37-38). Therefore, for those who long have been in positions of dominance, any space that students of color occupy appears excessive and their voices sound loud, demanding, and offensive" (Patai, 1991).

Proponents of multicultural education are taking the blinders off. Academe should not be the last to collectively embrace this movement. In an environment where intellectual acumen abounds, it is disturbing to encounter people in positions of authority who refuse to be open to ideas and information which conflict with their beliefs.

The major theorists and researchers in multicultural education agree that the movement is designed to restructure educational institutions so that all students, including middle-class white males, will acquire the knowledge, skills, and attitudes needed to function effectively in a culturally and ethnically diverse nation and world. Multicultural education, as its major architects have conceived of it during the last decade, is not an ethnic- or gender-specific movement. It is a movement designed to empower all students to become caring, knowledgeable, and active citizens in a deeply troubled and ethnically polarized nation and world (Banks, 1993).

❖ NECESSARY ACTIONS

While students, faculty, staff, and administrators of color must take significant action and serve as catalysts in improving and changing the academic environment to embrace inclusivity, it is obvious they cannot do it alone (Reyes and Halcon, 1990). Much is required of each individual as well as the collective units and systems of academia. Each IHE must reexamine its specific initiatives, programs, and commitment to multicultural education and take proactive steps to assure that what is being done is adequate and appropriate. While recommendations are offered in this section which suggest steps IHEs could take to improve inclusivity, these recommendations are by no means exhaustive. Additionally, while there has been some logical attempt to present the recommendations as the topics were discussed throughout this chapter, many recommendations are applicable across topics.

General Recommendations

Inclusivity must be reflected from the top down. A "do as I am doing" posture must be adopted as opposed to a "do as I say" position. Unless members of the academic community see changes

Students, faculty, staff, and administrators from IHEs can collaborate with schools to jointly make improvements which benefit both schools and IHEs.

in top level administration, they will continue to know that it is nothing but business as usual. Seeing people of color predominantly in custodial positions within IHEs does not constitute an acceptance of diversity. When budget constraints result in personnel reductions, people of color, women, and disabled employees should not bear a disproportionate amount of the cutbacks.

Institutionally sponsored activities, purchases of services and goods, and distribution of available resources are all avenues for promoting inclusivity. Academic units or departments within IHEs could adopt local schools which would be advantageous for the IHE as well as the local schools. In this type of partnership, IHEs could collaborate with schools which enroll diverse ethnic populations. Students, faculty, staff, and administrators from IHEs would contribute time and resources to schools. Using such a model, not only would education majors from IHEs be involved in schools, but in other disciplines as well. Table 5-4 outlines ways that various academic disciplines can contribute to elementary and secondary schools. Many other activities can be provided as a way to deepen the university student's mastery of his/her discipline and to broaden their experience and understanding of different ethnic groups.

TABLE 5-4. Sample Activities That Academic Disciplines Can Contribute To Schools

Discipline	Types of Contributions
All	Tutor children who need extra help.
	Share a hobby or collection.
	Discuss your job.
	Tell stories about your cultural heritage.
	Share your professional skills.
	Assist in the school's office, computer, lab, library, or lunchroom.
Journalism	Help schools organize parent newsletters.
	Help students develop writing skills by writing about items of interest to them in the school or community.
Economics	Work with students on age-appropriate projects or units on various monetary concepts.
Art	Help art teachers with projects; help beautify schools.
Music	Help music teachers with projects; teach children to play musical instruments and/or read music; give voice lessons to children.
Drama	Teach children the rudiments of drama.
	Give assistance on school plays.
Foreign Languages	Teach children a foreign language.

Currently, IHEs are judged on the basis of efforts made toward addressing diversity issues. The emphasis should be redirected from assessing academia's efforts toward achieving inclusivity to assessing the actual results. Maintaining extensive documentation indicating a search for candidates or students of color should no longer be sufficient. Hiring qualified people of color or members of disenfranchised groups and cultivating a supportive environment go beyond complying with federal and accrediting regulations. Funding, development strategies, and opportunities for career advancement within academia should be assessed in terms of evidence of inclusivity. Performance evaluations should be revised to include assessments of academic personnel (presidents, provosts, deans, chairpersons, etc.) in this area.

Programs, policies, and procedures should be reexamined to assure that they do not adversely affect people of color's access, hiring, retention, and advancement opportunities. Workshops and seminars that sensitize participants to inclusivity issues should be a part of orientation procedures for everyone involved in the academic process. Many acts of covert exclusiveness occur because individuals are not conscious of the effect of their behavior on diverse groups. Workshops and seminars could also serve as professional development units for current academic personnel. Additionally, extensive education is required to help academic participants realize the diversity within groups as well as among groups.

An atmosphere of appreciation of diversity should permeate the campuses at IHEs. Leisure activities which attract people from all walks of life should be part of the life at university campuses. For example, musicals, art shows, and festivals that have wide appeal should be scheduled. Intolerance of racism, classism, sexism, and the like should be part of the fabric of IHEs. Regardless of whether the issue involves students, faculty, administrators, or curriculum, this intolerance should be openly communicated and acknowledged.

Some IHEs are creating top administrative positions to coordinate diversity efforts on their campuses. However, caution should be exercised in defining specific goals, responsibilities, evaluations, and the degree of authority involved in the role to ensure that it does more than just cosmetically address diversity issues.

Finally, the paradigms in most disciplines at IHEs must continue to be expanded. Currently, most disciplines have began to appreciate qualitative as well as quantitative research (Allender, 1986). Likewise, personal stories and anecdotes are given more credence as valid scholarship, giving credence to non-European and feminist styles, and denouncing the false dichotomy between subjective and objective data. Allender notes that there is evidence of IHEs not only being more responsive to qualitative data, but there is also an acknowledgement that it can also be as scientifically rigorous as quantitative data grounded on linear, Eurocentric principles reputed to be objective. Other examples of this trend are listed below (Allender, 1986).

- Acceptance of quasi-experimental research (versus strictly experimental methods).
- Acknowledgement that research can be sound without being externally valid.
- A growing number of arguments against the use of statistical significance tests because they tend to attribute misleading meanings to data. Common sense interpretations and replications are suggested as a more powerful means of producing understanding.
- Arguments that more valid generalizations are likely to come from studies using case study methods.
- Arguments for the use of introspection, self-reports, and speculation as valid aspects of a more complete set of scientific methods. This adds a more humanistic perspective.
- Interaction is encouraged between the researchers and participants in the research process, using primarily qualitative methods such as phenomenology, conceptual empiricism, and qualitative evaluation. Dialogue between an experimenter and a participant is emphasized.
- New kinds of data are now considered relevant, emphasizing personal meaning, holistic explanations, and societal change. Bronfenbrenner (1979) refers to these types studies as "transforming experiments" since they systematically challenge the form of social organizations, belief systems, and lifestyles prevailing in a particular culture or subculture.
- Refereed journals publish more qualitative research than in the past.
- More humanistic textbooks are being published and more qualitative dissertations are being written.

The multicultural implications of this paradigm shift is that research about women, ethnicity, disability, and the like are viewed as more valid than they once were. Hence, faculty members who choose these topics for their research agendas will not likely be penalized in the tenure and promotion process. Also, graduate students are now afforded more flexibility in their choices of research.

Faculty And Administration

IHEs must develop innovative and creative strategies for recruiting and retaining people from diverse cultures. Prudent judgment must be exercised in order to avoid obstacles in recruitment of people of color. Light's (1994) article, "Not Like Us," identifies and discusses fifteen possible obstacles which should be avoided. Light also offers fifteen alternative approaches for successfully recruiting faculty of color. Additionally, recruitment efforts should not be centered around ivy league or highly ranked institutions since most students of color cannot afford to attend such institutions. Students may be recruited from historically black colleges and universities (HBCUs). Recruiting in business and industry to redirect individuals to academia should be considered.

Comprehensive orientation procedures should be developed to promote inclusivity for faculty and administrators. Diverse populations should be informed of and have access to supportive networks. Mentoring relationships should be effectively formulated and developed within departments and across disciplines. These relationships should be monitored and reviewed frequently to ensure that the relationships are beneficial.

There is a need to restructure tenure and promotion requirements on service, scholarship, and teaching to reflect the diversity in those areas rather than constrain them to Eurocentric definitions of those components. For example, the culture of personnel of color may suggest extensive efforts in service to the neighborhood, community, and church. These efforts may not be recognized by tenure and promotion committees as "significant" service units if they are not associated with service units defined from a Eurocentric perspective, such as speaker's bureaus, civic clubs, etc.

Diverse populations of faculty and administrators must also take active steps themselves to organize and network both within groups and among groups. Strategies and opportunities to promote inclusivity could be presented and implemented collectively.

Students

IHEs should build liaisons between local schools and two-year institutions to recruit students of color. As in recruiting faculty and administrators from prestigious institutions, the key to increasing ethnic diversity in enrollments may be to seek students in previously overlooked places. Having a presence of faculty and administrators of color also increases enrollment decisions for students.

Financial assistance for students presents major obstacles. Providing substantial or alternative funding for students and disseminating this information about funding promptly and adequately is crucial for recruitment as well as retention.

Comprehensive orientation procedures as well as peer matching and mentoring relationships are also necessary for students of color. Many today are still first-generation college students and are unfamiliar with the environment and requirements or criteria for success.

Providing a supportive, encouraging environment where student diversity is acknowledged is essential. The diversity of the student population should be apparent in public relations material, representation on committees and student boards, and access to and use of institutional facilities. Access to and respect from academic personnel is also equally important.

The Curriculum

Massive changes must occur in the curriculum. What is considered accepted knowledge must be reexamined and redefined. As Minnich (1990) indicates, a true transformation of knowledge must occur. The concern from women, people of color, immigrants, etc. indicates that a tremendous amount of information about non-Europeans has been omitted from what is studied in the core curriculum. Moreover, what is included presents a distorted view of their actual contributions.

It is incumbent upon faculty members to develop and rewrite course texts or adopt new textbooks which more adequately reflect the contributions and presence of the diverse populations of this country. Courses must be redesigned and restructured to enhance students' learning experiences about the influences of all cultures. Simply adding ethnic courses or infusing supplementary material is not enough. Cultural pluralism in course content must be encompassing and indiscriminant.

Course requirements, assignments, teaching methodology, and assessments should reflect the objectivity in and acceptance of diversity. As Wilkerson (1992) indicates, "the new curriculum allows for subjective ways of knowing, as well as for the accepted 'objective' ways" (p. 63). Presentations from guest speakers of various ethnic backgrounds should be solicited for classes. Student presentations and reports on diverse cultures should also be encouraged. Class projects or collaboration with diverse community, civic, non-profit, and business establishments should be considered.

Developing activities or simulations to help students discover the diversity within the class is also beneficial. The cultural pursuit activity mentioned in Chapter Two is just as effective and enjoyable for college students as it is for young children. The activity can be structured to gather information about different cultures in the class or information about various cultures in general. Games and activities such as Barnga (description in Thiagarajan, n. d.), Bafa Bafa (Shirts, n.d.), The Diversity Game, Diversity Bingo, and Diversophy help students realize, appreciate, and understand how differences in cultures influence our thoughts and actions. These games as well as personality inventories such as the Myers-Briggs Indicator or The Cross-Cultural Adaptability Inventory can be used to address diversity issues. Feeble excuses that some college classes do not lend themselves to inclusion of diverse material is passé. The development of knowledge, like the development of civilization, has always been multi-faceted. While some exercises or activities may not be appropriate for all classes, the multicultural nature of each course should be naturally unveiled.

Group projects and collaborative assignments allow students to study and work with different cultures, thereby promoting inclusivity. The games and activities mentioned earlier are also useful tools in assigning students to groups. Courses should be structured to encourage students to get to know one another within the class. Students could introduce one another to the class during the initial class period, reporting basic information such as name, major, classification, hometown, special talents, hobbies, etc. They could also be encouraged to form and join study groups across cultural lines.

❖ SUMMARY

A rebirth of this nation is required. Only then can it be said, without reservation, that the mottoes, creeds, and inclusive statements at the beginning of this chapter are bona-fide truths. The acknowledgment that this society has never been monocultural is essential. Like schools, IHEs play an important role in in addressing national ideals of equality and inclusivity. IHEs must work toward eradicating racism, classism, sexism, and helping society realize how each culture influences and enriches others.

IHEs are not immune from and in most instances reflect the conditions of the larger society. The opportunities, however, are infinite for IHEs to ensure that all students and citizens benefit from the discovery and acquisition of knowledge which will enable them to live, work, and function in a multicultural, global economy. IHEs engaging in practices or procedures which continue to preserve or condone an environment where all participants are not accepted and respected, or are graduating students who are culturally incompetent, do a disservice to all of society. Individually and collectively steps must be taken out of defined comfort zones to ensure that the truths purported to be self-evident—that all individuals are created equal and are endowed with certain inalienable rights to life, liberty, and the pursuit of happiness—are fundamentally true.

The IHEs which have already taken steps to address the issues of a multicultural society, by implementing some or all of the suggestions mentioned here (and more) must help others do so and lead the way into the twenty-first century with clear vision, conscience, and fortitude.

❖ RECOMMENDED ACTIVITIES

1. *Journal entry*—Reflect on school experiences that you had, or teachers who best prepared you for college. As an adult, how are the views that you hold about other cultures affected by your school experiences? How do your school experiences affect how you will teach or educate your students? How did your prior school, family, and community experiences prepare you for teaching in a diverse society? How did your schooling, family, and community experiences affect the type of school that you would like to work in?

2. Interview two African American college students—one who attends a Historically Black College or University and one who attends a predominantly white institution. Ask them to delineate the pros and cons of each. Compare and contrast their responses.

3. Interview a faculty member who is the minority in terms of ethnicity to find out race-related dilemmas that he or she faces.

4. Think about all of your college courses. Share examples of courses and assignments which focused on diversity with the rest of the class. Are there any glaring omissions? If so, how can they be addressed? Is there evidence that your university or college values diversity? Give examples.

5. Do a panel discussion with college students from one particular ethnic group (European, African, Asian, Native, or Latino American). Try to get students who hold a wide range of viewpoints. Volunteers can probably be found on any college campus. Ask students to share their viewpoints on a wide variety of topics (e.g., racism in this country, Affirmative Action, sexism, multiculturalism, ethnic studies).

6. Interview international students and ask them how their educational experiences in their countries of origin compare to their educational experiences in the United States.

7. Use culturegrams developed by Brigham Young University to acquaint faculty and students with an overview of other cultures.
8. Interview white students and ask them how they think their educational experiences compare to students of color.
9. Have a panel discussion of whites and students of color discussing similarities and differences on social, political, economical, and educational issues.
10. Debate the pros and cons of Affirmative Action as it relates to recruitment of faculty members and admission of students to IHEs.

❖ REFERENCES

Allen, W. R. 1992. The color of success: African-American college student outcomes at predominantly White and historically Black public colleges and universities. *Harvard Educational Review* 62 (Spring): 26-44.

Astone, B. and E. N. Wormack. 1990. *Pursuing diversity: Recruiting college minority students*. ASHE-ERIC Higher Education Report No. 7. Washington, D. C.: The George Washington University School of Education and Human Development.

Banks, J. A. 1993. Multicultural education: Development, dimensions, and challenges. *Phi Delta Kappan* 75(1): 22-28.

Bernstein A. and J. Cock. 1994. A troubling picture of gender equity. *The Chronicle of Higher Education* 40(41): B1-B3.

Bronfenbrenner, U. (1979). *The Ecology of Human Development*. Cambridge, MA: Harvard University Press.

Brown, C. 1991. Increasing minority access to college: Seven efforts for success. *NASPA Journal* 28(Spring): 224-230.

Carter, R. T. 1990. Culture and Black students' success. *Educational Considerations* 18(Fall): 7-11.

Chira, S. 1992. Minority students discouraged from post-graduate education. *The Houston Chronicle* 9 August, Two Star Edition, A: 12.

Chronicle of Higher Education Almanac. (1995, September 1). Vol. XL11, No. 1, Editor: Corbin Gwaltney, Almanac Editor: Jean Evangelauf, Publisher: Robinette D. Ross.

Cibik, M. A. and S. L. Cambers. 1991. Similarities and differences among Native Americans, Hispanics, Blacks, and Anglos. *NASPA Journal* 28 (Winter): 129-139.

Copeland, E. 1995. There is still an urgent need for doctorates of color. *Black Issues in Higher Education* 12 (10): 96.

Diaz, C. F. 1994. Dimensions of multicultural education Implications for higher education. *National Forum* 74 (1): 9-11.

Drummond, M. 1995. Minorities in higher education leadership positions: A report of eight years of disappointment: 1986-1993. *Black Issues In Higher Education* 12 (2): 43-47.

Dual, P. A. 1992. Diversity in higher education: Challenges and opportunities for the next decade. *American Educational Research Association.* ED 345658 Note: this is an ERIC document. It is classified as "Speech/Conference Paper", April 22, 1992.

Evangelauf, J. 1992. Minority-group enrollment at colleges rose 10% from 1988 to 1990, reaching record levels. *The Chronicle of Higher Education* 38 (20): A33, A37.

————.1993. Number of minority students in colleges rose by 9% from 1990 to 1991, U. S. Reports. *The Chronicle of Higher Education* 39(20): A30-A31.

Feagin, J. R. 1992. The continuing significance of racism: Discrimination against Black students in white colleges. *Journal Of Black Studies* 22 (4): 546-578.

Fishkin, S. F. 1995. The multiculturalism of 'traditional' culture. *The Chronicle of Higher Education* 41(26): A48.

Fordham, S. 1988. Racelessness as a factor in black students' school success: Pragmatic strategy or Pyrrhic victory? *Harvard Educational Review* 58(1): 54-84.

Gose, B. 1995. Growth of minority enrollment slowed to 2.6% in 1993. *The Chronicle of Higher Education* 41(27): A34.

Graff, G. 1992. *Beyond the culture wars: How teaching the conflicts can revitalize American education.* New York: W. W. Norton & Co.

Gunsch, D. 1993. Games augment diversity training. *Personnel Journal* 72(6): 78-83.

Haro, R. P. 1991. Search firms should work harder to find minority candidates for academic jobs. *The Chronicle of Higher Education* 37(13): B2.

Hawkins, B. D. 1993. New voices: Women and people of color forge new perspectives on legal education for fairness at law schools. *Black Issues In Higher Education* July 1: 10-14.

Hayes, D. W. 1995. Recruitment and retention. *Black Issues In Higher Education* 12(20): 30, 35.

Hayes-Bautista, D. E. 1992. Academe can take the lead in binding together the residents of a multicultural society. *The Chronicle of Higher Education* 39(10): B1-B2.

Howard, G. R. 1993. Whites in multicultural education: Rethinking our role. *Phi Delta Kappan* 75(1): 36-41.

Hu-DeHart, E. 1993. The history, development, and future of ethnic studies. *Phi Delta Kappan* 75(1): 50-54.

Kelley, C. and J. E. Meyers. 1992. *The cross-cultural adaptability inventory.* National Computer Systems, P. O. Box 1416, Minneapolis, MN 55440.

Ladson-Billings, G. 1994. *The dreamkeepers: in Successful teachers of African American children.* San Francisco: Jossey-Bass.

Lang, M. 1992. Barriers to Blacks' educational achievement in higher education: A statistical and conceptual review. *Journal Of Black Studies* 22(4): 510-522.

Leatherman, C. 1994. Number of Blacks earning Ph.D.'s rose 15% in year. *The Chronicle of Higher Education* 41(7): A16.

Light, P. 1994. "Not like us: Removing the barriers to recruiting minority faculty. *Journal of Policy Analysis and Management* 13(1): 164-180.

Logan, S. L. 1990. Promoting academic excellence of African-American students: Issues and strategies. *Educational Considerations* 18: (Fall): 12-15.

Lomawaima, K. T. 1995. Educating Native Americans. In *Handbook of research on multicultural education,* edited by J. A. Banks and C. A. M. Banks. New York: Macmillan.

Magner, D. K. 1993. Blacks earned fewer doctorates in 1992 than in 1991, study finds. *The Chronicle of Higher Education* 40 (6): A18.

Mattai, P. R. 1992. Rethinking the nature of multicultural education: Has it lost its focus or is it being misused? *Journal of Negro Education* 61 (1): 65-77.

McIntosh, P. 1995. White privilege and male privilege: A personal account of coming to see correspondences through work in women's studies. In *Race, class, and gender: An anthology.* (2nd ed.), edited by M. L. Anderson and P. H. Collins. Belmont, CA: Wadsworth.

McMillen, L. 1991. Women in academe say they bear brunt of staffing cutbacks. *The Chronicle of Higher Education* 38 (12): A31, A37.

Mercer, J. 1994. Ambitious program aims to produce minority Ph.D.'s. *The Chronicle of Higher Education* 40 (35): A36.

Minnich, E. K. 1990. *Transforming knowledge.* Philadelphia: Temple University Press.

Morgan, J. 1995. The sisterhood and the academy. *Black Issues In Higher Education* 12 (4): 20, 22-23.

Morton, C. N. 1982. Higher education's response to the needs of minority students: Leadership and institutional issues. *Society of Ethnic and Special Studies Southern Illinois University at Edwardsville.* Another ERIC document: ED 224853 (classified as "speech/conference paper", October 14, 1982).

Moses, Y. T. 1993. The roadblocks confronting minority administrators. *The Chronicle of Higher Education* 39 (19): B1-B2.

Nieves-Squires, S. 1992. Hispanic women in the U. S. academic context. In *Perspectives On Minority Women In Higher Education,* edited by L. B. Welch. Westport: Praeger.

Nora, A., and A. F. Cabrera. 1996. The role of perceptions of prejudice and discrimination on the adjustment of minority students to college. *Journal of Higher Education* 67(2): 119-148.

Obiakor, F. E. 1992. Multiculturalism in higher education: A myth or reality? Paper presented at the Multicultural Fair, 6 February, The University of Tennessee at Chattanooga, TN.

Painter, N. I. 1994. It's time to acknowledge the damage inflicted by intolerance. *The Chronicle of Higher Education* 40(29): A64.

Patai, D. 1991. Minority status and the stigma of 'surplus visibility.' *The Chronicle of Higher Education* 38(10): A52.

Ramey, F. 1995. Obstacles faced by African American women administrators in higher education: How they cope. Section II. Issues in African American Education. *The Western Journal of Black Studies* 19(2): 113–119.

Reyes, M. L. and J. J. Halcon. 1990. Racism in academia: The old wolf revisited. In *Facing racism in education*, edited by N. M. Hidalgo, C. L. McDowell, and E. V. Siddle. Cambridge: President and Fellows of Harvard College.

Richardson, R. C., Jr. and E. F. Skinner. 1991. *Achieving quality and diversity*. New York: American Council on Education and Macmillan Publishing Company.

Rodriguez, R. 1994. HACU examines status of Hispanic education; session also discusses media and legal challenges. *Black Issues in Higher Education* 11(18): 8-12.

Scheurich, J. J. 1993. Toward a white discourse on white racism. *Educational Researcher* 22(8): 5–10.

Shea, C. 1994. Women and minorities led the way in a year of slow enrollment growth. *The Chronicle of Higher Education* 40(21): A32.

Shirts, G. R. n.d. *Bafa Bafa: Cross-cultural orientation.* P. O. Box 910. Del Mar, California, 92014.

Sleeter C. E. and C. A. Grant. 1990. An analysis of multicultural education in the United States. In *Facing racism in education*, edited by N. M. Hidalgo, C. L. McDowell, and E. V. Siddle. Cambridge: President and Fellows of Harvard College.

Smith, V. W. 1995. Minorstreaming: Resolving problems of the color line in the 21st century. *Black Issues In Higher Education* 12(8): 30-31.

Thiagarajan, S. n. d. *Barnga: A simulation game on cultural classes.* Intercultural Press, Inc., P. O. Box 700 Yarmouth, ME 40496.

Treadwell, C. G. 1992. Demographic changes and higher education. *The Education Digest* 57 (6): 33-35.

Trueba, H. T. 1995. Race and ethnicity: The role of academia in healing multicultural America. In *Sources Notable Selections in Race and Ethnicity*, edited by A. Aguirre, Jr., and D. V. Baker. The Dushkin Publishing Group, Inc.

Welch, L. B. 1992. *Perspectives on minority women in higher education.* Westport: Praeger.

West, C. 1993. *Race matters.* Boston: Beacon Press.

Wharton, C. R. 1986. Public higher education and Black Americans: Today's crisis, tomorrow's disaster? Address at a National Urban League Conference. Albany, State University of New York. (ERIC document) ED 276388 (speech/conference paper). July 21, 1986.

Wilkerson, M. B. 1992. Beyond the graveyard: Engaging faculty involvement. *Change* 24(1): 59-63.

Wilson, R. 1995. Among white males: Jokes and anecdotes. *The Chronicle of Higher Education* 41(33): A20-A21.

Wright, S. J. 1981. Education of minority students: Problems and challenges? ED 243979

Young, H. A. 1983. Cultural differences that affect retention of minorities on predominately white campuses. Paper presented at the Annual Meeting of The American Educational Research Association. Montreal, Quebec, Canada.

Multicultural Issues Confronted by Parents and Families

Schools should welcome parents from all walks of life.

INTRODUCTION

Miss Mack is a Latina parent of four children—all under six years of age. She is a welfare recipient who lives in a housing project. Her English is not very good at this point. She loves her children very much. Her oldest child, Juarez, is a first grader at school. The teacher sent a note to parents encouraging them to volunteer in the classroom. Since Miss Mack's other children are visiting her sister, Miss Mack decides to visit Juarez's class.

School is just beginning when Miss Mack arrives and many parents come in and sign the visitor's book and proceed to their children's classrooms. Miss Mack is confused and does not know what to do and does not know where her son's class is. The office secretary does not greet or smile at her, but looks at Miss Mack and then turns her head and returns to work. After a few minutes of waiting. Miss Mack stutters, "Ah wanna volunteer."

Without getting out of her seat, the secretary looks at her, frowns, and says, "What?" Miss Mack nervously repeats, "Ah wanna volunteer in my son's class." *"Who* is your son?" asks the secretary, looking at Miss Mack with disapproval. (Miss Mack is wearing a brightly colored outfit and has on heavy makeup). The dialogue continues in this manner for a few moments and finally, the secretary tells Miss Mack how to find her son's classroom. After leaving the office, Miss Mack is so embarrassed that she goes home instead of visiting her son's class as planned.

Although schools generally espouse a policy welcoming parent involvement, parents such as Miss Mack who are from non-mainstream families are often treated with disdain and are not made to feel welcome in their children's schools. Furthermore, many of these parents may not be convinced that an education will help their children.

While the teacher in the scenario may have sincerely wanted to involve her student's parents, Miss Mack was unwelcomed before she even reached the teacher's classroom. Schools must become more cognizant of the ways that they "disinvite" parent involvement. Furthermore, they must insist that all parents are welcome in the school regardless of the parent's marital status, dress, language, socioeconomic status, religion, or ethnicity. Without strong parent-school relationships, many children's chances of success are greatly reduced. Schools must accept parents as they are if effective relationships are to be established. Although it may be difficult to do so in many cases, educators must learn to focus on the strengths that parents have rather than on their liabilities. In the scenario, Miss Mack cared about her son enough to come to school. This is a strength that can be used to help her son reach his fullest potential educationally. It is unlikely that children will be successful without such parental involvement. Most parents care about their children and will try to help them succeed if they are encouraged by their child's school and if they realize that they are expected to be involved. When parents are treated with respect, they are more likely to work with their children's teacher in a mutually rewarding relationship (Boutte, Keepler, Tyler, and Terry, 1992).

The organizing theme of this chapter is the importance of contemporary educators identifying, acknowledging and applying knowledge of multicultural issues surrounding parent involvement in school programs. To achieve effective parent involvement in classrooms and schools, teachers and administrators will need to increase their cultural awareness about the many different patterns of parenting which now exist. This is essential, for the day is long past when parents left their children at the school door and then knew nothing of their days. Research from the 1970s onward confirms that parent involvement in the educational process results in longer lasting gains for children—cognitively, socially and emotionally (Bredekamp, 1987).

Still, at this point in history, many teachers need to continue to examine their past assumptions that most of the students they teach will come from traditional two-parent families. School personnel may also need to divest themselves of ingrained prejudices against divorce and divorced people, against single parents and against certain ethnic groups and cultures. It is particularly important that teachers accept the fact that there is nothing wrong with parents who are no longer married or never have been, and to realize that it is remarkable that so many single fathers and mothers have succeeded in holding their families together, and continue to do so (Belton-Owens, 1993). Often, school personnel have focused only on problems and weaknesses of fatherless homes, which distorts the true picture and obscures clues to ways of building on strengths (Hale, 1988).

Although it is true that in the 1990s parent involvement in the education process has become more established, our limited knowledge of multicultural factors still regards progress in implementing school programs with families who may fall outside traditional parameters. In an effort to partially overcome the deficit of information, this chapter will review the last three decades of parent's involvement in their children's schooling, look at multiculturalism and families, and examine some related research findings. The final section of the chapter discusses specific questions teachers can consider to enhance parent involvement in education programs.

❖ PARENT INVOLVEMENT DURING THE LAST THREE DECADES

The 1960s saw the birth of very active parent involvement efforts among early childhood educators in this country. Bronfenbrenner's (1974) comments on the effects of varieties of intervention programs (planned to enhance children's development) summarize the case for parent involvement. In his findings Bronfenbrenner emphatically concluded:

> The evidence indicates that the family is the most effective and economical system for fostering and sustaining the development of the child. The evidence indicates further that the involvement of the child's family as an active participant is critical to the success of any intervention program. Without such family involvement, any effects of intervention, at least in the cognitive sphere, are likely to be ephemeral, to appear to erode rapidly once the program ends. In contrast, the involvement of the parents as partners in the enterprise provides an on-going system which can reinforce the effects of the program while it is in operation, and help to sustain them after the program ends (p. 55).

Other research findings over the past several decades led to a variety of program models and services developed to involve parents, particularly African American parents, in early childhood programs. Among them are an Infant Stimulation through Family Life Education program in Schenectady, New York (Ligan, Barber, and Williams, 1971) and Ira Gordon's (1971) well-known home visitation programs in Florida that utilized paraprofessionals. The Carnegie Infant Education Project (Lambie, Bond and Weikart, 1974) had as its main developmental objective the construction of curriculum to increase a mother's awareness of and her ability to enhance her infant's growth.

At the George Peabody College Demonstration and Research Center for Early Education (DARCEE), Susan Grey (1971) and her colleagues developed home visitation techniques and tasks for mothers of preschoolers. Levenstein's (1970) Verbal Interaction Project was based on the belief that parents could be taught to stimulate their children's intellectual development. Many early programs of parent involvement relied exclusively on parent group meetings, such as that conducted by Karnes, Hodgins, Teska, and Kirk (1969). Nimnich and others (1972) at the Far West laboratory pioneered a toy-teasing and demonstration program, and, in the early 1970s Home Start was launched as an adjunct to Head Start. The Home Start program utilized home visitors, whose qualifications were friendly attitudes, suitability of cultural and language background and successful experience as a parent, rather than academic credentials. It is important to note that this, and many other early intervention programs of the era did emphasize the importance of cultural and language awareness (MIDCO, 1972).

Some of the significant attributes best taught by parental involvement in the home are cited in research reports from the thirteen-year Harvard University Preschool Project (Winter, 1985). The project used trained parent educators in a program called Parents as First Teachers. According to the study, the degree of a child's competence in language, curiosity, social skills, and cognitive intelligence led to improved positive home-school relationships during the school years. In describing the study, the author makes a powerful argument for providing families with timely, practical information to use in "fostering optimal development" as a cost-effective investment to improve schooling in the United States. That is, the absence of parental participation and involvement in school activities implies that current parent involvement strategies may be ineffective and costly.

There were many preschool programs which made an effort to hire parents and others, such as cooperative preschools that used parents as teachers (many of whom were African-American). There also was a trend toward helping parents to become early childhood personnel through the use of trained staff as models in actual work situations. This was one of the thrusts in the Child Development Associate (CDA) program (Klein, 1982). The CDA program certified competence through supervised experience in actual child-care centers rather than by formal training.

At about this same period (early to mid 1970s) television programs began to be used as a component of early education programs involving parents. In Appalachia, a television program called Home-Oriented Preschool Education (HOPE) instructed children and parents in positive parent-child interaction skills. Each week a home visitor took booklets called Parent Guides to families. There were also many "omnibus" programs that included research as well as comprehensive services and instruction. Special programs existed in churches, and there were also programs such as the Nurseries in Cross-Cultural Education (NICE) program for children and parents in San Francisco (Lane, Elzey, and Lewis, 1971) which searched actively for varieties of experiences through which parents of children in a multicultural preschool could become more inolved with their children's learn-

Cross-cultural communication is important
for effective parent teacher conferences.

ing, and could enhance their own growth and development as
adults. The NICE program's emphasis was an important one,
which can still be revisited as a model for present involvement
programs.

In those early days, efforts to involve parents included ways
to measure changes in parenting skills, self-esteem, trust, and parent's acceptance of educational values for their children, as well as
many other changes that may have occurred. The research findings often showed that many conditions existed that were caused
by poverty, minority status or personal stress. Parents found the
effort that was involved in participating in parent education programs to be just another impediment or *life stresser*. Parents knew
all too well, then, as they do now, that such programs could not
change the larger or broader conditions of poverty and racism.

Some findings of these earlier programs have significant,
long-range implications for today's educators. The more basic of
these findings are summarized here:

- All parents need to fully understand and appreciate the
  significance of their behavior in shaping children's lives—
  the attention paid to a child's expressions of pleasure, and
  parent's listening skills and demonstrations of interest.
- Parent involvement should be cross-cultural. Involvement
  is certainly not a problem only for the poor or people of
  color. Parenting skills are needed at all levels of society—
  everyone can use more skills in this area.

- Teaching parents by modeling and demonstration works better than talking.
- Parents need to be involved early on in the school life of their children if they are to become active participants in later school activities.
- No one approach matches every parents' ability to participate.
- There must be a *wide variety* of outreach efforts made by school personnel to meet the developmental and educational needs of children and parents.
- Parent involvement efforts may require a lot of patience and the results may not be apparent immediately.
- Regardless of the level of involvement in their children's learning experiences, parents can benefit from knowledge about how children develop emotionally, socially, physically and cognitively, and how this relates to the growing child's personality and ability to succeed in school.
- Parents must feel *positively rewarded* when they are involved in educational progress.
- Observation skills are very important for parents to acquire; that is, becoming informal child-watchers in order to understand the relationship between a child's developmental stage and their ability to learn new skills.
- Parents need to know how to take advantage of many opportunities to learn routines and activities in the home environment that create learning and problem-solving experiences, as well as positive socialization experiences.
- Do not look for cognitive gains alone. Affective goals may be more lasting and more significant. Social development outcomes are also a very important aspect of parent involvement. Zigler (1970) noted that "we must be just as concerned with the development of positive attitudes and motives as the development of the intellect." (p. 408)
- The interactions of teachers with parents were found to strongly affect children's learning. Beller's (1969) research on teacher attitudes showed that when some teachers "exhibited greater respect than other teachers for the child's family," (p. 39) such respect was associated with a child's readiness to gain from educational experiences in the classroom.

There were three historical trends in the 1970s that were largely responsible for the active interest and realization of the importance of involving parents in early education programs. First, there was the undisputed failure of programs planned without parent involvement to sustain the cognitive gains made during the time when children participated in such programs. Second, research into parent-child exchanges revealed differences in the abilities of parents to teach their children effectively (Brophy, 1970; Caldwell, MIDCO, 1972; Kamii and Radin, 1965; Schaefer, 1972; Swan and Stavros, 1973). Since this time, parent involvement in the educational process has become part of the American political system, and as Datta (1973) said, "parent involvement as a philosophy is now seen as consistent with the political system of participatory democracy." (p.68)

The third factor that strengthened the parent-involvement movement was the accumulation of positive evidence about the effectiveness of parent involvement in young children's education as an influence on their children's academic motivation (Beckwith, 1972; Jones 1970; Schaefer, 1973; Swan and Stavros, 1973; among others). Of course, teachers of children of all ages have long perceived the importance of parental involvement in a child's school success. But they also have known that traditionally, the parents they welcome at school functions are not those they probably need to see most!

❖ RESEARCH PERSPECTIVES ON MULTICULTURAL ISSUES

Many of our current problems in schools exist because of teachers' lack of understanding of children's cultural differences, and a consequent variance in learning styles (Claxton, 1990; Milner, 1989). Teachers of all races are frequently unable to adjust to differences in attitude and values with the family structure and child-rearing practices in their own backgrounds (Clark, 1983; Daniel, 1985; Ogbu, 1990). In the United States there is also a long history of viewing African American, Latino and Native American families negatively in the research literature. Their various problems were often viewed as evidence of their racial or ethnic status, rather than as a manifestation of external factors imposed upon their lives by the effects of poverty and racism.

Because there has been recent awareness of the need for research focused on multicultural families, there is now increased knowledge that families are diverse entities, and the stereotypical family studied in the past, which consisted of dad, mom, brother, sister, dog, and cat, is now no longer typical. It has become clear that now we, as a nation, must come to grips with present realities and develop an appreciation for different family systems.

In particular, past research in the United States has frequently characterized African American families as pathological.

Many anthropologists, such as Stack (1974), Hannerz (1969), Ashenbrenner (1975), and Lein (1975) have consistently described African American behaviors they observed as starting to transcend their origins and move toward white norms, or they attributed the differences they observed between blacks and whites as emanating from African origins. Whichever route taken, African American cultures studied by white anthropologists were largely examined in terms of "something or someone else" (Fraser, 1991, p. 407). The researchers seemed to be either fascinated with African Americans as though they were set apart from the predominant Euro-American culture, or ignored what were very apparent differences. But whether they neglected or investigated black culture, anthropologists treated it as set apart from "American" culture (Fraser, 1990).

Most past research has not examined how history has shaped the differences found in families, although there has been an apparent need to "explain" many differences (Belton-Owens, 1993). These deficiencies in research are apparent at all levels of United States society, and the omissions have taken a heavy toll on schools and schooling. The repercussions of these failures are felt by many United States families; today's educational systems badly need the benefit of multicultural research to allow teachers and researchers to gain new insight into the nature and importance of cultural pluralism. At this point in history there is a critical need for much more research to contribute to the body of knowledge concerning people of color's family structure, which may provide teachers with insights about the diverse families of children of differing races and social class. Now, at last, multicultural or cultural difference theory has begun to be recognized as a positive perspective from which to look at non-traditional American family life. Some research (Hilliard, 1989; Irving, Harold, and Rickett, 1984) has shown a lack of sensitivity to cultural differences can cause teachers to misinterpret students of color's behavior and devalue the true academic potential of their pupils.

Baratz and Baratz (1970) believe that failure of psychology and other disciplines to recognize distinct cultural issues of people of color have four main sources: the basic ethnocentrism of psychology, the socio-political myths surrounding our conception of assimilation, ignorance concerning the fundamental notion of culture, and the embarrassment of the African American middle class and the white liberal community in dealing with culturally-rooted behavioral differences. Unfortunately the African American family has been depicted historically as lacking family traditions because it has always been compared to the European nuclear family. Writing about this misplaced emphasis Billingsley

(1968) stated that no other area of United States life was "more glaringly ignored, more distorted, nor more systematically devalued than black family life" (p. 49). This statement is still true today, and what was devastating for African Americans is also problematic for other people of color in America.

Studies of people of color's family life in the United States have too frequently "blamed the victim" when they identified weaknesses in black families (Daniel, 1985; Gibson, 1972; Hare and Castenell, 1986). Susan Toliver (1982) contends that the most popular variant of blaming the victim has been to talk about the weaknesses in African American, Latino American and other ethnic minority families. Rawick (1972) wrote that in the 1960s cultural deprivation/cultural enrichment theories were used to "prove" racial inferiority. She contended that without understanding the historical development of people of color's societies, cultures, and communities, comprehension of the totality of the development of the United States is impossible. The failure to approach this understanding from a scientific perspective can be attributed in large part to the prevalence of theories of racial inferiority which have existed in United States society since the eighteenth century (Gossett, 1963).

This failure has been partially addressed in recent years with the emergence of a renewed cultural approach to the study of African American family life (Fraser, 1991; Goodwin, 1990; Heath, 1983). This approach recognized African American and other people of color as characterized by cultural values and beliefs that are distinct from European American values and beliefs (Foster, 1983; Meyers, 1982; Nobles, 1978) and acknowledges that all family structures vary widely according to demographic and personal parameters (McAdoo and McAdoo, 1986). (Examples of differences in cultural behaviors can be found in Chapter Three). A culturally based study examines the family when the unit analysis is the extended family structure.

Despite the emergence of some culturally based studies in the 1970s and 1980s, there continues to be a great need to have more reliable information about parents' interactive functions within non-traditional families; particularly the father's role when he is not married to the mother and does not live with his children, but does contribute to their welfare. This and similar cultural information can give us some guidance in solving our present school, home, and community problems. Over time, an increased awareness about non-traditional African American and Biracial families may bring important insights and information to present and future teachers of all races, with the common task of educating children.

Shadow Family Research

A recent research study (Belton-Owens, 1993) challenges current assumptions regarding African American family structure, particularly the research assumptions which too often underlie such studies. Some of these assumptions, when depicting serious problems in African American families, have been that they are fatherless, disorganized, and dysfunctional, and are dominated by females. The term "Shadow Families" was introduced in Belton-Owens' 1993 ethnographic study, to describe families in which the male parent is not openly acknowledged and does not live with the children, but does have an active role in their lives. Little or nothing has been written about these families, although they comprise a significant number of African American families. Instead, they are among those families generally lumped together and labeled "single parent" or "fatherless" homes with all the stigmas our society attaches to them.

In the past, a failure to look realistically at the family functioning and structure of families of color has been one of the significant barriers in creating truly multicultural school programs. Little knowledge of black families has been gained, because it has always been difficult for researchers to positively analyze cultures other than their own. In the United States, our experiences and perceptions have long been dominated by the blinding effects of racial prejudice. Unfortunately, many scholars have not chosen to study or write about aspects of African American family life that were viewed as morally or socially incorrect, as seen from a traditional Eurocentric perspective. Regardless of a reluctance to study them realistically, many non-traditional family patterns do exist and the children of such families are enrolled in school. Therefore, it is imperative that the families of all children be more fully understood by educators with the responsibility for educating children.

Because educators of all races often lack knowledge of other cultures' unique values and customs, the behavior of students of different cultures may be unintelligible to their teachers, many of whom have been less than successful in planning and conducting instruction based on differing learning styles (Clark, 1983; Edelman, 1989; Hale, 1986; Heath, 1983; Hilliard, 1989). There continues to be very limited recognition that since our beginnings, we in the United States have been continuously forming multicultural customs related to family life that are not clearly understood, articulated, or interpreted by black or white researchers.

When the research on Shadow Families began in 1992, a review of past studies of family structure, race, and culture showed that this phenomenon was part of what is a hidden multicultural society seldom described and usually denied. In fact, Shadow Families have been growing since the days of slavery. They were formed when a relationship existed between couples of different races—often with the father being white. During slavery, white men fathering children in a second family (with black mothers) was not unusual. Thus began in the United States a tradition which continues into present time. When fathering children in a second family was done by white men it was considered a privilege of race/class; however, when this was done by black men, it was considered pathological.

Belton-Owens' study of Shadow Families was conducted in two rural towns in the Southeast called Blackbanks (pseudonym). It revealed much that contradicts traditional assumptions. The finding of the study indicated that black families were very different from the way they have been described in the literature and the media. Belton-Owens reported that many of the negative aspects attributed to black family life were untrue in Blackbanks. Most of the families studied were not fatherless, matrifocal, unstable, and disorganized, as they are often described. In Blackbanks, families were discovered to have an organized, active lifelong familial network. Their family functions were just different, not dysfunctional. There existed in the Blackbanks community a kind of extended family network within which both families and community placed great value on education and took pride in children's school achievements. (Many of these children are taught in current public school systems that their family structure is abnormal, dysfunctional, and aberrant.) Table 6-1 shows the values of the families studied toward children and their education. The data showed definite patterns of child-centered behavior (which in this study was called kindercentric). These behaviors, shown in Table 6-1, were tabulated according to observations in Phase I, II and III of the Shadow Family study. In the rural southern community where the research was conducted, many adults are observably preoccupied with the lives of children; their own and those of their friends, neighbors and kin. The concern for children's education dominated conversations in Blackbanks.

The Shadow Family study presents a convincing view of how difficult it is for many black and white researchers to positively analyze another culture if their personal experiences with that culture have been negative. Now, with many more students of color in the United States schools, it is essential for teachers to recognize and understand the cultural backgrounds of children, and to be able to recognize the effects of past, misguided racial

TABLE 6-1. Frequency of Kindercentric Comments Among Shadow
Families in Blackbanks

Phase I

Categories	Frequency of Observations Over Four Months				Totals	%
Concern for Education	4	3	2	5	14	12.7
Protectiveness	2	3	3	4	12	10.9
Financial Welfare	5	3	4	6	18	16.4
Male Parent Involvement	7	5	4	10	26	23.6
Paternal Family Involvement	4	6	4	5	19	17.2
Pride in Children	4	3	4	5	16	14.5
Other	2	0	1	2	5	4.5
Total	28	23	22	37	110	99.8

Phase II and III

Categories	Frequency of Observations Over Four Months						Totals	%
Concern for Education	4	3	3	4	4	2	20	12
Protective	5	4	6	4	3	4	26	15
Financial Welfare	4	3	3	4	5	3	22	13
Male Parent Involvement	7	8	6	6	7	5	39	23
Paternal Family Involvement	4	3	4	5	3	4	23	14
Pride in Children	4	3	4	3	4	3	21	12
Other	2	4	3	3	4	3	19	11
Total							170	100

attitudes in present school practices. It takes a great deal of cross-cultural experience, or living in an environment different from one's own, to learn about another culture. One must learn another's culture from the inside out—that is, from another cultural perspective (Spradly, 1979).

In summary, the research on Shadow Families provides greater knowledge of family life in our multicultural society, which could possibly be of value in bringing recognition to the many cultural differences children bring to school. The outcome of the research indicates that we in the United States have long been forming diverse customs which have gone unrecognized. It is hoped that increased awareness of the strengths of nontraditional families of color and biracial families may bring important insights and information, and can underline the importance of improving school programs for young children by creating truly multicultural classrooms where all children may learn more effectively.

Implications for Educators

Many, if not most of the issues addressed in research about the life and schooling of African Americans also have significance when analyzing the importance of parent involvement of all ethnic groups. One clear area of similarity across ethnic boundaries concerns the language of development of children. For example, everybody speaks a dialect, which is of course a dialect of their native language (Heath, 1983). As dialects are not related to intellectual development, schools are remiss if they fail to recognize the importance of teachers demonstrating sound attitudes towards a child's dialect.

Teachers can benefit from knowledge of such factors as the "style shifting" in Black English, and of the rhetorical devices that add richness to BE, such as "signifying", "rapping", "woofing", and the "dozens". Educators need to be aware that in all languages there are different ways of storytelling, as well as different ways of questioning and verbal and non-verbal communicating (Heath, 1983).

Parents who have difficulty speaking English are often unaware of educational services that could help their children in school (Huang and Oei, 1996). Consequently, many students who need academic help are not receiving it. For example, many teachers who tend to view Asian Americans as high achievers may not notice when these students are struggling in school. Furthermore, if their parents are not fluent in English and teachers are not sensitive to the language needs of bilingual children, the students needs will not be met (Huang and Oei, 1996).

Teachers need to know more about the history of all children's family life in order to more fully understand the background for many of the problems people of color have always faced. As noted in previous chapters, many perspectives of United States history need to be told when educational programs and curricula are designed for children. Among other aspects of history, all children need to know the stories of slavery, and the extent and pervasiveness of the denial of educational opportunities for African Americans, Native Americans, and other ethnic people of color in this country. For example, many of us do not realize most African Americans received little or no secondary education until after World War II, or that historically they paid taxes to support public schools, but had to build and support schools themselves if their children were to be educated. We badly need to have knowledge of such historic injustices as the effects of sharecropping and of mass rural-to-urban migration, as well as unbiased portrayals of the economic and occupational hardships of men of color have suffered. And to help teachers in their efforts, there must be readily accessible resources to assist them in planning applicable, inclusive, curriculum approaches—including films, books, consultants, and community involvement. In the past, many African American teachers have stood alone in now-integrated schools trying to forge out culturally inclusive programs in relative isolation, battling to make small gains when monumental change was required. Educational materials that are truthful and realistic will create a wide range of cross-cultural curricula to enrich the lives of all children, regardless of their ethnicity.

❖ MULTICULTURALISM AND FAMILIES

In a multicultural and democratic society, extensive parent participation is essential, for today there remains a crucial need in our schools to link the homes and communities of children to their learning environment. The very real challenge of parent involvement in school programs is to overcome professional, political, and institutional prejudices and insensitivities, and bring positive changes to the culture of schools. This is difficult to achieve, for both historical and contemporary conditions have conspired to create great barriers between many homes and schools. Although in today's world parents provide a broad spectrum of services in schools—often sharing their cultural background, raising money, tutoring, serving on boards, and providing input about schooling issues—there is still limited knowledge of how multicultural issues impact on parent involvement in school programs.

Differences of all kinds—race, religion, economics, and many forms of social behavior—may be barriers between home and school. Because there is such a wide variation within traditional ethnic groups in the United States, it is a formidable task for teachers to understand cross-cultural differences, much less to ameliorate the effects of such differences on children's ability to learn in schools. For example, there are approximately 500 American Indian groups, with variance in their culture, languages, communication and organizational styles, and family structures (Little Soldier, 1992). Widespread variance also exists within Latino, Vietnamese and Cambodian families and numerous other ethnic groups (Holloway, 1992).

We also find many differences within these groups, based on the attitudes and behaviors of different families, such as:

- different levels of acculturation (that is, the extent to which individuals from one cultural background adapt to life in another cultural environment)

- a family's prior history with discrimination

- the degree to which extended family members play a role in family life

- the particular disciplinary styles found in the family

- variance in the interactive "mix" of linguistic factors that influence the communication process families employ

The last point was emphasized by Salend and Taylor (1993) when they stressed the importance of educators realistically interpreting both the verbal and non-verbal behaviors of parents within their social and cultural context. (This would seem to be a polite way of saying that what may seem less than agreeable to middle-class teachers of all races may be normal for individuals from other social classes or ethnic groups.)

This is also referred to as cultural sensitivity, which is an "awareness, appreciation, and understanding of the unique cultures of families" (LaPoint, Boutte, Swick and Brown, 1993). Educational programs which apply cultural sensitivity in their various activities use a "bicultural" approach, which means helping families keep and appreciate their own values while adopting new ideas from the mainstream of American cultures. Bicultural programs are planned to give credence to the significance of family history and language, for in the past, many culturally and linguistically diverse families have been discriminated against (Japanese Americans, Puerto Ricans, Italian Americans, Mexican Americans, Chinese Americans) (Ramirez, 1989; Taylor-Gibbs, and Huang-Nakme, 1989). Additionally, many poor and rural families are denigrated by schools. Table 6-2 presents sample bicultural activities that schools can use to demonstrate both appreciation for and extension of students' culture.

In some instances, culturally sensitive interpreters and cultural informants can help bridge the communication gap between home and school (Salend and Taylor, 1993). These issues become more and more imperative to address as the numbers of school-age children of color and native speakers of non-English continue to grow in the United States. Great care needs to be

---

TABLE 6-2. Sample Bicultural Activities

---

1. *Field Trips*—Visit museums, special exhibits or festivals that feature both ethnic cultures and mainstream groups (e.g., Mainstream: Dinosaur exhibit; Cultural: Greek Festival).

---

2. *Literature*—Include a balance of mainstream books and books about different cultural groups (see previous chapters for additional discussion). Books written in mainstream language and dialects should be part of the collection.

---

3. *Resource Speakers*—Invite parents/community members from both mainstream and nonmainstream culture. Seek a balance and try to show people of color in many different professions (e.g., blue-collar; white-collar).

---

taken not to label the values and behaviors of the children from these families as "deviant, defiant or dysfunctional" (p. 9).

Swick, Boutte, and Van Scoy (1994) stress the need for initiating multicultural learning in the early years by creating new approaches to parent involvement. The authors introduce a framework for "initiating multicultural learning in early childhood that includes a rationale, opportunities for learning, issues, strategies and resources," all of which are related to ways in which families can foster more positive multicultural learning in young children and in themselves. In the arena of cross-cultural experiences, children see more of the universe through the worldwide window of television than they find in school classrooms. An enriched school-family curriculum can improve the classroom environment and bring a view of the larger world into the school.

Children's involvement at an early age with other cultures can also help them learn the "rules" of other groups; ways of dressing, styles of interacting, taboo words or actions, and the deeper, embedded meaning of much behavior (Delpit, 1988). As noted in Chapter Two, Delpit believes there is a "culture of power" that is enacted in traditional school classrooms. She asserts that many parents of color transmit another culture that children must learn at home in order to survive in their communities. Delpit also suggests educators need to learn to listen to the voices of oppressed groups in terms of what is the most effective way to teach children of color. Teachers and administrators must learn to understand parents' unspoken messages as well as spoken ones. Table 3-2 in Chapter Three should be helpful. However, we reiterate a major point that has been emphasized throughout this book—cultural norms are only one piece of information that educators can use to inform them about children and families. Because of the tremendous amount of variation within groups, other information should be regarded as well.

Essentially, adoption of multicultural approaches in schools involves expansion of traditional parent roles, beyond that of spectator, room parent, and resource person to include roles as policy makers and decision-makers and guides to teachers. To achieve optimum multiculturalism, schools must demonstrate genuine acceptance of parents, and plan activities and experiences that permit a partnership between parents and schools. To achieve this goal, there is a critical need to provide parents a place within the school where they can meet, share information, work and relax (Jones, 1970).

What is probably more essential in achieving multiculturalism involving families is to introduce the ideas about the importance of such involvement in teacher education programs. This training should include:

1. knowledge of the special problems parents face, and how to deal with them
2. education about how to prepare programs of cooperative education that de-emphasize competitiveness
3. ways to teach knowledge of multicultural options across the curriculum
4. ways to foster teaching strategies that build on bicultural foundations
5. training in how to achieve awareness of the importance of enculturation (enculturation focuses upon "the things that families do to enable children to know and understand society's shared ideas about values, attitudes, beliefs, and behaviors") (Phillips, 1992).

The college curriculum needs to prepare teachers to plan programs that permit children to be active constructors of their own knowledge. College students should also become familiar with developmentally appropriate school practices and cultural values (Bredekamp, 1987). Prospective teachers must understand and accept that schools serve a growing number of students from diverse cultural and linguistic backgrounds who may not respond to traditional instructional approaches. Future teachers can learn how to find their own alternative ways of showing students how to develop (both for poor and minority students) essential academic skills *and* how to help them acquire creative and critical thinking skills.

❖ SUMMARY: KNOWLEDGE TEACHERS NEED TO IMPLEMENT MULTICULTURAL PARENT INVOLVEMENT

Throughout this book, the roles of families and parents have been discussed. Developing effective partnerships between parents, families, and school requires that schools be familiar with the cultures of the children and their families. This is an enormous, but necessary, task if educators are to do an effective job of working with families from all walks of life. When developing a culturally inclusive classroom, some of the following questions should be addressed.

1. What subtle, as well as obvious, cultural and familial differences affect behavior of children of color in schools?
2. What are the levels of differences in childrearing patterns in nontraditional families (e.g. mother's and father's roles; discipline, communication)?
3. In what specific ways can knowledge and understanding of cultural diversity affect school programming (for example, the inclusion of more music and bodily-kinesthetic activities for children who come from families where these activities are valued)?
4. How can application of culturally inclusive school programs bring greater incentives to learn into the classroom? When children are valued for their diversity, can this genuinely affect their academic progress? Are they then more motivated to learn?
5. Can teachers' knowledge of language diversity change their attitudes towards students' cognitive ability? By what names do children of color prefer to be addressed? What are some of the colloquial expressions used in the child's home and community?
6. Can school personnel and significant adults have a role in socializing children if a need exists to provide help for children when biological parents fail to provide an adequate learning environment?
7. Do we fully understand the kinds of language adjustment many children of color need to make to succeed in schools?
8. In what ways can knowledge of the patterns and functions of families of color build bridges between children's natural learning styles and the very different styles traditionally introduced in schools?
9. How can we design better ways to realistically involve all parents in our childhood programs in a relevant way, regardless of the parent's social class, ethnicity, gender or religion?

10. Can we genuinely acknowledge that current standardized measures of children's ability measure only *very limited* aspects of the children's ability, skills, talents and interests?

11. Will teachers have the resources and assistance they must have to give individual learners appropriate instruction? Can teachers understand the need for ways to empower young learners and bring cooperative and constructive philosophies of education into their lives?

The cultural issues raised in this chapter are relevant to all levels of schooling. By addressing these and other questions, educators can begin to build an ecologically-balanced program which bridges the school and home culture of their students.

❖ RECOMMENDED ACTIVITIES

1. *Journal entry*—How did your family influence your views about people from different ethnicities, socioeconomic statuses, religions, sexual preferences, physical or learning abilities, and so forth? What biases will you have to overcome when working with families who are different from your family? How will your family values affect the way you interact with parents from different walks of life? Can you learn to respect families whose values are diametrically opposed to yours? How can you find common ground with such families in order to be successful educating their children. How can you convey to parents the long-term effects of schooling (especially for parents who may not be readily aware of this)?

2. NOTE: *This activity requires an extraordinary amount of sensitivity and respect for families who differ from the mainstream. Readers who have difficulties accepting this lifestyle should not interview the families.*

Try to locate a "shadow family." Interview the mother (and father if possible) to find out what they think of their child's school. Ask if they are involved in the school. If they are, ask why? If not, find out why also. How can schools involve these parents more? When interviewing the family, be sensitive to cultural issues discussed throughout this book (especially in Chapter Three). *Do not ask questions that are offensive or imply disrespect for the family's lifestyle* (e.g., "Don't you think that a child needs to grow up with two married parents? How can you say you support the child when you do not work? What do you think of being a "shadow family"? (NOTE: Avoid psychological jargon). You should approach the situation with the attitude that you want to learn more about various types of families to increase your effectiveness as an educator.

3. Schools must learn to be bidirectional in their interactions with parents. This means not only telling parents what the school needs, but soliciting information from the parents as well. Try to interview parents from different socioeconomic status levels or ethnicities. Find out what they like and dislike about their children's school. How can you use this information as an educator?

4. Interview a teacher or administrator at school to determine the type of parent involvement at the school. List all parent activities that the school offers (e.g., PTA, open houses, "fun day," performances, class volunteers, home visits). In small groups, decide which activities require little or no authentic parent involvement. That is, which activities simply require parents to physically attend versus which ones ask parents to provide input. Does the school seek and respect parent involvement? Did the school staff make comments about the nature of the parents and why they do or do not participate? For example, do school officials make comments about parents being on drugs and not being interested in their children's education, or do they make comments about parents being from upper or middle income homes being very involved? How can such comments and attitudes affect the school's interactions with the parents and children? Can these attitudes become self-fulfilling prophecies for the families?

5. Often as educators, we tend to view poor and/or non-white children from a middle-class perspective. Many teachers do not live in the same neighborhood as their students and have never visited the students' neighborhoods. Without intending to, we may view these children from a "deficit" model. That is, we may focus on what they don't have or know rather than on what they do have or know. In an effort to see things through their lens, walk or ride slowly through their neighborhood. Talk to some of the people that you see (if it is safe to do so). You may want to do this in groups of twos or threes. Try to view things from the children's perspective. Instead of seeing a house that needs repair, realize that this may be the home of one of your children's relatives or friends. In other words, the child may have fond memories of a house that looks poor to you. Think of ways that you can use this experience to understand your students better.

6. If you are unable to do activity #5, you may have a discussion with your students about the type of activities that they do

after school. Find out who are some of their favorite people in their neighborhoods. Find out as much as you can about your students' communities and families. How can you use this information to better reach the children and their families?

7. Analyze the two letters in Figures 1 and 2 in terms of their tone, general message, and potential for eliciting parental support. How will each letter affect students' view of school? What subtle messages (expectations) are conveyed in each letter?

Figure 1

Dear parents:

We are having a lot of disciplinary problems with your children. For example, many children are bringing candy and snacks to school and dropping the wrappings on the school yard. This must stop! From this point on, we are not allowing children to bring ANY candy or snacks to school. Effective immediately, if we catch children with snacks, they will be suspended immediately (please refer to school codes of behavior). We will also do random locker searches to ensure that this policy is being followed.

Please sign the form below and have your child return it tomorrow. Thank you.

Sincerely,
School Staff

Figure 2

Dear Parents:

The year is off to a great start. Most of the students seem to be reacclimated to the school routines and rules. However, over the past two weeks, we have noticed an increase in the amount of litter that students are dropping on the campus. Most of the litter seems to be candy wrappers and other snacks. We have held an assembly on the topic and have asked teachers to speak with their classes. We are also considering undertaking a school-wide study of ways we can all help the environment. Yet, the problem has not gotten much better.

Congruent with our motto: "Strong Home/School Partnerships: Let's Work It Out," we are seeking your help resolving this problem. Teachers, students and principals have made a number of suggestions for resolving this problem. Check the ones that you prefer, or write in other suggestions. The teachers and students will tally the answers and we will decide as a school on the best approach to take.

Please talk to your child(ren) about this issue at home. Feel free to talk to your child's teacher as well. Thank you for your support and assistance! Please detach the bottom of the letter and return to school by next week. Thanks.

Sincerely,
School Staff

- -

Name _____

Check the ones you prefer or add alternatives.

____ Assign student, parent, and teacher monitors during lunch and recess to identify people who litter. (Anybody caught littering will have to pick up trash around the school for one week). Parents will be contacted also.

____ Conduct a school-wide study of the environment.

____ Do not allow students to bring snacks to school. Students who break this rule will have to pick up trash around the school for one week. Parents will be consulted.

____ Other suggestions.

❖ REFERENCES

Aschenbrenner, J. 1975. *Lifelines: Black families in Chicago.* New York: Holt, Rinehart, and Winston.

Aston, P. T. 1975. Cross-cultural Piagetian research: An experimental perspective. *Harvard Educational Review* 45(4). 475-506.

Banks, J. A. and C.A.M. Banks. (Eds.) 1993. *Multicultural education: Issues and perspectives.* 2nd ed. Boston: Allyn and Bacon.

Baratz, J. C. and S. S. Baratz. 1970. Early childhood intervention: The social science base of institutional racism. *Harvard Education Review* 40: 29-50.

Becher, R. M. 1986. Parent involvement: A review of research and principles of successful practice. In *Current topics in early childhood education* Vol. VII, edited by L. G. Katz. Norwood, NJ: Ablex Publishing Corp.

Beckwith, L. 1972. Relationships between infants' social behavior and their mothers' behavior. *Child Development* 43: 392-411.

Beller, E. K. 1969. The evaluation of effects of early intervention on intellectual and social development of lower-class, disadvantaged children. In *Critical Issues in Research Related to Disadvantaged Children,* edited by E. Grotherg. Princeton, N. J.: Educational Testing Service.

Belton-Owens, J. 1993. *Blackbanks: An ethnographic study of child-centered (kindercentric) attitudes of fathers and community members in southern rural black shadow families.* Ph. D., University of South Carolina.

Berry, M. F. and Blassingame. 1982. *Long memory: The Black experience in America.* New York: Oxford University Press.

Beuf, A. H. *Red children in white America.* Philadelphia: University of Pennsylvania Press.

Billingsley, A. 1986. *Black Families in white America.* Englewood Cliffs, NJ: Prentice-Hall.

Boutte, G. S., D. L. Keepler, V. S. Tyler, and B. Z. Terry. 1992. Effective techniques for involving "difficult" parents. *Young children* 47(3): 19-22.

Boyle-Boise, L. and C. Grant. 1992. Multicultural teacher education: A proposal for change. In *Students at risk in at-risk schools: Improving environments for learning,* edited by H. C. Waxman, J. Walker de Felix, J. E. Anderson, and H. Prentice Baptiste. Newbury Park, CA: Corum Press.

Bredekamp, S., ed. 1987. *Developmentally appropriate practice in early childhood programs serving children from birth through age eight.* Washington, D. C.: National Association for the Education of Young Children.

Brim, O. G. 1965. *Education for child rearing.* New York: Free Press.

Bronfenbrenner, U. 1974. *Is early intervention effective? A report on longitudinal evaluations of preschool programs.* Washington, D. C.: Office of Child Development, United States Department of Health Education and Welfare.

Brophy, J. E. 1971. Mothers as teachers of their own preschool children: The influence of socioeconomic status and team structure on teaching specificity. *Child Development* 41: 79-94

Caldwell, B. M. 1967. What is the optimal learning environment for the young child? *American Journal of Orthopsychiatry* 37(1), 8-21

Clark, R. M. 1993. Family life and school achievement: *Why poor Black children succeed or fail*. Chicago: University of Chicago Press.

Claxton, C. S. 1990. Learning styles, minority students, and effective education. *Journal of Developmental Education* 14(1): 4-8.

Comer, J. and M. Haynes. 1991. Parent involvement in school: An ecological approach. *Elementary School Journal* 91: 271-278.

Comer, J. P. 1986. Parent participation in the schools. *Phi Delta Kappan* 65(6) 442-446

Cunningham, C. E. and D. K. Osborne. 1979. A historical examination of Blacks in early childhood education. *Young Children* 34(3): 20-29.

Daniel, J. H. 1985. *Cultural and ethnic issues: The Black Family*. In *Unhappy families*, edited by E. H. Newburger and R. Bourne. Littleton, MA: PSG Publishers.

Datta, L. E. 1973. Parent involvement in early childhood education: A perspective from the United States. Paper presented at the Organization for Economic Cooperation and Development, Centre for Educational Research and Innovation Conference on Early Childhood Education, Paris, France.

Davies, P. 1976. *Schools where parents make a difference*. Boston: Institute for Responsive Education.

de Anda, D. 1984. Bicultural socialization: Factors affecting the minority experience. *Social Work* 29: 101-107.

Delpit, L. D. 1988. The silenced dialogue: Power and pedagogy in educating other people's children. *Harvard Educational Review* 58(3):L 281-298.

Edelman, M. W. 1989. Black children in America. In *The State of black America,* edited by J. Dewart. New York: The National Urban League.

Edwards, C. P., M. E. Logue, S. Loehr, and S. Roth. 1986. The influence of model infant group care interaction at home. *Early Childhood Research Quarterly* 1(4): 317-332.

Foster, H. J. 1983. African patterns in the Afro-American family. *Journal of Black Studies* 14: 201-232.

Fraser, G. 1991. Race, class and differences in Hortense Powermaker's *After Freedom: A cultural study in the deep south. Journal of Anthropological Research* 47: 403-415.

Gibson, G. 1972. Kin family network: Overheralded structure in past conceptualizations of family functioning. *Journal of Marriage and the Family* 34: 13-23.

Goodwin, M. H. 1990. *He-said-she-said: Talk as social organization among black children*. Bloomington: Indiana University Press.

Gordon, I. J. 1971. Early child stimulation through parent education. *Final Report.* Project no. PHS-R-306. Children's Bureau, Social and Rehabilitation Service, United States Department of Health, Education, and Welfare.

Gordon, I. J. and W. Breivogel. 1976. *Building effective home-school relationships.* Boston: Allyn and Bacon.

Gossett, T. 1963. *Race: The history of an idea in America.* Provo: Brigham Young University Press.

Greenberg, P. 1989. Parents as partners in young children's development and education. *Young Children* 44: 61-75.

Grey, S. 1971. *Home visiting programs for parents of young children.* Demonstration and Research Center for Early Education *Papers and reports* 5, no. 4. Nashville, Tenn: George Peabody College for Teachers.

Hale, J. 1988. *Black children: Their roots, culture, and learning styles.* Baltimore: John Hopkins University Press.

Hannerz, U. 1970. *Soulside: Inquiries into ghetto culture and community.* New York: Columbia University Press.

Hare, B. P., and L. A. Castenell. 1986. No place to run, no place to hide: Comparative status and future prospects of Black ways. In *Beginnings: The social and affective development of Black Children,* edited by M. B. Spencer, G. K. Brooks, and W. R. Allen. Hillsdale, NJ: Earlbaum.

Heath, S. B. 1983. *Ways with words.* Cambridge: Cambridge University Press.

Henkin, A. B. and L. T. Nguyen. 1981. *Between two children: The Vietnamese in America.* Saratoga, CA: Century Twenty One Publishing.

Hill, S. and B. J. Barnes. *Young children and their families: Needs of the nineties.* Lexington, MA: D.C. Heath and Co.

Hilliard, A. G. 1989. Teaching and cultural styles in a plurastistic society. *National Education Association* 7(6): 65-69.

Hohmann, M., B. Banet, and D. P. Weikart. 1979. *Young children in action: A manual for preschool educators.* Ypsilanti, MI: High Scope Educational Research Foundation.

Holloway, S. D. and B. Fuller. 1992. The great child-care experiment: What are the lessons for school improvement? *Educational Researcher* 21: 12-19.

Huang, A., and T. Oei. 1996. Behind the myth. *Teaching Tolerance* 5(2): 57.

Irving, J. P., P. Harold, and E. J. Rickett. 1984. Minority curricula or a curriculum of cultural diversity? Differences that make a difference. *American Psychologist* 39: 320-21.

Jones, E. 1970. Involving parents in children's learning. *Childhood Education* 47(3): 126-130.

Jones, P. and S. Jones. 1978. *Parents unite: The complete guide for shaking up your child's school.* New York: Wideview Books.

Kamii, C. and N. Radin. 1965. The childrearing attitudes of disadvantaged Negro mothers and some educational implications. ED002088 (ERIC document Abstract)

Karnes, M. B., A. S. Hodgins, J. A. Teska, and S. A. Kirk. 1969. *Investigations of classroom and at-home interventions. Final Report.* Washington, D. C.: Bureau of Research, Office of Education, United States Department of Health, Education, and Welfare.

Kendall, E. D. 1983. *Diversity in the classroom; A multicultural approach to the education of young children.* New York: Teachers College Press.

Kitano, H. H. L. 1969. *Japanese Americans: The evolution of a subculture.* Englewood Cliffs, NJ: Prentice Hall.

Klein, J. W. 1982. Symposium/CDA: The Child Development Asociate. *Childhood Education* 49(6): 288-291.

LaPoint, S. A., G. S. Boutte, K. J. Swick, and M. H. Brown. 1993. Cultural sensitivity: How important is it for effective home visits? *Day Care and Early Education* 20(4): 10-14.

Lambie, D. Z., J. T. Bond, and D. P. Weikart. 1974. *Home teaching with mothers and infants.* Ypsilanti, Mich.: High Scope Educational Research Foundation.

Lane, M. B., F. F. Elzex, and M. S. Lewis. 1971. *Nurseries in Cross-cultural Education (NICE). Final Report.* San Francisco: San Francisco State College, School of Education.

Lein, L. 1975. Black American migrant children: Their speech at home and school. *Council on Anthropology and Education Quarterly* 6: 1-11.

Levenstein, P. 1970. Cognitive growth in preschoolers through verbal interactions with mothers. *American Journal of Orthopsychiatry* 40: 426-432.

Ligon, E. M., L. W. Barber, and H. J. Williams. 1971. *Let me introduce myself: A guide for parents of infant children.* Schenectady, N. Y.: Union College Research Project.

Lightfoot, S. L. 1978. *Worlds apart: Relationships between families and schools.* New York: Basic Books.

Little Soldier, L. 1992. Working with native American children. *Young Children* 47(6): 15-21.

Low, V. 1982. *The unimpressible race: A century of educational struggle by the Chinese in San Francisco.* San Francisco: East/West Publishing Co.

Lucas, T. R. Henze, and R. Donata. 1990. Promoting the success of Latino language-minority students: An exploratory study of six high schools. *Harvard Educational Review* 60: 315-340.

Lynch, E. W. and R. C. Stein. 1987. Parent participation by ethnicity: A comparision of Hispanic, Black, and Anglo Families. *Exceptional Children* 54: 105-111.

McAdoo, H. P. and J. McAdoo, ed 1986. *Black children: Social, educational and parental environments.* Beverly Hills, Sage.

Midco. 1972. *Perspectives on parent participation in Head Start: An analysis and critique.* Washington, D.C.: Project Head Start, Office of Child Development, U.S. Department of Health Education and Welfare. New-05-72-45.

Milner, D. 1989. *Children and race.* Newbury Park, CA: Sage Publications.

Munroe, R. R., R. L. Munroe, and B. B. Whiting. 1981. *Cross-cultural human development.* New York: Garland Press.

Myers, H. F. 1982. Research on the Afro-American: A critical review. In *The Afro-American Family: Assessment, treatment and research,* edited by B. Bass, G. E. Wyatt and G. Powell. New York: Grune and Tratter.

Neugebauer, B., ed. 1992. *Alike and different: Exploring our humanity with young children.* Washington, D.C.: National Association for the Education of Young Children.

Nimnicht, G. P., E. Brown, B. Addison, and S. Johnson. 1971. *Parent guide: How to play learning games with a preschool child.* Morristown, N. J.: General Learning Corporation.

Nobles, W. 1978. Toward an empirical and theoretical framework for defining Black families. *Journal of Marriage and The Family* 40: 679-688.

Office of Child Development. 1973. *Children Today. Special Issue: Education for Parenthood.* 2(2).

Ogbu, J. 1990. Minority education in comparative perspective. *Journal of Negro Education* 59(1): 45-47.

Phillips, C. 1992. Culture: A process that empowers. *Infant/toddler caregiving: A guide to culturally sensitive care.* Sausalito, CA: Far West Laboratory for Educational Research and Development.

Powell, D. R. 1989. *Families and early childhood programs.* Washington, D. C.: National Association for the Education of Young Children.

Powell, G. J., ed. 1983. *The psychosocial development of minority children.* New York: Brunner/Mazel Publishers.

Ramsey, P. and L. Derman-Sparks. 1992. Multicultural education reaffirmed. *Young Children* 47(2): 10-11.

Ramirez, O. 1989. Mexican American children and adolescents. In *Children of color: Psychological interventions with minority youth,* edited by J. Taylor, H. Gibbs, and L. Huang-Hahme. San Francisco: Jossey-Bass.

Rawick, G. P. 1972. *American slaves: A composite autobiography. Vol. I. From Sundown to Sunset.* Westport, CT: Greenwood Publishing.

Roberts, J. and S. Akinsanya. 1976. *Schooling in a cultural context.* New York: David McKay.

Salend, S. J. and L. Taylor. 1993. Working with families: A cross-cultural perspective. *Remedial and Special Education.* Austin, TX: Pro-Ed.

Schaefer, E. S. 1972. Parents as educators: Evidence from cross-sectional, longitudinal, and intervention research. *Young Children* 27: 227-239.

Schlossman, S. L. 1976. Before Home Start: Notes toward a history of parent education in America, 1897-1929. *Howard Educational Review* 46(3): 436-467.

Shade, B., ed. 1989. *Culture, style, and the educative process.* Springfield, IL: Charles C. Thomas.

Sleeter, C. E. and C. A. Grant. 1988. *Making choices for multicultural education: Five approaches to race, class, and gender.* Englewood Cliff, NJ: Merrill/Prentice Hall.

Slonim, M. 1991. *Children, culture, and ethnicity.* New York: Garland.

Spradley, J. P. 1979. *The ethnographic interview.* Orlando: Holt, Rhinhart, and Winston.

Stack, C. 1974. *All our kin: Strategies for survival in the Black community.* New York: Harper and Row.

Swan, R. W. and H. Stavros. 1973. Child-rearing practices associated with the development of cognitive skills of children in low socioeconomic areas. *Early Child Development and Care* 2: 23-38.

Swap, S. M. 1993. *Developing home-school partnerships: From concepts to practice.* New York: Teachers College Press.

Swick, K. 1987. *Perspectives on understanding and working with families.* Champaign, IL: Stripes.

Swick, K. J., G. Boutte, and I. Van Scoy. 1994. Multicultural learning through family involvement. *Dimensions of Early Childhood* 22(4): 17-21.

Taylor-Gibbs, R. J. and L. Huang-Nakme, eds. 1989. *Children of color: Psychological interventions with minority youth.* San Francisco: Jossey-Bass.

The CDA Program: The Child Development Associate training guide. 1973. Washington, D.C.: Office of Child Development, United States Department of Health, Education and Welfare. Publication no. OCD 73-1065.

Tobin, J. J., D. H. Y. Wu, and D. H. Davidson. 1989. *Preschoolers in three cultures: Japan, China, and the United States.* New Haven: Yale University Press.

Toliver, S. D. 1982. *The Black family in slavery; The foundation of Afro-American culture: Its importance to members of the slave community.* Ann Arbor: University Microfilms International. University of California, Berkeley.

White, B. L. 1980. Primary prevention: Beginning at the beginning. *The Personal and Guidance Journal.*

Whiting, B. B. and C. P. Edwards. 1988. *Children of Different Worlds: The Formation of Social Behavior.* Cambridge, MA: Harvard University Press.

Williams, T. M. 1974. *Infant care: Absracts of the literature (Supplement).* Washington, D.C.: Consortium of Early Childbearing and Child-rearing, Research Utilization and Information Sharing Project.

Winters, W. G. and C. M. Schreft. 1977. *Developing parent-school collaboration: A guide for school personnel.* New Haven: Yale Child Study Center.

Zigler, E. 1970. The environmental mystique: Training the intellect versus development of the child. *Childhood Education* 46(8): 402-412.

The Problems, Prospects and Implications of Standardized Testing in a Multicultural Climate

Test results based on one point in time are insufficient measures of children's development.

INTRODUCTION

Randall and Jabari are two African American brothers who typically score exceptionally high on the annual standardized tests. However, they rarely turn in school assignments and frequently receive D's and F's on their report cards. Because of their extremely high test scores (usually at or above the 95th percentile), they are promoted each year even though they have missed more days from school than they have attended.

Often, schools place more value on test scores than on classroom performance. Students' lives can be transformed as the result of standardized test scores. Students who perform poorly on these measures are normally placed in a remedial curriculum with the potential for impeding their performance on subsequent tests.

The utilization of instruments which purport to measure intelligence and achievement have become part of the social fabric of our society. Standardized test results influence students' access to knowledge and social resources. For example, standardized tests are frequently employed to classify students as "gifted" or "slow learners."

African Americans, Latino/a Americans, Native Americans and women have borne the brunt of the misappropriation of the results of standardized measures. Hilliard notes that "much of this injustice and malpractice grows out of prevailing, long-standing misconceptions about the nature of intelligence and the use and interpretations of measures employed in these classifications of students in schools" (1990, p. 147).

This chapter investigates the problems of standardized testing in a national climate of multiculturalism. Particular attention is given to the evolution of intelligence and achievement tests and the implications of the use of these instruments for students from different socioeconomic backgrounds, ethnicities, and gender groups. The approach employed recognizes that:

1. Awareness on the part of educators, psychologists, social workers, employers, and others about the effect of standardized measures on various groups can lead to the modification of testing practices to better take into account diversity
2. Performance on standard measures is influenced by the students' educational and family environment
3. Knowledge and awareness of issues can, in fact, stimulate the utilization of testing in ways which more equitably influence the distribution of knowledge and social resources.

While we are optimistic that awareness of testing issues can facilitate changes in the way tests are used and interpreted, we are also cognizant that knowledge alone does not produce structural change. Indeed, structural change often necessitates social action (Mullings, 1989). Therefore, we do not believe that changes will take place rapidly.

Consequently, this work hinges on two assumptions. First, although standardized achievement tests are being challenged on social, cultural, and political grounds, they remain the predominant means of assessing student learning (Powell, Zehm, and Garcia, 1996). Standardized testing will prevail as a means by which society classifies and assigns its members with respect to the distribution of knowledge and consequent social resources. Second, standardized testing has operated and will continue to operate as part of a broader educational ideology which legitimizes the institutionalization of racism, classism, and sexism. Thus, testing, like other educational issues discussed throughout this book, cannot be examined in a vacuum, given the complexity of issues surrounding multiculturalism.

❖ HISTORICAL BACKGROUND AND PERSPECTIVE

The problems which confront students of color and women in the educational arena must be viewed in light of the subjugation of these groups in the formative years of the nation. For example, African Americans who lived during the period from 1619 to 1870 were often physically punished by slave masters for being able to read, write, and articulate their opinions. Despite the best efforts of groups such as the Quakers in the northern states to help educate African Americans in the southern states, the slave codes forbade teaching African Americans to read (Bennett, 1975; Quarles, 1976).

The first public school in the British colonies was established as early as 1635 in Boston, Massachusetts. The school's curriculum was adopted from England's educational system where students were taught Latin and Greek for entrance to college. The first African American school was the Snowden School of Alexandria, Virginia founded in 1870 (Kane, 1981).

In 1636, Harvard University became the first college founded in the United States for whites. In 1854, over two hundred years later, Lincoln University, the first predominantely African American college, was founded. Amherst College, founded in 1821 in Amherst, Massachusetts, awarded the first bachelor degree to an African American in 1826. Between 1865 and 1900, only 1,195 African Americans earned bachelor degrees (Kane, 1981). The two-hundred year gap between the secondary and postsecondary educational experiences of blacks and whites, the forgotten factor, may be crucial to the explanation for differences in achievement scores among African Americans, other students of color, and whites. Women were also denied the right to attend school and institutions of higher education.

Politically and economically, most people of color and women (particularly non-Asian and non-white women), have been and continue to be disadvantaged from a practical vantage point. Specifically, African Americans, Latinos and Latinas, Puerto Ricans, and Native Americans are disproportionately concentrated at the lower end of the socioeconomic scale as compared to whites (Mullings, 1989). One reason for these discrepancies is the lack of educational training and opportunities at selective colleges, agencies, and companies (see chapters on higher education and the workplace for further discussion).

As noted in previous chapters, access to some institutions is frequently determined by performance on intelligence or other standardized tests. Thus, the use of achievement tests is a pressing concern for many people of color and females. That these groups have been limited in their educational opportunities, and in the enjoyment of the benefits of United States society, is apparent by their underrepresentation in occupations and professions requiring extended education, especially in science and mathematics.

The reality that historically educational inequities have led to differentiation by class, ethnicity, and gender cannot be overstated (Susser, 1989). Achievement testing, however, is not a causal agent in the education and employment of people of color. Rather, it is part of a societal ideology that attempts to legitimize educational and employment inequalities (Kozol, 1991).

❖ FACTORS INFLUENCING STANDARDIZED TEST OUTCOMES

Psychological research seems to cherish the "African Americans, Native Americans, and Latino/a Americans score lower on standardized tests than whites" theme. By and large, the research in the field fails to acknowledge the affects of historical and contemporary social forces on the test performance. Rose (1990) has astutely observed: "The manner in which given individuals are able to optimize whatever innate potentialities they may possess are dependent, in part at least, upon the opportunities afforded in the social milieu into which they are born and in which they are raised" (p. 92).

However, little consideration has been given to the cultural content of standardized measures on the performance of African Americans, Native Americans, Latino/a Americans, and women. Student performance is largely dependent on linguistic and communicative behavior styles that differ depending on ethnicity, socioeconomic status, and gender. Moreover, culturally biased test items can be particularly problematic. All assessments are inevitably culture-bound since the items used to assess students' knowledge and skills reflect the standards of language and the perspectives of the test writers. Standardized tests typically reflect the vocabulary, topics, and life experiences typical of the mainstream cultures. As a result, the tests do not measure what the students are able to do relative to their own cultures (Powell, Zehm, and Garcia, 1996).

Environment also has a considerable influence on how individuals perform on standardized measures. Consider the following scenario. A family's twins attended the same schools. One twin was enrolled in the regular curriculum and the other twin was enrolled in the college preparatory curriculum. If the twins were given the same achievement test, which would be most likely to score the highest? The twin enrolled in the college preparatory curriculum would likely score better. This scenario suggests that a quality education can have a major influence on achievement. It implies that achievement levels can be directly affected by manipulation of the individual's home and school environment.

Since children of the same ethnic and social class background vary in IQ and test performance, many studies support the conclusion that environmental factors contribute to these differences (Berk, 1994). A stimulating physical environment, encouragement to achieve, and affection are linked to intelligence and test performance, regardless of the child's background (Bradley and Caldwell, 1981; 1982).

❖ TESTING IN REVIEW

The social and educational climate of the late nineteenth and early twentieth centuries led to the rise of the testing movement. One of the most important influences was the beginning of universal public education in Europe and the United States. Once schools opened their doors to children of all social classes, educators sought methods that would identify pupils who could and could not profit from regular classroom instruction. The first intelligence test, created by Alfred Binet and Theodore Simon in 1905, responded to this need (Berk, 1994). It was extremely successful in predicting school performance and became the basis for new intelligence tests. However, Binet was very insistent that his test did not measure intelligence as a fixed entity—a claim that is antithetical to the use of IQ tests today. Nonetheless, Louis Terman, who revised the original IQ test created by Binet, assumed that these tests measured intelligence quantitatively, without any regard for the students' experience, culture, age, or gender. IQ tests were designed to provide a more "scientific" and "efficient" assessment of students' intelligence (Powell, Zehm, and Garcia, 1996).

Since their inception in the late 1890s, standardized tests have affected the lives of all U.S. citizens. Two of the most widely accepted tests of intelligence at the turn of the century were the Stanford-Binet scales and the Yerkes Alpha and Beta tests. These tests were employed extensively by the Army on soldiers during World War I. Psychologists such as Carl C. Brigham and others, who had long maintained the intellectual inferiority of African Americans, analyzed the data gathered by the Army and concluded that whites were intellectually superior not only to blacks but to immigrant groups as well (e.g., Jewish people). The College Board and the Educational Testing Service (ETS) are quick to disown the prejudices of Brigham. Brigham fashioned the Scholastic Achievement Test (SAT) (now named Scholastic Assessment Test) to weed out immigrants who wished to attend Columbia University in the early 1900s. While the ETS maintains that the current SAT is a far cry from the intentionally discriminating, original version of the test, many critics claim that subtle bias endures (Sadker and Sadker, 1994).

The 1983 publication of *A Nation at Risk* spurred a movement of educational reform in the United States. Consequently, standardized testing was implemented at strategic points in kindergarten through twelfth grades and higher education. Examinations were more widely employed for purposes of placement, promotion, admission, and exit in many programs. These examinations had a detrimental effect on students of color. Not only were students of color affected by the new wave of testing, but the numerous professions were also affected.

Hardest hit was the teaching profession, which had been a major route to upward mobility for many people of color. It is crucial that teachers of color be included in the teaching profession if schools are to better reflect the diversity of this country. In addition to serving as positive role models, teachers of color can assist in promoting racial understanding among all students and discouraging cultural misconceptions (Valencia and Aburto, 1991).

A study conducted by the University of North Florida (Smith, 1987) found that a disproportionate number of prospective teachers were being sifted from the teaching profession through admissions testing and/or certification. It was revealed that veteran teachers were increasingly being removed from the field on the basis of test scores. Moreover, the tests were purported to reflect the quality of teaching of individuals going into the profession. Interestingly, however, the following finding from the Florida study suggests that standardized tests may not be accurate indices of quality teaching.

> In the only study of beginning teacher programs conducted to date that reports data by race, black teachers out-performed white teachers on beginning teacher classroom performance

evaluations. Measures of applied knowledge may be more appropriate instruments than pencil-paper tests for selecting qualified minority teachers (Smith, 1987, p. 12).

Notwithstanding the apparent career implications, standardized tests have hindered prospective teachers professionally by holding them up to public ridicule (Hilliard, 1991). Negative interpretations of standardized tests have been particularly detrimental to African American educators.

ETS, the developers of the National Teacher Examination (NTE), has introduced a more sophisticated battery of tests for initial teacher certification. In addition to measuring teachers' mastery of academic skills and knowledge of student needs, the new battery of tests (known as the PRAXIS) includes a performance-based assessment system (Parkay, 1995). The performance portion of the PRAXIS, known as PRAXIS III, is based on the concept of authentic assessment. That is, the PRAXIS III evaluates the performance of beginning teachers according to how effective they are in real classrooms. One of the dimensions that observers of beginning teachers will look for is the teacher's sensitivity to students' cultural differences. States that use the PRAXIS III will likely obtain a better assessment of teachers' competencies.

Many of the standardized tests used in public school settings implicitly make the assumption of conformity to the values, standards, and norms of the majority. Hence, the ethnic and cultural group within which one is socialized can affect performance negatively or positively. Low performance results in placement in remedial and "slow learner" tracks, special education, and low ability reading classes (Oakes, 1985). The cycle of testing and placement serves to cultivate and sustain a society which has become increasingly polarized in both racial and economic terms.

❖ RACE AND SOCIOECONOMIC STATUS

The argument of intellectual inferiority continues to be made with respect to African Americans, Native Americans, and Latino/a Americans. Major institutions of higher learning in the nation have emerged as hotbeds for the controversial debate. Two such examples include the work of Audrey Sheuey (1958) of Columbia University and Arthur Jensen (1969) of Harvard University. Sheuey concluded that the difference between the scores of African Americans and whites was attributable to the innate intellectual inferiority of African Americans. More than a decade later, Jensen asserted that genetic factors largely explain the fifteen-point difference between the scores of blacks and whites on IQ tests (Jensen, 1969). Translated into percentiles, the average white person tests higher than approximately eighty-four percent of the population of African Americans. Inversely, the average African American tests higher than approximately sixteen percent of the population of whites (Herrnstein and Murray, 1994). The average white and African American differ in IQ at every level of socioeconomic status, but they differ more at high levels than at lower levels. In the past few decades, the gap between blacks and whites has narrowed by approximately three points. Herrnstein and Murray attribute these changes to improvements in economic circumstances of blacks, the quality of schools they attend, better public health, and diminishing racism.

While the literature is dominated by black-white differences in IQ, studies of differences between whites and other ethnic groups exist as well. For example, intelligence tests tend to be biased against Latino/a American and Native American children who do not speak English (Herrnstein and Murray, 1994). Standardized achievement tests used with students for whom English is not the first language gives unreliable and invalid results of student learning (Powell, Zehm, and Garcia, 1996). In contrast, East Asians (e.g., Chinese, Japanese), whether in America or in Asia, earn higher scores on intelligence and achievement tests than European Americans (approximately ten points) (Herrnstein and Murray, 1994). Interestingly, the academic community is relatively silent about the superior performance of Asian Americans in comparison to that of whites.

The 1994 publication of *The Bell Curve* is indicative of a resurgence of the national debate about racial and class differences in intelligence. This debate has unfolded in an ideologically laced climate focused on the dismantlement of Affirmative Action, Aid to Families With Dependent Children (AFDC), Medicaid, and other social programs instituted to facilitate the upward mobility of groups historically excluded from the social mainstream. Theories of genetic and cultural inferiority used during slavery to justify and legitimize oppression and economic exploitation persist as we approach the twenty-first century. Attempts to explain the continuation of social deprivation insist on the relative genetic intellectual inferiority of non-whites and women.

Because of the complexity of issues surrounding IQ, neither genetic nor environmental models and arguments have been found to be very helpful in resolving the nature versus nurture issue. Viewing differences in IQ in terms of racial differences treats race as a separate issue and oversimplifies the fact that individuals hold multiple group memberships which include (but are not limited to) race, gender, and Socioeconomic status.

Regardless of the models used to study intelligence, the ultimate goal should be to gain a better understanding of intelligence and its origin and to use these findings in ways that will best help individuals reach their full potential.

However, to argue simply that tests are inappropriate measures of intellect and have low predictive validity for many Native Americans, Latino/a Americans, and African Americans addresses only one dimension of the problem. The consequences of testing also chisel away the success of students of color in the educational arena, including the success of practicing professional educators who are role models of professionalism for all students to emulate. The role of multiculturalism in the arrangement and delivery of education presents both the opportunity and context for raising and addressing these issues.

Standardized tests, including IQ tests, carry tremendous long-term implications for academic, occupational, and social success. Hilliard (1991) lamented that:

> The negative effects of present practice fall heavily upon minority racial or cultural groups and upon poor children in general. These children are found disproportionately in low academic tracks and in special education classes for the mentally or emotionally impaired. The gross injustice here is that the number of children so classified is large. Most of those classified as learning-impaired are fully capable of meeting the regular academic requirements of school. However, many perform at a low level merely because they have not been exposed to high-quality instruction and are not expected to do well (155).

Thus, students often are the victims of a system of testing that is manipulated by administrators, politicians and "concerned citizens" who believe that low national scores are the fault of some individuals or ethnic groups. Blindly ignored is the reality of an educational system cocooned in racism and classism which consequently skews the distribution of educational resources, cultural experiences, and employment possibilities.

In the United States there are only two nationally recognized college entrance examinations: American College Test (ACT) and Scholastic Achievement Test (SAT). The majority of colleges require or recommend that college-bound students take one examination or the other for admissions purposes. Institutions with open admissions policies that do not require admissions test scores recommend that students take these examinations to facilitate advising, diagnosis and placement, and the awarding of scholarships.

Table 7-1 presents first year test scores of college-bound students who took the SAT between 1987 and 1996. The table shows that the test scores of college-bound students of color have increased since 1987 with the exception of Mexican American students who showed a slight decline (minus two points) on the verbal portion. The greatest gains were made by students in the category labeled "other national." As a group, Asian American students made the next largest gains, followed closely by Native Americans and Puerto Ricans. It should be noted, however, that white students and "other national" students are the only groups above the overall means on both the verbal and math parts of the SAT. Not surprisingly, Asian students continue to have the highest means on the math portion for the ten-year period.

Native Americans on the average decreased four points on the verbal test and six points on the mathematics test from 1993 to 1994. Over time, the scores for the group rose eight points to 396 and twenty-one points to 441, respectively. Of all ethnic groups, Mexican Americans made the lowest gain (plus one point) on the verbal section of the test and other Latino/a Americans achieved the lowest gain (plus ten points) on the mathematical section of the test. The average verbal score of all students of color increased by at least one point. Mathematics scores on the average increased by at least ten points. Whites were the only group whose average verbal score dropped (eight points between 1976 and 1994). During the same period, the average mathematics score for whites increased by two points, the lowest increase among racial and ethnic groups. For the years reported, whites had the highest average verbal scores and the second highest average mathematics scores. Asian Americans were the only group whose average mathematics scores were higher than whites.

According to *Education Week* (1994), the College Board published a guide for parents of elementary and middle school students to help them prepare their children for college. The guide, *Planning for Your Child's Future*, emphasizes the importance of course work. The publication urges parents to assist children with selecting classes which will improve writing skills, critical-thinking ability, vocabulary, and will enhance problem-solving and math reasoning skills. The emphasis on course work is not new to parents who understand the importance of a quality education. These individuals typically demand that their children be enrolled in college preparatory curricula. Indeed, students who complete a core curriculum perform better on college entrance examinations than those who complete less than a core curriculum. ACT defines "core or more" as a typical college preparatory

TABLE 7-1. SAT Averages by Ethnicity, 1987–1996 Range =200-800 Points

	1987	1988	1989	1990	1991	1992	1993	1994	1995	1996	CHANGE 1987-1996
TOTAL											
Number of Students	1,080,426	1,134,364,	1,088,223	1,025,523	1,023,685	1,034,131	1,044,465	1,050,366	1,067,993	1,084,725	
SAT V-MEAN	507	505	504	500	499	500	500	499	504	505	-2
SAT M-MEAN	501	501	502	501	500	501	503	504	506	508	+7
NATIVE AMERICAN											
Number of Students	10,107	12,330	18,005	10,466	7,843	7,412	7,488	8,150	8,936	8,737	
SAT V-MEAN	471	471	462	466	470	472	477	473	480	483	+12
SAT M-MEAN	463	466	461	468	468	471	476	470	476	477	+14
ASIAN AMERICAN											
Number of Students	58,216	64,102	71,792	76,703	78,287	78,693	81,097	81,514	84,319		
SAT V-MEAN	479	482	483	483	485	487	489	489	492	496	+17
SAT M-MEAN	541	541	545	548	548	551	553	553	555	558	+17
BLACK											
Number of Students	88,037	97,483	96,615	94,311	100,208	99,126	102,939	102,679	103,872	106,573	
SAT V-MEAN	428	429	428	428	427	428	429	428	432	434	+6
SAT M-MEAN	411	418	421	419	419	419	421	421	422	422	+11
MEXICAN AMERICAN											
Number of Students	20,714	22,722	25,207	26,073	28,602	30,336	32,355	35,397	36,323	36,689	
SAT V-MEAN	457	459	459	457	454	449	451	448	453	455	-2
SAT M-MEAN	455	460	462	460	459	457	458	458	458	459	+4
PUERTO RICAN											
Number of Students	10,304	11,497	11,415	11,400	12,065	12,091	12,645	13,036	13,056	13,103	
SAT V-MEAN	436	431	437	435	436	442	443	444	448	452	+16
SAT M-MEAN	432	434	438	437	439	438	440	442	444	445	+13
LATIN AMERICAN											
Number of Students	18,895	20,213	21,242	23,608	25,584	26,766	28,420	29,395	30,713	32,193	
SAT V-MEAN	464	463	466	459	458	459	460	460	465	465	+1
SAT M-MEAN	462	463	466	464	462	463	463	464	468	486	+4
WHITE											
Number of Students	788,613	813,116	752,257	694,976	687,231	680,806	670,965	682,107	674,343	681,053	
SAT V-MEAN	524	522	523	519	518	519	520	520	525	526	+2
SAT M-MEAN	514	514	515	515	513	515	517	519	521	523	+9
OTHER NATIONAL											
Number of Students	13,102	14,094	13,454	14,632	16,300	17,771	19,614	22,198	25,113	28,099	
SAT V-MEAN	480	485	490	484	486	491	497	500	507	511	+31
SAT M-MEAN	482	487	493	492	492	498	501	504	510	512	+30

Courtesy of College Board, 1996

program. According to the *1994 ACT Assessment Results Summary Report* (ACT, 1994), "core or more" is comprised of the following four components:

1. **English** (four years or more). One year credit each for English 9, English 10, English 11, and English 12.
2. **Mathematics** (three years or more). One year credit each for Algebra I, Algebra II, Geometry. One-half year credit each for Trigonometry, Calculus (not pre-calculus), other mathematics courses beyond Algebra II, Computer Math/Computer Science.
3. **Social Studies** (three years or more). One year credit each for American History, World History, American Government. One-half year credit each for Economics, Geography, Psychology, other History (European States, etc.).
4. **Natural Sciences** (three years or more). One year credit each for General/Physical/Earth Science, Biology, Chemistry, Physics. A "less than core" program refers to any high school program consisting of fewer courses than those included in "core or more." Table 7-2 presents the ACT scores of college-bound students who completed "core or more" or "less than core." Caution should be exercised in interpreting Table 7-2 since ACT tested seniors may not be representative of the total population of graduating seniors. College-bound students who completed a college preparatory core curriculum tended to score higher on the ACT than students who did not complete core course work, regardless of racial or ethnic background. For example, African Americans in 1994 who completed "core or more" had an average ACT score of 18.0 compared to 16.0 for those who completed "less than core." The data used in this illustration and past research show that although academic preparation—the kind of courses students take in high school—is not the only factor involved, it is one of the factors most strongly associated with performance on the ACT assessment.

In order for students of color to perform as well as whites on college entrance examinations they must obtain the same quality of education in the home and school. Coleman (1966) stated that children of color were below white children by the time they entered school, but that the difference grows larger as the children grow older and move through successive grades in school. The reality, however, is that many students of color do not receive the same quality education as whites. The misuse of standardized tests has led to critics' refusal to acknowledge that the educational system is failing students of color.

Table 7-2 Trends in average ACT composite scores across five years by type of High School program and Racial-Ethnic group.

National Reference Group	Core or More		Less Than Core	
	N	Composite	N	Composite
All Graduates				
1990	370379	22.3	394540	19.1
1991	387404	22.1	374976	19.1
1992	419073	22.0	372166	19.1
1993	453064	22.0	374256	19.1
1994	478885	22.0	359974	19.1
Afro-American/Black				
1990	29814	18.2	40127	16.1
1991	32468	18.2	39729	16.1
1992	35166	18.1	39465	16.1
1993	38893	18.1	40620	16.1
1994	41533	18.0	39275	16.0
American Indian/Alaskan Native				
1990	3163	19.9	5208	17.1
1991	3727	19.8	5098	17.2
1992	4026	19.8	5255	17.1
1993	4537	20.0	5390	17.3
1994	4995	20.0	5533	17.3
Caucasian				
1990	290929	22.8	301253	19.7
1991	299557	22.7	282708	19.7
1992	320849	22.6	277995	19.7
1993	342884	22.6	275294	19.8
1994	356512	22.6	260155	19.8
Mexican America/Chicano				
1990	9770	19.9	12349	17.2
1991	11143	19.9	12555	17.2
1992	12787	19.8	13185	17.1
1993	13764	19.8	13753	17.2
1994	15411	19.6	13918	17.1
Asian American/Pacific Islander				
1990	11734	22.8	6714	20.0
1991	13401	22.6	7173	19.8
1992	14945	22.5	7336	19.8
1993	16600	22.5	7649	19.8
1994	17686	22.5	7952	19.9
Puerto Rican/Cuban/Other Hispanic				
1990	5250	20.9	4886	17.6
1991	5991	20.7	5006	17.6
1992	7026	20.7	5608	17.6
1993	7693	20.5	5799	17.6
1994	8685	20.5	5950	17.6

Courtesy of ACT, Iowa City, IA.

In 1990 Jeannie Oakes completed a comprehensive study entitled *Multiplying Inequalities: The Effects of Race, Social Class, and Tracking on Opportunities to Learn Mathematics and Science.* Oakes' findings demonstrate what is occurring in public schools. For example, white students tend to be clustered in courses that are academic in their orientation, while those in which students of color are clustered tend to be non-academic in their focus. While achievement test scores provide a lens for viewing the academic and developmental experiences of African American and non-Asian students of color in the school system, the curriculum should be examined in order to derive a more comprehensive understanding of the problems.

The gap in the scores of students of color and whites will continue until more students of color complete college-preparatory core curricula. Bills (1982) stated that ". . . teachers usually advise their 'better' students to be prepared for college and their 'poorer' students to enter vocations." If large numbers of the "poorer" students are students of color, it follows that it will be almost impossible for them to perform as well as whites on college entrance examinations. An inadequate education influences not only the achievement scores of individuals, it also influences their thinking. Woodson ([1933]; 1990) so aptly observed that, "When you control a man's (sic) thinking, you do not have to worry about his actions" (p. xiii).

❖ GENDER

While there is much discussion surrounding racial differences on tests, substantially less is heard about gender differences. Females are the only group in the United States to begin school testing ahead and exit school behind the norm. The fact that this decline receives so little national attention is a powerful indicator of the persistence and pervasiveness of sexism in schools (Sadker and Sadker, 1994).

The only test where the female decline in test performance has received public attention is the SAT. Required for admission to most colleges and universities, males typically receive scores that are fifty to sixty points higher on the math and verbal portions of the test (Sadker and Sadker, 1994; Beidleman and Cole, 1991; Navarro, 1989). However, male-female test performance differences are not limited to the SAT. For example, performance differences have been found also for the Graduate Record Examination (GRE) subject tests and the Miller's Analogies Test (MAT) (Hirschfeld, Moore and Brown, 1995; House and Keely, 1995). Research has also suggested that being female may be a key factor in the labeling of students as learning disabled (LD) with evidence of a severe disability (Payette and Clarizio, 1994; Leinhardt, Seewald, and Zigmond, 1982).

When females begin school they outperform males on almost every measure. Their test scores start declining around middle school and males' test scores overtake females' at that point. The small lead that males hold in science widens in middle school and is further expanded in high school. Thus, the longer females stay in school, the further they fall behind, especially in mathematics and science (Sadker and Sadker, 1994).

During their junior year in high schools many college-bound students take a scaled-down version of the SAT called the Preliminary Scholastic Assessment Test (PSAT). The PSAT gives students opportunities to win scholarships. The high performance differential between females and males on the PSAT results in two out of three National Merit Scholarship semifinalists being male. The Educational Testing Service (ETS) tackles this disturbing problem by rigging the score to reduce the gender gap (Sadker and Sadker, 1994).

SAT scores send an even more devastating message to non-Asian, minority females who do not perform as well on the SAT as white students. The gap is the largest between Latino American males and Latina American females (an average of sixty-two points). There is a fifty-point difference between the sexes of students whose families are originally from Asia, Mexico, or Puerto Rico; for Native Americans, the gender gap is forty-six points. The gender gap is the narrowest (nineteen points) for African Americans (Sadker and Sadker, 1994). However, regardless of ethnicity, United States females share a common bond—a gender gap in test performance that places them behind males.

One of the problems with standardized admissions tests is their low predictive validity. For example, the SAT overpredicts the college performance of male high school students and underpredicts the performance of high school females. Males answer more questions correctly when the items include male characters; females achieve more on questions with female characters or an equal number of males and females (Sadker and Sadker, 1994). While many questions on the SAT do not include people, those that do are more likely to represent the male world. Sadker and Sadker cited a recent group of reading comprehension questions which mentioned forty-two men, but only three women. They note that "one of these women was anthropologist Margaret Mead, whose work was criticized throughout the passage" (p. 153). Even themes and topics included on the SAT tend to be more male-oriented, e.g., sports, measurement, money, science, dates, and wars, all areas in which males excel. Females, however, surpass males on questions concerning personal relationships, aesthetics, civil rights, women's rights, abstract concepts, and topics traditionally thought to interest women (Sadker and Sadker, 1994).

SAT critics suggest several strategies for making the test more fair to females. First, eliminate or revise items on which females tend to do poorly. Second, change the format of the test. Males tend to do better on multiple choice tests, (Anderson, Benjamin, and Fuss, 1994; Heath, 1989; Ferber, Birnbaum, and Green, 1983; Lumsden and Scott, 1987) while females tend to perform better on essay questions (essay questions are more difficult and time-consuming to grade and rarely found on these exams) (Lumsden and Scott, 1987). Likewise, males do better on the "beat-the-clock," pressure cooker items created by timed tests, while girls perform better when tests are not timed (Sadker and Sadker, 1994).

There are doubts that improved tests will dramatically alter the gender gap since it is likely to be the result of the different educational experiences of males and females. Males still take more high school math and science courses which contribute to their test performance (Navarro, 1989; Loewen, 1988). Additionally, more females than males take college achievement tests, which may mean that more under-prepared females are taking the test and lowering the average for all females.

Females perform better on the ACT than on the SAT (Sadker and Sadker, 1994). On the ACT, females score almost one full point higher than males on the English section. But on the rest of the test, males are ahead, from a small lead in reading, to more than one full point on the math and science sections. Thus, despite the fact that the ACT was designed to mirror school learning, males' composite scores are higher (Sadker and Sadker, 1994).

Even on examinations for graduate school, women score lower than males. For example, on the Graduate Record Examination (GRE), women score lower than men on all three sections: verbal, quantitative, and analytical (Sadker and Sadker, 1994). The Miller Analogies Test (MAT) has also been found to overpredict and underpredict graduate school grade point averages (GPA) of males and females respectively. The result of one study revealed that despite their relative underperformance on the MAT, females tended to earn grades that exceeded those of their male counterparts (House and Keely, 1995).

Standardized tests are crucial in the competitive application for professional schools, including law, medicine, and business. Although these professional examinations differ in content and approach, they share a common bond: women score lower than men on all three of them (Sadker and Sadker, 1994). In the final analysis, gender inequities in school and society reveal a dire need for a multicultural approach to student assessment.

❖ THE USES AND ABUSES OF STANDARDIZED TESTS

Standardized testing has traditionally served both administrative and instructional functions. Administratively, tests are used regularly to determine whether a student is eligible for special services or to place students in ability tracking, remedial programs, gifted programs, or advanced placement programs (Powell, Zehm, and Garcia, 1996). Instructionally, standardized tests are used to evaluate the effectiveness of educational programs.

Theoretically, a test score is simply a number until an interpretation is made (Hanford, 1991). The interpretation of test scores can have devastating effects for many students of color and women. Research in the social and behavioral sciences has been instrumental in the dismantling of the long-standing convention that the white majority is more intellectually capable than Native Americans, Latino/a Americans, and African Americans, and that males are more capable than females. However, despite the refutation of these arguments the same theories and themes continue to be rehashed. The timing with which these themes resurface seems to correlate with the ideological trajectory of politics and policymaking in American society. For example, *The Bell Curve* (Herrnstein, 1994) revisits a number of well-worn issues and theories.

Using a test score as the sole determinant of students' placement is not the best practice. The continued use of standardized tests to identify a disproportionate number of students of color for ability tracking is a *de facto* form of segregation. Schools continue to use test scores to justify the placement of large numbers of people of color in classrooms where they are often provided with a custodial form of instruction for example, doing busywork that requires lower levels of thinking (Powell, Zehm, and Garcia, 1996). In these types of environments, the expectations for achievement tend to be decidedly low. When these children are tested later their test scores tend to be much lower. This is due partially to the low level of instruction that they receive. As noted in Chapter Two, this becomes a test-placement-test cycle (Powell, Zehm, and Garcia, 1996).

The politics of testing remain intense. Although standardized tests are constructed to create a bell curve in which fifty percent of the students score above the national percentile and fifty percent below, most states report the average student scores *above* the national percentile. Because of such practices, the stakes are high for students, teachers, and schools. Success is typically defined in terms of higher test scores; hence, there is much pressure on schools and teachers to increase scores. To avoid the high-stakes consequences, some teachers result to teaching to the test. Some districts place more students in special education in order to exclude them from taking standardized tests (Powell, Zehm, and Garcia, 1996). Typically, these students are low-income, students of color, or ESL students.

While some have argued that more attention needs to be given to understanding environmental differences among groups that may explain their performance on standardized examinations, it is rarely acknowledged that slavery and the vestiges of racism, classism, and sexism continue to pervade the lives of many students. As mentioned in Chapter One, people of color frequently encounter institutional and personal racism on a day-to-day basis, as well as various forms and manifestations of discrimination. Until schools and society begin to address these deeply rooted issues, testing misuses and abuses will continue. Using a multicultural education approach ensures that educators are sensitive to the complexity of the testing problem.

❖ SUMMARY AND IMPLICATIONS

This chapter has examined the problems of standardized testing in a multicultural setting. Special attention was given to the impact of standardized testing on students of color and women. Traditional social values have circumscribed the role of women in much the same way that racism and discrimination have influenced the social position of African Americans and other people of color, consequently affecting the performance of both groups on standardized tests. The permanence of standardized testing in United States society, and its significance as a component of a broader educational ideology were important underlying assumptions of this work.

The results of our investigation indicate that there are some significant problems related to testing in the United States which must be addressed. Chief among these is that the results of standardized tests are frequently used to deny poor students and students of color equal access to educational opportunity by serving as a justification for their lack of educational success (Oakes, 1990). Females are also disadvantaged. At the same time, the test results provide a convenient explanation for teachers who would otherwise be held accountable for the academic and personal growth and development of students (Deyhle, 1986; Mercer, 1989).

The results of standardized testing in recent years indicate some improvement among students of color, suggesting the importance of pursuing academic paths at the high school level consisting of college preparatory courses in cases where ability and interest warrants it. However, elementary students also need to receive challenging course work for satisfactory performance in college preparatory courses when they reach high school. The fact of modest improvement in standardized test scores among non-Asian students of color, however, should not preclude efforts to improve the instruments of assessment and the utilization of their results.

The theory of multiple intelligences (MI Theory) presents one possible alternative to the current approach. This approach views intelligence as a complex set of "intelligences". Gardner and Hatch (1990) have stated that "MI Theory requires a fresh approach to assessment, an approach consistent with the view that there are a number of intelligences that can be developed—and can best be detected—in culturally meaningful activities" (p. 5). The approach is based on the idea that intelligence is too complex to be reflected by a single test score. Reiff (1996) observed that the Western education system overemphasizes the linguistic and logical/mathematical intelligences. In the final analysis, consideration of alternative approaches to viewing and assessing human intelligence may do much to eradicate social inequalities.

It is important also to minimize the negative effects of standardized tests. The following actions may help to attain this end (Powell, Zehm, and Garcia, 1996). First, educators need to learn more about assessing the learning of all students—particularly students of color, low-income students, females, and students for whom English is a second language. Educators must have a more complete understanding of assessment if they are to make informed decisions regarding the learning needs of students.

Second, educators can help their students become more proficient in test-taking skills. Since we live in a "testing" society, students will not be able to go to college, serve in any military branch, or get certain jobs (e.g., postal employment) unless they can pass a test. There is nothing unethical or illegal about teaching test-taking skills. Test taking is a survival skill for students, and educators are remiss if they do not help children become proficient. There are a number of "testwise" programs on the market that can be purchased, or teachers can develop their own.

Third, educators can help parents become more informed about testing issues. As with other educational issues, bridging the bond between the school and the home benefits the students in the long run. Many parents of color, speakers of English as a second language (ESL), or low income parents may not be aware of the biases inherent in standardized tests, or of the consequent placements. When parents and educators work together, the results can be mutually beneficial since parents can help children prepare for tests (Powell, Zehm, and Garcia, 1996).

Fourth, educators need to be aware that some students do well academically, but test poorly because of test biases. The negative effects of testing may be minimized if greater attention is given to matters of validity and reliability with the goal of eliminating test bias against non-traditional groups. Standardized tests are mirrors that reflect the socioeconomic realities of the test-takers' lives and the dimensions of social problems which beg for solutions (Hilliard, 1990). However, for the majority of African Americans, Latino/a, Native Americans, women, and others, standardized tests continue to pose problems that society has chosen to ignore. The activities presented in the remainder of this chapter will help educators become more knowledgeable about testing so that they can take action.

❖ RECOMMENDED ACTIVITIES

1. *Journal entry*—Reflect on your standardized test-taking abilities. How have these abilities (or lack thereof) influenced the level of instruction and placements that you received in school? How do (or will) you view children who obtain extremely high test scores? Very low test scores? Do you think that standardized tests are currently given more weight and credence than they deserve? Why or why not?

2. Research position papers on the use of standardized tests in schools (e.g., the National Association for the Education of Young Children (NAEYC) or the Southern Association for Children Under Six (SACUS). Do you agree or disagree with these positions? Why or why not?

3. Go to the library and research one or both of these topics: "Authentic Assessment" and/or "Portfolio Assessment." Do you agree or disagree with these approaches?

4. Interview an early childhood education teacher and a high school teacher about their views on the value of standardized testing. Compare and contrast their points of views.

5. Contact your State Department of Education and obtain test scores for children in your state. You may opt to contact a

local district instead. (Test scores are public information). What information can be gleaned from the test scores in terms of racial, gender, and SES differences? What implications can be drawn?

6. Brainstorm about what measures would be used to assess students' achievement if standardized achievement tests did not exist. Discuss the feasibility of using alternative methods of assessment.

7. In small groups, discuss the role that tests have played in your life. Are you good at taking standardized tests? Why or why not? Have tests been accurate predictors of your success in school or work? Why or why not? What conclusions can you draw?

8. Which of the following testing issues do you feel most comfortable discussing: race, socioeconomic status, or gender? Why? Discuss testing issues that are common to all three factors.

❖ REFERENCES

American College Testing Program. 1994. *1994 ACT assessment results summary report.* Iowa City, Iowa: ACT.

Anderson, G., H. Benjamin, and M. A. Fuss. 1994. The determinants of success in university introductory economics courses. *Journal of Economic Education* 25: 99-119.

Beidleman, D. C. and C. L. Cole. 1991. Scholastic aptitude test gender gap. *American Secondary Education* 19(2): 2-5.

Bennett, L., Jr. 1975. *Before the Mayflower.* New York: Penguin Books, Inc.

Berk, L. 1994. *Child development.* 3rd ed. Needham Heights, MS: Allyn and Bacon.

Bills, R. E. 1982. *Education for intelligence? Or Failure?* Washington, DC: Acropolis Books.

Bradley, R. H., and B. M. Caldwell. 1981. The HOME Inventory: A validation of the preschool scale for black children. *Child Development* 52: 708-710.

————.1982. The consistency of the home environment and its relation to child development. *International Journal of Behavioral Development* 5: 445-465.

Coleman, J. S. 1966. *Equality of educational opportunity.* Washington,DC: U. S. Office of Education.

Colleges. 1994. *Education Week,* 14(7): page 8.

Deyhle, D. 1986. Success and failure: a micro-ethnographic comparison of Navajo and Anglo student's perceptions of testing. *Curriculum Inquiry* 16(4): 365-389.

Ferber, M. A., B. G. Birnbaum, and C. A. Green. 1983. Gender differences in economic knowledge: A reevaluation of the evidence. *Journal of Economic Education* 20: 24-37.

Gardner, H. and T. Hatch. 1990. Multiple intelligences go to school: Educational implications of the theory of multiple intelligences. *Educational Researcher* 18: 4-10.

Hanford, G. 1991. *Life with the SAT: Assessing our young people in own times.* New York: CEEB.

Heath, J. A. 1989. An econometric model of the role of gender in economic education. *American Economic Review* 79: 226-30.

Herrnstein, R. J. and C. Murra. 1994. *The bell curve: Intelligence and class structure in American life.* New York: The Free Press.

Hilliard, A. G., III. 1990. Misunderstanding and testing intelligence. In *Access to knowledge: An agenda for our nation's schools,* edited by J. I. Goodlad and P. Keating. New York: College Entrance Examination Board.

Hirschfeld, M., R. L. Moore, and E. Brown. 1995. Exploring the gender gap on the GRE subject test in economics. *Journal of Economic Education* 26: 3-15.

House, D. J. and E. Keeley. 1995. Gender bias in prediction of graduate grade performance from Miller Analogies Test scores. *The Journal of Psychology* 129: 353-355.

Jensen, A. R. 1969. How much can we boost I.Q. and scholastic achievement? *Harvard Educational Review* 39: 1-123.

Kane, J. N. 1981. *Famous first facts: A record of first happenings, discoveries, and inventions in American history.* 4th ed. New York: H. W. Wilson Company.

Kozol, J. 1991. *Savage inequalities. Children in America's schools.* New York: Harper.

Leinhard, G., A. Seewald, and N. Zigmond. 1982. Sex and race differences in learning disabilities classrooms. *Journal of Educational Psychology* 74(6) 835-43.

Loewen, J. W. 1988. *Gender bias in SAT items.* Report no. TM 011 635. Washington, DC: Women's Educational Equity Act Program, ERIC ED 294 915.

Lumsden, K. G. and A. Scott. 1987. The economics student reexamined: Male-female differences in comprehension. *American Economic Review* 79: 226-30.

Mercer, J. R. 1989. Alternate paradigms for assessment in a pluralistic society. In *Multicultural education: Issues and perspectives,* edited by J. A. Banks and A. M. Banks. Boston: Allyn and Bacon.

Mullings, L. 1989. Gender and the application of anthropological knowledge to public policy in the United States. In *Gender and anthropology: Critical reviews for research and teaching,* edited by S. Morgen. Washington, DC: American Anthropological Association.

Navarro, C. 1989. *Why do women have lower average SAT-MAT scores that men?* Report No. TM 014 018. San Francisco, CA: American Educational Research Association, ERIC ED 312 277.

Oakes, J. 1985. *Keeping track: How schools structure inequality.* New Haven: Yale University Press.

———.1990. *Multiplying inequalities: The effects of race, social class, and tracking on opportunities to learn mathematics and science.* Santa Monica, CA: The RAND Corporation.

Parkay, F. W. 1995. *Becoming a teacher.* 3rd ed. Needham Heights, MA: Allyn and Bacon.

Payette, K. A. and H. F. Clarizio. 1994. Discrepant team decisions: The effects of race, gender, achievement and IQ on LD eligibility. *Psychology in the Schools* 31: 40-48.

Powell, R. R., S. Zehm, and J. Garcia. 1996. *Field experience: Strategies for exploring diversity in schools.* Englewood Cliffs, NJ: Merrill.

Quarles, B. 1976. *The Negro in the making of America.* New York: Collier Books.

Reiff, J. C. 1996. Bridging home and school through multiple intelligences. *Childhood Education* 72(3): 164-166.

Rose, P. I. 1990. *They and we: racial and ethnic relations in the United States.* 4th ed. New York: McGraw Hill Publishing Company.

Sadker, M. and D. Sadker. 1995. *Failing at fairness: How schools cheat girls.* New York: Touchstone.

Sheuey, A. 1958. *The testing of Negro intelligence.* Lynchburg, Virginia: Randolph-Macon Women's College.

Smith, G. P. 1987. *The effects of competency testing on the supply of minority teachers.* A report prepared for the National Education Association and the Council of Chiefs State School Offices. ED 302 521. Washington, DC.: National Education Association.

Susser, I. 1989. Gender in the anthropology of the United States. In *Gender and anthropology: Critical reviews for research and teaching*, edited by S. Morgen. Washington, DC: American Anthropological Association. 343-359.

Valencia, R. R. and S. Aburto. 1991. Research directions and practical strategies and teacher testing and assessment: Implications for improving Latino access to testing. In *Assessment and access: Hispanics in higher education*, edited by G. D. Keller, J. R. Dennen, and R. J. Magallan. Albany, NY: SUNY Press.

Woodson, C. G. [1933] 1990. *The miseducation of the Negro.* Trenton, NJ: African World Press, Inc.

Executive Suites: Off Limits to People of Color and Women (Diversity and the Workplace)

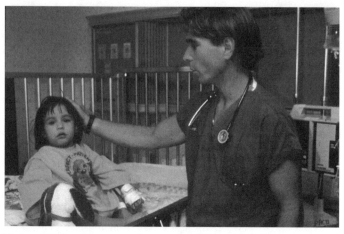

Women and other groups are underrepresented in some professions.

INTRODUCTION

Tonya, a young interracial (black-white) woman is beginning her career as a middle school teacher. Since Tonya is Jewish, she celebrates a number of religious holidays (e.g., Yom Kippur, Rosh Hashanah, Passover, and the Feast of Eleven Breads). When Tonya told her principal that she would not be working on these days, the principal objected. Tonya explained that because of her religion, there was no way that she could work. Additionally, she pointed out that legally, she had the right to take leave on her religious holiday. She emphasized that these are not days of leisure for her; rather, she spends most of the time fasting, praying, and the like. However, the principal felt that Tonya was not dedicated to her job since she was unwilling to work on these days.

Dilemmas like this one often arise in the workplace. This chapter will discuss how religion, ethnicity, gender, ability levels, and socioeconomic status affect one's work experiences. In the scenario, Tonya's holidays conflicted with standard Christian holidays; therefore, her loyalty to her job was questioned. Should Tonya not celebrate the holidays in order to avoid reprisal from her principal? How will her decision to take leave affect the principal's subsequent treatment and opinion of Tonya? Should workplaces allow for such leave? There are no easy solutions to such problems, as this chapter will reveal.

Like testing, the workplace is an example of a setting that educators do not have a *direct* influence on. Yet, the relationship between education and future employment opportunities is clear. Education has become an important requisite for future success for most people. Since education affects future income, occupations, tastes, interests, grammar, and accents, it is a powerful divider and classifier (Herrnstein and Murray, 1994).

More and more people of color are excluded from reaching the "American dream" of obtaining viable employment (Berns, 1993). An assumption of this chapter is that both blue and white collar positions are respectable. Yet, it is important that students have opportunities to *choose* the nature of their work rather than have it chosen for them by educational limitations. Therefore, they need to be exposed to skills, competencies, and the like that will prepare them for future employment. Additionally, they must be familiarized with both white and blue collar jobs and made aware that they are attainable.

While reading this chapter, educators must constantly examine the role that they play in contributing to students' future employment choices (or nonemployment or illegal employment). Educators must be knowledgeable of the role that school experiences play in later employment opportunities. Parents' workplaces are exosystems that affect children's lives. That is, the nature of parents'/guardians' jobs will inevitably affect children's motivation to learn and the value they place on education. Depending on the demographics of the student population at a particular school, parents may be more concerned with merely meeting *basic* needs rather than educating their children. Information presented in this chapter should help educators become cognizant of the type of issues that need to be addressed during the school years in order to give all students the opportunity to be gainfully employed later in life. Specifically, this chapter will highlight professions which are in dire need of particular genders, ethnicities, people from varied socioeconomic backgrounds, and the like. This information should be used to inform curricular decisions and instructional styles.

❖ LABOR MARKET FORECAST FOR PEOPLE OF COLOR

For the past decade, many labor market analysts have projected optimistic employment trends for people of color because of the changing demography. Accordingly, people of color will comprise a large share of the labor pool in the twenty-first century. As a result,

> If companies are to meet their labor needs, they will have to broaden the ethnic and gender makeup of this force. In other words, affirmative action will no longer be a matter of social responsibility, but of economic necessity. (Opportunity 2000, US Labor Department, 1988, as cited in Tidwell, 1995, p. 134).

According to the U. S. Bureau of Labor Statistics, employment in major occupations should grow by twenty percent between 1990 and 2005 (see Table 8-1). The challenge for minorities is to be academically prepared for this window of opportunity since this new labor force must be intellectually and technologically advanced for global competitiveness.

TABLE 8-1. **Distribution of Employment by Major Occupational Groups**

Occupation	1990	2005	Percent Change 1975-1990	Percent Change 1990-2005
Total	100%	100%	37.4%	20.1%
Executive, administrative, and managerial	10.2	10.8	83.1	27.4
Professional	12.9	14.2	59.9	32.3
Technical and support	3.4	3.9	75.7	36.9
Marketing and sales	11.5	11.9	55.1	24.1
Administrative support, including clerical	17.9	16.9	33.9	13.1
Service	15.7	16.9	36.1	29.2
Agriculture, forestry and fishing	2.9	2.5	−9.8	4.5
Precision production, craft, and repair	11.5	10.8	28.9	12.6
Operators, fabricators, and laborers	14.1	12.2	6.7	4.2

Courtesy of: *The State of Black America*, 1995. New York: National Urban League 1995, p. 142.

The optimism surrounding the projected labor market trends for people of color must be approached with a certain amount of caution due to unforeseeable economic and technological advances that could drastically alter labor demands (see Table 8-2).

People of color are caught in a trend that is both "promising and perilous" (Tidwell, 1995, p. 133). Promising, in that the demographics of the labor force are expanding to accommodate shifts in technology and the level of education required for certain occupational professions. People of color are increasingly part of a growing labor pool, and employers are selecting from

TABLE 8-2. Twenty Fastest-Growing Occupations (Numbers in Thousands)

Occupation	Projected Employment Growth 1990-2005	
	Number	**Percent**
Home health aides	263	91.7
Paralegals	77	85.7
Systems analysts and Computer scientists	366	78.9
Personal and home care aides	79	76.7
Physical therapists	67	76.0
Medical assistants	122	73.9
Operations research analysts	42	73.2
Human services workers	103	71.2
Radiologic technologists and technicians	103	69.5
Medical secretaries	158	68.3
Physical and corrective therapy assistants & aides	29	64.0
Psychologists	79	63.6
Travel agents	82	62.3
Correction officers	142	61.4
Data processing equipment repairers	50	60.0
Flight attendants	59	58.5
Computer programmers	317	56.1
Occupational therapists	20	55.2
Surgical technologists	21	55.2
Medical records technicians	28	54.3

Courtesy of: *The State of Black America*, 1995. New York: National Urban League. p. 143.

this market of available workers. Perilous, in that the ticket to success in this contemporary labor market is built upon a foundation of assimilation into European culture, ideals, and values. To make this sword double-edged, "much of White America has come to equate Affirmative Action and civil rights with preferential treatment for African Americans, and has come to believe that 'unqualified minorities' are taking jobs, promotions, or seats in college classrooms from 'qualified white males'" (Watson, 1995, p. 199). As with schools, diversity in the workplace in America is largely unappreciated.

❖ THE IMPACT OF AFFIRMATIVE ACTION

Affirmative Action has been blamed for nearly every shortfall in income and inequality in the United States. Labor Secretary Robert Reich, addressing the issue of wage stagnation, says it is forming a "politics of stagnation," with disgruntled workers supporting curbs on immigration, Affirmative Action, welfare, and foreign trade (*US News and World Report*, 1995). Wage stagnation, along with massive layoffs and uncertainties in the economy, has fueled a backlash from the economic "victims" against anything and anybody perceived to be responsible for their condition. Many politicians have seized this issue with fervor.

The "Golden State" is on the forefront in banishing all Affirmative Action programs. California Governor Pete Wilson has led the charge to end Affirmative Action in California. During the 1996 elections, the so-called "California Civil Rights Initiative," a proposed constitutional amendment, ended state programs that give gender or racial preference in government hiring, contracting, and public education.

Republican political consultant Sal Russo, in reaction to the California Civil Rights Initiative, stated "We have such a slow economic growth rate and weak economy that it makes people particularly sensitive about something that might give somebody else a preference" (Stewart, 1996, p. A2). The recession and continuous reductions in public expenditures for social services and education have sent distress signals all across the nation. The truth of white male fear has been exposed—it appears that their power structure, steadily maintained for virtually over 400 years in these United States, has been shaken.

Perhaps the best way to explain the need for Affirmative Action is to distinguish between equality and equity (G. N. Carnes, personal communication, April 7, 1997). Equity assumes that diversity among people exists; therefore, there is sometimes a need to do different things for disadvantaged groups to give them a fair chance. In other words, in order to ensure equity, "unequal" strategies may be used. An example is presented to illuminate this point. Since there is an underrepresentation of women in administrative positions in schools (e.g., principal's or superintendent's positions), women may be recruited to apply for such positions in an effort to bring parity to the situation.

Equality, on the other hand, assumes "sameness" and does not acknowledge that differences in opportunities exist. There is the fallacious belief that everyone has a fair chance to get any job. Therefore, this approach would not make any special arrangements to ensure that more women become administrators. As history has aptly demonstrated, without some interventions, women, people of color, and other groups may not be given fair opportunities even when they are qualified. Affirmative Action seeks to remedy this. Unlike the "equality" approach which would not alter procedures under any circumstances, equitable approaches such as Affirmative Action do.

What Is Affirmative Action?

Affirmative Action is a mechanism designed to represent the interests of candidates who fall within the following categories: people of color, women, persons with disabilities, Vietnam Era veterans, and disabled veterans (B. D. Gist, personal communication (letter), July 17, 1995, University of South Carolina, Columbia, SC 29208). These groups are protected classes for which employers are allowed to take affirmative action to employ and advance in employment. Hiring goals for these groups are based on underrepresentation in particular positions. According to Affirmative Action principles, it is permissible to be race- or sex-conscious in recruitment under the following conditions:

1. certain groups are underutilized by employers and hiring goals are projected in the employer's Affirmative Action plan
2. the candidate is fully qualified for the position
3. race or sex is not the sole criterion used in the selection process, but merely one of several factors given consideration.

Affirmative Action procedures should be used during the recruitment process to ensure that the position is advertised in a manner that will reach prospective people of color and women applicants. Additionally, adequate time should be allowed so that the search process is conducive to an active search for women, people of color, and other protected groups. This is extremely important, since such applicants are frequently not included in the applicant pool. Affirmative Action tries to ensure that objective, job-related, selection criteria are established early in the process and that these criteria are applied equally to all persons. The selection criteria should not cause a disproportionate number of applicants from protected groups to be eliminated. During the interview process, Affirmative Action seeks to ensure that discriminatory questions are not posed (e.g., inquiries about the applicant's name that would indicate his/her lineage or national origin; information regarding child-care arrangements or pregnancies that results in a limitation of job opportunity; questions that require the applicant to state his or her age; questions about religious backgrounds). In sum, the purpose of Affirmative Action is to ensure that protected groups are given a fair opportunity to apply for and obtain positions that may otherwise be closed to them.

Contrary to popular belief, Affirmative Action does not mean setting and meeting quotas. A quota requires that a business hires or promotes a fixed percentage of people of color and women. Quotas are prohibited by the Civil Rights Acts of 1964 and 1991. The only exception is when a court orders a fixed percentage because of legal findings of past discrimination; however, employers are not required to hire unqualified people.

Title VII of the Civil Rights Act of 1964 prohibits employment discrimination. This act covers private firms with fifteen or more employees, educational institutions, state and local governments, employment agencies, and unions. This law does not require Affirmative Action programs unless court-imposed after a finding of discrimination, nor does it ensure effectiveness.

Affirmative Action is designed to increase the number of women, people of color, and other protected groups in the workplace, and to improve their status because of historical patterns of employment discrimination against these groups. The reality of the situation is that federal contractors routinely do not meet Affirmative Action goals with no penalty imposed (Joint Center for Political and Economic Studies, 1995).

In 1965, President Lyndon B. Johnson issued Executive Order 11246 extending previous presidential directives against employment discrimination by establishing the Office of Federal Contract Compliance. The Order applies to federal contractors with fifty or more employees and contracts over $50,000. The Joint Center for Political and Economic Studies (1995) asserted that it . . .

> will take affirmative action to ensure that applicants are employed, and that employees are treated during employment, without regard to their race, creed, color, or national origin. Such action shall include, but not be limited to the following: employment, upgrading, demotion, or transfer; recruitment or recruitment advertising; layoff or termination; rates of pay or other forms of compensation; and selection for training, including apprenticeship. (no pagination)

A study by Badgett and Hartmann (as cited in Joint Center for Political and Economic Studies, 1995) concluded that Affirmative Action does not come at the expense of either employer's competitiveness or fairness of employment practice. Rather, the practice means a "greater effort in hiring protected groups in growing firms without sacrificing quality." (no pagination)

Furthermore, Affirmative Action has not equalized earnings between women, people of color and white males. A *U. S. News and World Report* study found that between 1975 and 1993, a twenty-six percent to forty-six percent differential in earnings existed between women and people of color as compared to white males (see Table 8-3).

It is clear from this data that the misinformation and unfounded rhetoric about Affirmative Action claiming that black men take jobs from white men is factually flawed. If people of color are in positions previously held by white men, then they obviously are making a lot less. With the realignment of the global economy and the tendency of many politicians to blame America's wage stagnation and slow economic growth on Affirmative Action, the United States' goal of inclusion and equal opportunity for all is at great risk.

Why Affirmative Action Is Needed

Many analyses of the workplace suggest that African Americans are slowly spiraling downward in the United States labor force. In 1990, African Americans accounted for 10.7 percent of the total civilian labor force. By the year 2005, African Americans will account for 13.0 percent of the civilian labor force (Tidwell, 1995).

There are millions of African Americans in desperate situations, yet another million African Americans are increasingly

TABLE 8-3. Median Annual Earnings Compared to White Men's

Year	Black Men	Hisp. Men	White Women	Black Women	Hisp. Women
1975	74.3%	72.1%	57.5%	55.4%	49.3%
1980	70.7%	70.8%	58.9%	55.7%	50.5%
1985	69.7%	68.0%	63.0%	57.1%	52.1%
1990	73.1%	66.3%	69.4%	62.5%	54.3%
1993	74.0%	64.8%	70.8%	63.7%	53.9%

Courtesy of: *U. S. News and World Report.* February 13, 1995.

becoming upwardly mobile. This may be attributed to ambition, determination, a solid education, family support, or other factors, but the inclusive nature of mandatory Affirmative Action policy is the infrastructure of middle class Black America. Affirmative Action erodes nepotism and other exclusive, discriminatory practices so blatantly used against people of color. The testimonies of the effectiveness of Affirmative Action are loud and clear. Oliver Lee a successful African American corporate lawyer is convinced that Affirmative Action transformed his life. He participated in a program called, "Chosen for a Better Chance," which invited talented low-income youth to attend elite private schools to help them gain entry to the middle class. Mr. Lee says that the program lifted his horizons and that he could not imagine a life beyond selling insurance or teaching before then (Sharpe, 1995). While both selling insurance or teaching are respectable and viable careers, the point is that they have traditionally been among the only professions open to African Americans.

Affirmative Action opens doors of opportunity, but only for those who are the most prepared and the most qualified. Its effectiveness is limited, however. African Americans represent twelve percent of the nation's population, and only three percent of the lawyers, physicians, college professors and corporate executives (*National Catholic Reporter*, 1995). The triumphs of defeating discrimination in the office or at school are short-lived; for every success, there may be one thousand failures.

African Americans are the only group who suffered a tremendous employment loss during a 1993 recession (*Wall Street Journal*, Sept. 14, 1993), which resulted in a net loss of 59,479 corporate jobs and 180,210 blue collar jobs. Essentially, "the recession in America means depression in the black community" (Sharpe, 1993).

> The losses can be partially explained by blacks' relatively low seniority in companies and their heavy concentration on the types of jobs eliminated. Corporations' continuing decisions to abandon inner-city offices, factories or franchise outlets didn't help blacks, either (Sharpe, 1993, A1, A12).

The gains illustrated by Oliver Lee and others are not the norm—actually, relatively few gains have been made. Attempts by the Republican Congress, California State Legislature, and corporate America to end Affirmative Action policy and programs are based on myths, untruths, and fear. The need for Affirmative Action is necessary as long as racism, sexism, and classism exist.

Since passage of legislation promoting Affirmative Action, people of color and women have made some progress in the work environment. The extent of this progress in upper management is debatable. People of color and women describe their progress as slow. On the other hand, white male corporate executives generally disagree, and feel as though these groups have made great progress.

People of color and women who have moved into the executive suites attribute their success to being better qualified than their white counterparts—they are better educated and consistently excel. Yet, they recognize breakdowns in the system when they experience difficulty obtaining a job, are discriminated against, or face glass ceiling despite their educational and experiential preparation. Having an influential mentor is a plus since a mentor can open doors to the informal channels of organizations that are essential to upward mobility.

In his keynote address at the 1995 National Urban League Conference, President and CEO Hugh B. Price proposed "Five Commandments for an Inclusive America," which he believes can be embraced by Americans who are genuinely committed to equal opportunity.

1. **The goal is genuine inclusion.** We do not condone quotas, but neither will we tolerate tokenism or total exclusion of any segments of American society from the opportunity structure.

2. **Only the qualified should be included.** Candidates who aren't qualified ought not be in the applicant pool. For those with potential who lack the requisite skills, let there be intensive remediation programs to help them get quickly up to speed so that they too can qualify some day soon.

3. **Selection should be based on a broad understanding of what "qualified" and "merit" mean in the real world.** Those who do the picking should be free to weigh traditional indicators, such as test scores and grades, along with intangible attributes like grit and determination.

4. **Inclusion is morally virtuous, economically advantageous, and demographically inevitable.** Our population is diverse by definition—50 percent female, and more and more multiethnic by the day. Americans must accept this reality and incorporate it into the allocation of opportunities to learn, work and do business in our society.

5. **To achieve inclusion, those who allocate opportunity should take many factors into account, among them geography, gender,ethnicity, economic status and cultural diversity.** Gender

or race needn't be the deciding factors, but they definitely should be among the criteria used to overcome exclusion and promote inclusion of all those who are qualified. (pp. 12-13)

A commitment to inclusion is the only way to ensure that people of color and women will continue to have access to the executive suite. American demographics are changing and we must make equal opportunity available to all, if we are to continue to be a competitive force in the global economy.

❖ THE RELATIONSHIP OF EMPLOYMENT CHOICES TO OTHER FACTORS

The type of work that a person will do as an adult is influenced by a number of factors. It is a result of the complex interplay of factors outlined in previous chapters of this book, such as family background and educational experiences. A person's ethnicity, gender, socioeconomic status, and physical/mental abilities may also affect the type of work that is chosen.

The Relationship of Employment Choices to Family Background

> Clifford (Vietnamese): "My parents said to me, 'Living in the white man's world, to compete with them, you have to be able to hang with them in society—you have to be able to speak like they do, know their culture. You don't want to be an outcast. Yet you want to be above their standards of intelligence, because if it comes down to the worst, a white person is going to hire a white.'" (Oei and Lyon, 1996, p.56)

Family variables which influence an individual's employment choices include his/her socioeconomic status, the work status of his/her parents (unemployed, blue-collar, white-collar, self-employed), ethnicity, cultural customs and values. Early in life, young children begin to decide (either consciously or unconsciously) on a career trajectory. Some parents actively guide these career decisions while others do not. The type of early cultural exposure that children have also affects their later career choices. Children may change their minds about their career choices because of messages received from society, schools, or families. For example, when females consistently do not see themselves represented in a particular field or if no members of the child's family or community has pursued a certain career, the child may view that career choice as unattainable.

The Relationship of Education to Employment Choices

The cumulative effect of a person's educational experiences becomes evident when a person reaches adulthood. Students who performed poorly in elementary and high school may have limited skills and may not graduate from high school or attend college. Hence, their prior educational experiences have limited their future employment possibilities. The type of educational exposure that students have will direct them to particular professions. A student who has not had an adequate background in English, for example, will find it difficult or impossible to pursue a career in journalism.

Some ethnic groups seem to have a better chance of obtaining higher status positions in our society, while other groups are relegated to lower status positions. Asian Americans, as a group, appear to be able to excel in the workplace because their educational preparation and subsequent opportunity to attend college puts them at an advantage in the workplace. Because of extremely high SATs and academic records, Asian Americans enter universities at record rates (Bell, 1994). On the SATs, Asian Americans score an average of 519 in math, which surpasses whites by thirty-two points. At Harvard, Asian Americans barely made up three percent of the freshmen class ten years ago (Bell, 1994). Currently, the figure is ten percent—five times their share of the population. Similar figures can be noted at Brown, Berkeley, UCLA, MIT, the Julliard School of Music in New York, and medical schools around the nation (Bell, 1994).

Among the Asian American population, approximately thirty-three percent of the largely foreign-born citizens over twenty-five graduated from college. In contrast, approximately sixteen percent of the general population over twenty-five graduated from college. Eighty-eight percent of third-generation Japanese Americans graduated from college (Bell, 1994).

As noted in Chapter Two, educational outcomes are vastly different for various racial, language, economic, and gender groups in this nation (Pine and Hilliard, 1990). Children from different social classes are likely to attend different types of schools, receive different types of instruction, study different curricula, and leave school at different rates and times. As a result, children end their school careers more different from each other than they were when they entered (Persell, 1993; Wilcox, 1982). Differences in dropout rates, suspensions, expulsions, academic achievement indices, and patterns of coursework contribute to the disparities among children from different social classes. As with gender

---

Even primary classrooms prepare children for certain
employment opportunities.

issues, many people feel more comfortable dealing with socioeconomic status rather than race. Certainly, both are interrelated and
affect teacher expectations. Lower expectations are generally held
for children from low socioeconomic status groups. Kathleen
Wilcox's (1982) ethnographic study demonstrated how teachers
unknowingly channel children into different vocational paths
(blue vs. white collar) based on children's socioeconomic statuses.
Interestingly, the channeling process begins during the early
childhood years. For example, Wilcox's study (1982) compared
two first grade teachers who were reputed to be outstanding
teachers. The teachers were from two different schools that served
children from middle-income homes. One school served lower-
middle-class children from families that primarily worked in fac-
tories. The other school served professional families. Although
the schools were fifteen-minutes apart, the families lived in neighborhoods that were different socially and economically: small
tract houses showing signs of age versus large, stately houses,
architecturally individualized and surrounded by lush and
immaculately groomed landscaping. The lower-middle-income
school spent $840 per student during the school year (1973-1974)
versus $1,350 per student at the high-middle-income school.
Teachers' salaries differed also: median salary for the lower-middle-income school was $12,800 as compared to $16,200 for the
high-middle-income school.

Significant differences were found in the nature of instruction in the schools: the way that cognitive skills were taught and
tested; the way students were taught to present themselves in

terms of appropriate manners of speech and demeanor; and the sense of personal capability and likely future role conveyed to students. Wilcox compared how "Show and Tell" was carried out in both school. The findings provide much insight into how teachers and schools unintentionally affect students' future employment choices.

"Show and Tell" was one technique by which teachers gave students a chance to "present themselves." In the lower-middle school, the teacher used the sharing time only about once every three days at irregular times. She appeared to think that sharing time was nice, but not important enough to happen daily. She seemed to think of sharing time as the children's time and was relatively unobtrusive during this time. Half of the time, she did not comment; however, when she did she frequently asked a factual question (that required a specific answer) or made a positive closing remark such as "That's nice." She only offered procedural instruction about how to make presentations eight percent of the time (and then it was usually a specific direction about what else to say). For example in response to a student's comment "My family bought a new car," the teacher replied, "Tell us the color."

On the other hand, at the high-middle-income school, the first ten minutes of every day began with sharing. The teacher used the time to review academic materials through her follow-up questions and to give procedural suggestions to individual speakers about grammar and presentation. She would frequently draw the child and/or class into further presentation or discussion based on what the child had originally said. She also used the child's presentation as a basis for a discussion question for the class.

During ninety percent of the observations, Wilcox noted that the teacher in the high-middle-income school followed student presentations with a response. Twenty-five percent of the time, the teacher made specific comments such as:

> What nice sentences you made. You told us so many things. We know exactly when and where and what. (p. 292)

> I like the way Joanne shared yesterday. She called it a "poster"; she could describe it more than "this." (p. 292)

> I really like the way Matt spoke so nice and loud. Although I was looking in my desk and rattling papers, I could hear every word he had to say. When we have something that's important to say, then we should say it so people can hear it. (p. 292)

Indeed, as Wilcox's study graphically demonstrates, education divides children according to social class and that educators hold political power which can influence their students' future employment choices. Wilcox concluded that the lower-income children were being socialized to perform before a group in a relatively haphazard way. Little attention was placed on developing extended verbal skills appropriate for the upper levels of the occupational hierarchy. Contrastingly, the high-middle-income children were being prepared for the types of interactions that characterize the upper occupational echelons of the culture of the United States. Consider the following contrasting examples.

In the low-middle school, external control was the overriding control mechanism used by the teacher. Many commands were used, for example, "I want that done now" or "You have an assignment; sit down and get busy." (Wilcox, 1982, p. 288). Rule repetition was also common. Other examples are listed below.

> You have work to do and I want it done. (p. 288)
>
> I won't accept backwards numbers on your arithmetic paper. (p. 288)
>
> Here's a star for everybody who finished. (p. 288)
>
> Sit down and do that work; this is a work time. (p. 288)

Contrastingly, the teacher at the high-middle school consistently refused to act as an external authority when disputes arose among children, urging them to take responsibility for resolving their own differences. She also encouraged children to engage in self-directed academic endeavors.

> [To a boy who came to her during art because he couldn't find the glue] You've been in this classroom since September and you still can't handle that? You can solve that problem yourself. (p. 288)
>
> Our fifteen minutes are up. Have you used them wisely? (p. 289)
>
> That's being a real independent worker. (p. 290)
>
> If you're talking to your neighbor, you're probably not looking at the clues and remembering what the answers are. (p. 289)

At the high-middle-income school, students learned that they had positive futures ahead of them.

> Good thinking. See, you're really thinking like a mathematician [after a review of geometric shapes]. You'll be a good scientist [writing fantasy stories]. You were artists—now you're authors. (p. 293)
>
> It's real important to be a good listener. What you said wasn't wrong, but it didn't answer the question. This is important for taking tests, and you'll have them from now on, even if you get to Harvard. (p. 294)

In contrast, while the teacher at the low-middle school at times reinforced the progress they had made in first grade, she rarely extrapolated it beyond that level. The few references made to second grades were negative ones.

> When the class failed to bring a seed from home, as she had asked: "We're not getting ready for second grade. This was homework." (p. 294)

> After struggling with several children about writing their letters properly: "In second grade they don't teach you printing. That's why you have to know it now." (p. 294)

> When the class was not paying attention during math, in exasperation: "We've got to get this before we get to second grade." (p. 294)

Children in the low-middle schools were taught to follow rules and obey authority, and focus on the here and now—skills that are important for success on blue-collar jobs. In contrast, children in high-middle-income school were taught to think independently, which will be useful when working without supervision later in life.

All of this was done under the vestiges of effective teaching and it is doubtful that either teacher was aware of the amount of influence that they had on the children's futures. Indeed, teaching is a powerful position. Schools implicitly expect and accept vastly different levels of performance, depending on the population. This does not imply that factors other than education do not influence future employment decisions; however, it does point out how education can facilitate or hinder employment opportunities.

Wilcox (1982) suggests that the "hidden curriculum" of schools is difficult to change. Children continue to be sorted into particular careers/jobs based on their social class. Interestingly, in Wilcox's study, educational reforms which suggested that schools for low-income children become less restrictive and rigid had been "implemented" at the lower-middle-income school. However, the substance of what was being transmitted remained.

Teachers who bring real thoughtfulness into the nature of their interactions with students can break down the promotion of stereotypes about socioeconomic status (Wilcox, 1982). Additionally, sensitizing parents about differential socialization also helps. The practices of schools need to be scrutinized for various levels of expectations as discussed in previous chapters. Heterogeneously grouped classes by socioeconomic status and race may also help diminish differential socialization.

In the final analysis, educators must understand the dynamics at work in the part and in the whole. Education is a complex process and it is difficult for educators to overcome the influence of mainstream enculturation (Wilcox, 1982).

The complexity of the situation is compounded by the gross inequities that exist between schools of mainstream children and schools for many poor children and/or children of color. Based on extensive visits to schools across the nation, Kozol (1991) graphically illustrated how existing systems of school funding perpetuate cycles of educational inequities which greatly influence differences in the types of jobs (if any) that individuals hold later in life. The reliance of public schools on property taxes and the localization of the uses of those taxes combine to make public school into an educator for the educated rich and a keeper for the uneducated poor (Kozol, 1991). There exists no more powerful force for the rigidity of social class and the frustration of nation potential than the public school system, contends Kozol.

Even when low-income districts go to court to challenge the existing system of school funding, the present public school finance system is defended on a platform of economic or political freedom. There "is no graver threat to the capitalist system than the present cyclical replacement of the 'fittest' of one generation by their artificially advantaged offspring." (John Coons as cited in Kozol, 1991, p. 206). This situation is made worse since that advantage is proffered to the children of the successful by the State. Kozol laments that free enterprise has sold its birthright. The freedom claimed by the rich to give their children preferential education by inheritance denies the children of others the freedom inherent in the notion of free enterprise. Without doubt, democracy can stand certain types and amounts of inherited advantage. On the other hand, **what a democracy cannot tolerate is an aristocracy padded and protected by the State itself from competition from below**. Ironically, according to rhetoric espoused in textbooks, North Americans abhor a social order in which economic privilege and political power are determined by heredity or class. Yet, such a system prevails, unbeknownst to many educators who are part of the system. In theory, we live in a society in which a family's wealth has no relation to the probability of future educational attainment and the wealth and station in life it affords. Using this line of reasoning, education for poor children should be at least as good as that which is provided to the children of the upper-middle class. Conclusively, educators who really wish to help **all** children have a better chance of employment success later in life should organize as a group to begin to dismantle the deeply entrenched and unfair system of education.

The Relationship of Employment Choices
And Ethnic Group Membership

Historically, some ethnic groups gravitated toward certain professions. Chinese Americans owned laundries and restaurants; Japanese Americans pursued the grocery business and truck farming; and Koreans worked in the grocery business. Recently, however, Asian Americans have diversified their employment choices and have become prominent in several other professions and trades. Filipino doctors outnumber African American doctors and have become general practitioners in thousands of rural communities that previously lacked physicians. East Indian Americans own approximately 800 of California's 6,000 motels. In parts of Texas, Vietnamese Americans control eighty-five percent of the shrimp-fishing industry (Bell, 1994). In New York City, where the Asian American population increased tremendously in the seventies and eighties, it is estimated that Korean Americans run 900 of the city's 1600 corner grocery stores.

Asian Americans also tend to pursue careers in science (Bell, 1994). However, an unequal distribution of Asian Americans in science professions limits their possibilities for pursuing other professions such as history, sociology, or journalism (Takaki, 1994). Many Asians pursue scientific rather than more language-oriented professions because of difficulties mastering English.

Parallels are often drawn between the Jewish and Asian communities' success in this country. Like the Russian and Polish Jewish population who came to this country in the late 19th and early 20th centuries who worked primarily in the garment industry, today thousands of Chinese American women fill the sweatshops in New York City doing the same work of stitching and sewing (Bell, 1994). Many members of the Jewish population became retail or wholesale proprietors. Likewise, many Koreans in Los Angeles are also becoming retailers and wholesalers.

As a group, Jewish and Asian Americans have fared well in the workplace. This is because sociologically, both Jewish and Asian populations came to this country with certain advantages. Jewish Americans who came to this country had extremely high literacy rates, a long tradition of scholarship, and useful skills. Likewise, Japanese, Filipino, and Vietnamese immigrants during this century have come exclusively from the middle class (Bell, 1994). Bell notes that seventy percent of Korean male immigrants are college graduates. Since both Jewish and Asian Americans fully understand the importance of a college education, they have pushed their children to attend college from the very start. Thus, their chances of attaining higher status positions are greatly increased.

African and Irish Americans have not made the same types of economic advances in the workplace, since they have had to depend largely on political action for advancement (Bell, 1994). In contrast, Jewish, Chinese, and Japanese Americans with educational and work skill advantages have not depended on the political process for economic advancement. Rather, they relied on community organization and self-sufficiency. Even during the Great Depression, few Asian Americans required public relief. Both Jewish and Asian Americans also tend to help one another with business skills information, cluster in particular industries, and purchase ethnic commodities. Typically, when they need financial help, it comes from their own community.

As a result of these factors, the median income of Asian Americans exceeds that of whites ($22,713 versus $19,917). However, the differences in the income levels are attributed to the fact that generally Asians live almost exclusively in urban areas where incomes are higher (Bell, 1994). Moreover, they generally have more people working in each family and are better educated than whites. Traditionally, Asian Americans have entered into family businesses with all the family members pitching in long hours to make them a success (Bell, 1994). Therefore, in terms of individual incomes, Takaki (1994) notes that Asian Americans have not reached equality with white men. In fact, many Asians note that they are typically underpaid based on their high levels of education. Because of language difficulties and professional standards that differ from their native standards, many new Asian immigrants initially work in jobs where they are overqualified. The image of the "model minority" obscures the difficulties confronting many Asian Americans (Huang and Oei, 1996). Asian Americans who have "made it" frequently do not earn as much as their white counterparts, even with equal or better education and experience. Essentially, many Asian Americans work harder for less money.

It may sound as if Asian and Jewish Americans have been extremely successful in the workplace; however, this is not always the case. Hmong tribesmen who arrived in the United States with little money, few valuable skills, and extreme cultural disorientation have not fared well (Bell, 1994). Almost a decade after arriving here, they are still heavily dependent on welfare. Other Asian groups that are not doing well include the elderly Japanese and Filipinos who were once farm laborers. Because of the dubious reputation of Asian Americans as the "model minority," the government has sometimes denied funding for social service programs designed to help them learn English and find employment. Asian Americans have also been excluded from Educational Opportunity Programs intended for low-income families because college administrators do not realize that there are poor Asians. Such discrimination also limits the success of this group of Asians in the workplace. Additionally, the percentage of Asian Americans below the poverty line is 12.2 percent—exactly the same as the national rate and double that of European Americans (Huang and Oei, 1996).

The relative success that Asians face in the workplace causes racial strife. Many white Americans have resorted to Asian-bashing because they feel as if Asians are taking their jobs and places in universities. To make matters worse, industrial workers in this country have been advised to emulate Asian Americans and work harder (Takaki, 1994). Additionally, many African Americans condemn Asians for taking over black businesses. A number of African Americans also resent Asians for profiting from black communities.

Another problem faced by Asian Americans in the workplace is that they often face "glass ceilings." That is, they hold middleman jobs and are basically absent from the higher levels of management and administration. Although the number of Asians are increasing as university employees, they are virtually nonexistent as administrators (Takaki, 1994). Asians blame these inequities on cultural differences such as speaking with an accent. Asians have also often been stereotyped as being passive and lacking aggressiveness. However, Takaki argues that it is not cultural differences that prohibit Asians from reaching higher management levels; rather, it is the deeply ingrained "good old boy" network that keeps them out. The glass ceiling effect is also faced by African Americans, Latino Americans, and Native Americans.

Many Native Americans do not attend college; thus, the types of positions open to them are limited. In terms of professional jobs, many Native Americans are concentrated in the education profession (Lomawaima, 1995). Science professions are in dire need of Native Americans.

As discussed in previous chapters, many African Americans experience cultural conflict and ambivalence in Eurocentric schools and workplaces (Fordham, 1988). When they try to "assimilate," they often worry about how they will be accepted by blacks and whites. In professional settings, many African Americans who gain entry into predominantly white institutions are not only likely to experience enormous stress and feelings of isolation, but they are often viewed suspiciously by other African Americans who do not work in such institutions. African Americans who work for predominantly white institutions may try to disassociate themselves with other African Americans in an effort to "fit in" the mainstream; hence, many members of the African American community may consider them "un-black."

Fordham presents the following examples of African American professionals who have sought to become raceless.

> They consciously choose their speech, their walk, their mode of dress and car; they trim their hair lest a mountainous Afro set them apart. They know they have a high visibility, and they realize that their success depends not only on their *abilities* [emphasis added by Fordham], but also on their white colleagues' feeling comfortable with them. (p. 60)

> Many times, other blacks feel that these strange creatures with three-piece suits and briefcases have sold out. "A black manager can have a multi-million dollar deal on his mind," explains Dr. [Ronald] Brown of San Francisco. "But when he passes that black janitor, he knows that he'd better remember to speak; otherwise, he'll be labeled as 'acting white.' " (p. 60).

> The voice is quiet thunder. Seductive. He stretches words, rolls them around in his mouth. Because his voice is neither black nor white and favors no geographical region, there has been some confusion about his racial identity. "I've had people look at me like I'm a ghost," says the 30-year-old disc jockey. "Some of them were expecting a white person. I hate for people to say I sound white. I don't. It's a matter of speaking properly, and anyone can do that." (p. 58)

> **(Max Robinson, former ABC news reporter)** "One of the problems that I have is that we tend to separate everything, so at ABC Roone [Arledge; the director in charge of hiring news personnel] . . .mentioned on three occasions, he said, 'I told you when I hired you, I didn't think you were black, or I didn't think of you as a black man.' That's an incredible statement. I mean, I must be the funniest looking white man in this country. And the fact is, what he was trying to say, 'I am going to give you credit. I admire you greatly, so therefore I will not think of you as black.'" (pp. 58–59)

> **(In reference to ex-Governor Doug Wilder of Virginia)** "In the state with the lowest percentage of blacks (17) of any southern state, he [Wilder] announced his candidacy in front of a picture of Harry Byrd and down-played race until 'people never perceived a Black candidate running.' A statewide trek, backed up with television ads that included an archetypal white deputy sheriff endorsing Wilder, paid off. Wilder undid his tie and rolled up his sleeves in front of Confederate flags at country stores. Instant press, statewide and local, at every stop." (p. 59)

> **(Oprah Winfrey, talk show host)** They [the students at Tennessee State] all hated me—no, they resented me. I refused to conform to the militant thinking of the time. I hated, hated, hated, college. Now I bristle when somebody comes up

and says they went to Tennessee State with me. Everybody
was angry for four years. It was an all-black college, and it was
in to be angry. Whenever there was any conversation on race,
I was on the other side, maybe because I never felt the kind
of repression other black people are exposed to. I think I was
called 'nigger' once, when I was in fifth grade." (p. 59)

Cultural conflict and ambivalence appear to be more pronounced among African Americans who achieve the greatest
degree of success, as defined by the dominant society, relative to
the success of peers in the African American community
(Fordham, 1988). As these examples demonstrate, race influences
employment choices in complex ways. How closely one aligns
himself with their indigenous culture versus the mainstream culture has tremendous implications for success in this society. Since
some ethnic groups are underrepresented in certain professions,
educators can ensure that all students are prepared academically
for many possible professions.

The Relationship of Gender
and Employment Choices

In many professions, women are generally paid less than men.
Female-dominated professions such as teaching, nursing, and
secretarial positions pay less than male-dominated ones. From
the perspective of the macroculture, professions that appeal to
females (often caring professions) are not valued in society.

College-educated women make only sixty-nine cents for
every dollar earned by their male colleagues (Kaplan and
Aronson, 1994). However, women who have taken eight or more
mathematics classes in college earn virtually the same amount as
their male counterparts. (Presently, males are more likely than
females to take higher-level math courses in high school.) A number of programs (such as the EQUALS program) have been
implemented in schools to give females an equal chance of succeeding in math-related careers in the future.

Historically, many professions excluded women (e.g., construction, military). Although women now have an "equal opportunity" to choose almost any profession, many professions are
still dominated by men. In these professions women, like many
ethnic groups, also face "glass ceilings" and are generally promoted at lower rates than men and paid less. Interestingly, even
in female-dominated professions such as teaching, males often
hold the administrative positions which pay more. For example,
most superintendents are men (ninety-six percent) and most are

European American (ninety-seven percent). Additionally, seventy-five percent of principals are men and ninety-percent are European American. More than eighty-percent of all administrators are over forty years of age; hence, credence is given to the notion of the "old boys club" (McNergney and Herbert, 1995).

In addition to being promoted and paid less than men, women often face other types of discrimination in the workplace. For example, they may face sexual harassment on the job. Pregnant women and women with young children may not be hired or promoted. Indeed, because of the structure of our society, women are more willing than men to accommodate their careers around family obligations (Flanagan, 1993). Employers in a diverse society must learn to value the different roles played by males and females. Employers must learn to accommodate women's needs in a better manner than is currently being done. As a multicultural society, we must learn that both genders have unique roles to contribute to the survival and betterment of the family, and society at large.

Women of color are virtually nonexistent at the upper levels of most positions. Women of color face gender as well as racial issues in the workplace. This is fondly referred to as the "double whammy." Although many white females would deny having an advantage over females from other ethnic groups, white women are probably discriminated against less than other females. White women who justifiably view themselves as being oppressed by white men find it difficult to separate themselves from the effects of power shared with white men (Bulter, 1993). As Bulter (1993) adds, white women share with white men an ethnicity, an ancestral heritage, racial dominance, and certain powers and privileges by virtue of white skin privilege. This does not imply that white women intentionally contribute to discriminatory actions; rather, the point is made to illustrate the depth of institutional racism and sexism in the workplace.

Males are not immune to gender discrimination. They may also be sexually harassed, although it is unlikely that the harasser will be their boss or supervisor since only a small number of women hold such positions. Additionally, although the Family and Medical Leave Act of 1993 allows both parents to take leave without pay from their jobs, most employers will not allow men to take paid paternity leave. The decision allowing only mothers to take leave with pay is sexist and based on the premise that the male is the primary breadwinner and the female is the caregiver. However, today more males are assuming the role of primary caregiver. Employers should view paternity leave as a benefit which not only supports the family, but one that is beneficial to the employer as well, since it is likely to increase job satisfaction. As pointed out in Chapter One, the welfare of the family is inextricably tied to the welfare of all parts of society—including the workplace.

The Relationship of Physical/Mental Abilities to Employment Choices

Not only do the disabled have a right to receive an appropriate education, they also have the right to be employed and to enjoy the services provided by the community (Berns, 1993). The Vocational Rehabilitation Act of 1973 required that federal agencies and all organizations holding contracts or receiving funds from the United States government have Affirmative Action programs to hire and promote qualified disabled persons. It enforced an earlier law requiring that all buildings constructed with federal funds or buildings owned or leased by federal agencies have ramps, elevators, or other barrier-free access for disabled employees. In 1990, the Americans with Disabilities Act barred discrimination in employment, transportation, public accommodations, and telecommunications. The law guarantees access to all aspects of life—not just those that are federally funded—for disabled individuals. For example, telephone companies must make whatever adaptations are necessary so that individuals with hearing or voice impairments can use ordinary telephones (Berns, 1993).

Although there are laws prohibiting discrimination toward people with disabilities, it still exists in the workplace. Additionally, many employers do not have physical accommodations such as ramps, elevators, and handicapped parking spaces. It is noteworthy that many people do not become disabled until they are adults. Therefore, any of us are likely to become disabled. No one could have predicted that Christopher Reeves (the actor best known for his role as Superman) would become a quadriplegic in 1995. Most employers offer temporary disability benefits, but do not have any policies or plans for long-term disabilities.

As a society, we must learn to embrace disabled people in the work force. We must realize that often their disability does not interfere with their competence. Yet, because we see so few images of competent disabled people in the media or in society at large, we tend to feel a sense of discomfort around people who are disabled. We must move beyond this discomfort and find ways of accommodating people with different abilities. The more students with disabilities are included in classrooms, the more familiar future generations will be with them; hence, they may be less likely to discriminate against them in the workplace.

❖ RECRUITMENT AND RETENTION OF PEOPLE OF COLOR

In recent years, many professions which lack diversity among their employees have attempted to recruit people of color and women. Some of these attempts are half-hearted and only seek "token" representation rather than the diversity of opinions that the new recruits will bring. Such employers typically hire people of color who will "fit in" or assimilate rather than challenge the status quo. Other efforts are more serious and the employer (and other employees) truly values diversity and realizes that the essence of their workplace may change drastically as problems are examined through different lenses.

Since recruitment and retention of people of color and women in these professions is frequently problematic, special strategies are frequently employed. For example, new positions may be advertised in places where people of color and/or women are likely to see the advertisement (e.g., at Historically Black Colleges and Universities or in publications that cater to these populations). Salaries offered to new employees of color are more equitable. Once hired, people of color and women may be assigned a mentor who is responsible for guiding and/or supporting the new employee's progress. The new recruits may be placed on committees or included in the decision-making process in other ways.

Although employers are making overt efforts to eliminate the effects of discrimination in the workplace, covert discrimination continues to exist. One problem that these new recruits may face is resentment from other employees. Many feel as if people of color and women are receiving preferential treatment. Additionally, the work or decisions of recruits may be questioned unnecessarily, or they may be subjected to other covert discriminations.

Kozol (1991) identified a recruitment trend that has historically had a negative impact on employees of color. People of color, notes Kozol, are often hired in high profile positions in which success is basically impossible. For example, administrators of poor rural and urban schools, administrators of homeless shelters or welfare offices, or chiefs of police in urban cities festering with crime, often actively recruit among people of color for these positions. Kozol observes that since having a white superintendent at the head of a school district which "warehouses" African American children would be too suggestive and provocative, efforts are made to find African Americans, Asian Americans, or Latino/a Americans to fill these positions.

Kozol (1991) equates placing an African American in control of dysfunctional entities such as social agencies or urban schools with placing them in an essentially apartheid system (whether welfare or public schools). According to Kozol, hiring persons of color in these cases serves three functions: it offers symbolism that protects white officials against charges of racism; it offers enforcement, since people of color are expected to be more severe in putting down unrest than white officials; and it offers a scapegoat. When the situation is unchanged, the employee of color may be condemned for corruption, ineptitude, or lack of vision. In such cases, people of color are placed in a no-win situation. While employees of color often enthusiastically accept the positions with the hope that THEY can make a difference (even though countless able predecessors have failed), they soon discover that bureaucratic chaos prevents them from making the necessary changes or receiving additional funding. Readers may wish to view movies suggested in Chapter Four (*Lean on Me*, *Stand and Deliver, Dangerous Minds*, or *Conrack*) for fictional examples of this real phenomenon. These patterns point out the endemic nature of institutionalized discrimination. The information presented here regarding the difficulty of changing some school settings is not intended to frustrate educators. Rather, it is offered so that educators do not lose sight of the complexity of issues involved in changing classrooms and schools so that all children have a reasonable chance to be successful. However, it is our hope that this information motivates educators to become active advocates for children.

We are not suggesting that people of color absolutely should not be hired in such positions; however, they must be given the proper financial, community, and political support necessary to succeed. Otherwise, hiring them in lose-lose situations raises the question: Do we really want the children and families in this system to succeed? Another important point is that people of color in education and social disciplines should also be sought after to work in mainstream districts as well.

As the workplace continues to become more diverse, employers will face dilemmas such as the one noted in the scenario at the beginning of this chapter. When holiday celebrations or other cultural behaviors and beliefs interfere with the employer's policy, policies may have to be changed or negotiated. Employers will be forced to examine the underlying premises of their policies and expectations. For example, at one time African American women were discouraged from wearing braids or other cultural hairstyles on professional jobs because they were viewed as unprofessional. The definition of professional in this case was hairstyles that had a European American flavor. Such hairstyles are more difficult to maintain for many African American women. Additionally, braids and other cultural hairstyles reflect cultural pride. Today, such cultural expressions are rarely questioned. It is not uncommon to see an individual garbed in ethnic attire such as a sari or headwrap. In a diverse workplace, the fabric of the environment is altered and one can expect anything other than business as usual. Cultural clashes have the potential for extending the culture of the workplace so that views and behaviors which deviate from European-oriented perspectives are accepted.

❖ SUMMARY

Most United States residents view themselves as fair and most favor equal opportunities for all people (Monk, 1994). However, the way to accomplish such fairness is the subject of much controversy in this country. The civil rights movement and legislation at the state and federal level prohibited discrimination in jobs, education, and housing. Affirmative Action programs were implemented to take steps to ensure equity in hiring of minority group members according to predetermined numerical goals.

A number of people of color and whites oppose Affirmative Action because it implies that certain quotas are met with no regard to qualifications (Monk, 1994). Additionally, many whites strongly disagree with Affirmative Action because they do not want to be required to hire people of color. As a result, many deliberately sabotage affirmative action guidelines in a number of ways. Recently, white men have protested that Affirmative Action discriminates against them. The crucial question surrounding Affirmative Action is how can the playing fields be leveled in the workplace? Wahisi (1995) notes that if it were not for affirmative action, neither Clarence Thomas or Sandra Day O'Connor would be on the Supreme Court. Most high level positions in industries, higher education, and other fields are dominated by white males. Even white females are not represented. One only has to examine the racial and gender composition of our national lawmakers to see who holds the power in this country.

If Affirmative Action is not used, what mechanism will be used to ensure that all individuals in this country, regardless of race, religion, ability, gender, and socioeconomic status, have equal opportunities? If the United States were a country where "isms" did not exist, perhaps no mechanism would be needed. However, in light of our history and present conditions, we must continue to address inequities in the workplace and in the classroom.

❖ RECOMMENDED ACTIVITIES

1. *Journal entry*—Reflect on how your school experiences influenced your career choice in the field of education. Were there other disciplines that you wanted to pursue but could not because you lacked the necessary academic preparation, encouragement, or exposure? Discuss these. Did you receive subtle or overt messages in school or at home that certain careers were not appropriate (e.g., too challenging, "beneath you," not for your gender, ethnicity, and the like)? Elaborate on your response. Think about the children you work with (or would like to work with)? What type of employment do you envision them doing later in life? How is your vision for them affected by their personality, physical characteristics, academic abilities, family background and parental employment, and other factors? How will your expectations and instructional approach affect their future employment choices?
2. Interview people from a variety of cultural groups (e.g., whites, males, disabled) to get their view on Affirmative Action. What conclusions can be drawn from your interviews?
3. As a class, debate whether or not an African American should be able to take annual leave on the Martin Luther King Holiday if the employer has not designated it as one of the approved holidays. Should the employee be penalized for taking the day off? Should other ethnic groups be required to take the day off?
4. Observe two schools that serve students from distinctly different socioeconomic status groups. Write down instructional and disciplinary comments made. Did you find examples of differential socialization? Alternately, if you are a teacher, you may have yourself videotaped and analyze the nature of your interactions/comments with students. Think carefully about how you are preparing children for certain types of employment. It would be helpful to locate and read the Wilcox (1982) study which elaborates on the issues, and presents numerous examples of comments and interactions.
5. Think retrospectively about your own school experiences. In small groups, name projects, assignments, instructional styles, and so forth that prepared you for college.

❖ REFERENCES

Bell, D. A. 1994. Are Asian Americans a "model minority"? In *Taking sides: Clashing views on controversial issues in race and ethnicity*, edited by R. C. Monk. Guilford, CT: Dushkin.

Berns, R. 1993. *Child, family, community: Socialization and support.* New York: Harcourt Brace College Publishers.

Butler, J. E. 1993. Transforming the curriculum: Teaching about women of color. In *Multicultural education: Issues and perspectives*, edited by J.A. Banks and C. A. M. Banks. Needham Heights, Mass.: Allyn and Bacon.

Flanagan, C. 1993. Gender and social class: Intersecting issues in women's achievement. *Educational Psychologist* 28(4): 357–378.

Fordham, S. 1988. Racelessness as a factor in black students' school success: Pragmatic strategy or Pyrrhic victory? *Harvard Educational Review* 58(1): 54–84.

Herrnstein, R. J., and C. Murray. 1994. *The bell curve: Intelligence and class structure in American life.* New York: The Free Press.

Huang, A. and T. Oei. 1996. Behind the myth. *Teaching Tolerance* 5(2): 57.

Kaplan, J., and D. Aronson 1994. The numbers gap. *Teaching Tolerance* 3(1): 21–27.

Kozol, J. 1991. *Savage inequalities: Children in America's schools.* New York: Harper.

Lomawaima, K. T. 1995. Educating Native Americans. In *Handbook of research on multicultural education*, edited by J. A. Banks and C. A. M. Banks. New York: Macmillan.

McNergney, R. F., and J. M. Herbert. 1995. *Foundations of education: The challenge of professional practice.* Needham, Heights, MA: Allyn and Bacon.

Monk, R. C. 1994. Is affirmative action reverse discrimination? In *Taking sides: Clashing views on controversial issues in race and ethnicity*, edited by R. C. Monk. Guilford, CT: Dushkin.

National Catholic Reporter. Editorial: "When we don't need it, we will know it." 17 March, 1995. [no pagination].

Oei, T. and G. Lyon. 1996. In our own words. Asian American students give voice to the challenges of living in two cultures. *Teaching Tolerance* 5(2): 48–59.

Persell, C. H. 1993. Social class and educational equality. In *Multicultural education: Issues and perspectives*, edited by J. A. Banks and C. A. M. Banks. Boston: Allyn and Bacon.

Pine, G. J., and A. G. Hilliard. 1990. Rx for racism: Imperatives for America's schools. *Phi Delta Kappan* 71(8): 593–600.

Price, H. B. 1995. *Five commandments for an inclusive America.* National Urban League. 1995 Annual Conference, 23 July. Miami, Florida.

Sadker, M., D. Sadker, and L. Long. 1993. Gender and educational equality. In *Multicultural education: Issues and perspectives*, edited by J. A. Banks and C. A. M. Banks. Boston: Allyn and Bacon.

Sharpe, R. 1995. Affirmative Action lifted Mr. Lee, and he has never forgotten. *The Wall Street Journal*, 27 December Eastern ed., p. A1.

Sharpe, R. 1993. In latest recession, only Blacks suffered net employment loss. *The Wall Street Journal*, 14 September Eastern ed. pp. A1, A12.

Economic perspectives on Affirmative Action. edited by M. C. Simms. Washington, D. C.: Joint Center for Political and Economic Studies.

Stewart, S. A. (1996. February 22). Affirmative action faces showdown, *USA Today*, natl. ed.: A2.

Takaki, R. 1994. The myth of the "model minority." In *Taking sides: Clashing views on controversial issues in race and ethnicity*, edited by R. C. Monk. Guilford, CT: Dushkin.

Tidwell, B. J. 1995. African Americans and the 21st century labor market: Improving the fit. In *The State of Black America*, edited by P. J. Robinson and B. J. Tidwell. New York: National Urban League, Inc.

US News and World Report. (1995, February 13). [No Title, No Pagination]

Wahisi, T. T. 1995. Des Moines NAACP sends clear message to Clarence Thomas. *Crisis* 102(7): 2-3.

Watson, B. C. 1995. The demographic revolution: Diversity in 21st century America. In *The State of Black America*, edited by P. J. Robinson and B. J. Tidwell. New York: National Urban League, Inc.

Wilcox, K. 1982. Differential socialization in the classroom: Implications for equal opportunity. In *Doing the ethnography of schooling*, edited by G. Spindler. Prospect Heights, Illinois: Waveland.

Conclusion

Multiculturalism requires that educators from all walks of life work together.

INTRODUCTION

Simultaneously thinking about all the multicultural issues presented in this book may be mind boggling and overwhelming, to say the least. Because of the complexity of the issues involved, the problems facing schools may seem insurmountable. However, the reader is encouraged to regard major historical struggles such as the ones presented at the beginning of the book (e.g., slavery, the holocaust, women's suffrage) and realize that even in these depressing instances, change did occur—albeit slowly. We encourage readers to do their small part in making a difference in the lives of children, in the future of this country, and in the world. The resolution of all historical struggles undoubtedly began with a few people who were willing to take a stand.

Throughout this book, we have tried to capture the complexity of the issues and realize that at times it may have seemed as if information contradicted other information (e.g., the recommendation to consider cultural learning styles and individual differences). Although it may be difficult to hold two seemingly opposing issues in one's mind, it is necessary to do so. Effective educators realize this and negotiate many variables in order to contribute to the holistic development of their students. Understanding children's development both between and within cultures is important.

This book has recognized that schools and educators do not operate in a vacuum. A holistic model of human development acknowledges that a person's development is influenced by numerous factors. Therefore, schools do not bear the sole responsibility for children's welfare and futures.

While it is clear that racism, sexism, classism, and other "isms" cannot be wiped out by schools, "the role of schools should not be underestimated either" (Nieto, 1992, p. 249). "Business as usual" cannot be tolerated if schools intend to address diversity issues which affect students' performance and behavior in schools (Banks and Banks, 1997).

> If we are to confront the persistence of racism and other forms of discrimination, we must do so within the broad sociopolitical context in which they occur. Racism, classism, ethnocentrism, sexism, linguicism, anti-Semitism, handicapism, and other forms of discrimination exist in schools because they exist in society. To divorce schools from society is impossible. Although schools may with all good intentions attempt to provide learning environments free from such discrimination, once students leave the classroom and building they are again confronted with an unequal society. (Nieto, 1992, p. 249).

The attack on discrimination must be multi-faceted. For example, Nieto (1992) points out that even if schools decide to do away with standardized tests because of their discriminatory nature, the implications might be far-ranging and have adverse effects on the desired goals. Students' performance on tests may in fact determine whether or not they go to college, what college they attend, and what they will study. Their entire future may depend on knowing how to take tests. If legislation is passed to exclude testing throughout elementary and secondary school as well as higher education, then students' futures are less likely to be directly affected by this decision. Yet, many careers may require test scores (e.g., National Teacher's Exam). As this example demonstrates, the issues are complex and multi-faceted. The importance of examining issues holistically and developmentally is apparent. In the short run, educators cannot change society. However, educators can make schools less alienating. Multicultural education, especially anti-bias approaches, is a way to change "business as usual" (Banks and Banks, 1997). Educators must be realistic about how rapid and smoothly change will occur. Undoubtedly, it will take years before progress will be seen. Additionally, a sense of disequilibrium is an expected, necessary, and healthy part of the process. Moving out of one's comfort zones will be necessary for development to occur. While this may seem risky to some, the ultimate benefit (successful students) outweighs the risks by far.

Currently, many educators and schools remain inactive because they are not sure of *what* to do or *how* to do it. Being inactive and uninformed are not viable options, since both inactivity and ignorance can be detrimental to children's development. **Additionally, silence on important issues connotes acceptance.** As professional leaders, educators must have a strong understanding of many historical, political, economic, and social issues. Importantly, educators must be able to speak assertively on the issues and to mobilize support from people who agree with the basic tenets of fairness and equality for all. This book and thousands of other works can lead the way, in conjunction with professional judgment and common sense. However, as the book has emphasized throughout, there are no simple solutions.

❖ FINAL THOUGHTS REGARDING THE NEED FOR MULTICULTURAL EDUCATION

Our society is becoming increasingly more diverse each day. No longer can we speak of European American culture as the embodiment of all things "American" (Snow, 1992). Critics of multiculturalism say that it is divisive. Questioning the status quo and the melting pot conception is taboo. A common assertion is that people should either accept America as it is or leave. However, arguments against multiculturalism often fail to acknowledge the dynamic nature of culture. As individuals and as a nation, we are in a constant state of flux. From this perspective, change is viewed positively rather than negatively. Developmental theorists such as Piaget (1969), Vygotsky (1978), and Bronfenbrenner (1979) have always acknowledged the important role of change and adaptation in life. In order to survive as a species, change is inevitable.

Change has always been the norm, but more so in today's society. When I was growing up, a typical adult goal was to get married, buy one's "dream house," and live in the same house until death. If extra space was needed, the house was renovated and expanded. The expectation was that the house would be passed on to another family member and remain in the family. People generally lived in one community for most of their lives. Today families live in three or four dream houses (each bigger and better) and move to states or countries far beyond their home-towns. It is not atypical to see neighborhoods where people do not know one another. Real estate signs proliferate in many neighbor-hoods and real estate advertising brochures are abundant in most places. Because people are frequently zooming from one place to the next, and simply MUST get there in a hurry, the number of air-lines and airplanes has increased greatly since I was a child.

Few could have predicted a generation ago the significant role that technology now plays in our lives. It is almost incon-ceivable for some to imagine life without a computer. Our lexi-cons continue to change rapidly with the addition of new words such as: "E-mail," "AIDS," and the like. Foods that were once rarely eaten have become the norm (e.g., Chinese food, tacos, sushi). All these examples indicate that the magnitude of change in one's life is unpredictable. However, it is not likely that com-munities and society at large will become less diverse in terms of population. Educators have the responsibility and joy of prepar-ing children to live in this diverse and ever-changing world.

Kozol (1991) points out that many children today learn a type of ethical exemption. That is, they learn that inequality is not their responsibility, and they should not be blamed for things which happened before they were born. As was mentioned in Chapter One, how each of us lives affects how others live. "A cul-ture of satiation for some will necessarily create a culture of poverty for others" (Montgomery-Fate, 1997, p. 20). "(North) American innocence has been historically nurtured and protect-ed by a conveniently selective memory (Stuart Creighton Miller as cited in Montgomery-Fate, 1997, p. 20). The voices of many people of color and disenfranchised groups have been written out of United States history. Until we as a country fundamental-ly believe every culture and person has value, we will not be able to truly be a UNITED States of America.

As we continue to expand and broaden our horizons, both the uniqueness and commonalities that humans bring to society must be acknowledged. Many writers have used the metaphor of a "tossed salad" to describe our society (versus a melting pot conception). An increasing number of people now realize that the United States never was a melting pot (Grant, 1994). Many peo-ple of color have not been able to "melt" and other groups such as women, the physically challenged, and the poor have not been fully accepted into the mainstream of American society. Many realities invalidate the melting pot thesis:

1. the glass ceiling in corporate America that prevents women and people of color from reaching top leadership positions
2. inequities in salaries between men and women, and between people of color and white people
3. the exclusion of women, people of color, and the poor from much of the political system
4. the increasing division into a two-class society of "haves" and "have nots" (Grant, 1994).

Recently, I heard someone say that they preferred a quilt metaphor instead since a quilt is made of many different pieces woven together. Our commonalities (the thread) hold us together as a nation, while our differences add variety and beauty to the quilt. With a tossed salad, one might decide to "toss out" the ingredients (read cultural groups) that they do not like.

In a diverse society, both American and individual cultures can co-exist. Individuals do not need to eradicate their cultures or histories, nor is it possible to really lose one's indigenous culture. We can camouflage or suppress aspects of our culture (and many people do a credible job); however, it remains a part of us even though its original form may be altered.

❖ CHALLENGES FOR MULTICULTURALISM

One of the greatest challenges of multiculturalism will be to get to the root of fundamental and covert issues of injustice. Increasing educators' and students' awareness of the hidden curriculum in schools is difficult but necessary in order to facilitate change (Zisman and Wilson, 1992).

Recently, I shared Peggy McIntosh's (1995) chapter, from *Race, Class, and Gender*, on white and male privileges with some of my white colleagues. One of them said that she believed that the discrimination problems (e.g., housing and school issues) outlined by McIntosh were no longer true. The relative nature of truth was readily apparent to me, since I had found McIntosh's work to be extremely relevant and timely. I remember thinking it is indeed a privilege NOT to be aware of such issues. From my perspective, racism, sexism, and classism abound. I do not have to search hard to find these issues. In fact, it seems as if these social ills actively pursue me and many other people of color. Consequently, when many of my African American students read McIntosh's work, they exclaim, "Amen!" They also frequently add that they are glad that there are some whites who are aware of such issues as well. Contrastingly, a number of European American students find McIntosh's work "too direct." If simply reading about such issues is too direct, imagine what experiencing them on an almost daily basis does to one's psyche. I am reminded of a young white male who once appeared on "The Oprah Winfrey Show." The young man had decided to see for himself what life was like as a young African American male. He ingested chemicals that changed his color, cut his hair, and dressed in sagging clothes typical of many African American adolescents. After one day of this experience, he was so overwhelmed by the continuous negative experiences that he encountered that he quickly discontinued his "experiment." Oprah Winfrey kept repeating in amazement, "I have been black for 40 years and lived with it, while you were black for only one day and could not tolerate it." (not a direct quote) The point is that it is a privilege (versus a choice) not to be aware of the "isms."

Perhaps on paper and in rhetoric, white privilege is no longer the norm; however, from my African American cultural perspective, it is very real, and many people of color and other marginalized groups do not have the luxury of overlooking or failing to acknowledge it. Although we have made great strides towards reducing racism, classism, and sexism, we have a long way to go. Many of the historical injustices presented in the preface still exist in altered states. Parallels between the historical injustices mentioned in the preface and present-day injustices are presented on Table 9-1. Although tremendous progress has been made by most groups, I will highlight areas that still need to be addressed.

Try as we may, we cannot deny the inequities that exist at the many levels of society (school, workplace, society at large). For some, it is easier to put on blinders, and act like there are equal opportunities for all. But viewed through the lens of presently oppressed and devalued groups, many would beg to differ.

As Table 9-1 indicates, we have made progress, but there is still much to be done. Many people believe that the problems of racism and sexism were resolved during the sixties (Sleeter, 1995; West, 1994). When multiculturalism is mentioned, they often claim, "Been there, done that!" indicating that we are simply "going through a phase" that has already been visited and solved during the Civil Rights Movement. From this perspective, multiculturalism is viewed as being politically correct rather than as a dynamic process inherent in a polyethnic society. Typical responses assert that schools have been desegregated for years, old offensive textbooks have been discarded, and new curriculum materials portray "minority groups" in a positive manner (Pang, 1988). The general impression is that all is well and that there is nothing

TABLE 9-1. Parallels Between Historical And Present day Injustices

Historical Version	Contemporary Version
Lords live in mansions; servants in huts	Many similar examples still exist (e.g., migrant workers and their employers; Hollywood celebrities living in close proximity to fans who live in housing projects or low-income environments).
Indentured Servants (European immigrants)	Non-citizens from other countries are hired illegally to work in "sweat shops" in the United States making products like designer clothing and being paid less than $1.00/hr just to remain in this country.
Stripping of Native American land; genocide of Native Americans	Although most overt brutality has been eliminated, evidence of psychological damage is still present. Native Americans as a group are one of the least educated, most unemployed, poorest, and least healthy groups in America (Snipp, 1995). Alcoholism and violence continue to be problems (Snipp, 1995). Negative myths continue (e.g., Native Americans are savages).
Africans enslaved; culture denigrated	As with Native Americans, the psychological damage of slavery is still present. Inequities in education, employment, housing, and the justice system abound. Negative stereotypes about African and African American culture still exist.
Chinese subjected to pervasive legal anti-Asian discrimination; lived in virtual slavery	Deemed one subgroup of the "model minority" because of successes. Difficulty gaining access into some professions. Often face "glass ceiling" because of discrimination. Subjected to violence and negative stereotypes because of Asian appearance.
Japanese internment	Deemed one subgroup of the "model minority" because of successes. Subjected to "Japan-bashing." Still face discrimination because of physical features.
Jewish holocaust	Still subjected to Anti-Semitic violence and discrimination, especially by hate groups such as Neo-Nazis and skinheads. As a group, this culture has experienced a fair amount of success.
Schools for white males and financially privileged.	Both males and females are privy to an education. However, in some disciplines a disproportionate number of females are not represented. Male/female achievement differences in math and science continue to be debated.
Disabled children not allowed to attend public schools.	Laws have been passed to allow all children to attend public schools. However, inclusion and high quality education for people with exceptionalities (all types) continue to be issues of concern.

else that needs to be done. However, remarks like these fail to acknowledge that multiculturalism is an ongoing process. Many educators would be shocked to discover the dilapidated state of many urban and rural school districts. Many students do not have books, use old texts and materials, and are in buildings that would be considered uninhabitable to most of us, including dysfunctional toilets, no heating or cooling, holes in ceilings, overflowing sewage in buildings, and rat infestations (Kozol, 1991).

Contrary to popular myths about the sixties, this era represented only one brief moment during which we bravely confronted our most explosive issues of racial hierarchy and maldistribution of wealth and power (West, 1994). However, this period did not last long. Ethnic and other prejudices remain prevalent in the United States education system, just as they persist in the larger society (Pang, 1988; McIntosh, 1995). Educators must be aware of possible attitudes, behaviors, situations, and expressions that reinforce prejudice. If the educational community continues to examine itself, then it can lead society in reducing unintentional prejudice (Pang, 1988). However, many educators and others remain unconvinced that multiculturalism is a worthwhile effort.

The idea that multiculturalism needs to be "sold" to the public and approached in a way that is nonthreatening to everyone is an unachievable and thankless task (Sleeter, 1995). Multiculturalism is for those who have a moral commitment to equity and integrity, not only in this country but throughout the world. Multiculturalism unveils many of the unpleasantries of history for both genders, many ethnicities, socioeconomic status groups, religions, and members of differently-abled communities. In order for healing to occur, both positive and negative aspects of history must be acknowledged.

As a consequence of structural inequalities in access to knowledge and resources, students from certain ethnic groups face persistent and profound barriers to educational opportunity in the United States (Darling-Hammond, 1995). Institutionally sanctioned discrimination in access to educational resources is deeply ingrained in the fabric of this country beginning with the "colonization" of the Native Americans and enslavement of African Americans (Darling-Hammond, 1995). Denial of access to books, libraries, and schools ensured an unequal and cumulative disadvantage to this type of education. Although many argue that such practices occurred centuries ago, tracking, inequities in the funding of schools, and other institutional mechanisms ensure the continuation of these trends.

Racism, sexism, classism, and other "isms" will continue to rear their heads in the future. Every time we are convinced that the nation is rising above the persistance of "isms," there are reminders of how little headway has been made—even at eliminating the most vulgar and conspicuous manifestations of the diseases ("isms") (Pine and Hilliard, 1990). Educators should not be surprised by these instances and should address the issues when they arise in classrooms in a straightforward manner. Care should be taken to avoid blowing these situations out of proportion. Yet, educators should view these instances as opportunities to determine how their own curricula and classroom/school atmosphere could do a better job of addressing diversity issues.

Although the previous examples point out that the "isms" are still alive and well, I am not pessimistic about the future. Many schools, colleges, universities, and workplaces are seeking information on diversity. Learning to live together and respect each other's differences, as well as similarities, is being done one school at a time, one college at a time, one workplace at a time. The melting pot conception of America continues to be questioned. People of color and other disenfranchised groups insist on equal rights, and macrocultural values and practices are slowly changing.

❖ RECOMMENDATIONS FOR EDUCATORS

Educators who are committed to diversity will continue to make a difference in the lives and futures of all children. This book will be most effective for educators who are open to continuous change (refer to the Reach Model [Table 1-2] in Chapter One). Multiculturalism is for those who wish to change (Sleeter, 1995). Without true convictions, educators will simply regurgitate appropriate phrases and use multicultural materials, but will not truly demonstrate an appreciation for diversity. Respecting diversity begins with the individual. Self-reflection is a valuable tool that must be utilized if educators wish to change. They must continuously acknowledge, evaluate, and confront biases and move forward. This book has provided many opportunities for educators to engage in self-reflection. The overt information that is taught in schools is secondary to the covert messages and systemic inequities and negative attitudes that exist. As I have noted elsewhere, racism and other "isms" are real and ongoing issues in schools today (Boutte, LaPoint, and Davis, 1993). As observed by Phil Donahue, "Racism is so insidious. It's like cancer. You don't know you have it." (Phil Donahue Show, August 30, 1996). Donahue asserts that we are reared in the midst of a society where white is revered (e.g., Jesus is white; angel food cake is white).

Educators need to scrutinize the structures, policies, and practices of schools for prejudice and educational inequities

(Pang, 1988). Complex issues such as the disproportionate numbers of children of color who fail in schools and the disproportionately larger number of white children in high-track classes must continue to be addressed.

Darling-Hammond (1995) asserts that even *teachers* are tracked in schools. Those who are judged to be the most competent, experienced, or with the highest status are assigned to the top tracks. Since expert and experienced teachers are in great demand, they are rewarded with opportunities to teach the students who already know a lot. On the other hand, novice teachers, unprepared teachers, and those teaching outside their field of preparation are often assigned to students and classes that others do not care to teach. Essentially, these teachers end up practicing on students who would benefit most from the skills of expert, experienced teachers.

Effective teachers must be lifelong students of culture (Ayers, 1993). Ayers points out that culture is an important window into understanding a child. It is an essential part of the child. Teachers must continuously seek to understand children, families, and the communities in which they live. Educators have a tendency to blame students when failure occurs. It is time to closely examine the system that has not engendered success for most ethnic groups (Kasten, 1992).

Educators who teach children from non-mainstream backgrounds need to understand the ambiguity, confusion, and double-consciousness associated with negotiating two cultures in a society where only one of them is respected by the macroculture (Fordham, 1988). Educators must also encourage students to work across racial, gender, socioeconomic status, and other cultural lines. Currently, in many integrated schools, cross-racial contact is confined to formal settings (Rizzo-Tolk and Varenne, 1992). Interracial violence in schools is common. If acceptance of others permeates classrooms and schools from elementary school through high school, it is likely that interracial strife can be diminished. Classroom and school practices which do not consistently show respect for diversity send subtle messages to students. When the mission of schools strongly conveys appreciation of diversity, students and their families quickly get the message.

White, middle-class teachers with primarily monocultural schooling experiences who are being prepared for teaching by teacher educators with similar backgrounds to teach ethnically and socioculturally diverse students face the greatest challenges (Powell, Zehm, and Garcia, 1996; Sleeter, 1993). Without adequate knowledge and experience, such educators will view diverse students with limited cultural perspectives and, hence, will be unable to connect educational problems experienced by students with the cultural disparity between the students and the school (Powell, Zehm, and Garcia, 1996). Several activities throughout this book have been designed to help readers determine their readiness for teaching students from diverse cultures. Table 9-2 may be used as a comprehensive assessment of teachers' preparation to teach in diverse settings. It is anticipated that all readers will have voids and should use this assessment as a guide for seeking additional information and experiences.

In the final analysis, educators must acknowledge that knowledge is neither neutral or apolitical. Yet, many schools and educators continue to treat it as if it were (Nieto, 1992). Consequently, educators tend to present knowledge of the lowest common denominator, that which is sure to offend the fewest and is least controversial. However, history, is full of debates, controversies, and ideological struggles (e.g., the current debate over the canon, and cultural literacy versus multicultural literacy)

TABLE 9-2. Comprehensive Assessment of Preparation For Working With Diverse Students

Directions: Put a check in each column if you have the type of preparation listed. You may also list or count the number of experiences in each category.

Students	Actual Experiences (teaching, practicums, tutoring)	Readings	Video/Films	Classes, Seminars, Workshops
African Am.				
Asian Am.				
European Am.				
Native Am.				
Latino Am.				
English as a second language				
Interracial				
Low socioeconomic status				
Middle socioeconomic status				
High socioeconomic status				
Non-Christian				
Special Needs				
Rural				
Urban				

(Nieto, 1992). Educators must understand that all decisions that they make, regardless of how neutral they appear, impact in unconscious, but fundamental ways on the lives and experiences of students (Nieto, 1992).

A major problem with a monocultural curriculum is that it gives students only one way of viewing the world. Nieto notes that "Reality is often presented in schools as static, finished, and flat" (1992, p. 219). For example, most schools have presented limited images of whites, just as they have with other people of color. Rarely do schools teach about poor (e.g., "hillbilly") cultures. Educators must constantly present information which demonstrates how the intersection of race, gender, socioeconomic status, religion, and ability manifests itself among humans. To be truly informed and active participants in a democratic society, students need to understand the complexity of the world and a variety of perspectives. Students must learn that there are more than one, two, or three ways of viewing the world (Nieto, 1992).

In sum, educators should attempt to adhere to the following guidelines.

1. Examine all aspects of curriculum and school policies for biases.
2. Think critically about instruction (e.g., isolated units, holiday celebrations, interactions with students).
3. Conscientiously and critically examine book collections.
4. Actively address racism, classism, sexism, and other forms of discrimination.
5. Teach students to address stereotypes and discrimination.
6. Abolish the rightness of "whiteness" (white superiority).
7. Consider and respect students' home setting, but also ensure that they acquire skills, behaviors, and attitudes necessary for functioning in a dominant society.
8. Stay abreast of information and trends to inform teaching.

❖ WHERE DO WE GO FROM HERE?

"If we believe in the Constitution, the Bill of Rights, and the Declaration of Independence, that's all we need to know." (President Bill Clinton, 1996). The basic premises of these documents are still relevant. Indeed, multiculturalism seeks the same goals: life, liberty, and pursuit of happiness. As Banks and Banks (1997) explain, "A major goal of multicultural education is to 'Americanize' the United States by helping the nation realize in practice ideals that are part of its founding documents." (p. xiv) Banks and Banks further assert that the challenge to multicultural educators is to determine how to increase equity for a particular victimized group without further limiting the opportunities of another.

Cornell West (1994) notes that none of us alone can save the nation or the world. However, he adds, each of us can make a positive difference if we commit ourselves to do so. West urges us to have courage, vision, and analysis in order to highlight the best in each other as we point out the vicious effects of the "isms" and the pernicious consequences of the maldistribution of wealth and power.

The incentive for becoming multicultural *is* the mutual benefit of all humans living together in relative harmony and respect. All cultural groups face challenges, but European Americans (as a group) probably face the biggest challenge. European Americans have the awesome task of learning to recognize and acknowledge white privileges inherent in this society in order to learn to share power. As my graduate student pointed out in Chapter One, this is no easy task. Yet it seems to me that a tremendous amount of energy must be expended to maintain the current societal structure which is built on the premise of white supremacy (Ayers, 1993; Delpit, 1988; Howard, 1993; McIntosh, 1995). It is unlikely that typically marginalized cultural groups will stop demanding equal rights. Therefore, either the power will be shared or energies will be continuously expended in fighting for or against power.

Whites must recognize that criticisms of "white America" are not criticisms of them individually; rather, they are criticisms of the institutionalized ethnocentrism. It is important for whites to move past their initial reactions of guilt, anger, fear, denial, and so forth in order to take action against the many "isms" that exist in our society. Failing to acknowledge the existence of racism and remaining color-blind enables racism to continue.

White males have been the greatest benefactors of racism and sexism and, admittedly, they have the most to "lose" (or gain—depending on how one looks at the situation) in terms of yielding to the inevitable changes (McIntosh, 1995). However, it seems that sharing power is easier and simpler than living in constant fear of losing power or working hard to oppress others and, thus, maintaining the institutions of racism, classism, sexism, and the like.

Being a person of color in this country is often wrought with emotional trauma, and frequently causes anger and resentment toward "white America." People of color must redirect anger typically directed at European Americans toward addressing the larger issues of living together as humans. In an effort to be proactive rather than reactive, people of color must continue to share their perspectives and worldviews with whites. Nevertheless, people of color also need to vigorously fight the "isms" every chance that they get.

People of color also need to recognize the tremendous diversity that exists among whites. Viewing all whites in an adversarial role is counterproductive since many whites are and have been in the forefront in terms of fighting discrimination. All ethnic groups must seek to understand and analyze their historical trajectories and how they relate to the current state of affairs.

The poor face a tremendous challenge in this country. Recognizing the value of education for future success is important. People of color from low-income homes face an even greater challenge since they must fight classism and racism. While I am not so naive as to believe that we will eliminate the "underclass" in the United States, I do think that we can greatly reduce the numbers of those living in poverty by systematically providing access to knowledge to all children (rather than excluding children from low socioeconomic status groups). Education can be the gateway to better lives for many children. Indeed, for many poor children, it is the *only* possibility.

Women face many challenges as well. However, if women from all ethnic groups work together, the inequities they face can be greatly reduced since there is power in numbers.

Individuals with special needs will continue to face discrimination in schools, on tests, and in the work world. Massive campaigns to educate society about the number of disabilities that exist may help sensitize people to issues faced by individuals who are physically and mentally challenged. Additionally, the realization that any of us can become disabled within moments should enlighten all of us. All of us need to be more sensitive to issues of access to buildings, parking spaces, and the like, and do our part to promote accessibility for all individuals.

As humans, we must work together for the mutual benefit of all. The legacies that we leave for future generations should not be a shameful replay of the atrocities cited at the beginning of this book. Rather, it should be a legacy that instills pride rather than guilt and embarrassment. The legacies that we leave should be so great and promising that when future generations examine history, they will wonder in awe, *"How* on earth could they have been so forward-thinking? How *did* they ever overcome discrimination?"

In light of the issues raised in this book, the limitations of teaching from an ethnocentric perspective, which perpetuates many myths and much misinformation, should be obvious. I end this book by urging educators to work toward ensuring that all children reach their highest potentials. It may be necessary for educators to convince some children of color, poor children, and other children from non-mainstream backgrounds that it is in their own best interest to become bicultural. The goal of biculturality (maintaining their home culture while also mastering mainstream culture, and knowing when and how to negotiate both) is crucial for educators at all levels of schooling. During the early childhood years, young children typically have no idea of what lies ahead of them. Because of their limited view of the world, conceptualizing the future is just too enormous to do in any realistic way. Therefore, educators, along with caregivers, must help children develop the requisite skills needed for success later in life. During the elementary years, children's visions continue to be nearsighted. Being like peers and fitting in is normally too important for them to see the value of skills needed to succeed in society. Finally, during adolescence, young people begin to gain some vague notions of the future. However, because of vast hormonal changes, philosophical (versus realistic) views, and other turbulence that may occur during this period, teens are generally pretty focused on the here and now. By the time young adults (and sometimes older ones) recognize the value of an education, it is often seen as being too late. Additionally, opportunities to change may not be readily available, or patterns of behaving may be so deeply set that change is difficult, if not impossible. This may explain why some high school graduates who did not master Standard English during the elementary years seldom do so afterwards. In sum, teaching is an awesome task and educators at all levels must assume the responsibility for children's long term predicaments. This can only be done when educators respect differences, view them as assets rather than deficits, have high expectations for students, and teach in a relevant way. The principles espoused in this book should pave the way.

One generation plants the tree; another gets the shade .
Chinese proverb

❖ RECOMMENDED ACTIVITIES

1. *Journal entry*—Reflect on insights you have gained from this book. How can you implement some of the recommendations in your professional setting or personal life? Go back to Chapter One (Table 1-2) and re-evaluate your stage of ethnic awareness. The ultimate goal is toward global awareness.

2. Have any of your views changed after reading this book? Why or why not?
3. Reread the section of the preface where some of the historical and current injustices were mentioned. Discuss some of the positive changes that have transpired.
4. Write a paper presenting two opposing sides of an issue raised in this book. Present literature to demonstrate the pros and cons of each side of the issue. For example, you may research the advantages and disadvantages of tracking.

❖ REFERENCES

Ayers, W. 1993. *To teach: The journey of a teacher.* New York: Teachers College Press.
Banks, J. A., and C. A. M. Banks. 1997. *Multicultural Education: Issues and perspectives.* 3rd. ed. Boston: Allyn and Bacon.
Berns, R. M. 1994. *Topical child development.* Albany, NY: Delmar.
Boutte, G. S., S. LaPoint, and B. Davis. 1993. Racial issues in education: Real or imagined? *Young Children* 49(1): 19–23.
Bronfenbrenner, U. 1979. *The ecology of human development.* Cambridge, MA: Harvard University Press.
Clinton, B. 1996. *The 1996 Presidential Debate.* October 16. American Broadcasting Company.
Darling-Hammond, L. 1995. Inequality and access to knowledge. In *Handbook of research on multicultural education,* edited by J. A. Banks and C. A. M. Banks. New York: Macmillan.
Delpit, L. D. 1988. The silenced dialogue: Power and pedagogy in educating other people's children. *Harvard Education Review* 58(3): 280–298.
Fordham, S. (1988). Racelessness as a factor in black students' school success: Pragmatic strategy or pyrrhic victory? *Harvard Educational Review,* 58 (1): 54 - 83.
Graff, G. 1992. *Beyond the culture wars: How teaching the conflicts can revitalize American Education.* New York: W. W. Norton and Co.
Grant, C. A. 1994. Challenging the myths about multicultural education. *Multicultural education,* 2(2): 4–9.
Hale-Benson, J. 1986. *Black children—Their roots, culture, and learning, rev. ed.* Baltimore: John Hopkins University Press.
Hilliard, III., A. G. 1991/1992. Why we must pluralize the curriculum. *Educational Leadership,* 12–15.
Hillis, M. R. 1996. Multicultural education as a moral responsibility. *The Educational Forum* 60(2): 142–148.
Howard, G. R. 1993. Whites in multicultural education: Rethinking our role. *Phi Delta Kappan* 75(1): 36–41.
Kasten, W. C. 1992. Bridging the horizon: American Indian beliefs and whole language learning. *Anthropology & Education Quarterly* 23(2): 108–119.
Kunjufu, J. 1990. *Countering the conspiracy to destroy black boys.* Vol. II. Chicago: African American Images.
Mackenzie, B. 1984. Explaining race differences in IQ. *AmericanPsychologist,* 39(11): 1214–1233.

McIntosh, P. 1995. White privilege and male privilege: A personal account of coming to see correspondences through work in women's studies. In *Race, Class,and Gender: An anthology. 2nd ed.* edited by M. L. Anderson and P. H. Collins. Belmont, CA: Wadsworth.

Montgomery-Fate, T. 1997. Beyond the multi-culture. *The Other Side* 33(2): 16–20.

Murphy, D. 1986. Educational disadvantagement: Associated factors, current interventions, and implications. *Journal of NegroEducation* 55(4): 495–507.

Nieto, S. 1992. *Affirming diversity/ The sociopolitical context of multicultural education.* New York: Longman.

Oakes, J., and M. Lipton. 1990. Tracking and ability grouping: A structural barrier to access and achievement. In *Access to knowledge: An agenda for our nation's schools,* edited by J. I. Goodlad and P. Keating. New York: College Entrance Examination Board.

Pang, V. O. 1988. Ethnic prejudice: Still alive and hurtful. *Harvard Educational Review* 58(3): 375–379.

Piaget, J., and B. Inhelder. 1969. *The psychology of the child.* New York: Basic Books.

Pine, G. J., and A. G. Hilliard, III. 1990. Rx for racism: Imperatives for America's schools. *Phi Delta Kappan* 71: 593–600.

Powell, R. R., S. Zehm, and J. Garcia. 1996. *Field experience: Strategies for exploring diversity in schools.* Englewood Cliffs, NJ: Merrill.

Rizzo-Tolk, R., and H. Varenne. 1992. Joint action on the wild side of Manhattan: The power of the cultural center on an educational alternative. *Anthropology & Education Quarterly* 23(3): 221–249.

Scarr, S. 1981. Testing for children. *American Psychologist* 36(10): 1159–1166.

Scheurich, J. J. 1993. Toward a white discourse on white racism. *Educational Researcher* 22(8): 5–10.

Schlesinger, A. M., Jr. 1994. The disuniting of America. In *Taking sides: Clashing views on controversial issues in race and ethnicity,* edited by R. C. Monk. Sluice Dock, Guilford, CT: Dushkin.

Sleeter, C. E. 1995. An analysis of the critiques of multicultural education. In *Handbook of research on multicultural education,* edited by J. A. Banks and C. A. M. Banks. New York: Macmillan.

Sleeter, C. E. 1993. How white teachers construct race. In *Race identity and representation in education,* edited by C. McCarthy and W. Crichlow. New York: Routledge.

Snipp, C. M. 1995. American Indian studies. In *Handbook of research on multicultural education,* edited by J. A. Banks and C. A. M. Banks. New York: Macmillan.

Snow, M. A. 1992. *The multicultural classroom: Readings for content-area teachers.* New York: Addison-Wesley.

Tribe, C. 1982. *Profile of three theories: Erikson, Maslow, Piaget.* Dubuque, IA: Kendall/Hunt.

Vygotsky, L. S. 1978. *Mind in Society: The development of higher psychological processes.* Cambridge, Mass: Harvard University Press.

West, C. 1994. *Race matters.* New York: Vintage Books.

Zisman, P., and V. Wilson. 1992. Table hopping in the cafeteria. An exploration of "racial" integration in early adolescent social groups. *Anthropology & Education Quarterly* 23(3): 199–220.

Appendices

Appendix A
Answers to Cultural Pursuit

1.
2.
3.
4.
5.
6.
7.
8. An African American holiday celebrated from December 26 - January 1.
9. Refused to give up her seat on a bus. Started the Montgomery Bus boycott.
10. "Abuela" is Spanish for grandmother.
11. No correct response.
12. Jewish festival of lights.
13. A term sometimes used to refer to the texture of African American hair; kinky.
14. Perms generally straighten black hair and curl white hair. Another interesting tidbit is that many white females wash their hair daily while many black females wash their hair less frequently (typical range is once weekly to every two weeks). Differences have to do with the texture of the hair and hair styling processes. Blacks typically add oil to their hair, while whites typically wash oil out of their hair. Think of implications of this information when teaching hygiene.
15. A traditional dress worn by Indian (east) females.
16. A Caribbean or Gullah term which is used instead of "you all." Refers to more than one person (e.g., "How oonu doing?").
17. An African American magazine.
18. An Indian (east) bread. Also refers to Italian noodles.
19. Write a cultural term that you know with which others may be unfamiliar.
20. Write another cultural term that you know with which others may be unfamiliar.

Index